Shindō Yōshin Ryū
History and Technique

Tobin Threadgill
and
Shingo Ohgami

**Dedicated to
Takamura Yukiyoshi (1928-2000)**

"Our predecessors in the koryū were giants among men, and what they passed forward to us is a sacred trust. As inheritors of their knowledge it is our duty to preserve not just the techniques of the art, but the wisdom that inspired and sustained them."

- Takamura Yukiyoshi

About the Authors

Tobin Threadgill

Tobin Threadgill was born in January, 1959. He is the Shihan/Kaichō of the Takamura ha Shindō Yōshin Kai and Honbuchō of the Takamura ha Shindō Yōshin Ryū Honbu Dōjō in Evergreen, Colorado, United States.

He is a graduate of the Brooks Institute of Photography in Santa Barbara, California, worked as a professional advertising photographer for over 25 years and was the owner of Threadgill Productions with studios in Dallas, Texas and Long Beach, California.

He started his martial arts training in western fencing with Captain Hart Kait in 1978 and started training in Wadō Ryū karate in 1981 under J. Gerry Chau. He also trained in Jeet Kune Do, Muay Thai boxing, and Aikijūjutsu.

In 1985, he met and became a student of Takamura Yukiyoshi, the headmaster of the Obata/Takamura line of Shindō Yōshin Ryū and was awarded a Kirigami Shoden in 1986. He was subsequently awarded a Chūden Menkyo in 1990 and a Jōden Menkyo in 1995. In 2001, a Menkyo Kaiden issued by Takamura was awarded to Threadgill during a ceremony at his Soryūshin Dōjō. In 2003, the retirement of branch directors Takagi Iso and David Maynard led to Threadgill being asked to assume the position of kaichō or administrative head of the Takamura ha Shindō Yōshin Kai. Today, he oversees private instruction at the honbu dōjō while also maintaining a busy seminar schedule, supporting associated Takamura ha Shindō Yōshin Ryū dōjō and study groups around the globe.

Ohgami Shingo

Ohgami Shingo was born in November, 1941. He is the chief instructor of Swedish Karatedō Wadōkai and Karate Club Samurai-Dōjō in Gothenburg, Sweden.

He studied at Tōkyō University from 1960 to 1965 and started training in karate there, under Ōtsuka Hironori sensei, the founder of Wadō Ryū karate. He worked at Toyōbō Co. as an engineer from 1965 to 1969, where he started his first karate club. In 1969, he moved to Sweden as a guest researcher in chemistry at Chalmers Technical University in Gothenburg, where he started a second karate club. In 1971, he left his career in chemistry and has since been engaged in teaching karate full time while also studying and researching other forms of budō.

He is a member of the Japanese Budō Academy (Nippon Budō Gakkai), eighth dan in Japan Karate Federation Wadōkai, fifth dan in Mugai Ryū Iai Hyōhō, and Gomokuroku in Shindō Mūso Ryū jōdō.

Publications:

- Introduktion till Karate (Swedish 1974).
- Karate Katas of Wadō Ryū (English 1981).
- Introduction to Karate (English 1984).
- Karate för Nybörjare (Swedish 1985).
- Introduktion till Budō (Translation from Japanese into Swedish 1992, original in Japanese Nakabayashi Shinji 'Budō no Susume').
- Tai Chi för Nybörjare (Swedish 1993).
- Fem Ringars Bok (Translation of Japanese text 'Gorin no Sho' into Swedish 2010).
- A series of articles about the history of karate (Swedish) in 'Svenska Fighter'.
- Editor of quarterly magazine 'Svenska Wadōkai' 1977-2013, 148 issues.

Shindō Yōshin Ryū

New Willow Press
31979 Quarterhorse Rd.
Evergreen, Colorado 80439
USA

First Edition:

Copyright © 2019 by Tobin E. Threadgill and Shingo Ohgami

All Rights Reserved. Published, October 2019

Printed in the United States of America

No part of this book may be reproduced, distributed or transmitted in any form or by any means including photocopying, recording or other electronic or mechanical methods without prior written permission of New Willow Press. Exceptions exclusively include brief passages embodied in critical reviews, scholarly works and certain other non-commerical uses permitted by copyright law.

Illustrations by Jaclyn Threadgill / Hexasketch Design & Illustration

Book and Jacket Design, New Willow Press

ISBN:978-1-7334223-0-7 (Softbound)

Library of Congress Control Number: 2019912061

Foreword

Very few non-Japanese have achieved what I would call a truly professional level in the Japanese classical martial traditions, or koryū. Most of us who have pursued this path know one another from the decades we spent together in Japan, training under the headmasters and shihan of our chosen traditions. But it wasn't until a few years after I returned to the U.S. that I first met Toby Threadgill. We were introduced by a student of mine, and we sat together at lunch sharing stories of our teachers, training, and visions of the koryū. Threadgill's training experience was unusual in that he spent his formative training years with his teacher Takamura Yukiyoshi in California, not Japan, but it was immediately obvious to me that what his teacher transmitted to him was the "real deal." We have been friends and confidants ever since.

Although relatively young in its current incarnation, Takamura ha Shindō Yōshin Ryū traces its lineage back to some of the earliest Japanese jūjutsu traditions. The ryū also had a distinctive influence on Ōtsuka Hironori, founder of modern Wadō Ryū karatedō. Today there are more than 250 Shindō Yōshin Ryū members worldwide, all under the supervision of kaichō Toby Threadgill. The transmission has been remarkably preserved and maintains the full range of both esoteric and physical training; many Japanese traditions have lost huge chunks of their curricula to the ravages of time.

Well-researched books by non-Japanese who are also practitioners are rare. Even the Japanese books on the classical arts are either fairly light on historical details or are focused on technical explanations. Researcher and practitioner Donn F. Draeger began to pull back the curtain on these often secretive traditions with his ground-breaking books in the 1970s, and set a high bar for subsequent publications.

With the depth of meticulously researched detail, illuminating illustrations, range of topics, and rigorous presentation of contextual information, Threadgill and Ohgami have risen to Draeger's challenge handily. This duet between Japanese native historical researcher and the enquiring practitioner/teacher, with the spirit of Takamura Sensei at the core, chronicles the evolution of the art from its inception until the present. They have collected and presented information on the personalities and events of the ryū's history that was in real danger of vanishing; many of those who the authors talked to have since passed away. Without the efforts of Threadgill and Ohgami, much of the rich Shindō Yōshin Ryū lore would be lost. Ryū members and those interested in the classical Japanese martial traditions are in their debt.

Naturally, every practitioner of Takamura ha Shindō Yōshin Ryū and Wadō Ryū will need to read this book, and it contains much that will interest followers of other Yōshin Ryū lineages, and even other jūjutsu schools. Chapters on Shintō, densho, and the moving interview with senior students about Takamura Sensei will provide insight for the serious student of any tradition, as will the Japanese cultural and historical details throughout the text.

And while this is not a "how-to" book — these arts can only be transmitted by a qualified teacher — illustrated sequences provide an overview of the technical corpus of the ryū as well.

In short, this unique bi-cultural team has produced the most comprehensive study of a Japanese classical martial tradition ever published in English; it has established a standard that others may aim at, but are not likely to surpass.

Phil Relnick
Shintō Musō Ryū, Menkyo Kaiden
Tenshinshō-den Katori Shintō Ryū, Shidōsha Menkyo
Dōjōchō, Shintōkan, Woodinville, WA

Acknowledgements

The authors of this book are indebted to a great number of individuals, without whose contribution, commentary, expertise, and guidance this work would not have been possible. In particular, we would like to thank Matsuoka Takeshi and Matsuoka Masahiro for providing details about Matsuoka Katsunosuke, Shindō Yōshin Ryū's founder, their family history; as well as access to never-before published Matsuoka family photographs. We would also like to thank Inose Katsuei and Saitō Takao, of Shimotsuma Daiichi High School, for providing access to documentation and photos related to Nakayama Tatsusaburō, the school's past martial arts teacher, and his students Matsuoka Nobuatsu and Ōtsuka Hironori.

We would also like to thank:

- Norma Foster, Kathryn Douglass, Arthur Ginley, and Michael Heiler, whose preliminary editing and compositional input helped craft the work of two separate authors into one informative volume. We would also like to thank Ben Reus for his final editing and indexing. And lastly, Karen Hensley-Chelstowska, whose meticulous proofreading polished the work, making it ready to publish.

- Phil Relnick, Meik and Diane Skoss, Wayne Muramoto, Ellis Amdur, Kuroda Tetsuzan, Karl W. Garrison, David Maynard, Paul Manogue, Doug Walker, and Steve Delaney for their input, proofreading, advice, and critique concerning the organization and scope of this book.

- Tahara Setsuko, Miyamoto Kozue, Suzuki Naoko, Nobuko Relnick, Bob Nash, Andre Martinez, Kobayashi Toshishiro, as well as Nathan Scott and Tae Iio of Nichigetsukai Honyaku for their assistance in translating both modern as well as arcane Japanese language documents.

- Dr. David Hall for consultation about Marishiten, Sōjōbō, and other esoterica related to Mikkyō Buddhism and Shintō contained in various Yōshin Ryū and Shinkage Ryū-related documents.

- Jaclyn Threadgill of Hexasketch Design and Illustration for the excellent artwork utilized in Chapter 7.

- The individuals and organizations that allowed the authors to use their photographs and other artwork. These include: Miyamoto Kozue, Mark Raugas, Doug Walker, Adam Coleman, Steven F. Radzikowski, Karl W. Garrison, John Lovato, Osano Jun, Matsuoka Masahiro, Ludwig Binder via Andreas Sparmann, Miles Kessler, Mariko Takamura-Thomas, David Maynard, Nicolas Delalondre, Christina Gutz, Jon Classic, Jen Yamada, Kuroda Tetsuzan, Kurama Temple (Kyōto, Japan), Hōzanji Temple (Nara, Japan), Odawara Library (Kanagawa, Japan), Shimotsuma Daiichi High School (Chikusei City, Japan), and Tsubaki Grand Shrine of America. Those images whose sources are not noted are either the property of the authors, subject to fair use, in the public domain, purchased from a stock photography agency, or were created by the authors themselves.

- Nakayama Tsuyuko for access to information related to her ancestor, Nakayama Tatsusaburō.

- Ōta Yoshio for access to rare books such as "Goshinjutsu Okugi by Hoshino Sentarō (1924)".

History And Technique

- Mariko Takamura-Thomas for providing access to family documents and other materials related to her father's life and career in budō.

- Frederick Ōta, lifelong friend of Takamura Yukiyoshi, for participating in an exclusive interview where he provided documents, insights, and information about Takamura's early life, his move to Europe, and his eventual relocation to California in the early 1960s.

- Fujiwara Ryōzō for access to information related to the Shindō Yōshin Ryū Dōmonkai and Matsuoka Tatsuo.

- Patrick Peschke for his intercession, investigation, and translation of German language materials related to Erwin Baelz, his son Erwin Toku Baelz, Heiko Bittmann, and Susanne Germann.

- Aikidōka Ulf Evanas, whose support and encouragement convinced the authors to pursue this project.

- Those Takamura ha Shindō Yōshin Kai members who took time out of their busy schedules to demonstrate the kata and allowed themselves to be photographed for inclusion in this book: Juergen Baier, Erica Bollon, Brent Carey, Adam Coleman, Piotr Chelstowski, Sasha Corchado, Kathryn Douglass, Valentino Elias, Miguel García de Leaníz, Troy Gehrett, Arthur Ginley, Rafa Girón Calvente, Sven Gerstendörfer, Kevin Hayles, Kimberly Henderson, Paul Henderson, Karen Hensley-Chelstowska, Miki Koshio, G. John Lewis, Chuck McCollum, Chris McMahon, Craig Moore, Patrick Peschke, Marco Pinto, David Ruttinger, David Sasaki, Peter Smith, Linda Tuzzolino, Doug Walker, and Eric Winters.

- Finally, all the unnamed friends and members of the Takamura ha Shindō Yōshin Kai who offered us encouragement and expertise, as well as much-appreciated feedback in the pursuit of this project.

Authors' Preface

Tobin Threadgill

One afternoon during a seminar in Spain, a student asked me how a non-Japanese obtains a Menkyo Kaiden and becomes the legitimate headmaster of a koryū jūjutsu school. I was so dumbfounded by the question I didn't know how to respond to it. I finally said "In my case, accidentally." I had never considered the possibility of leading Takamura ha Shindō Yōshin Ryū. The principle reason for this was I had several senpai (seniors) whom I knew to be more experienced, and in my mind, were more well-suited for such a demanding position. Even after I received notice I would receive a Menkyo Kaiden, and Takamura Sensei told me he was grooming me to be capable of leading the organization, I still did not take the possibility seriously. I had two seniors who had received complete transmission of the school's teaching, and one was Japanese. For this reason, I saw myself as a Takamura ha Shindō Yōshin Ryū insurance policy, one that would never mature. All of that changed after unfortunate events related to the health of my two senpai demanded I step into the leadership position.

The conversation in Spain reminded me of several discussions I had with friends when I finally accepted the reality of my situation. The first person I consulted was my good friend Stanley Pranin, the publisher of Aikidō Journal magazine. Stanley, who had extensive correspondence with Takamura Sensei during the crafting of an interview for his magazine, gave me no quarter. He even chastised me for not considering the possibility of someday leading the ryūha the very first day I walked into Takamura Sensei's dōjō. Later, I would discover that Takamura Sensei had already consulted Stanley Pranin about the subject of my suitability to receive a Menkyo Kaiden, and Stan had given his enthusiastic support of the decision. Another memorable moment came from my friend Phil Relnick, arguably the most senior practitioner of koryū outside Japan, and himself holder of a Menkyo Kaiden in Shintō Musō Ryū. Phil actually laughed at the news of my status, and while shaking his head, said to me: "For years, a group of us foreigners who trained in Japan wondered who would be the first non-Japanese to inherit a koryū school. Toby, you're the guy. Do you have any idea what you're in for? I don't envy you." I understood that the scrutiny I would confront in the ensuing years would be intense, but I also knew the legitimacy of my position was never really in question. The Obata/Takamura line of Shindō Yōshin Ryū is a well-documented school, and all the materials required to confirm the veracity of my position were easy to access. Just as importantly, I also knew I had the technical knowledge to go with the position. Takamura Sensei had taught me well, and no one familiar with the technical or historical legacy of the school could dismiss the ryūha's claim of my position as headmaster.

Takamura Sensei did an admirable job of preparing me for the task I faced, but his first priority had to be technical. For the sake of the school, he had to guarantee that the entire mokuroku (technical catalog) was passed to me, as well as the gokui (deepest mysteries) and okugi (secret teachings). Only after he was convinced I was fully initiated, and had received complete transmission of the school's knowledge, did he start passing on the political and administrative insights I would need to properly lead the organization. I remain impressed at the man's wisdom and his ability to discern the strengths and failings of human nature, regardless of cultural indoctrination. Many of the hypothetical situations he used to convey administrative and political competence to me actually came to pass. When an incident he had admonished me to be wary of started playing itself out in plain view, I wondered if he had been psychic. He not only knew the political minefield, but also taught me how to recognize the mines and avoid them. Before he could complete my instruction on the finer points of Japanese social etiquette and protocol, his illness had progressed to the point he told me I would have to seek counsel on this knowledge elsewhere. In the years following his passing, many Japanese friends and members of the koryū community have generously provided me with sound counsel on a wide range of related topics. These included Stanley Pranin, Phil and Nobuko Relnick, Meik and Diane Skoss, Ellis Amdur, Kuroda Tetsuzan, Ohgami Shingo, Norma Foster, and Tahara Setsuko. I will always be in their debt for their counsel.

The aforementioned 1999 interview with Takamura Sensei in Aikidō Journal resulted in my introduction to this book's co-author, Ohgami Shingo, a JKF Wadōkai eighth dan and koryū practitioner of Shintō Musō Ryū and Mugai Ryū. In 2004, Ohgami invited me to Gothenburg, Sweden, to introduce Shindō Yōshin Ryū jūjutsu to a group of his advanced Wadō Ryū karate students. I found Ohgami to be a fascinating person, as not only was he a dedicated budōka, he was also an adept budō historian and curator of an extensive martial arts library. When Ohgami and I started to compare notes on Shindō Yōshin Ryū history, we realized our combined resources and knowledge represented a more complete depiction of the art and its history than had ever been available. It was this realization that led us to produce this book.

Myths die hard, and during the writing of this book, we uncovered documented information which led us to conclude that many stories repeated by third parties about Takamura Yukiyoshi's early life, the life of his well-known grandfather Obata Shigeta, as well as other Shindō Yōshin Ryū and Wadō Ryu budōka, simply weren't accurate. Sometimes these stories were speculations, which over time morphed into innocent myths, but other times they were irresponsible fabrications intended to exaggerate or distort certain details surrounding these men's amazing lives. Why would someone misrepresent a fascinating history with intentional fakery? Such transgressions remain perplexing to me, as the truth weaves a sublime tapestry of history, adding important context to the lives of the individuals who passed the arts of Shindō Yōshin Ryū and Wadō Ryū forward to the present.

Through my interaction with Ohgami Shingo, I have developed a deeper appreciation of how proper historical research is conducted, and how dispassionate one must be in the quest for accuracy. Ohgami's meticulous attention to detail, his dogged determination to follow what appeared to be the most trivial lines of research, and his refusal to accept hearsay as fact is a testament to the veracity and passion of his work. In 2007, Ohgami and I traveled to Japan in a quest to find answers for some of the remaining questions we had about Shindō Yōshin Ryū's legacy. We were graciously invited to meet with the descendants of the founder of Shindō Yōshin Ryū at the original location of the Ueno Matsuoka/Shindōkan dōjō. There, the Matsuoka family allowed us access to a treasure trove of photos and documents, and enthusiastically participated in an extensive recorded interview where they provided new facts and clarified many of the confusing myths about their famous ancestor. We were also kindly received by Dr. Fujiwara Ryōzō in Tōkyō, where we discussed his experiences as the leader of the Shindō Yōshin Ryū Dōmonkai. We were further greeted by JKF Wadōkai eighth dan, Dr. Hakoishi Katsumi, who provided us with his insights into the technical evolution of the Shindō Yōshin Ryū kata which were eventually integrated into Wadō Ryū karate.

Inevitably, there will be questions raised as some sources of information we confronted were ambiguous. Other information presented will raise eyebrows as the relevant sources for our conclusions have simply been so obscure that they were overlooked by the greater budō community. Regardless, we did our best to stick to a narrative supported by multiple documented sources. When that was impossible or we confronted vague information, we fell back on Occam's razor (the philosophical principle of parsimony), and followed a reasoned path which required the least number of assumptions. Lastly, we gave weight to proprietary sources of information held by the Takamura ha Shindō Yōshin Kai. These include historical records, essays penned by Takamura Yukiyoshi as well as a diary kept by Obata Shigeta. As an active koryū jūjutsu school, many of our proprietary documents function as a denki (historical biography) of our legacy, something I have taken a blood oath to maintain and protect.

Over a decade in the making, this book presents historical insights into the individuals, history and technical legacy of Shindō Yōshin Ryū, supported by information that has never previously been accessible to the public. I hope the readers find it to be an illuminating window into the personalities and evolution of a koryū jūjutsu tradition whose origins are found in the early Edo period, continued through the turbulent years of the Bakumatsu period, and which miraculously survived the cultural realignment that defined Japan's Meiji period.

Ohgami Shingo

I have been practicing karate since 1960 when I entered Tōkyō University. Ōtsuka Hironori, the founder of Wadō Ryū karate had been a shihan at the university karate club from 1936 until 1981. Tōkyō University Karate Club, founded in 1925, is one of the oldest university karate clubs in Japan, as is the Tōkyō University Wadō Ryū karate club, founded in 1936.

I came to Sweden as a guest researcher in chemistry in 1969. Ōtsuka Sensei encouraged me to promote Wadō Ryū karate in Sweden while I was working at the university. Over time I became more and more involved in karate and finally resigned from the Japanese company that had sent me to Sweden in 1971. I took a risk in abandoning my career in chemistry research to devote myself to karate, but this path allowed me to dedicate all my time to karate and its research.

In order to more deeply understand my training in Wadō Ryū, I endeavored to study other styles of karate; Gōjū Ryū, Shōtōkan, and Shitō Ryū. Though the other schools of karate are definitely not enemies, I viewed my pursuit of knowledge in the spirit of Sun Tsu when he said:

"Know your enemy, know thyself, and you shall not fear a hundred battles".

Shiokawa Hōshō Sensei was from my home town of Shimonoseki. He was my sensei not only in Shitō Ryū karate, but also in Mugai Ryū iaidō and Shindō Musō Ryū jōdō. He practiced Mugai Ryū and Shindō Musō Ryū because he believed they reflected principles and movement very similar to karate. For this reason, I became involved in them too. In time, I realized the principles of proper movement were basically the same whatever school of karate or other martial arts you practice.

Because karate had been influenced by Chinese systems throughout its history, I began the study of Chinese martial arts to research the origins of karate. I traveled to Taiwan several times in the 1970s to study Tai Chi Chuan and Ton Lon Chuan under Lin Chin Fu Sifu. I traveled to China twice, in 1983 and 1984, to study Chen style Tai Chi Chuan, because it was reportedly the older form of Tai Chi Chuan, and closer to Shaolin Chuan, which is said to have influenced karate. I also traveled to Okinawa three times, in 1989, 1991, and 2001. Of course, this was because Okinawan karate is the direct root of Japanese karate.

Through my research, I became aware Ōtsuka Sensei was photographed performing Tankendori (Tantōdori) in the book Karatedō Taikan, published in 1938 and I reasoned that the Tankendori in that book must have been taken from Shindō Yōshin Ryū jūjutsu. Since only 200 copies of the book were originally published, very few people had seen it. I heard Nagamine Shōshin of Shōrin Ryū (Matsubayashi) in Okinawa, owned a copy and I strongly wanted to have one myself. He was kind enough to make me a copy when I met him in Okinawa in 1989. A year later, a reprint edition of Karatedō Taikan was published, so today anyone can acquire one.

Although karate has dominated my interest in martial arts, I have investigated many martial arts systems, not only those originating in Japan, but also those existing all over the world. My broader interest in martial systems from all over the globe has inspired me write quite a few articles about my studies in various Swedish magazines. I have given lectures about the history of karate, the history of martial arts around the world, the concept of budō, and even the history of aikidō, as I have been interested in aikidō, and even practiced it for a while, because I felt aikidō seemed rather similar to my karate in the principles of body movement.

One thing that unsettled me for a long time though was Shindō Yōshin Ryū jūjutsu. Because Ōtsuka Sensei claimed he practiced, and gained Menkyo Kaiden in the art, I had been looking for the opportunity to study Shindō Yōshin Ryū in the 1970s and 1980s, but my efforts were in vain. Although I had known Dr. Fujiwara Ryōzō, the representative of Shindō Yōshin Ryū Dōmonkai since the 1970s, and he had published the book 'Shindō Yōshin Ryū no Rekishi to Gihō' in 1983, no opportunity to train in the art was forthcoming. I asked him quite a few times about the possibility of studying Shindō Yōshin Ryū jūjutsu, but eventually I came to realize there were no longer any Shindō Yōshin Ryū Dōmonkai dōjō active in Japan.

Then, in 1999, Takamura Sensei was interviewed. Due to my interest in aikidō, I have always collected books, videos, and even magazines about the art, and I subscribed to the Japanese language version of Aiki News. I was astonished to read there were people apart from the Dōmonkai practicing Shindō Yōshin Ryū. I immediately wrote to the editor of the magazine, Stanley Pranin, who sent my letter to Takamura Sensei. I received an answer from him telling me he was quite ill and getting treatment in Sweden. He told me he could not help me with the matter of teaching Shindō Yōshin Ryū, but that one of his students was going to contact me. That student was Tobin Threadgill, the co-author of this book. Tobin made a special video for me presenting Shindō Yōshin Ryū jūjutsu following the instructions of Takamura Sensei. Tobin visited Gothenburg, Sweden for the first time in 2004 and taught Shindō Yōshin Ryū jūjutsu to the higher graded students in Swedish Wadōkai. I was deeply impressed by his skill in Shindō Yōshin Ryū and its underlying theory. Since then, he has visited Sweden more than 10 times and has frequently taught Shindō Yōshin Ryū jūjutsu in my dōjō.

Because I have studied the history of Wadō Ryū and Ōtsuka Sensei, the history of Shindō Yōshin Ryū jūjutsu has been of great interest to me. This book has evolved to become a much deeper investigation than I originally intended and this is due to Tobin, who is an extraordinary researcher in the history of jūjutsu. I think his knowledge about koryu culture may be deeper than many Japanese. I am very grateful to have had the opportunity to work with such a seasoned budō practitioner and diligent researcher.

Shindō Yōshin Ryū

*"Gusting winds blow and sweep the willow trees.
Ride these winds.
There you will find victory."*

-Akiyama Yōshin Ryū koka (didactic verse)

Table of Contents

Authors	v
Foreword	vii
Acknowledgments	viii
Authors' Preface	x
Table of Contents	xv
Special Subjects Included in Inserts	xvi
Notes on Japanese Language and Romanization	xvii

1. Studying Nihon Koryū Outside Japan	2
2. The Origins of Koryū Jūjutsu	12
3. The Origins of Shindō Yōshin Ryū	28
4. The History of Shindō Yōshin Ryū	72
5. The Technical Legacy of Shindō Yōshin Ryū	128
6. The Shindō Yōshin Ryū Mokuroku	141
Te Hodoki	142
Tachiai Kuzushi	164
Idori	176
Tachiai Taijutsu	202
Tantō Toriage	228
Ken Toriage	240
Kenjutsu	250
Battō/Iaijutsu	264
Battō Torikaeshi	274
7. Shisei no Gyō: Teaching Body Structure	283
8. Nairiki: Internal Power	300
9. On Shintō	322
10. Koryū Densho	332
11. Recollections on Takamura Yukiyoshi	345
12. Bibliography	370
13. Glossary	377
14. Index	399

Special Subjects Included in Insets

Yōshin Ryū and the Takeda Clan of Kai and Aki	33
Kurama Yōshin Ryū	33
Dai Nippon Butokukai	37
Inagaki Yōshin Ryū, the Kai Takeda, and the other Akiyama	49
The Bakufu Kōbusho	50
Edo Hantei	50
1906 Dai Nippon Butokukai Jūdō/Jūjutsu Conclave	51
Shintō Rikugō Ryū	56
Tenjin Shinyō Ryū and Shishin Takuma Kyūdai Kinnichi Ryū	69
Shindō Yōshin Ryū and Its Evolving Name	74
Sei Kotsu Shi	89
Nakayama Tatsusaburō 1870-1933 or 1945?	89
Nakayama Tatsusaburō, Ōtsuka Hironori, and Issues of Succession	101
Bakumatsu no Sanshu	103
Matsuzaki Namishiro/Matsuzaki Shinkage Ryū	118
On Kata	163
Sōdansha - Kai Advisors	175
Jogensha - Outside Kai Advisors	201
On Teaching	227
Adam Coleman, Kaji/Japanese Bladesmith	239
Katchū Kenjutsu/Shinaigeiko	249
Tameshigiri/Test Cutting	263
Richard Elias/Tsukamaki-shi	273
Akiyama Lineage Internal Strength Training	299
Jogensha Rev. Koichi L. Barrish	331
Eimeiroku/Student Register	331

Notes on Japanese Language and Romanization

Japanese is a highly contextual language. The precise meaning of a word is dependent on the context in which the word is being used, who is speaking, who is listening, the physical location of the communication, and if a third party is involved. Consequently, context and social dynamics can give one word multiple meanings, sometimes subtle, and sometimes significant.

Syllabary and Alphabets

Another complicating characteristic of Japanese is the use of an ideographic syllabary and multiple phonetic alphabets. The ideographic syllabary is called kanji and is directly sourced from China. When the Chinese syllabary was imported into Japan, any familiar concepts or meanings brought with them an associated Chinese pronunciation. These new Chinese sourced pronunciations were simply added to the native Japanese pronunciations. Therefore, each kanji ideogram will generally represent two different pronunciations, one called "on" (Chinese origin) and another called "kun" (Japanese origin).

The phonetic alphabets are hiragana and katagana. Hiragana represents Japanese language sound changes, while katagana attempts to replicate foreign language sound changes as accurately as possible within the norms of Japanese phonetics. Maintaining two phonetic alphabets allows a native Japanese speaker to immediately identify if the word being referenced is a Japanese word or a foreign word.

Romanization

For romanization of Japanese terminology and names, we have adhered to the modified Hepburn System as introduced in the fourth edition of Kenkyusha's New Japanese-English Dictionary (1974). Occasionally we have deviated from this system in special cases where the terminology or naming conventions of a specific ryūha utilize an alternate system of romanization.

Japanese syllabaries have only one stand-alone consonant, and that is "n" as in "senmon", "Daimon", "Sadauemon" etc. All other consonants are paired with a following vowel (e.g., ka, hi, bo). Commonly when "n" precedes "b" it is pronounced "m" but written "n"; Examples: "Honbu" is voiced as "hombu" but written as "honbu" because the character is "本" hon" and not "hom". Another example is "Shimbashi" written as "Shinbashi", because the character is "新" "shin" and not "shim". Consistent with the modified Hepburn System, the romanization in this book will not use stand alone "m" as it should be followed by a vowel.

Plural nouns are not created in Japanese by adding "s". They are inferred from context; that is, one dōjō, two dōjō, 10 dōjō.

Consistent with the modified Hepburn System, we have chosen macrons to distinguish long vowels "u" and "o" in authentic Japanese words and we have added an "i" to a long "e" to construct "ei", pronounced as in "bay" when a name is of Chinese origin.

Instead of writing the long "u" vowel as "uu, u-u" or "u", which can lead to mispronunciations such as found in English "uhuh", "you-ooh" or "up", a macron is applied "ū" to indicate that it should be pronounced as in English "you". Consider, "ryū" and "Shinshū".

Instead of writing the long vowel "o" as "oo", "o-o", "o" or "ou" which can lead to mispronunciations such as in "look", "oh-oh", "lot" or "shout", a macron is applied to "ō" to indicate that it should be pronounced as in English, "low". Consider, Tōkyō.

For long "e", we have selected "Shirōbei", not "Shiroobee", and "Ōi Senbei", not "Ooi Senbee".

Japanese names are rendered traditionally with the family name first, followed by the given names.

Pre-Taisho era Japanese ages are rendered traditionally reflecting kazoedoshi (age one at birth).

Shindō Yōshin Ryū

"As a young man I was fortunate to be counseled by Katsu Kaishū, the samurai, statesman, and aristocrat. He stressed upon me to never incite violence. Through his counsel I came to realize victory is best achieved through skilled negotiation, but I further understood you must always negotiate with your swords in plain sight."

-Obata Shigeta, Obata ha Shindō Yōshin Ryū

History And Technique

Studying Koryū Outside Japan

古流武道

Studying Koryū is not for everybody.

Koryū (classical Japanese budō) is an undertaking that can be in conflict with contemporary ideals of western thought, individuality, and self-determination. It is unique and not for everyone - even those interested in martial arts. Significant debate surrounds how successful any transmission of koryū can be outside Japan. Only time will reveal the outcome. Headmaster Takamura Yukiyoshi of Shindō Yōshin Ryū jūjutsu believed koryū could be successfully taught and transmitted outside Japan, but acknowledged its transmission faced serious challenges.

Shindō Yōshin Ryū

Koryū is unquestionably antiquated by nature, with many schools requiring exposure to obscure Japanese social customs and participation in rituals far outside the experience of the average non-Japanese, and even most contemporary Japanese. A teacher of modern budō is unbridled by strict adherence to classical Japanese ideals, and is thus free to indulge the desires and individuality of themselves and their students. In contrast, maintaining the traditions and technical legacy of a classical school of budō is the driving force behind participation. Individual desires are of little concern.

Koryū is a pursuit that presents a significant challenge to non-Japanese attempting its study. Koryū does not allow the freedom to choose which aspects of the art to study. Curricula are strictly defined and the learning process is based on a long-standing traditional process. Training in koryū is best facilitated by embracing a mindset called "nyūnanshin", that is, to release personal desire and open the mind to alternatives. Preconceived notions and expectations about what will be learned must be discarded, and practitioners must become immersed in the experience of being shaped by an entity charged with maintaining centuries of unique cultural and martial tradition.

What is Koryū?

The structure of Japanese culture and politics during the Tokugawa Shogunate, before 1868, was feudal and dominated by daimyō (military warlords). Japanese society was stratified to include a military warrior class, identified as samurai, who worked for and maintained the authority of the daimyō via administrative duties and force. However, this feudal political system collapsed in 1868 after a series of intense civil uprisings and was replaced by a monarchy, with Emperor Meiji in political control. One outcome of this political shift was the samurai, as a unique social class and military force, were abolished and replaced by a conscripted military force, which was separated from the constraints of social hierarchy.

Koryū literally translates as "old tradition", and it refers to the Japanese martial traditions associated with the samurai class before 1868. Koryū are very diverse traditions reflecting martial disciplines which endured throughout many centuries. The oldest surviving schools of Japanese martial study were founded in the 1400s and include legendary schools such as Maniwa Nen Ryū and Tenshinsho-den Katori Shintō Ryū. Shindō Yōshin Ryū was one of the last koryū schools formulated and es-

Sensei Doug Walker and Troy Gehrett training at the Takamura ha Shindō Yōshin Ryū Murakumo Dōjō, Portland, Oregon.
(Photo courtesy of Mark Raugas.)

The Takamura ha Shindō Yōshin Ryū Honbu Dōjō in Evergreen, Colorado, 2018.

tablished by a samurai, Matsuoka Katsunosuke Hisachika, who lived during the twilight years of the Tokugawa Shogunate.

Organizational Structure

Koryū are relics of a feudal past with sole authority vested in the headmaster, unlike modern budō, which frequently functions through a democratic organizational structure. The authority within koryū is absolute and intolerant of dissension, debate, or negotiation. The headmaster approves everything a teacher or student undertakes in relation to the study of the art. The teachings and individual authority granted instructors in authentic koryū are passed from teacher to student via the issuance of menjō or menkyo (formal documents or scrolls). Although knowledge, once given to a student remains with the student, the authority to formally teach under the auspices of the ryūha does not. A headmaster in koryū enjoys absolute control over virtually every aspect of the school and can provide and withdraw teaching authority as deemed necessary. The survival and health of a koryū is facilitated by a unique relationship forged among three entities: the students, the teacher, and the ryūha. Members of koryū, including the instructors and headmaster, are very much aware they are temporary custodians of the entity to which they have become obligated. The ryūha always takes precedence over any individual member, regardless of position. Some koryū schools require all members to ultimately undergo keppan (a ritual blood oath), to emphasize that the members are formally committed to maintaining a tradition that is larger, more important, and more enduring than any personal desires. A koryū instructor, who accepts the responsibility of teaching, vows never to abuse their authority over others for selfish gain or behave in a manner which could be deemed harmful to the reputation of the ryūha.

Training and Commitment

Access to the knowledge contained within the mokuroku (curriculum) of a koryū is viewed as a privilege. It is not a commodity or right. This is important to understand when contemplating the study of koryū. Many students of modern budō view martial training as a sport, hobby, or financial agreement, and believe they are consumers whose needs should be satisfied. Such an attitude is out of step with the mindset required of a koryū member. A koryū student must realize a financial contribution to the school does not automatically guarantee anything will be received in exchange. Knowledge is provided to students based on criteria that transcend financial compensation. The acquisition of important knowledge and understanding requires dedication, character, and an appropriate mental attitude. The information within the koryū curriculum is provided in measured doses and is often individualized. A koryū instructor will frequently choose to teach two students with similar experience in a different manner or sequence. This is unlike a modern budō school, where all members study in unison towards a definable goal, with progress being measured in terms of colored belts. Consequently, technical ranking systems similar to those in modern budō are rare in koryū, and when recognized, are interpreted as a modern convention.

The priorities of koryū do not focus on the modern stage; they heed the tactics and principles of a bygone world and mindset. Therefore, topics such as modern self-defense must be balanced against maintaining traditions that do not necessarily lend themselves to the realities confronted in current society. Although modern self-defense is certainly a training component of many koryū schools, such considerations are always secondary to the prime objective, which is to maintain the history, traditions, and legacy of the school. Shindō Yōshin Ryū headmaster Takamura Yukiyoshi once admonished his students during a class on modern self-defense applications:

> *"Self-defense is an important consideration in all budō, and should be in Shindō Yōshin Ryū. The waza must maintain technical effectiveness, but this is not a modern school of self-defense after all. We are a classical school and practice fighting with classical weapons. Beyond the dōjō, the decision to apply jūjutsu in actual self-defense should be viewed with grave seriousness."*

Another aspect of koryū training, which exists beyond that of most modern budō, concerns exposure to obscure Japanese cultural and spiritual practices. These aspects of study seem irrelevant to most non-Japanese, who envision training in martial arts as a pursuit simply connected to fighting or fitness. Immersion in the study of esoteric Shintō or Mikkyō Buddhism is unlikely to seem relevant to such individuals. Such spiritual pursuits and their accompanying mental disciplines are at the very core of understanding koryū. Without first-hand experience of these esoteric practices, many koryū believe a student cannot grasp the mindset required to internalize the foundations of the ryūha. After all, sitting under an ice-cold waterfall while reciting a Shintō

Tobin Threadgill, teaching iaijutsu in the Takamura ha Shindō Yōshin Ryū Honbu Dōjō.

norito (prayer) or chanting a Buddhist sutra connected to the deity Marishiten is unusual, even for a Japanese. However, the importance of the arcane as an element of koryū practice becomes more obvious to students as they experience such practice. To accurately explain this to people outside koryū can be challenging, as it is easily misinterpreted as new-age metaphysical pretentiousness. These ancient mental/spiritual exercises serve a very important purpose, as they have a concrete and definable objective in koryū. The intense stress and mental discipline demanded in such training seeks to create a mental state that affects a member in distinct ways. After regularly engaging in such practices, students can begin to appreciate how samurai, steeled by years of cultivating powerful mental and physical discipline, could wade into the gore and horror of an ancient battlefield without losing their emotional bearings or mental focus. Mental training seeks to instill the capacity for hyper-awareness and emotional detachment. Consider the modern psychological phenomenon of post-traumatic stress disorder. Many modern soldiers, due to a lack of mental and emotional preparedness, have survived intense combat only to suffer debilitating emotional trauma later. The samurai of feudal Japan were well acquainted with this phenomenon and developed methods of mental forging to prepare themselves for this eventuality. The founders of many koryū understood that ignoring the effects of intense emotional trauma could fracture a person's mental and spiritual equilibrium. Therefore, many classical schools still include mental exercises in their advanced teachings as a vehicle for instilling the appropriate mindset required for full initiation into the curriculum.

Loyalty

If any one concept threatens the survival of koryū outside Japan, it is the trivialization of loyalty. In western culture, where notions of individuality hold powerful intuitive sway, loyalty, in the context of koryū culture, can be difficult to embrace and properly prioritize. When a student formally joins a koryū through the process of nyūmon (initiation), he must familiarize himself with the context of what loyalty really is, why it is indispensable, and what it demands of every member. Loyalty must be approached as a conscious decision, not as some implicit abstraction spoken about in flowery language during a lecture, but then simply ignored when the full weight of its demands bears down on one's ego. Every member of a koryū will eventually come face to face with the unrelenting force of real loyalty. How a member interprets and reacts to the challenges demanded by such loyalty can be revealing. All too often rationalization is the method used to justify behavior that circumvents the persistent demands of proper loyalty. I have heard excuses made which used loyalty to the ryūha as a justification for betraying a teacher. I have also heard similar excuses made by teachers to justify the betrayal of a student. When the marginalization of loyalty is motivated by one's ego or political gain, it is an assault upon of the very foundations of a ryūha.

Even in Japan, where individuality is culturally subordinate to group benefit, loyalty can become corrupted or abused. There was a case where a koryū preservation society in Japan inserted itself into the internal politics of a member ryūha. This society, in a rationalized and corrupted sense of loyalty, betrayed a school's deceased sōke (headmaster) by trying to insert an unqualified and previously hamon (formally ejected) member into the ryūha's leadership position. This was a gross violation of everything the organization supposedly stood for, and fortunately the attempt was rejected. In an example of proper loyalty, the seniors of the ryūha rose up and made it clear they would not tolerate inappropriate outside interference in the internal administration of their ryūha. Today, the individual appointed by the now deceased headmaster leads the school because the members understood where their loyalty truly belonged. Loyalty in a koryū must be a selfless endeavor and remain an immutable commitment to your teacher, your fellow students, and the ryūha itself.

Finding an Authentic Koryū School

Koryū dōjō are rare inside Japan, and even more scarce outside it. Sadly, there's no shortage of frauds in the martial arts community, ready to prey on the public by misrepresenting their credentials or what it is they are teaching. Despite the prevalence of koryū tricksters, if you follow a fairly simple and logical process, you can significantly improve your chances of weeding out any frauds and locating an authentic koryū instructor.

The first thing to remember is the internet is a great resource for information and networking. Despite the fact that frauds are using the internet to promote themselves, it is also where legitimate teachers communicate and openly discuss their arts. A good starting point would be to visit koryū websites and read the information available there. Longtime practitioners, Meik and Diane Skoss, have compiled an impressive amount of information about legitimate koryū on their website, which you can trust without reservation. Next, join an internet koryū discussion group and simply ask around. People in the legitimate koryū community are more than happy to help potential members find authentic teachers and avoid frauds. My last suggestion is to read books and articles written by adept koryū instructors. Authors Donn Draeger, Meik & Diane Skoss, Wayne Muramoto, Karl Friday, Dave Lowry, Ellis Amdur, Hunter Armstrong, William Bodiford, and David Hall have published numerous works that can introduce an uninitiated but interested person into the world of authentic koryū.

One phenomenon that has muddied the water in recent years, and deserves mention, is the confusion existing between schools identified as gendai budō, neo-koryū, and faux-koryū. Gendai budō are martial arts schools of modern creation; meaning they were founded after the end of the Tokugawa era. Shinkendo, founded by Obata Toshishiro in 1990, and its parent

Chūden instructors gasshuku at the Takamura ha Shindō Yōshin Ryū Honbu Dōjō, June, 2018.
(Photo by Doug Walker.)

History And Technique

Phil and Nobuko Relnick's Shintōkan Dōjō in Woodinville, Washington. Tenshinshō-den Katori Shintō Ryū and Shintō Musō Ryū are taught here. These koryū schools are predominantly influenced by esoteric Buddhism.

Tobin Threadgill's Soryūshin Dōjō in Evergreen, Colorado. This dōjō is presently the Takamura ha Shindō Yōshin Ryū Honbu Dōjō. This ryūha is predominately influenced by esoteric Shintō and this dōjō functions as a minor shrine.

art, Toyama Ryū, founded by Nakamura Taizaburō in 1925, are both well-known examples of gendai budō. These two schools do not trace their origins directly to any koryū, but instead to the swordsmanship originating at the Rikūgūn Toyama Gakkō (Toyama Military Academy).

Neo-koryū are essentially a subset of those schools identified as gendai budō. Most neo-koryū are founded by students of legitimate koryū who do not hold licenses of complete transmission in the school of their study. These students have made the decision to end their koryū study and create their own modern variation. Sometimes neo-koryū represent a technically sound and cohesive entity, created by a koryū instructor who is competent and highly skilled, but is not fully licensed due to some political disagreement or technical schism that has occurred within a ryūha. Other times they represent a technically discordant entity; carelessly cobbled together from different sections of previously unconnected schools. If the founder of a neo-koryū school is honest about his background and aims, it's up to the potential student to determine if pursuit of such study is what is desired. From a purely technical standpoint, there are some neo-koryū that are widely admired for their excellent training. In the opinion of the authors, studying a neo-koryū is a riskier proposition than studying a koryū, because many examples of neo-koryū are incompetently created and do not honestly reflect their claimed origins.

That said, there is no guarantee a koryū surviving into the modern era is necessarily a vibrant example of the school as it existed in centuries past. Some koryū schools have degenerated significantly through the ages. However, it is important to remember, when evaluating any classical school, the individuals who have received full transmission in a koryū did not receive such recognition, and the associated authority that comes with it, frivolously. These individuals have proven themselves worthy of such responsibility in the eyes of their headmasters, and are passionately engaged in the historical preservation of their ryūha. The same level of competence and dedication to excellence cannot be automatically assumed about most people who found a neo-koryū.

Faux-koryū are a completely different subject. Faux-koryū are made up schools that misrepresent themselves as being connected to a legitimate koryū. The people founding these schools are frauds. They are essentially doing live action role-play and passing it off as an authentic

John Lovato's Takamura ha Shindō Yōshin Ryū Kenshinyōkan Dōjō in Lakewood, Ca.
(Photo by John Lovato.)

Nicolas Delalondre's Tesshinkan Dōjō in Osny (Paris), France.
(Photo by Nicolas Delalondre.)

representation of a classical Japanese samurai tradition. They may appear authentic to the untrained eye, but to a genuine initiate of a koryū their ruse is easily identified. A few characteristics commonly associated with faux-koryū include:

- Teaching performed in garish or flamboyant costumes.
- Ignorance of how to wear traditional training attire.
- The use of grandiose titles and/or absurdly high ranks.
- The inability to discuss or authenticate their school's lineage.
- Historical documentation which is unavailable for inspection by experts.
- Contrived or nonsensical reigi, or no reigi at all.
- Unfamiliarity with koryū lexicon and terminology.

Let us assume you have avoided the frauds, successfully navigated the koryū maze, located a koryū group in your city, and want to visit the dōjō to observe a class. First, and very critically, you must follow proper social protocol. Japan is a nation built on strict and long-held social courtesies. Koryū, as an old and highly traditional pursuit, can be even more demanding. Any time a potential student sends an instructor an inquiry, be it hardcopy or email, it creates a critical first impression. If someone does not properly introduce himself or herself, or addresses an instructor in an overly casual manner, it creates the perception they are not really serious about training. Such inquiries are usually relegated to the trash can. How difficult is it to write a proper letter of introduction? Koryū is, by its very nature, a socially rigid undertaking, so any appearance of flippancy or social negligence indicates an individual is not suited for such a culturally punctilious undertaking.

Let's now assume you have been formally invited to observe a class by the instructor of a legitimate koryū dōjō. You must respond, accept the invitation, and show up on time. Whether you know it or not, you are not the only one doing an evaluation during this visit. Everything you do will be observed and evaluated by the instructor and students during this first visit. Watch quietly, attentively, and do not appear bored or start looking at your smart phone. Do not, under any circumstances, leave the class before it concludes. It is considered disrespectful and only confirms to the instructor you are a not a serious candidate for dōjō membership. When the class is concluded, the instructor may ask if you have any questions. Now is the time to ask them. If you have no further questions at this point, politely excuse yourself, and send a thank-you letter to the instructor. If you decide you'd like to be considered for membership, send the request in a separate follow-up letter. From there the instructor will tell you what comes next in the process. This may include further visits and an interview.

There are many things to look for while observing a koryū class. Unless conducted at a multi-use public facility, like a YMCA or modern budō dōjō, a koryū dōjō will be imbued with a unique Japanese aesthetic characteristic, called shibui or sabi, one which exemplifies a clean and restrained elegance. If the art being taught is predominantly influenced by Buddhism, the dōjō can be almost severe and stark in its simplicity. It might be so modest as to have blank walls with just two or three vertical scrolls hanging in a tokonoma (elevated alcove) alongside a vase of fresh cut flowers. If the dōjō is more strongly influenced by Shintō, the environment might still demonstrate a restrained and elegant aesthetic, but it might also include many characteristics of a Shintō Shrine, like a prominently displayed kamidana (Shintō altar), kake-jiku (hanging scrolls), taiko (ceremonial drum), and maybe even the soft scent of hinoki, the cedar-like sacred wood of Shintō. You will most commonly observe aesthetic influences that are a mixture of both Buddhism and Shintō in a koryū dōjō but, regardless of the influences, there will be an unmistakable sense of austere refinement in the surroundings. You will not see glass cabinets full of shiny trophies, golden dragons bathed in red silk tassels, or other cheesy looking pseudo-Asian decor.

At the beginning of most koryū classes, students line up kneeling and facing the upper seat of the dōjō, an area identified by a tokonoma with a hanging scroll, a kamidana, or most probably both. The instructor will then lead the class by kneeling and bowing towards the kamiza, possibly reciting a short prayer in Japanese, and then clapping his hands methodically together. Following this demonstration of reigi (ritual formalities), the training will begin.

The training environment in an authentic koryū dōjō can vary a great deal from dōjō to dōjō or even day to day. Some dōjō environments are so strict that little talking is permitted between students during training, while other dōjō environments allow technical discussion, light

Ken Toriage training in Jürgen Buchwald's Takamura ha Shindō Yōshin Ryū Mitake Dōjō, Saarlouis, Germany.

banter and even frequent laughter. What should be obvious is that the instructor sets the training tone in both intensity and ambience in every class. The students should observe and follow the instructor's directions and intent intuitively. It is part of the student's training to observe, recognize, and follow the teacher's directions without constant verbal reinforcement. Takamura Sensei frequently changed his training intensity as a form of passive instruction. This encouraged the students to quickly perceive and instantly adjust to a changing environment and mood in the dōjō.

What you won't see in an authentic koryū dōjō is group teaching that includes the militaristic barking of orders, students yelling "osu", and the instructor loudly counting as students robotically march up and down the dōjō in lines. This teaching pedagogy originated in the early days of the Meiji Restoration, when Japan was adopting western military training methods for their conscripted soldiers. Most modern karatedō, kendō, and aikidō instructors employ versions of this teaching method. Conversely, teaching in a koryū dōjō reflects an intimate and personal level of interaction between student and teacher. You should likewise never observe something that appears like hazing in a koryū dōjō. In all my years of training in Shindō Yōshin Ryū, I never observed a student in Takamura Sensei's dōjō personally or physically humiliated as a form of retribution. Yes, the training was tough and could be both mentally and physically harsh at times, but it was never malicious, demeaning, or cruel.

Lastly, pay attention to your gut. If something just feels wrong or your intuition makes you think the instructor is not being honest with you, this needs to be addressed. If the instructor demands behavior that borders on cultishness or worship, walk away, because something is definitely wrong. A real koryū dōjō does not operate like a cult. You should never train in a dōjō where you do not perceive an ambience of trust. The environment should be intense and challenging, but always positive.

Conclusion

The level of dedication required to be a student of a koryū dōjō is extreme, yet many people who profess interest in koryū are unprepared for such a demanding undertaking. Joining a koryū school requires a commitment to the long-term pursuit of structured and uncompromising study. Koryū study is a discipline, not a hobby. A student who chafes at the uncompromising environment of a koryū dōjō might not be suited to such training. Unquestioned dedication to the traditions of the school and absolute acceptance of the headmaster's authority can be difficult to accept in an egalitarian society. The realization that self-determination is essentially non-existent in koryū and must be left at the dōjō door, is the simple fact of things. Likewise, that the curriculum is genuinely antiquated and steeped in a culture and era that may never be fully understood, is also difficult to appreciate. Every student must intellectually accept that they may train for at least a decade before they grasp the realities of what koryū really is. All students must recognize and commit to a rigid manifestation of authority, and the maintenance of traditions that are completely outside their previous experience. If not powerfully drawn towards a classical school of budō, then the decision to continue training will require re-evaluation. Many modern budō schools provide access to an excellent and flexible training experience. However, dedicated koryū training might be an experience that transcends initial expectations for those who believe in the importance of tradition and history, and perceive training as a long-term quest into the physical, metaphysical, and psychological depths of an ancient but enduring martial culture.

History And Technique

The Origins of Koryū Jūjutsu

Yagyū Shingan Ryū demonstration at the Meiji Jingū, 2015.
(Photo courtesy of S.F. Radzikowski.)

The Mythological Roots of Nihon Koryū

The martial arts traditions of Japan, more accurately called budō or bujutsu, trace their origins to fanciful ancient legends and archetypal myths. The oldest known written document in Japan, the Kojiki (Records of Ancient Matters; compiled ~ 712), is a mythological warrior tale that narrates a challenge between two deities: Takemikazuchi no Kami and Takeminakata no Kami. The Kojiki tells a story in which the sun goddess, Amaterasu Ōmikami, sends Takemikazuchi no Kami to earth, via a divine boat to pacify the terrestrial realm and quell a growing

Shindō Yōshin Ryū

Shintō kami of thunder and tutelary patron of martial arts, Takemikazuchi no Kami is the chief diety of Kashima Shrine in Ibaraki Prefecture. He is revered in many classical schools of budō.

rebellion. Perched among the waves, on the point of his sword, Takemikazuchi no Kami confronts the rebellious terrestrial deities, among whom is Takeminakata no Kami, who holds a massive stone on his fingertip and challenges Takemikazuchi no Kami to a test of strength. When Takeminakata attempts to grasp the arm of his adversary, Takemikazuchi frees himself by changing his arm into an icicle, and then into a sword. As Takeminakata recoils in confusion at this powerful feat, Takemikazuchi seizes and crushes one of Takeminaka's hands. Overwhelmed by Takemikazuchi's formidable strength, Takeminakata flees forever into exile to Suwa in Shinano. The remaining rebellious deities are awestruck by Takemikazuchi's martial power and pledge fealty to Ninigi no Mikoto, the grandson of Amaterasu and great grandfather of Jinmu, the first mortal emperor of Japan. Thus, the myth of Takemikazuchi no Kami forever links the martial disciplines of grappling and swordsmanship with the imperial house of Japan. Takemikazuchi no Kami is a patron kamisama (Shintō deity) of the martial arts, and is revered at Kashima Jingū (shrine) in Ibaraki prefecture. This mythological link among the divine, the martial, and the mortal is sustained in many Nihon koryū bujutsu ryūha surviving today, including the Takamura ha Shindō Yōshin Ryū.

Many other warrior myths are chronicled in six literary works of old Japan called the Rikkokushi. Among these works is the 30-volume chronicle, the Nihon Shoki, completed in 720. This work contains the oldest reference in any Japanese historical document to a grappling and striking contest by mortals. Dated to the seventh year of Suinin (23 CE), one passage describes a challenge match, called sumai no sechie (sumō) where two powerful adversaries, Nomi no Sukune and Taima no Kehaya, faced each other in mortal combat. During this contest, Taima no Kehaya succumbed to a powerful kick delivered by Nomi no Sukune. Considered the precursor to modern sumō, sumai no sechie was a contest, which drew combatants from all over Japan to compete in front of the Japanese emperor. Unlike modern sumō, the techniques included striking in addition to throwing and joint wrenching. The martial nature of the art is reflected in an imperial edict issued by emperor Ninmyō (833-850), proclaiming "sumai no sechie is not only a spectacle intended to appease the gods, but a superior method of cultivating warriors."

A sumai no sechie contest between combatants Nomi no Sukune and Taima no Kehaya, in 23 CE.

Bujutsu, Buddhism, and Kurama Temple

Kurama Temple, founded in 796 by Buddhist monk Gantei.

A Chinese priest named Ganjin (688-763), arrived at the Todaiji-temple in Nara, the ancient capital of Japan in 754, after many failed attempts. Elderly and suffering from poor eyesight by the time of his arrival, he committed the remainder of his life to spreading Buddhism in Japan. A student of Ganjin named Gantei (722-809) moved to Kurama, north of Kyōto, in 770. Gantei experienced a vision on Mount Kurama two years later, which convinced him the area possessed unusual spiritual power, and thus he and his followers founded a Buddhist temple near the summit of Mount Kurama in 796.

At that time, Buddhist monks commonly trained in martial arts to defend themselves and their temples. This tradition is most famously associated with the Shaolin Temple in Henan, China, but it was also common in Japan. Japanese Buddhist monks trained in martial arts were not initially permitted to possess deadly weapons, so their training was limited to empty-hand techniques and wooden staffs. However, as Buddhism spread across Japan, monasteries gained significant political influence. One of the most famous of these is Hieizan Enryaku-ji, founded in 806 by Saichō of the Tendai sect. Along with the proliferation of rival Buddhist sects, temples started employing their own trained warriors for self-protection. These warrior monk/mercenaries were called sōhei. Rivalry among sects resulted in political skirmishes and localized wars. The sōhei gained increased political sway in Japan between the 10th-12th centuries. Contemporary with the sōhei, the noble land-owning class started employing its own warriors for protection during this period due to increasing conflict. These bushi (warriors) evolved into a powerful warrior class, which eventually eclipsed the Buddhist sōhei, and were referred to as samurai (to serve).

Gantei, Founder of the Kurama Temple.
(Photo, courtesy of Kurama Temple, Kyōto.)

The most powerful of the early samurai were the Genji (Minamoto Clan) and Heike (Taira Clan). The Heike were

Shindō Yōshin Ryū

A sohei often wore his robes over his armor and covered his head with a sacred kesa. They were renown for their use of the naginata.
(Collection of the Takamura ha Shindō Yōshin Kai.)

initially successful in gaining power, and attained the prestige of protecting the emperor and capital city of Kyōto. However, the Genji overthrew the Heike during the Gempei Wars of 1185 and formed the first samurai-led government, the Kamakura Shogunate, in 1192.

The political influence of the sōhei waxed and waned until the Sengoku period (1467-1590). When the power of the sōhei threatened warlords such as Oda Nobunaga, Toyotomi Hideyoshi, and Tokugawa Ieyasu, the response was swift. Tokugawa Ieyasu attacked the Buddhist Ikkō sect of Mikawa at the Battle of Azukizaka in 1564, but initially lost. He then returned, aided by a contingent of warrior monks from his own Jōdo sect, and defeated the Ikkō and their partisans, burning their temples to the ground. An army of 30,000 samurai led by Oda Nobunaga attacked Mount Hiei in 1571 and destroyed Enryaku-ji Temple, then attacked the Ikkō in their fortresses of Nagashima and Ishiyama Hongan-ji. When Toyotomi Hideyoshi started to enforce a rigid class structure and restrict access to weaponry in 1588, it swiftly stifled the power of the warrior monks. The era of the warrior monks and their political influence finally ended with the powerful rise of the samurai and the victory of Tokugawa Ieyasu at the Battle of Sekigihara in 1600.

In the illustration above, Prince Morinaga Shinnō, sōhei and abbot of a Tendai Buddhist sect from Enryaku-ji Temple, is depicted drinking sake with other Buddhist warrior monks during the Genkō Wars (1331-1333).
(Collection of the Takamura ha Shindō Yōshin Kai.)

History And Technique

Bujutsu, Swordsmanship, and the Mythical Tengu

According to legend, the following Buddhist objects of worship reside in Kurama temple: Bishamonten (Buddhist patron of warriors), Sente Kanzeon Bosatsu (Buddhist goddess of compassion) and Gohō Maōson/Karuraten (Buddhist deity of protection with the power of the sun and fire). Gohō Maōson is artistically rendered at Kurama Temple with a long beard, long nose, and wings. In other locations throughout Japan, Gohō Maōson is birdlike in appearance with a crest running down his forehead. Related literature suggests the supernatural beings known as tengu originate with Gohō Maōson.

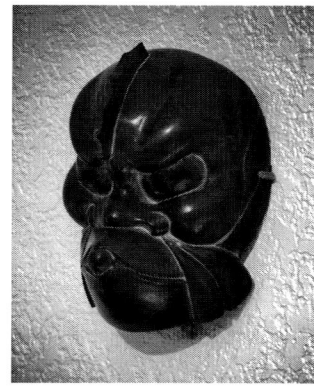

Gohō Maōson (Karuraten) mask in the Takamura ha Shindō Yōshin Ryū Honbu Dōjō.

Tengu are mythical creatures depicted in Japanese folklore as human-bird chimeras that reside in mountains and forests. Although the kanji characters (天狗) literally translate as "celestial dogs", the meaning is more commonly translated as amatsukitsune, or celestial foxes. Considered to be shapeshifters, tengu were originally described in popular tales as harbingers of evil or misfortune that sometimes assumed the appearance of foxes or tanuki (racoon dogs) to hide their true identity. Tengu are associated with the mountains and are said to be particularly fond of cryptomeria forests. The 12th-century Konjaku Monogatari (Anthology of Tales from the past), describes tengu as cunning adversaries who challenge arrogant, egotistical, and vain Buddhist priests by kidnapping them and then humiliating them by hanging them upside down in cryptomeria trees.

Karasu tengu statue at Yakuo-in Temple. Notice the yamabushi robes and tonkin (priest's cap) on his forehead.
(Photo courtesy of Karl W. Garrison.)

Tengu were also seen as dangerous to common people, as they were believed to spiritually possess individuals of weak constitution and drive them to commit mischievous acts, and even betrayal. However, the popular image of tengu softened over the centuries, and they have emerged as protectors of mountains, forests, and wildlife. Nonetheless, tengu have also been regarded as maintaining the duality of being exceedingly wise, yet unpredictably dangerous.

Three types of tengu are recognized. The first is the karasu (crow), tengu who most resemble a crow; having a beaked face, talons, and a dangerous disposition. They are portrayed as being particularly aggressive towards humans who cut down forests where they live. The second type is the konoha (foliage) tengu. The somewhat bird-like face of this type

16

Statue of Daitengu Naigubu in front of the Yakuo-in Temple of Mount Takao in Hachihōji City. Mount Takao, like Mount Kurama, is closely associated with its devotion to tengu.
(Photo courtesy of Karl W. Garrison)

evolved over time to acquire human features, such as a white beard and a long nose. The konoha tengu remained mischievous, unpredictable, and famously tormented arrogant Buddhist priests.

The third and most powerful tengu are the yamabushi (mountain warrior) tengu. They appear very human with a white beard and a long nose, but they have wings. Unlike the karasu tengu and the less evolved konoha tengu, with the legs and talons of birds, the yamabushi tengu have human-like legs. Yamabushi tengu are depicted wearing priestly robes and carry an uchiwa kagami (a mirrored fan backed by seven, eight, or 13 feathers). The most powerful is Sōjōbō, the daitengu (great tengu) of Mount Kurama. Sōjōbō is a manifestation of Sarutahiko, the leader of the earthly kami. Sōjōbō frequently appears in numerous folk tales, theater plays, and other esoteric writings.

During the medieval era of Japan, tengu came to be associated with the powerful mental practices of the yamabushi, mountain ascetics, who pursued Shugendō, a mix of regional shamanism, Shintō, Daoism, and Esoteric Buddhism. Tengu were commonly portrayed in art during the Japanese Middle Ages wearing the robes of warrior monks and roaming the mountains searching for humans to torment. A popular belief during this era was that tengu could see into human souls through their use of their feather-covered mirrors.

Tengu came to be associated with wisdom and great martial prowess by the 14th century and were portrayed as superb swordsmen and military strategists. Among the most popular fables associated with the tengu is that of Sōjōbō and his student, Minamoto no Yoshitsune (1123-1160). Historically, Yoshitsune was a heroic 12th-century samurai and strategist who led the Minamoto clan to victory over the Taira clan at Ichi-no-Tani, Yashima, and Dan-no-ura.

Yoshitsune and his exploits became the subjects of fantastic tales and supernatural legends in 14th-century literary works. Among them are dozens of Kabuki plays, Noh theater dramas, and Kōwakamai (dances), where Yoshitsune is portrayed as an unparalleled swordsman and virtuous warrior. In one tale, Yoshitsune, who as a youth was named Ushiwakamaru, avenges his father, Minamoto no Yoshitomo, who was assassinated by the Taira clan during the Heiji Rebellion. In this story, Kiyomori (1118-1181), head of the Taira, allows seven-year-old Ushiwakamaru to survive on the condition he be exiled to Kurama Temple and be trained as a monk. In the Tengu no Dairi version from the Muromachi period, 13-year-old Ushiwakamaru calls upon Bishamonten to introduce him to Sōjōbō and the other tengu generals in the tengu palace on Mount Kurama. Sōjōbō summons the other great tengu, enters into a conversation

Ushiwakamaru (Yoshitsune) with Sōjōbō training on Mount Kurama, by Oju Shunko, 1896
(Collection of the Takamura ha Shindō Yōshin Kai.)

with the young Minamoto heir, and is so impressed by the purity of heart of the young man that he introduces him to his human wife, Kinuhikihime. While momentarily alone, Kinuhikihime confides to Ushiwakamaru that his father, Yoshitomo, has achieved Buddhahood and is now the Dainichi Buddha. She further explains he resides beyond the human realm in Jōdo (pure land), and Sōjōbō sees him daily. With this revelation, Ushiwakamaru, recognizes the immense power of the daitengu Sōjōbō.

When Sōjōbō returns, Ushiwakamaru asks the daitengu to accompany him on a journey to Jōdo to meet his dead father. Sōjōbō initially resists this request but eventually acquiesces and accompanies Ushiwakamaru through the 136 realms of hell before finally reaching Jōdo and introducing him to his father, who tests his young human son to determine the depth of his character. When Ushiwakamaru answers all his father's questions correctly and demonstrates the deepest grasp of the Buddhist sutras, Dainichi rejoices at his son's accomplishments. He then instructs Ushiwakamaru to return to the earthly realm to avenge his murder and defeat the Taira Clan. Dainichi lays out Yoshitsune's entire life, victories, tragedies, and death, and even tells Ushiwakamaru the tragic tale of Lady Tokiwa at Yamanaka.

In this mythological tale, further expanded upon by Iwasa Matabei, Yoshitsune's mother and her handmaiden are brutally murdered at the hands of a group of bandits led by their leader, Kumasaka. Dainichi explains this event cannot be stopped, as it is related to the karmic destiny of his mother, Lady Tokiwa. However, Ushiwakamaru is permitted to avenge her death as quickly as possible. Yoshitsune unflinchingly accepts his destiny as conveyed by Dainichi, bids farewell to his father, and returns to the earthly realm. Upon his return to the tengu palace, Ushiwakamaru pledges to return and undergo training in swordsmanship and strategy, so he can fulfill his destiny as the leader of the Minamoto Clan.

Tengu mythology, which is specifically related to Mount Kurama and Sōjōbō, is common in the Shinkage Ryū schools of kenjutsu and the Yōshin Ryū schools of jūjutsu. In Takamura ha Shindō Yōshin Ryū, one advanced level teaching license uses tengu symbolism and mythology from the Tengu no Dairi to convey archetypal themes related to morality, conceit, enlighten-

Shindō Yōshin Ryū

One panel of Iwasa Matabei's tale of Yamanaka Tokiwa, a 12-scroll painting created 400 years ago. The scrolls, which total over 300 feet in length, depict the murder of Minamoto no Yoshitsune's mother and subsuquent retribution by her son. In the center is the legendary Yoshitsune, a student of the daitengu Sōjōbō, exacting his revenge.

(Yamanaka Tokiwa by Iwasa Matabei, fukusei makmono (replica) property of the Takamura ha Shindō Yōshin Kai.)

ment, and death. These timeless cultural tales are interwoven with the technical curriculum and transmit the ethos and moral ideals of the school through mysterious koka and sanbun (prose). Illustrated on one of these Shindō Yōshin Ryū densho are the tengu kings: Sōjōbō of Kurama, Jirōbō of Hira, and Tarōbō of Atago. One of several mythical tales on the tengu scroll explains how Sōjōbō uses his uchiwa kagami to see into the souls of men and extract their true nature. If the mirror reflects a pure heart, Sōjōbō and his karasu tengu minions will instruct the individual in swordsmanship and strategy. If the mirror reflects corruption, the penalty is a horrific death at the hands of the Sōjōbō's tengu minions.

Karasu tengu represented on the Tengushō section of a Shinkage Ryū Heihō Mokuroku dated 1601.
(Archives of the Hozanji Temple, Nara, Japan.)

Other high-level scrolls in Takamura ha Shindō Yōshin Ryū include esoteric teachings related to tengu. Several precepts from the Tengu no Dairi are included on the Shindō Yōshin Ryū Chi no Maki densho. It includes the following condemnation of lies and deceit:

"Hana yuki wo kōri to hito no nagamuru   Some people gaze at a snow of blossoms as if
wa mina itsuwari no tane to naru kana"   it were ice; they all become the seeds of lies.

History And Technique

Takamura ha Shindō Yōshin Ryū Okugi Tengu no Maki issued to Tobin E. Threadgill by Takamura Yukiyoshi in 1995.

Tengu maintain an important place in contemporary Japanese culture. They are revered in shrines throughout Japan and admired for their wisdom, but viewed with trepidation for their powers and desire to prey on the arrogant and prideful. Tengu festivals, such as that in Shimokitazawa, Tōkyō, are attended by thousands who revere these mythical challengers of hubris.

From Sengoku Period Bujutsu to Edo Period Jūjutsu

The oldest bujutsu ryūha that survive today were true martial disciplines created for battlefield applications against armored opponents during the Sengoku period (1467-1590). These schools, such as Kashima Shin Ryū, were systemized in the 15th century and are identified as katchū bujutsu ryūha (armored martial arts schools). Schools of this era generally embraced a wide array of skills, tactics, and emphasis. However, some schools, such as Hōzōin Ryū, which emphasize pole arm weapons, preferred a narrower focus, embracing a particular aspect of tactical engagement. The most comprehensive of the katchū bujutsu schools were focused on bugei (military science) and taught the 18 associated martial disciplines of the samurai Bugei Jūhappan, some of which are listed below.

Bugei Jūhappan *

1.	Kenjutsu	(剣術)	Swordsmanship
2.	Iaijutsu / Battōjutsu	(居合術 / 抜刀術)	Sword Drawing
3.	Sōjutsu	(槍術)	Spear
4.	Naginatajutsu	(長刀術 or 薙刀術)	Halberd
5.	Kyūjutsu	(弓術)	Archery
6.	Bajutsu	(馬術)	Horsemanship
7.	Kishajutsu	(騎射術)	Mounted Archery
8.	Kusarifundojutsu	(鎖分銅術)	Weighted Chain
9.	Kusarigamajutsu	(鎖鎌術)	Sickle & Chain
10.	Suijutsu	(水術)	Swimming in Armor
11.	Yoroi Kumiuchi	(鎧組み打)	Grappling in Armor
12.	Hōjutsu	(砲術)	Musket
13.	Shurikenjutsu	(手裏剣術)	Steel Blade Throwing
14.	Hojōjutsu	(捕縄術)	Prisoner Binding
15.	Juttejutsu	(十手術)	Truncheon
16.	Bōjutsu	(棒術)	Staff
17.	Jūjutsu	(柔術)	Grappling
18.	Torite	(捕手)	Capturing

* (It should be noted the disciplines that constituted the Bugei Jūhappan varied through time as influenced by the technical innovations encountered on the Japanese battlefield.)

Shindō Yōshin Ryū

Extant schools of today that identify as Japanese jūjutsu are assumed to be focused on unarmed combat or defense. In fact, many of the earliest jūjutsu-like schools were comprehensive and included the study of an extensive array of weaponry. The word jūjutsu was most likely derived from the word yawara (flexible), and it did not exist until the middle or late 15th century. Before this period, jūjutsu schools were described using the many words that represented the dominant technical features or categories of study. Examples include torite, taijutsu, koshi no mawari, hade, kogusoku, hakuda, kempō, shubaku, yawara, wajutsu, koppō, and kumiuchi. What distinguishes these early jūjutsu-like schools from other combat schools was the emphasis on employing minor weapons in close-quarter combat where the vulnerability of protective armor could be exploited.

Takenouchi Ryū is the oldest surviving jūjutsu school. Founded in the Sengoku era, it includes a comprehensive array of techniques and tactics intended for application during armored

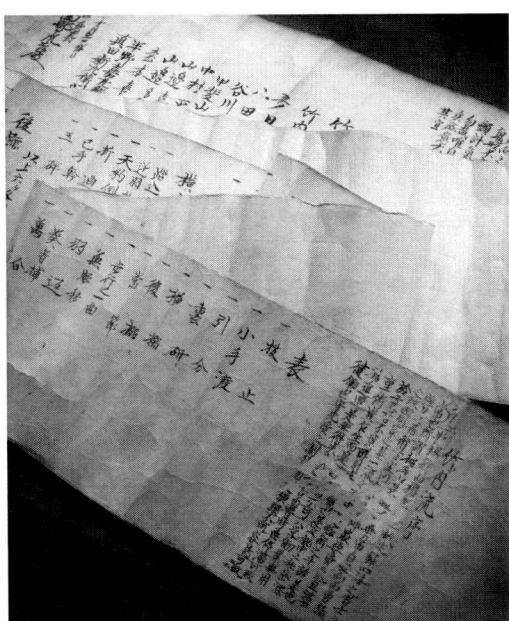

Takenouchi Ryū jūjutsu scroll, issued 1884.
(Collection of the Takamura ha Shindō Yōshin Kai.)

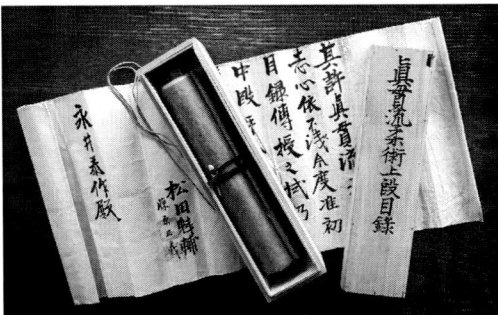

Shinkan Ryū jūjutsu Shoden Kirigami and Jōdan Mokuroku, issued in 1900 and 1902.
(Collection of the Takamura ha Shindō Yōshin Kai.)

Takenouchi Ryū includes:

- Jūjutsu — Flexible Technique
  - Tehodoki — Hand Escapes
  - Ukemi — Rolling and Falling
  - Nagewaza — Throwing
  - Kansetsuwaza — Joint Locking
  - Atemiwaza — Striking
  - Shimewaza — Strangling
  - Newaza — Ground Techniques
  - Kappō — Resuscitation
- Torite — Capturing
- Hōjō — Prisoner Restraint
- Koshi no Mawari — Small Weapon Grappling
- Kogusoku — Light Armor Grappling
- Kumiuchi — Heavy Armor Grappling
- Hade — Vital Point Attacks
- Kenpō — Fist Methods
- Taijutsu — Body Techniques
- Kenpō Saide — Grappling with a Sword
- Kenpō Iai — Sword Drawing
- Tessen — Iron Fan
- Jutte — Truncheon
- Bō — Wooden Staff
- Kusarigama — Sickle and Chain
- Shuriken — Throwing Blade
- Kasa — Hat
- Hobaku — Arresting
- Nabebuta — Cooking Pot Lid
- Naginata — Halberd

battlefield engagement. Other scenarios, such as armed ambush, attempted assassination, and empty-hand assault in a civilian environment are studied and trained, but the essence of Takenouchi Ryū lies in armored warfare of the Sengoku period. In contrast, the early Edo period (1603-1868) school, Shinkan Ryū jūjutsu, narrowed an originally comprehensive curriculum to exclusively focus on armored grappling and the use of a yoroidoshi (armor-piercing dagger).

Peace reigned during the mid-to-late Edo period, when katchū bujutsu evolved into an art dominated by the development of combat skills against adversaries without armor. These schools are generally categorized as suhada jūjutsu ryūha (unarmored martial arts schools). In suhada jūjutsu, empty-hand techniques are practiced and minor weapons skills are acquired during training while wearing kimono and hakama. Thus, suhada jūjutsu intends to thwart attempted assassinations, kidnappings, and counteract civilian violence using weapons such as tantō (dagger), tessen (iron fan), kōgai (skewer), kozuka (utility knife), torinawa (ensnaring cord), tetsubō (iron club), shuriken (throwing dart) and various hibuki (secreted weapons).

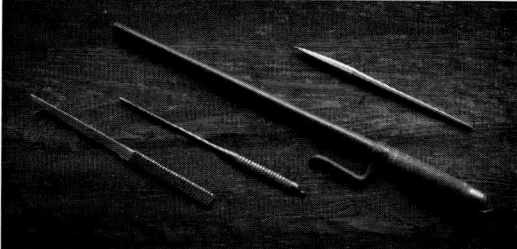

Left to right - kozuka/kogatana, kōgai, jutte and shuriken

Left to right - Tessen (iron fan): menhari-gata (folding), tenarashi-gata (solid), and motsu-shaku (wooden).

Striking was primitive in older katchū bujutsu schools, and was primarily used to physically disrupt an adversary during battle until a suitable weapon could be deployed. The absence of armor in suhada jūjutsu meant the study and application of punching, striking, and kicking skills (atemijutsu) acquired a more active role in combat and was rapidly absorbed into the curricula of many jūjutsu schools. The Akiyama Yōshin Ryū in particular, with a sophisticated understanding of kyūsho atemi (striking vital points on the body) acquired from Chinese martial arts, became one nexus for the deeper appreciation of how striking techniques could be applied to overwhelm adversaries. From the mid-15th century onwards, striking techniques became more sophisticated and practiced, resulting in dissemination throughout the Japanese martial arts community. Suhada bujutsu schools, such as Shin Musō Ryū kenpō, elected to focus almost entirely on the study and applica-

Exquisite menhari-gata (folding iron fan) with Nimatachi-do armor made by Myōchin Munedori, mid-Edo period.

Shindō Yōshin Ryū

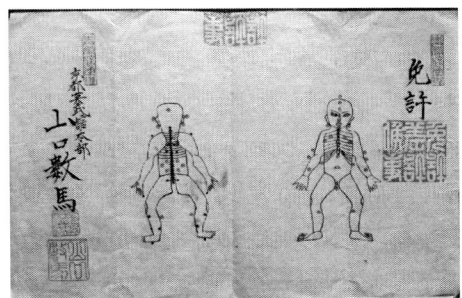
Seiun Ryū jūjutsu Kyūsho Atemi Zuhyō, from a Dai Gokui Kyūsho Kirigami, issued in 1898.
(Collection of the Takamura ha Shindō Yōshin Kai.)

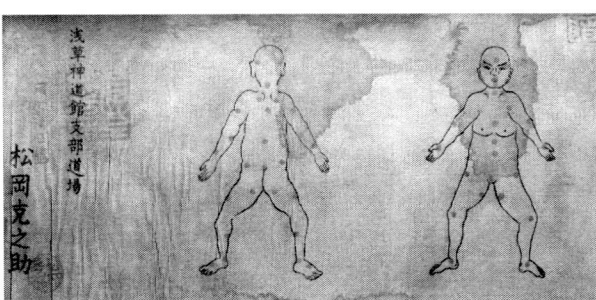
Shindō Yōshin Ryū Kyūsho Gokui no Maki issued by Ryūso (founder) Matsuoka Katsunosuke to Obata Shigeta, 1890.
(Collection of the Takamura ha Shindō Yōshin Kai.)

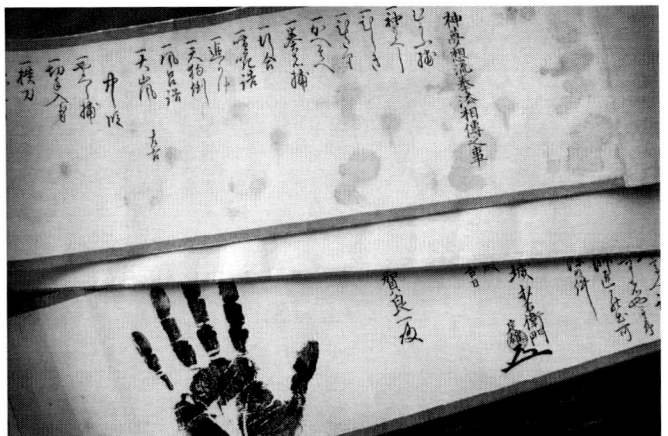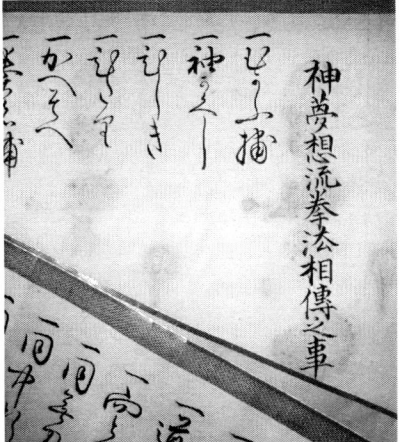
Shin Musō Ryū Kenpō Sōden no Maki, issued 1867. This Bakumatsu period school focused on striking skills.
(Collection of the Takamura ha Shindō Yōshin Kai.)

tion of striking techniques, notably pre-dating the introduction of the art of Okinawan karate to Japan by many centuries.

The Meaning of Jūjutsu

Jūjutsu is a difficult word to define because it has recently become interpreted as a generic form of unarmed combat of Japanese origin consisting of body grappling. Previously, unarmed grappling was of minor importance because of the arsenal of weaponry available to the samurai. However, unarmed combat started to assume a more important role during the enduring peace of the Tokugawa era, a fact that influenced the martial culture of Japan in general.

The simple translation of the word jūjutsu as "soft" technique does not reflect the term in its appropriate martial context. Jūjutsu is a set of combat principles and military tactics, which later came to represent a particular group of martial arts schools. Flexibility or pliability is probably a more accurate interpretation within the context of physical combat, where it represents the concept that dependence on raw physical strength should be avoided by implementing energy-conserving techniques via the application of superior body dynamics. Perhaps the defining characteristic of jūjutsu is the principle of nagashi (flowing). The strength of an adversary can be overcome by evasively flowing with an attack, and thus securing victory. Considering the psychological aspects of combat, nagashi manifests as the ability to maintain a state of mental detachment, alert relaxation, spontaneity, and situational flexibility. A practitioner of jūjutsu endeavors to blend with the psychological environment of combat, which avoids or forces physical conflict, and maintain an intensified but relaxed sense of awareness to dispassionately select the most effective strategy to overcome an opponent.

According to budō historian Dr. Imamura Yoshio,179 jūjutsu schools were registered and operating throughout the Japanese provinces during the 250-year reign of the Tokugawa Shogunate. The most influential of the era were Takenouchi Ryū, Kitō Ryū, Sekiguchi Ryū, Jikishin Ryū, Akiyama Yōshin Ryū, and Totsuka ha Yōshin Ryū.

Jūjutsu as an Art of Defense, Restraint, and the Police

Strict rules of physical behavior and social etiquette governed life behind imperial compounds and during political negotiations in feudal Japan. Such formality was initiated to maintain personal and political security and was never to be regarded as ceremonial pageantry. Negotiations between rival clans were often fraught with intense mistrust, so much so that passions could flare into violence or attempted assassinations. This problem became so pervasive during periods of political upheaval that formal court attire and etiquette were created, which restricted physical movements. Even reaching into a kimono sleeve could be perceived as a mortal threat and result in swift intervention. However, sanctions against the spilling of blood, considered a criminal act and a form of corruption, were absolute, making intervention in an assault a perilous undertaking. Thus, retainers who were loyal to dignitaries, involved in political and other negotiations involving important persons, often functioned as bodyguards in attempts to increase personal security. Such retainers were well trained in a specialized aspect of jūjutsu, which included subtle restraining techniques that did not violate the strictly enforced rules of court etiquette. While being able to apply non-lethal methods to intercede, restrain, and placate a perceived threat complied with court etiquette, such skills could rapidly ascertain and neutralize sources of threats.

During the extended peace of the Edo period, the restraining techniques that originated in the courts of nobles found new fans among the torimono-doshin and yoriki (police/constables) of the era. Notably, during this time of peace, Yamamoto Minzaemon Hidehaya of the Ōsaka Castle watch established Shin no Shindō Ryū jūjutsu based on Akiyama Yōshin Ryū in 1770. Shin no Shindō Ryū would become essential to the founding of Tenjin Shinyō Ryū jūjutsu.

Totsuka ha Yōshin Ryū would also be famously represented by the police in Chiba during the early Meiji period (1868-1912). As recounted by Dr. Erwin Baelz in his dairy "Awakening Japan: Diary of a German Doctor", it was the policemen in Totsuka Hidetoshi's Chiba dōjō who would totally dominate the jūdō students of Professor Kanō Jigorō during a famous jūjutsu contest in the late 19th century.

Yoriki (police). Jūjutsu skills were highly valued by Tokugawa law enforcement officials.

Shindō Yōshin Ryū

Extant Classical Jūjutsu/Torite Schools

Iga Ryūha Katsushin Ryū jūjutsu, Kashima Jingu, 2016.
(Photo courtesy of S.F. Radzikowski.)

Two organizations are under the umbrella of the Nihon Budōkan in Tōkyō, namely, the Nihon Kobudō Kyōkai (Japanese Ancient Martial Arts Association), which includes koryū jūjutsu, and the Nihon Budō Kyōgikai (Japanese Budō Association), which includes jūdō, aikidō, kendō, kyūdō, karatedō, sumō, jūkendō, naginata, and shōrinji kempō. Other preservation organizations in addition to those at the Budōkan are the Nihon Kobudō Shinkōkai (Japanese Kobudō Promotion Association) and the Kokusai Budōin (International Budō Institute).

Jūjutsu/Torite schools represented in the Nihon Kobudō Kyōkai (as of 2017):

School	Location
Araki Ryū Gunyō Kogusoku	Saitama
Araki Ryū Kempō (Kikuchi line)	Gunma
Daitō Ryū Aikijūjutsu	Tōkyō
Daitō Ryū Aikijūjutsu Takumakai	Ōsaka
Hasegawa Ryū Yawarajutsu	Saitama
Hontai Yōshin Ryū Jūjutsu	Hyōgo
Iga Ryūha Katsushin Ryū Jūjutsu	Ibaraki
Kiraku Ryū Jūjutsu	Gunma
Kitō Ryū Jūjutsu	Kyōto
Ryūshin Katchū Ryū Jūjutsu	Hokkaidō
Sekiguchi Shin-shin Ryū Jūjutsu	Wakayama

Takenouchi Ryū jūjutsu
Meiji Jingu, 2015.
(Photo courtesy of S.F. Radzikowski.)

- Shibukawa Ichi Ryū Jūjutsu — Hiroshima
- Shingetsu Musō Yanagi Ryū Jūjutsu — Hyōgo
- Shoshō Ryū Yawara — Morioka
- Takagi Ryū Jūjutsu — Hyōgo
- Takenouchi Ryū Jūjutsu (Hinoshita Torite Kaisan) — Okayama
- Takenouchi Ryū Jūjutsu (Koshi-no-Mawari, Kogusoku) — Okayama
- Tenjin Shinyō Ryū Jūjutsu — Saitama
- Tenjin Shinyō Ryū Jūjutsu — Tōkyō
- Yagyū Shingan Ryū — Kanagawa

The Shindō Yōshin Ryū Dōmonkai, representing the mainline, is no longer extant, but was a member of the Nihon Kobudō Kyōkai. Shindō Yōshin Ryū jūjutsu is listed in a 1989 survey of Japanese Kobudō (Nippon Kobudō Sōran) with Matsuoka Tatsuo (1892-1989) identified as the third-generation headmaster, and Dr. Fujiwara Ryōzō (1925-2017) as its representative.

Active koryū jūjutsu ryūha that are not members of the Nihon Kobudō Kyōkai include:

- Araki Ryū Kempō (Suzuki line)
- Araki Ryū Torite Kogusoku
- Asayama Ichiden Ryū
- Bokuden Ryū
- Enshin Ryū
- Fusen Ryū
- Inagaki Yōshin Ryū
- Ise Jitoku Tenshin Ryū
- Kurama Yōshin Ryū
- Nagao Ryū
- Seigō Ryū
- Shishin Takuma Yodai Kennichi Ryū
- Sōsuishi Ryū
- Takamura ha Shindō Yōshin Ryū
- Tenjin Myōshin Ryū.

Shingetsu Musō Yanagi Ryū jūjutsu Kashima Jingū, 2016.
(Photo courtesy of S.F. Radzikowski.)

Shindō Yōshin Ryū

"In the storm that shatters the oak, smothers the fire, and drives the waves, the willow tree dances."

- Akiyama Yōshin Ryū koka

History And Technique

The Origins of Shindō Yōshin Ryū

起源

There is a rather ubiquitous and romantic myth that persists among some in the Japanese budō community. This myth promotes the idea that the various koryū surviving through the centuries represent an almost pure compendium of martial knowledge passed down through many generations. The idea that the ryūgi (martial doctrines and insights) of these schools maintained a strictly orthodox and unchanging view of combat philosophy is simply untrue. In fact, most koryū were constantly evolving, challenged by the ever-changing innovations encountered on the field of conflict. Many of the more successful feudal warlords supported multiple ryū in their domains, because they knew diversity to be a strength. This led different schools to

Shindō Yōshin Ryū

exchange ideas and even spy on one another to remain combat-effective. In this vein, a famed Bakumatsu period samurai, Matsuoka Katsunosuke, founded an art he named Shindō Yōshin Ryū, by combining the ryūgi of five different schools of bujutsu to create his own expression of an older sōgō bujutsu (comprehensive martial art).

Yōshin Ryū or Yōshin Ryū?

The words "Yōshin Ryū" can refer to several budō traditions that are descended from up to six unrelated lineages, which still causes popular misunderstanding among jūjutsu practitioners. The Japanese linguistic penchant for homophones can easily confuse non-Japanese speakers. For example, over 100 kanji (Japanese characters) are pronounced "yō" and the meaning, nuance, or application between them can be quite different. The use of different kanji for yō is a feature among both the related and unrelated Yōshin Ryū schools. Inconsistencies among the related schools can be explained by calligraphic error, as two of the most popular characters are differentiated by a single brush stroke. However, others are clearly an intentional variation. The photographs below show four kanji combinations found on various Akiyama lineage densho, each of which differs, but all are correctly pronounced "Yōshin Ryū".

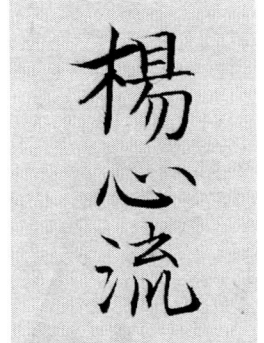
Willow Spirit Path

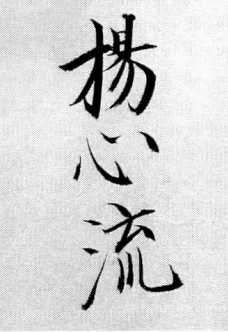
Rising Spirit Path

Cultivating Spirit Path

Positive Spirit Path

The Two Yōshin Ryū Jūjutsu Lineages Relevant to Shindō Yōshin Ryū

The shōgun (warlord) Tokugawa Iemitsu (1604-1651) officially adopted a policy of sakoku (closed country), a national isolation, which lasted from 1633 until 1867. Under this policy, foreigners could not enter Japan and Japanese could not leave under penalty of death. However, this policy was not absolute. Trade and cultural exchange with selected nations were permitted at four locations in Japan, the most significant being Nagasaki, where contact persisted with Dutch and Chinese merchants. Consequently, Nagasaki became the most important city in Japan, in terms of contact with the outside world, for over 230 years.

Chinese martial arts influenced several jūjutsu traditions with connections to Nagasaki during the first half of the 17th century. These include Miura Ryū, Miura Yōshin Ryū, and Akiyama Yōshin Ryū. The exact manner and origins of these Chinese influences are still debated by martial arts historians. There are likely several different sources for this influence. One commonly cited, but embellished source, is a Chinese philosopher/poet named Chin Genpin (Chinese: Ch'en Yuang Ping, 1587-1671). Chin Genpin's exploits were exaggerated by several of his students pursuing prestige due to his political connections to a famed retainer of Tokugawa Ieyasu named Ishikawa Jōzan. Although Chen Genpin apparently taught Chinese Kenpō at the Kokushōji monastery in Tōkyō, his instruction of Miura Yojiuemon, the founder of Miura Ryū jūjutsu, was minimal, lasting several months instead of years.

Miura Yōshin Ryū and Akiyama Yōshin Ryū are two schools with so many similarities they are often considered to be members of the same lineage. However, the most ubiquitous theory claims these two schools are actually independent lines of jūjutsu with coincidental technical and historical parallels. This "separate theory" holds that Nakamura Sakyodayu Yoshikuni, a Kōshū Takeda retainer who later changed his name to Miura Yōshin, founded Miura Yōshin Ryū. One claim is Nakamura Yoshikuni founded his jūjutsu school in Nagasaki around 1610 and based it on Taiin Ryū (or Daiin Ryū), an earlier school headed by his father. This theory also suggests Akiyama Yōshin Ryū was a totally unrelated tradition founded by Akiyama Shirōbei Yoshitoki, a doctor who either traveled to China to study medicine and martial arts or learned Chinese medicine and martial arts from a Chinese doctor in Nagasaki. The theory further posits Akiyama established his Yōshin Ryū jūjutsu school in Nagasaki around 1651. While these are the most commonly cited theories regarding the origination of these two schools, the authors of this book are convinced a mix of technical connections exist between Miura Ryū, Miura Yōshin Ryū, and Akiyama Yōshin Ryū.

Among various "connection theories," one postulates Miura Yōshin Ryū is actually a branch of Akiyama Yōshin Ryū and Miura Yōshin is the same individual who shows up on many Akiyama Yōshin Ryū genealogies, as Miura Sadauemon. Depending on the densho, an individual named Miura Sadauemon is identified as a second or third-generation Akiyama lineage shihan. An important aspect of this theory is that records identifying Miura Yōshin Ryū headmasters between the first and sixth generations are absent. The Miura Yōshin Ryū genealogy simply skips from the founder, Miura Yōshin, to an individual identified as the sixth-generation headmaster, Abe Kanryū (1712-1770). If Miura Yōshin is the same person as Miura Sadauemon, and this individual was a third-generation shihan of Akiyama Yōshin Ryū, who broke away to establish his own school, the number of generations listed on both Akiyama Yōshin Ryū and Miura Yōshin Ryū densho becomes fairly consistent. This would indicate Miura Yōshin Ryū is likely a descendant school of Akiyama Yōshin Ryū, and the tale of its founder, Nakamura Yoshikuni, is a later invention.

An additional connection theory postulates that the person identified as the second headmaster of the Akiyama lineage, Ōe Senbei, was a student of both Miura Ryū and Miura Yōshin Ryū. This theory suggests Ōe Senbei combined his knowledge of these two jūjutsu systems to establish Akiyama Yōshin Ryū in 1651, one year after the death of Nakamura Yoshikuni (Miura Yōshin) in 1650. This theory also surmises Akiyama Yoshitoki was not a real person, but a mythical individual created to embody the skill, wisdom, and character of its progenitors. In support of this notion, Nakamura Yoshikuni is said to have studied Chinese medicine, a characteristic commonly associated with Akiyama Yoshitoki. Further support is found in the densho collection of the Takamura ha Shindō Yōshin Kai, where keizu (lineage charts) included on several densho identify Ōe Senbei as the founder of Yōshin Ryū, eliminating the mention of Akiyama Yoshitoki altogether.

The most controversial connection theory is that Miura Ryū, Miura Yōshin Ryū, and Akiyama Yōshin Ryū all descended from an obscure grappling art taught by Yagyū Sekishūsai Muneyoshi, around 1585. This theory suggests three students of Yagyū Muneyoshi later studied with Chin Genpin and went on to establish the three famous jūjutsu schools, which are claimed to have originated in Nagasaki. This is a rather romanticized notion and evidence suggesting this theory deserves serious consideration is scant. Without convincing evidence to support this theory, it remains an outlier.

Shindō Yōshin Ryū

Historical Background of Akiyama Yōshin Ryū

Image taken from a series of woodblock prints titled Kenpōzu. This series of prints is extensive and said to depict yamabushi tengu and karasu tengu executing various Akiyama Yōshin Ryū jūjutsu techniques. Tengu mythology, particularly as associated with Sōjōbō and Mount Kurama, has long been associated with the Shinkage lines of kenjutsu originating with Kamiizumi Ise no Kami, and the Yōshin Ryū lines of jūjutsu originating with Akiyama Shirōbei Yoshitoki.

(Illustration from the Kenpōzu, courtesy of the Odawara Library, Kanagawa, Japan.)

Akiyama Shirōbei Yoshitoki is regarded as the founder of the Akiyama Yōshin Ryū jūjutsu lineage, yet his birthplace and birthdate remain obscure, and little else is known about him. Folklore about this legendary giant of jūjutsu history comprises several conflicting stories. All written references to Akiyama were created by third parties, after the 1670s, and any document personally written by Akiyama remains to be discovered.

The most common story about Akiyama is traceable to a mid-19th century document, the Tenjin Shinyō Ryū Tai-i Roku, which describes him as a doctor who traveled to China to study medicine. The Tai-i Roku states Akiyama learned 28 techniques of a martial art in China, which became the foundation of Yōshin Ryū jūjutsu.

According to another document from the Edo period, the Shinsen Bujutsu Ryūsoroku, Akiyama learned three jūjutsu techniques, identified as torite (restraining), and 28 kappō (resuscitation) techniques from a person identified as Mukan (military man), who lived in Higo Province in Japan. This document does not describe the nationality of Mukan or any journey to China, and does not imply any Chinese influence on Akiyama Yoshitoki or his creation, Yōshin Ryū jūjutsu.

A third variation is found in the Tenjin Shinyō Ryū Gokui Kyōju Zukai, published in 1896. It repeats the Chinese connection, claiming Akiyama traveled to China to study medicine, but names Hakuten as the Chinese teacher of the three torite techniques, and curiously attributes 28 katsu or katchū (armored techniques), not kappō, techniques to a man identified as Mukan.

The idea that Akiyama based such a comprehensive school as Yōshin Ryū on only three techniques or kata is difficult to accept historically. Takamura Yukiyoshi believed these three techniques actually symbolized the three foundational principles upon which Akiyama based his school of budō. He theorized these principles might have been identified as Ten (heaven), Chi (earth), and Jin (man).

Despite differences in origination stories, Yōshin Ryū lore is consistent in its fundamental principle of non-resistance, as well as with a legend. Akiyama is said to have meditated for 100 days at the Tenmangū Shrine in Dazaifu, Fukuoka (present-day Kyūshū) to expand the curriculum of Yōshin Ryū beyond his original learning. During a snowstorm at the shrine, Akiyama observed how snow building up on a willow tree fell harmlessly away when the flexible branch yielded to its weight and sprang back to its original position. He also observed that snow building up on oak tree branches eventually caused the branches to break. He realized the willow tree could not only survive the weight of the snow by yielding, but could also release stored energy through its flexible branches when the weight was removed. Thus, he reasoned, flexibility was superior to rigidity in both absorbing and releasing energy.

A unique feature of Akiyama Yōshin Ryū was its adoption of a liberal strategy related to awarding teaching licenses. Ōe Senbei Yoshitoki, the second-generation headmaster of Akiyama Yōshin Ryū, opened a dōjō in Ōsaka during the early 18th century and licensed a significant number of teachers. His most famous students were Hano Shinkurō, Miura Sadauemon, Satō Jirōbei, Ōi Uhei, Takemitsu Nobushige, and Yamamoto Minzaemon. Akiyama Yōshin Ryū had significantly grown by the third generation, having spread throughout southern Japan, and reached as far north as Edo. The Akiyama Yōshin Ryū dōjō in northern Japan ultimately became one of the most historically influential jūjutsu schools in the Japanese budō community.

Illustration of the kata Kekaeshi/Tsuka Guruma from an Akiyama Yōshin Ryū Inyō no Maki, issued by Morimoto Tokiuemon in 1845. (Collection of the Takamura ha Shindō Yōshin Kai.)

Yōshin Ryū and the Takeda Clan of Kai and Aki

The Takeda clan, in Kai (present day Yamanashi prefecture), was closely related to the Genji/Minamoto clan via Takeda Yoshikiyo, a nephew of Minamoto Yoshiie. The Takeda ruled Kai from the era of Takeda Nobuyoshi (1138-1186) until their defeat at Nagashino in 1575. Takeda Nobutake was the last Takeda governor of the three provinces of Kai, Aki, and Wakasa. His elder son, Nobunari, was selected to rule over Kai while his younger brother, Ujinobu, was selected to rule over the Aki and Wakasa provinces. The Aki line of the Takeda ended with the death of Takeda Nobuzane in 1555.

The Akiyama Yōshin Ryū and the Nakamura Yōshin Koryū lineages founded in Nagasaki had common roots in Kai. With the defeat of the Kai Takeda at Nagashino, the Akiyama family and the Nakamura family, both of the Kai Takeda, are said to have escaped and traveled to Aki province. The Akiyama and Nakamura families lived safely among other relatives of the Takeda, the Harada, and Yamaguchi families in Aki. The Harada and Yamaguchi were members of the Asano clan, itself descended from the Aki Takeda. The Akiyama and Nakamura families eventually moved and settled in Nagasaki, Hizen Province.

Legend holds a Takeda samurai living in Kai province, named Baba Mina no Kami, founded a jūjutsu school called either Taiin or Daiin Ryū. The second son of Baba Mina no Kami was Nakamura Yorifusa, the second headmaster of Taiin Ryū. Yorifusa's family, including his son Nakamura Sakyōdayū Yoshikuni, fled Kai around the same time as the Akiyama family. Nakamura Yoshikuni later founded Miura Yōshin Ryū. The dominant theory suggests the Akiyama and Nakamura Yōshin Ryū lines are completely separate, although if the Akiyama line did have a technical connection with Miura Yōshin Ryū, it could mean both Akiyama Yōshin Ryū and Miura Yōshin Ryū are descended from Taiin Ryū and share their origins in the Kai Takeda.

Whether this possible connection can explain the technical similarities between the curricula of these schools, or whether these similarities are due to later technical exchange, remains speculative. The similarities between Yōshin Ryū and Daitō Ryū in relation to their study of internal power offer plenty of possibilities to contemplate. Daitō Ryū is a school founded centuries later by Takeda Sokaku that traces its origins to a cryptically-referenced budō associated with the Genji/Minamoto clan.

Kurama Yōshin Ryū

Mount Kurama, with its mystical reputation, has been associated with budō for centuries. One composite school of bujutsu descended from Akiyama Yōshin Ryū is Kurama Yōshin Ryū. Its headquarters is located on Koshikijima Island, in Kyūshū. This school is a mix of Akiyama Yōshin Ryū jūjutsu, Nampa Ippo Ryū hojōjutsu, and Hikita Kage Ryū kenjutsu. The school's founder, Nakata Hikozaemon, added Kurama to the name in recognition of the esoteric tengu mythology included in the the school's teaching documents. Some kata in Kurama Yōshin Ryū mimic the movements and vocalizations of crows in a metaphorical manner which obscures the practical application of technique while preserving the kata's riai (theory). Other schools throughout Japan's budō history have similarly linked themselves to Mount Kurama and its famed tengu:

- Kurama Ittō Ryū
- Kurama Kō Ryū
- Kurama Shinden Zuisei Ryū
- Kurama Sōden Ryū
- Kurama Tōkin Ryū
- Kurama Nen Ryū
- Kurama Hachi Ryū
- Kurama Hiden Ryū

Technical Legacy of Akiyama Yōshin Ryū

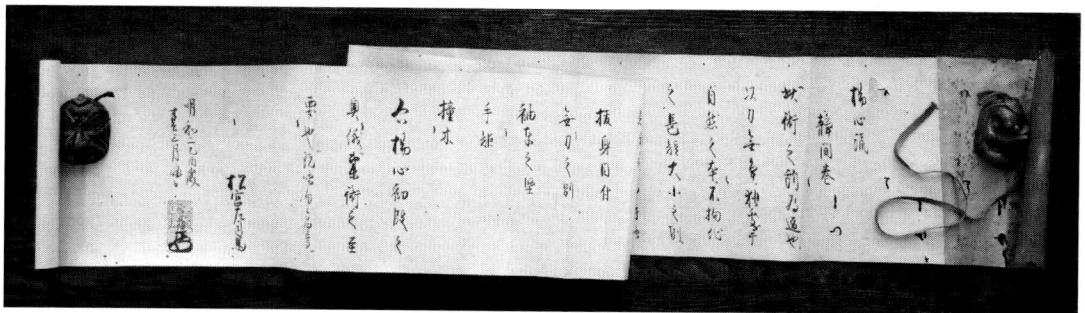

Akiyama Yōshin Ryū Seikan no Maki, issued in 1766.
(Collection of the Takamura ha Shindō Yoshin Kai.)

Akiyama Yōshin Ryū was conceived as a sōgō bujutsu, which principally reflected heifuku (civilian clothing/unarmored) kumiuchi (grappling), although a small portion of the study also involved training in katchū kumiuchi (armored engagement). In addition to the taijutsu (body techniques) curriculum, the school studied a substantial complement of weapons-based techniques, including bōjutsu, iaitachijutsu, kenjutsu, naginatajutsu, kusarigamajutsu, and sōjutsu. Since Akiyama Yōshin Ryū was founded by a doctor, a sophisticated understanding of anatomy, muscular dynamics, joint articulation, and neurological manipulation was reflected in the curriculum. Teachings also included medical training for treating injuries and illness. Several gokui (deepest secrets) densho of Akiyama Yōshin Ryū demonstrate a sophisticated grasp of body movement and joint manipulation, reminiscent of modern chiropractic medicine. This level of knowledge eventually resulted in many Yōshin Ryū shihan pursuing secondary careers in Seikotsu (bonesetting), a discipline similar to present-day physiotherapy.

As Akiyama Yōshin Ryū spread across Japan, various master instructors started emphasizing different aspects of its diverse curriculum. Most instructors by the mid-1800s focused on taijutsu through the study of kansetsu waza (joint locking), nage waza (throwing), shime waza (strangling), kyūsho atemi (vital point striking), nairiki (internal strength), and kappō (resuscitation). The lines of Akiyama Yōshin Ryū that predominately focused on taijutsu, evolved and

Kuruma Dori, from an illustrated Akiyama Yōshin Ryū jūjutsu Seikan no Maki, dated 1845.
(Collection of the Takamura ha Shindō Yōshin Kai.)

flourished, eventually becoming a dominant force among the jūjutsu schools of the middle-to-late Edo period.

Akiyama Yōshin Ryū extensively influenced the greater koryū community. Many older koryū jūjutsu schools started adopting elements of Akiyama Yōshin Ryū into their curriculum, particularly aspects related to striking and the generation of power. The supposedly Chinese-sourced knowledge within Akiyama Yōshin Ryū seems to have generated particular interest, and slowly migrated throughout the jūjutsu community of the Edo period. The Akiyama Yōshin Ryū knowledge of kyūsho atemi, and nairiki (internal power) represented a significant advance in sophistication compared with the practices originally taught in the older koryū jūjutsu schools. Kyūsho atemi densho of the older koryū jūjutsu schools practiced in the late Edo period reveal atemi kyūsho zuhyō (diagrams of vital points) which are very similar to those of Akiyama Yōshin Ryū. This indicates that such knowledge likely migrated backwards to these older schools from a more recent source. Akiyama Yōshin Ryū and Kitō Ryū appear to be the earliest nexus between Chinese-sourced kyūsho and the nairiki aspect of koryū.

Most students of koryū are familiar with kyūsho atemi zuhyō. This knowledge was uniquely sophisticated in Akiyama Yōshin Ryū by Japanese budō community standards because the vital points were divided into the following types at the highest level of study: akusho (evil points), ekisho (beneficial points), and kyoryokusho (potent points). When stimulated, these points are respectively considered dangerous, beneficial, and either beneficial or dangerous depending on how and when pressure is applied. Kyūsho knowledge within Akiyama Yōshin Ryū is likely derived from Chinese-sourced medical expertise related to acupuncture.

Akiyama Yōshin Ryū naginata performed at the Nippon Budōkan in 2017.
(Photo courtesy of S.F. Radzikowski.)

Female Akiyama Yōshin Ryū practitioners are taught sophisticated footwork that allows them to perform dramatic movements despite wearing restrictive furisode kimono.
(Photo courtesy of S.F. Radzikowski.)

Another example of the erudite knowledge of anatomy and body articulation associated with Akiyama Yōshin Ryū is illustrated in the Kyūsho Kiri Zuhyō (diagrams of vital-point cuts) of the school. Often mistaken for diagrams of atemi, these outline vital targets for bladed weapons, namely the most vulnerable points on the body associated with arteries, ligaments and tendons. A unique aspect of Akiyama Yōshin Ryū is the practice of starting a cut with pressure applied laterally to the skin of an adversary with the shinogi (sword blade ridge or side) of a bladed weapon. This depresses the skin at the site of contact between the weapon and the body. The aim is to facilitate the exposure of a tendon or artery. While the pressure is increased the blade is rotated 90°, allowing the cutting edge to sever the target. Appearing to the uninitiated as a mere flick of the wrist, this tactic is devastatingly effective when appropriately timed.

One Yōshin Ryū branch located in the Chūgoku region of southern Japan, selected a different path from the branches that focused predominantly on taijutsu. This branch was dominated by women and emphasized the study of weaponry, particularly naginata, kusarigama, yari, and hanbō (half staff). Today, the Akiyama Yōshin Ryū naginata school is located in Hiroshima, where it thrives under the direction of the 13th-generation headmistress, Koyama Takako. Men and women training in the school are notably taught in a different manner. The ladies-in-waiting of prominent lords of the Yanagawa domain (Fukuoka) were instructed in Akiyama Yōshin Ryū during the Tokugawa period. Consequently, female students of Akiyama Yōshin Ryū naginata train in beautiful, but apparently restrictive, furisode (long-sleeved) kimono, whereas the men train in traditional kimono and hakama. Yet many Yōshin Ryū naginata kata executed by women include dramatic leaps and sophisticated body movements that defy sartorial hindrance. Masterful footwork allows the Yōshin Ryū adept to move efficiently in any direction

Dai Nippon Butokukai / 大日本武徳会 (DNBK)

Butokuden, Kyōto next to Heian Jingū: It is classified as 'Jūyō Bunkazai' (Important Cultural Property of Japan).
(Photo courtesy of John Lovato.)

Popular understanding is Emperor Kanmu established a hall called the Butokuden in the newly designated capitol of Kyōto during 794 to encourage the study of martial arts in Japan. Heian Jingū was built 1100 years later in 1894 to commemorate the anniversary of Kyōto being selected as the capital city of Japan. The Dai Nippon Butokukai was established in Kyōto during the following year to promote bujutsu/budō. This event coincided with Obata Shigeta of Shindō Yōshin Ryū receiving a Menkyo Kaiden from Matsuoka Katsunosuke. A hand-brushed document in the possession of the Takamura ha Shindō Yōshin Kai, signed by the Butokukai patron, Crown Prince Komatsu no Miya Akihito, was presented to Obata Shigeta for preserving the ways of the samurai. Other surviving documentation indicates Obata Shigeta donated funds to the Butokukai in 1905.

The Butokukai aimed to accomplish the following in the years after its establishment in 1895:

1. To rebuild the Butokuden (Bujutsu hall) next to Heian Jingū. In 1899, Butokuden construction was completed.

2. To organize Butokukai festivals and Budō demonstrations at the Butokuden, and to issue titles. In 1903, Hanshi and Kyōshi (later Tasshi) titles were settled. In 1934, the Renshi title was added.

3. To build an educational system for Bujutsu, which included: the Bujutsu Kyōin Yoseisho (place to educate teachers in Bujutsu) in 1905, the Bujutsu Senmon Gakkō (special school for Bujutsu) in 1911, and the Budō Senmon Gakkō (special school for Budō) in 1919.

The Dai Nippon Butokukai voluntarily dissolved its charter in 1946 after the Allied GHQ issued a directive to dissolve all military-related organizations in Japan. Although a new organization was established under the same name in 1953, it is a private institution that issues modern budō ranks and maintains no influence within the greater community of koryū.

History And Technique

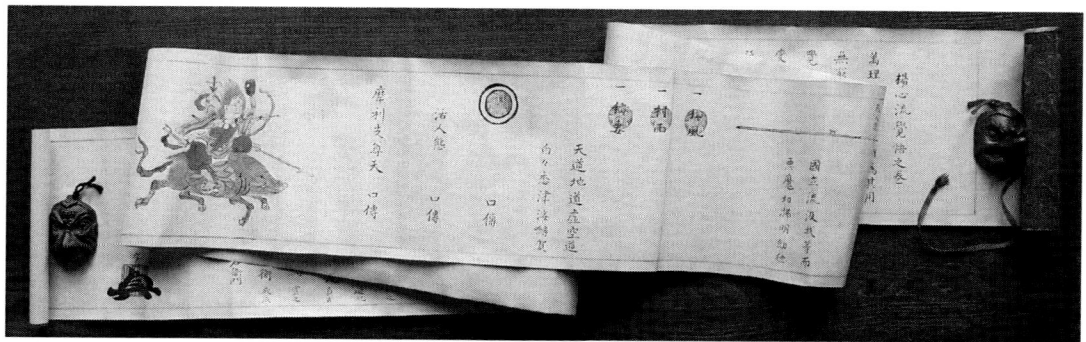

Akiyama Yōshin Ryū Kakugo no Maki. This densho of esoteric knowledge was issued by Morimoto Tokiuemon, 17th-generation shihan, in 1853.
(Collection of the Takamura ha Shindō Yōshin Kai)

and to leap and twist, achieving surprisingly fast cuts and powerful thrusts. Women are expected to execute these kata efficiently, with elegance and poise, whereas, men are taught to perform the kata in a manner focused entirely on pragmatic martial application.

Consistent with the defining principles of Akiyama Yōshin Ryū, kata performance is fluid and focuses on sophistication rather than strength or power. In particular, the naginata techniques capitalize on the momentum of the opponent's weapon in a parry or re-direction, which results in an immediate counter-attack to a vital target. All Akiyama Yōshin Ryū kata are executed against a tachi (sword), except the naginata kata, which are executed against either a tachi or a naginata in the following manner:

> *"Move gracefully and flow like a willow tree in the breeze. If an attacker cuts your flesh, flow with the attack and cut his bones."*
>
> -Akiyama Yōshin Ryū koka

Akiyama Yōshin Ryū burst into the Edo koryū community, immediately becoming popular and successful. A comprehensive and unique curriculum with unparalleled technical sophistication is one reason for this impressive success. However, issuing teaching authority outside ancestral lines was probably another key factor that contributed to the growth of this school. The number of students to whom Akiyama gave teaching authority is unknown, but surviving records confirm that the second-generation headmaster, Ōe Senbei, was a prolific teacher who conferred high-level teaching authority upon many students. The densho collection of the Takamura ha Shindō Yōshin Kai, contains numerous illustrated genealogies. Unfortunately, information about the total number of late Edo period Akiyama Yōshin Ryū lines is incomplete. Nonetheless, about 30 to 40 Akiyama Yōshin Ryū lineages and descendant schools with origins in Akiyama Yōshin Ryū are documented.

The following photographs show ten keizu (genealogies) representing a partial list of the Akiyama Yōshin Ryū densho residing in the Takamura ha Shindō Yōshin Kai collection.

Shindō Yōshin Ryū

Various Recorded Akiyama Yōshin Ryū Lineages

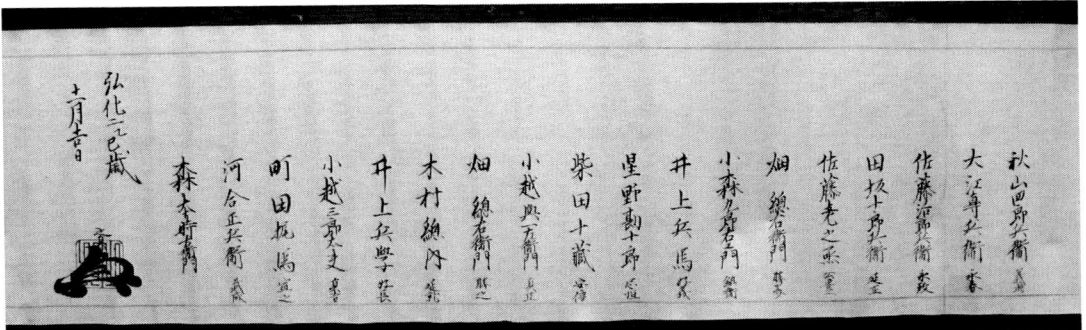

Akiyama Yōshin Ryū Inyō no Maki - issued by Morimoto Tokiuemon, 1845.
(Collection of the Takamura ha Shindō Yōshin Kai.)

Akiyama Yōshin Ryū Kakugo no Maki - issued by Morimoto Tokiuemon, 1853.
(Collection of the Takamura ha Shindō Yōshin Kai.)

1.	秋山四郎兵衛義時	Akiyama Shirōbei Yoshitoki
2.	大江千兵衛永春	Ōe Senbei Nagaharu
3.	佐藤治郎兵衛永政	Satō Jirōbei Nagamasa
4.	田坂十郎兵衛延正	Tasaka Jūrōbei Nobemasa
5.	佐藤老之蒸公豊	Satō Oinojō Kimitoyo[1]
6.	畑総右衛門勝義	Hata Sōuemon Katsuyoshi
7.	小森九郎右エ門鎮衛	Komori Kurōuemon Yasumori
8.	井上兵馬好義	Inoue Hyōma Sukiyoshi
9.	星野勘十郎忠恒	Hoshino Kanjūrō Tadatsune
10.	柴田十蔵安信	Shibata Jūzō Yasunobu
11.	小越興一左衛門貞正	Kogoshi Koichizaemon Sadamasa
12.	畑総右衛門勝之	Hata Sōuemon Katsuyuki
13.	木村総内延就	Kimura Sōnai Nobunari
14.	井上兵学好長	Inoue Heigaku Yoshinaga[2]
15.	小越三郎太夫貞吉	Kogoshi Saburōdayū Sadayoshi
16.	町田梶馬宣之	Machida Kajima Nobuyuki
17.	河合正兵衛武成	Kawai Shobei Takenari
18.	森本時右衛門	Morimoto Tokiuemon

弘化二乙巳歳 — Kōka 2 Kinotomi Sai, 1845
十一月吉日 — November Kichijitsu – Auspicious Day

[1] Satō Jirōbe Nagamasa has published 'Kenkanmon' in 1787.

[2] Omitted on the Inyō no Maki

References: *'Shindō Yōshin Ryū no Rekishi to Gihō'* (Fujiwara Ryōzō, Sōzō, 1983)

History And Technique

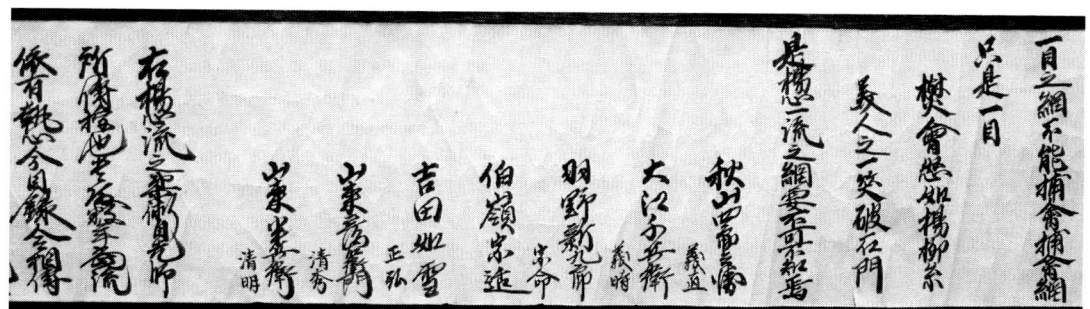

Akiyama Yōshin Ryū Jūjutsu no Maki - issued by Santo Hanbei Kiyoaki, 1863.
(Collection of the Takamura ha Shindō Yōshin Kai.)

1.	秋山四郎兵衛義直	Akiyama Shirōbei Yoshinao
2.	大江千兵衛義時	Ōe Senbei Yoshitoki
3.	羽野新九郎宗命	Hano Shinkurō Muneaki
4.	伯嶺宗造	Hakumine Uzō
5.	吉田如雪正弘	Yoshida Nyosetsu Masahiro
6.	山東彦右衛門清秀	Santō Hikouemon Kiyohide
7.	山東半兵衛清明	Santō Hanbei Kiyoaki

References: *'Higo Budōshi' (Budō History in Higo (Kumamoto), 1974, Kyōshinsha)*
'Shindō Yōshin Ryū no Rekishi to Gihō' (Fujiwara Ryōzō, Sōzō, 1983)

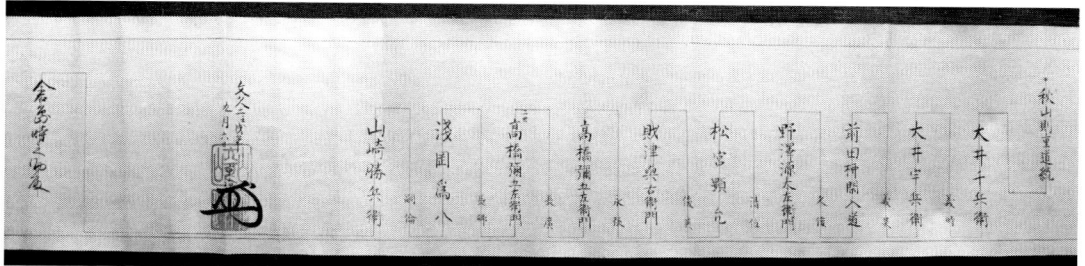

Akiyama Yōshin Ryū Kakugo no Maki - issued by Yamasaki Katsubei, 1862.
(Collection of the Takamura ha Shindō Yōshin Kai.)

1.	秋山則重道統	Akiyama Norishige Dōtō
2.	大井千兵衛義時	Ōi Senbei Yoshitoki (*大井 instead of 大江)
3.	大井宇兵衛義英	Ōi Uhei Yoshihide (*大井 instead of 大江)
4.	前田柳閑入道久俊	Maeda Ryūkan Nyūdō Hisatoshi
5.	野沢源太左衛門清信	Nozawa Gentazaemon Kiyonobu
6.	松宮顕充俊英	Matsumiya Akimichi Toshihide
7.	財津與右衛門永張	Zaitsu Youemon Nagahari
8.	高橋彌五左衛門長広	Takahashi Yagozaemon Nagahiro
9.	高橋彌五左衛門長郷	Takahashi Yagozaemon Nagasato
10.	浅岡為八嗣倫	Asaoka Tamehachi Tsugitomo
11.	山崎勝兵衛	Yamasaki Katsubei
	文久二壬戌九月六日	Bunkyū 2, Mizunoe, 1862
	倉島時之助殿	Kurashima Tokinosuke

Reference: *'Shindō Yōshin Ryū no Rekishi to Gihō' (Fujiwara Ryōzō, Sōzō, 1983)* shows 3 to 5 as:
Ōi Uhei Yoshihide
Maeda Nyūdō Hisatoshi
Nozawa Gengozaemon

Shindō Yōshin Ryū

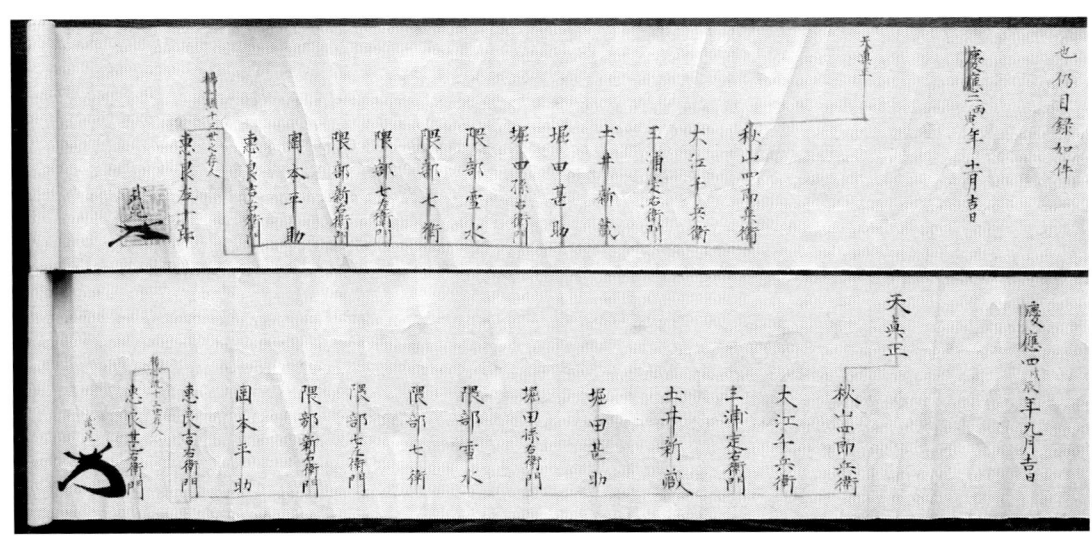

Akiyama Yōshin Ryū Iaitachijutsu - issued by Era Kichiuemon, 1866 & 1868.
(Collection of the Takamura ha Shindō Yōshin Kai.)

Akiyama Yōshin Ryū spread mainly in Kyūshū such as in Higo (Kumamoto), Hizen (Saga), Buzen (Fukuoka, Ōita), Bungo (Ōita), Hyūga (Miyazaki). The two licenses above are from a dōjō in Higo (Kumamoto).

	天真正	(Ten shin shō - Divine Transmission)
1.	秋山四郎兵衛	Akiyama Shirōbei
2.	大江千兵衛	Ōe Senbei
3.	三浦定右衛門	Miura Sadauemon
4.	土井新蔵	Doi Shinzō
5.	堀田甚助	Hotta Jinsuke
6.	堀田孫右衛門	Hotta Magouemon
7.	隈部雲水	Kumabe Unsui
8.	隈部七衛	Kumabe Hichiei
9.	隈部七左衛門	Kumabe Hichizaemon
10.	隈部新右衛門	Kumabe Shinuemon
11.	岡本平助	Okamoto Heisuke
12.	恵良吉右衛門	Era Kichiuemon

楊心流十三世之存人

| 13. | 恵左十郎 | Era Sajūrō (1866) |
| 13. | 恵良甚右衛門 | Era Jinuemon (1868) |

慶応二丙寅年	Keiō 2 Hinoe-tora, 1866
十一月吉日	November, Kichijitsu - Auspicious Day
慶応四丙寅年九月吉日	Keiō 4 Boshin, 1868
九月吉日	November, Kichijitsu - Auspicious Day

References: 'Higo Budōshi' (Budō History in Higo (Kumamoto), 1974, Kyōshinsha)
'Higo Hosokawa" (Hosokawa Samurai),(http://www.shinShindoh.com/samurai/01-a.htm)
'Shindō Yōshin Ryū no Rekishi to Gihō' (Fujiwara Ryōzō, Sōzō, 1983)

History And Technique

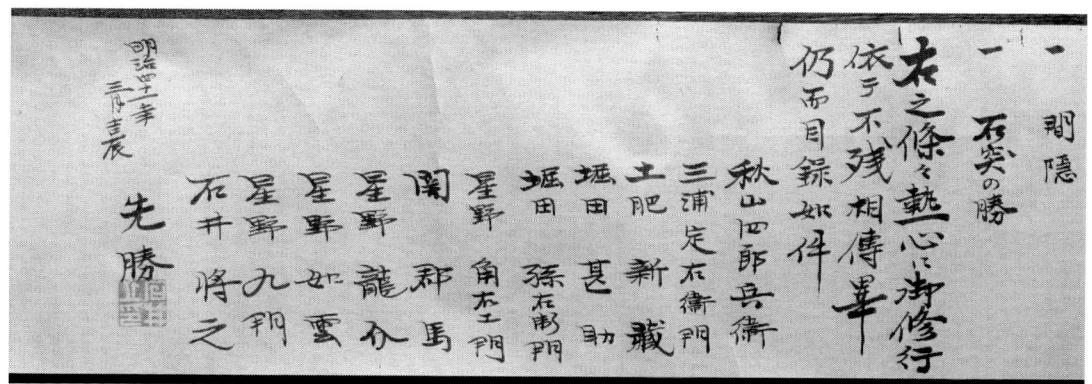

Akiyama Yōshin Ryū Naginatajutsu - issued by Hoshino Kumon, 1908.
(Collection of the Takamura ha Shindō Yōshin Kai.)

1.	秋山四郎兵衛	Akiyama Shirōbei
2.	三浦定右衛門	Miura Sadauemon
3.	土肥新蔵	Doi Shinzō
4.	堀田甚助	Hotta Jinsuke
5.	堀田孫右衛門	Hotta Magouemon
6.	星野角右衛門	Hoshino Kakuemon
7.	関郡馬	Seki Gunma
8.	星野龍介	Hoshino Ryūsuke
9.	星野如雲	Hoshino Joun
10.	星野九門	Hoshino Kumon
	石井将之	Ishii Masayuki
	明治四十一年三月吉辰	Meiji 41(1908) March, Kisshin
	先勝	Sengachi

星野如雲 (1805-1882)
Hoshino Joun, Shirozaemon, Higo (Kumamoto), Shihan in Hōki Ryū iai, Shiten Ryū kumiuchi, Yōshin Ryū naginata

星野九門 (1835-1916)
Hoshino Kumon, Higo (Kumamoto), Menkyo Kaiden in Hōki Ryū iai, Shiten Ryū kumiuchi, Yōshin Ryū naginata

(http://bujutsu.jp/h04.html)

Higo Budōshi shows:

Shiten Ryū kumiuchi: Narita Seibei - Nishi Yūheiji - Hotta Magouemon – Hoshino Kakuuemon - Seki Gunma - Hoshino Ryūsuke - Hoshino Shirōzaemon - Hoshino Kinuemon,

Yōshin Ryū naginata: Akiyama Shirōbei - Ōe Senbei - Miura Sadauemon – Doi Shinzo – Hotta Jinsuke – Hotta Magouemon – Hoshino Kakuemon – Seki Gunma – Hoshino Ryūsuke – Hoshino Shirōzaemon – Hoshino Kinuemon

Shiten Ryū kumiuchi and Yōshin Ryū jūjutsu are practiced by the same individuals in Higo (Kumamoto). Shiten Ryū kumiuchi was likely influenced by Yōshin Ryū jūjutsu. Higo Budōshi uses 揚心流 instead of 楊心流.

References: 'Higo Budōshi' (Budō History in Higo (Kumamoto), 1974, Kyōshinsha)
              'Higo Hosokawa" (Hosokawa Samurai),(http://www.shinShindoh.com/samurai/01-a.htm)
              'Shindō Yōshin Ryū no Rekishi to Gihō' (Fujiwara Ryōzō, Sōzō, 1983)

Shindō Yōshin Ryū

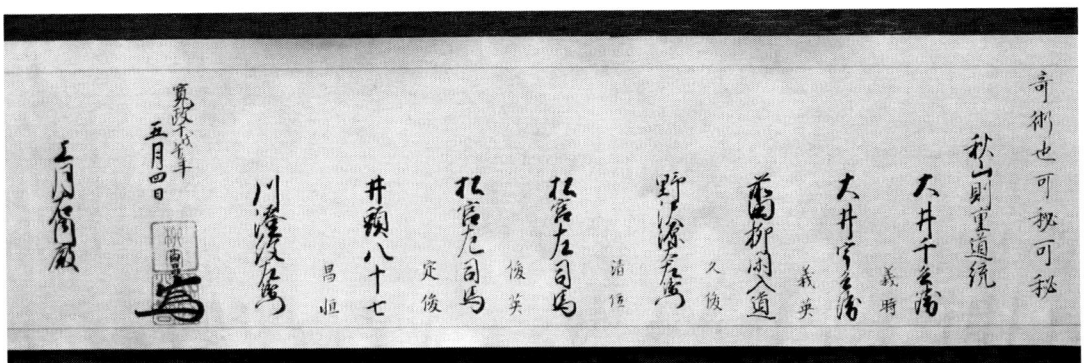

Akiyama Yōshin Ryū Jūjutsu Mokuroku - issued by Kawasumi Danzaemon, 1798.
(Collection of the Takamura ha Shindō Yōshin Kai.)

1.	秋山則重道流		Akiyama Norishige Dōryū
2.	大井千兵衛	義時	Ōi Senbei Yoshitoki (*大井 instead of 大江)
3.	大井宇兵衛	義英	Ōi Uhei Yoshihide (*大井 instead of 大江)
4.	前田柳閑入道	久俊	Maeda Ryūkan Nyūdō Hisatoshi
5.	野沢源太左衛門	清住	Nozawa Gentazaemon Kiyosumi
6.	松宮左司馬	俊英	Matsumiya Sashiba Toshihide
7.	松宮左司馬	定俊	Matsumiya Sashiba Sadatoshi
8.	井頭八十七	昌恒	Igashira Yasoshichi Masatsune
9.	川澄段左衛門		Kawsumi Danzaemon

寛政十戊午年　五月四日　　　　Kansei Jūnen Tsuchinoeuma, May 4th, 1798

上月右門殿　　　　　　　　　　Issued to Kōzuki Umon

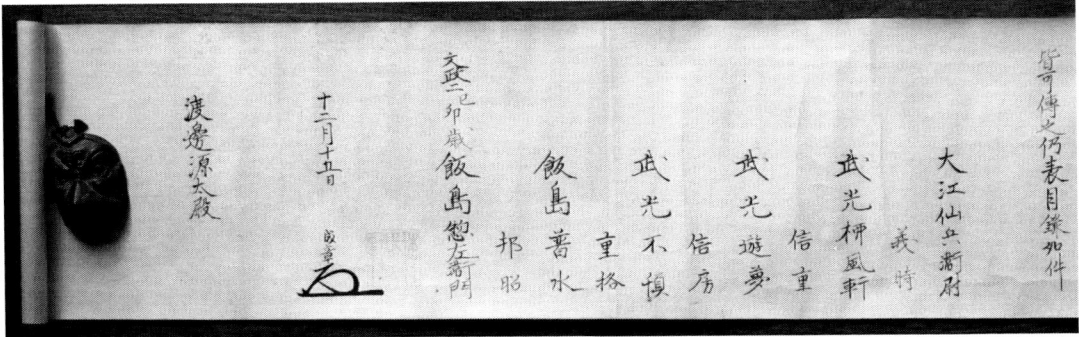

Akiyama Yōshin Ryū Yawara Omote Mokuroku - issued by Iijima Sōzaemon Nariaki, 1819.
(Collection of the Takamura ha Shindō Yōshin Kai.)

1.	大江仙兵衛尉	義時	Ōe Senbei Yoshitoki
2.	武光柳風軒	信重	Takemitsu Ryūfūken Nobushige
3.	武光遊夢	信房	Takemitsu Yūmu Nobufusa
4.	武光不	重格	Takemitsu Shigetada
5.	飯嶋普水	邦昭	Iijima Fusui Kuniaki
6.	飯嶋想左衛門	成章	Iijima Sōzaemon Nariaki
7.			

文政二　　　　　　　　　　　　Bunsei 2 (1819) December 15th

渡辺源太殿　　　　　　　　　　Issued to Watanabe Genta

History And Technique

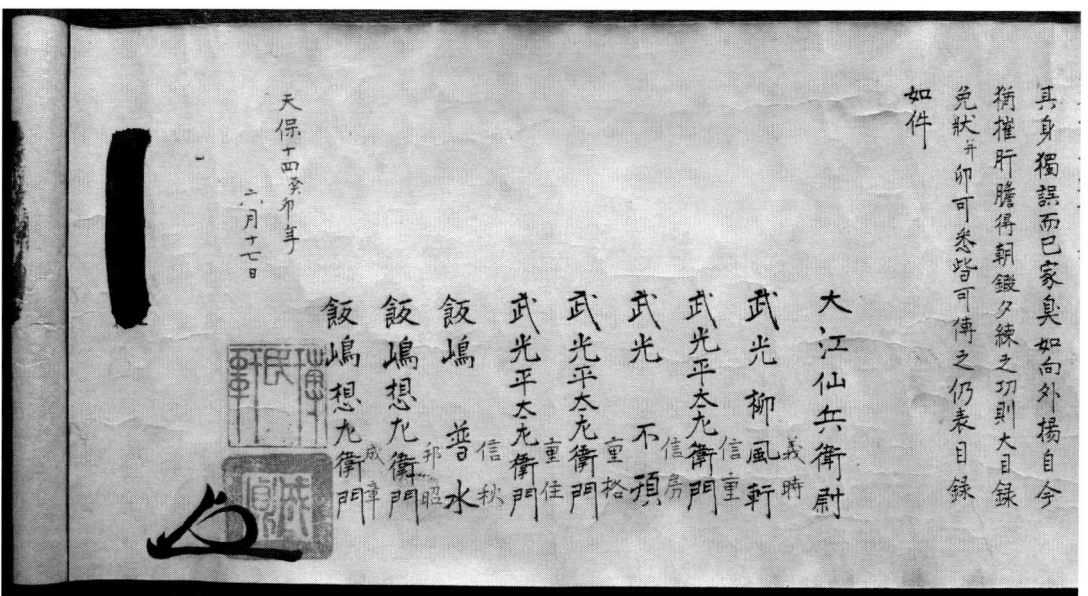

Akiyama Yōshin Ryū Yawara Mokuroku - issued by Iijima Sozaemon, 1843.
(Collection of the Takamura ha Shindō Yōshin Kai.)

1.	大江仙兵衛尉	義時	Ōe Senbei Yoshitoki
2.	武光柳風軒	信重	Takemitsu Ryūfūken Nobushige
3.	武光平太左衛門	信房	Takemitsu Heitazaemon Nobufusa
4.	武光不	重格	Takemitsu Shigetada
5.	武光平太左衛門	重住	Takemitsu Heitazaemon Shigesumi
6.	武光平太左衛門	信秋	Takemitsu Heitazaemon Nobuaki
7.	飯嶋普水	邦昭	Iijima Fusui Kuniaki
8.	飯嶋想左衛門	成章	Iijima Sōzaemon Nariaki
9.	飯嶋想左衛門	成章	Iijima Sōzaemon
	天保一四年		Tenpō 14 (1843) June 17th
	渡辺万太郎殿		Issued to Watanabe Mantarō

(Densho that list Ōe Senbei as the founder of Yōshin Ryū instead of Akiyama Shirobei Yoshitoki have led some historians to consider the possibility Ōe Senbei was the actual founder of Akiyama Yōshin Ryū. If this is true it is also possible that Akiyama might have been a mythological invention.)

44

Shindō Yōshin Ryū

Kakei (Lineage) / Akiyama Yōshin Ryū

History And Technique

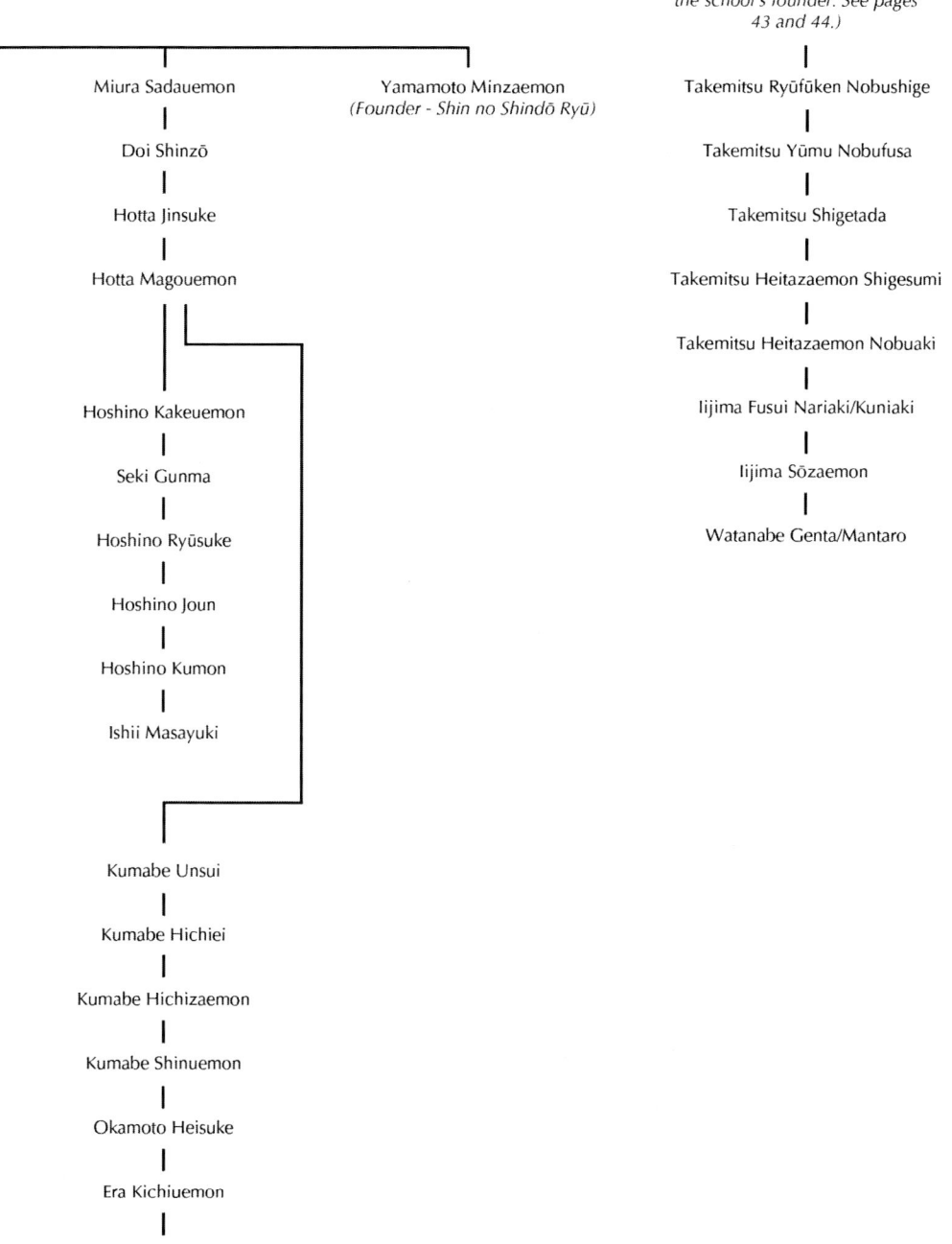

Miura Sadauemon   Yamamoto Minzaemon
                                (Founder - Shin no Shindō Ryū)

Ōe Senbei

(Kakei associated with this line of Yōshin Ryū omit Akiyama as the school's founder. See pages 43 and 44.)

- Miura Sadauemon
- Doi Shinzō
- Hotta Jinsuke
- Hotta Magouemon
- Hoshino Kakeuemon
- Seki Gunma
- Hoshino Ryūsuke
- Hoshino Joun
- Hoshino Kumon
- Ishii Masayuki
- Kumabe Unsui
- Kumabe Hichiei
- Kumabe Hichizaemon
- Kumabe Shinuemon
- Okamoto Heisuke
- Era Kichiuemon
- Era Sajūrō/Jinuemon

Ōe Senbei line:
- Takemitsu Ryūfūken Nobushige
- Takemitsu Yūmu Nobufusa
- Takemitsu Shigetada
- Takemitsu Heitazaemon Shigesumi
- Takemitsu Heitazaemon Nobuaki
- Iijima Fusui Nariaki/Kuniaki
- Iijima Sōzaemon
- Watanabe Genta/Mantaro

Shindō Yōshin Ryū

Akiyama Yōshin Ryū Jūjutsu Curriculum

Idori (7)

Shin no Kurai
Zanshin Metsuke
Mutō Wakare
Sode Guruma

Zen Goshi
Shaken
Chōdachi

Yukiai (7)

Ushiro Yamakage
Waki Yamakage
Mukau Yamakage
Shukin Ki

Umeorieda
Ate Nage
Koma Gaeshi

Iai (22)

Yubi Dori
Te Guruma
Ai Dori
Sode Guruma
Ude Guruma
Obi Hiki
Imon Kuzure
Kō Mawashi

Zō Oshi
Obi Guruma
Kōsode Gaeshi
Hiki Mawashi
Ōgoroshi
Matsuba Goroshi
Kō Mawari
Fushi Shika

Gen Seki
Kabe Zoe
Tōkyō Kuskaku-1
Tōkyō Kuskaku-2
Tōkyō Kuskaku-3
Shin Guruma

Tachiai no Maki (7)

Maki Komi
Sho Betsu
Tachiai Kobami
Kō Yōran

Koshi Tsuke
Ude Shitsu
Sune Shitsu

Kabezoe (7)

Kata Guruma
Gozen Dori
Tsuka Kudaki
Kobami

Iso Nami
Sayū Kyoku
Zū Dori

Shizuma no Maki (7)

Shin no Kurai
Zanshin Metsuke
Nukimi no Metsuke
Mutō Wakare

Tachiai Koiwakare
Kuruma Dori
Yōno Kurai

Kakugo no Maki (18) - *Oral Articles*

Keijutsu Fuyu Kon no Koto
Fuchin Bun no Koto
Byōki Ō Saru no Koto
Zanshin Metsuke
Dōsei Metsuke
Nishō no Metsuke

Chōtan no Metsuke
Mitsume Tebō
Yotsume Jiki Tebō
Seki Danosha
Enkin Hoyō
Nukimi no Metsuke

Ni no Tsume
Tachi Kakushi Tebō
Kami Kuzure Tebō
Satsujin Guma
Katsujin Guma
Marishi Sonten

Genmyō no Maki (15) *Jōdan Te Kazu*

Ushiro Dori Dokko
Shimo Fuji
Futari Zume
Ma Ate
Ryō Hizen

Shikkomi
Enkō Tsukimi
Shoryū
Shūkan
Fukaissoku

Uken
Saken
Fūken
Ryūko
Shaken Wakare

History And Technique

Akiyama Yōshin Ryū Jūjutsu Curriculum (Continued)

Jōdan Gokui Katame (5)

Kote Garame
Tomoe
Sansha
Tora Zume
Kata Haori

Unjō no Maki (7)

Matsukaze
Kyūu
Inazuma
Ganka
Suigetsu
Meisei
Tsuki Kage (Kuden)

Kokoromochi Kakugo no Maki (19)

Byoki Sari
Dōsei Metsuke
Chōtan Metsuke
Enkin Hoyō
Hiken
Seki Dome
Ōate
Ko Ate
Tsuri Ai
Senkei
Yotsume Tebō
Mitsume Tebō
Tachikage Tebō
Ran Hishi
Ganzen
Mikomi
Ranyaku
Fudōchii
Tenkanodaiji

Akiyama Yōshin Ryū Iaitachijutsu Curriculum

Iai (7) *Sho Volume*

Mukōzume no Koto, Shiden
Nigan Nukiuchi no Koto
Saten no Koto
Uten no Koto
Munadori Hanare no Koto
Ushiro Guruma no Koto
Seisen Ate no Koto, Shiden

Iai (8) *Ijo Volume*

Kodachi Kiritaisen no Koto
Dō Tsukidome no Koto
Sayūzume no Koto
Dō Tsume no Koto
Sayugiri no Koto
Sanpo Garami no Koto
Harakiri no Koto
Kaishaku Tachi no Koto

Akiyama Yōshin Ryū Naginatajutsu Curriculum

Omote (5)

Jōdan
Chūdan
Gedan
Asuka
Kuri

Naginata Roku no Hasuji (6)

Tsukikiri
Hikigiri
Age
Kage
Harai
Nagite

Tachiai (8)

Makiyubi
Makiotoshi
Sashitsuke
Yarika
Suigetsu
Uezashi
Degashira
Amazashi

Bōai (13)

Aigamae
Ganseki Otoshi
Hana Guruma
Sode Kakushi
Kage no Tō
Ryūka
Teito
Yukai
Ura no Nami
Matsukaze
Murasame
Maboroshi
Saru Kabuto

Hanbō (5)

Tai no Sen
Tsuba Dome
Kudaki
Makigoi
Asuka

Naginata (5)

Ran
Tadashi
Mizu Guruma
Main
Ishizuki no Kachi

Inagaki Yōshin Ryū Jūjutsu, the Kai Takeda, and the other Akiyama

Many independent koryū have adopted the name Yōshin Ryū throughout Japanese budō history. The most well-known and influential of all the Yōshin Ryū schools is the line attributed to Akiyama Shirōbei Yoshitoki, founded sometime in 1651. Akiyama Yoshitoki is said to have had family roots in Kai (present Yamanashi prefecture) province, which was under the control of the famed Takeda Clan. After the Takeda defeat at Nagashino in 1575, Akiyama Shirōbei's ancestors fled to Aki (present Hiroshima) where they lived among Takeda relatives in the Asano Clan. This line of Yōshin Ryū went on to become one of the most popular and influential jūjutsu schools in all of Japan.

Records indicate an earlier school also called Yōshin Ryū existed in Kai. This school is still extant and located in Okayama, in the southern part of Japan's main island, Honshu. This line of Yōshin Ryū is a sōgō bujutsu teaching jūjutsu, bōjutsu, juttejutsu, iaijutsu, hojōjutsu and kappō. This school's technical origins are claimed to have descended from an individual named Akiyama Hōkinokami (1527-1575), who was born in Suō (present-day Yamaguchi). Although there is a grave for Akiyama Hōkinokami and graves for the Akiyama family in Okayama, the dates surrounding this supposed connection are problematic. The school's actual founding as a unique ryūha is attributed to Inagaki Tatewaki (1539-1612), a samurai who was born in Mikawa (present-day Aichi) who eventually relocated to Okayama. The school was originally identified as Yōshin Ryū, but one line under the leadership of Yasui Shinzō Kiyomitsu, changed its name to Shinshin Ryū. Thirteenth-generation headmaster Nagase Keikichi Masamitsu changed the ryūha name to Inagaki Yōshin Ryū in 1901.

Most records indicate this school is a unique and isolated line of Yōshin Ryū, unconnected to the more famous school attributed to Akiyama Shirōbei Yoshitoki. Other records attempt to connect these two lineages by listing Akiyama's Yōshin Ryū as a descendant of Inagaki Yōshin Ryū but recent research by budō historians highlight facts that cast doubt on this claimed connection, supporting the contention that Inagaki Yōshin Ryū is an independent line of koryū bujutsu. Densho in the possession of the Takamura ha Shindō Yōshin Kai support the contention that these schools are independent as side-by-side comparisons of relevant documentation reveal numerous inconsistencies.

Inagaki Yōshin Ryū is currently led by 16th headmaster, Hoshijima Daigorō Masamitsu.

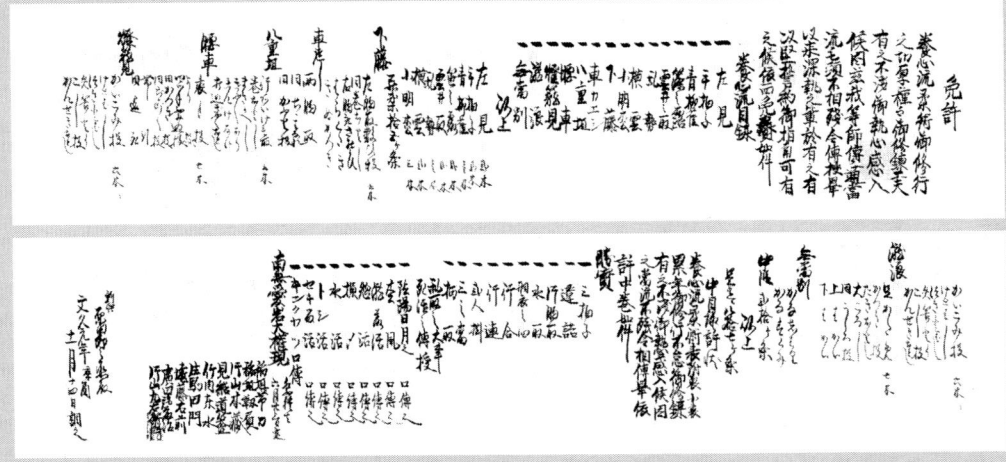

Bunkyū era (1861-1864) Inagaki Yōshin Ryū jūjutsu menkyo with lineage showing nine generations.
(Osano, Jun (1991) Yōshin Ryū Jūjutsu Denshoshu, Nihon Sōgō Budō Kenkyū)

The Bakufu Kōbusho
(Tokugawa Military Academy)

The Japanese were shocked by the advanced military technology of the Americans commanded by Admiral Matthew C. Perry, who arrived at Uraga, outside Tōkyō harbor, in 1853. The central Bakufu government under Tokugawa Iesada responded by establishing the Bakufu Kōbusho in Tsukiji, Tōkyō in 1856, to raise the standard of practical military training among the samurai. Trainees studied kenjutsu (sword), Western military science and teppō (firearms). In 1860, the Bakufu Kōbusho also became a training center for the Bakufu navy.

The government also built a new kōbusho in Kanda, in the middle of Tōkyō (near present-day Suidōbashi), where the trainees studied hōjutsu (rifle shooting), sōjutsu (spear arts), and kenjutsu, as well as two new subjects, kyūjutsu (archery), and jūjutsu (empty handed combat). Kyūjutsu and jūjutsu were dropped in 1862, as they were deemed impractical in modern warfare.

Edo Hantei
(Tōkyō Clan Residences)

Edo Hantei of the Kuroda han from Fukuoka. This was the birthplace of Matsuoka Katsunosuke.

Under the Tokugawa Shogunate during the Edo period (1600-1867), the wives and immediate family of clan lords had to permanently remain in Tōkyō as de facto hostages of the central government. These feudal lords spent part of their time in Tōkyō working for the central government, and part of their time at home ruling their domains. Consequently, all han (clans) had tei (residences) in Tōkyō that were referred to as Edo hantei. The lords had to travel between their domains and Tōkyō at least once a year on trips called Sankin Kōtai.

Many clans also had hantei in Kyōto, where the Emperor was located, and in Ōsaka, which was a large center of commerce. The hantei of the Kuroda clan, in which Matsuoka Katsunosuke of Shindō Yōshin Ryū was born and raised, became the Foreign Ministry Office in modern Japan.

Shindō Yōshin Ryū

1906 Dai Nippon Butokukai Jūdō/Jūjutsu Conclave

In 1906 Kanō Jigorō, under the auspices of the Dai Nippon Butokukai, called a conclave. This call summoned the most prominent jūjutsu masters from all over Japan. At this meeting, jūjutsu kata from the attending jūjutsu schools were demonstrated and evaluated for inclusion as part of the official Kōdōkan Jūdō curriculum. Sitting center front is jūdō founder, Kanō Jigorō. To Kanō's left is Totsuka Hideyoshi, the famed 10th-generation headmaster of Totsuka ha Yōshin Ryū.

(Front row, right to left): Hiratsuka Katsuta of Kagawa (Yōshin Ryū); Yano Kōji of Kumamoto (Takenouchi Santō Ryū Kyōshi); Sekiguchi Jūshin of Wakayama (Sekiguchi Ryū); Totsuka Hideyoshi of Chiba (Yōshin Ryū Hanshi); Kanō Jigorō of Tōkyō (Kōdōkan Jūdō Hanshi); Hoshino Kumon of Kumamoto (Shiten Ryū Hanshi); Katayama Takayoshi of Kagawa (Yōshin Ryū); Eguchi Yazō of Kumamoto (Kyūshin Ryū Kyōshi); Inazu Masamizu of Kyōto (Miura Ryū).

(Back row, right to left): Yamashita Yoshiaki of Tōkyō (Kōdōkan Jūdō Kyōshi); Isogai Hajime of Kyōto (Kōdōkan Jūdō Kyōshi); Yokoyama Sakujirō of Tōkyō (Kōdōkan Jūdō Kyōshi); Nagaoka Shuichi of Kyōto (Kōdōkan Jūdō Kyōshi); Takano Shikatarō of Okayama (Takenouchi Ryū); Tanabe Matauemon of Himeji (Fusen Ryū Kyōshi); Imai Kōtarō of Okayama (Takenouchi Ryū Kyōshi); Satō Hōken of Kyōto (Kōdōkan Jūdō Kyōshi); Ōshima Hikosaburō of Kagawa (Takenouchi Ryū Kyōshi); Tsumizu Mokichi of Wakayama (Sekiguchi Ryū); Aoyagi Kihei of Fukuoka (Sōsuishi Ryū Kyōshi).

Kyōto-shi o Butokukai Honbu (Butokukai Headquarters in the city of Kyōto)
Meiji 39-nen 7-gatsu 24-nichi (July 24, 39th year of Meiji - 1906)

History And Technique

Historical Background of Miura Yōshin Ryū (Totsuka ha Yōshin Ryū / Yōshin Koryū)

Totsuka ha Yōshin Ryū ninth headmaster, Totsuka Hidetoshi seated center. Tenth headmaster, Totsuka Hideyoshi is seated to his left.

The most popular story related to the founding of Miura Yōshin Ryū has been traced to Kai province, northwest of Edo, an area controlled by the legendary Takeda clan. A Kōshū Takeda samurai named Baba Mina no Kami, who lived in Kai, established a jūjutsu system called Taiin Ryū in the 16th century. When the combined forces of Oda Nobunaga and Tokugawa Ieyasu defeated the Takeda clan in 1575, the political administration of Kai fell into doubt. When Toyotomi Hideyoshi, under the authority of Nobunaga, assumed political control of Kai in 1590, many Takeda samurai fled. Among them was Nakamura Masayoshi (1537-1582), a loyal Takeda samurai and the second son of Baba Mina no Kami, who succeeded his father as the second lineal headmaster of Taiin Ryū. Following the Toyotomi conquest of Kai, Masayoshi and his only son, Nakamura Sakyōdayu Yoshikuni (1560-1625), escaped to the Aki domain where they joined the Asano clan, which was related to the Takeda clan. Upon reaching Aki, Masayoshi and Yoshikuni lost their professional status and became ronin (masterless samurai). They established a clinic near Hiroshima where they pursued occupations as doctors. After the death of his father, Yoshikuni furthered his medical education by studying with a doctor of Chinese medicine and herbology in nearby Hizen province. After completing his medical training, he settled in Miura village, where he changed his name to Miura Yōshin and worked as a doctor of Chinese medicine. Several years later, Miura Yōshin moved to Nagasaki where he opened his own medical clinic and a jūjutsu dōjō. As the third headmaster of Taiin Ryū, Miura Yōshin (Yoshikuni) combined his martial expertise and medical knowledge to create a unique jūjutsu system he named Miura Yōshin Ryū.

The names of the Miura Yōshin Ryū's lineal headmasters after Miura Yōshin are lost to antiquity, but the next documented headmaster is the sixth in line, Abe Kanryū (1712-1770). Historians assume Abe Kanryū studied with the unidentified fifth headmaster and records indicate Abe Kanryū established a Miura Yōshin Ryū dōjō in Ōsaka around 1730.

The seventh headmaster of Miura Yōshin Ryū was Abe Kanryū's nephew, Egami Shimanosuke Taketsune (1747-1795), who opened a dōjō in Shiba Akabane, Edo, in 1768. Egami was a popular and talented jūjutsuka as the Shiba Akabane Dōjō thrived for almost 100 years. After Egami's death 27 years later, Totsuka Hikouemon Hidesumi (1772-1847) became both the eighth headmaster of Miura Yōshin Ryū jūjutsu and the dōjō-chō of the Shiba Akabane Dōjō. Hidesumi changed the name of Miura Yōshin Ryū to Egami Ryū out of respect for his deceased teacher, but reverted to the name Miura Yōshin Ryū in 1836, when he was hired as an instructor to the Mizuno family in Numazu, Shizuoka prefecture.

Totsuka Hikosuke Hidetoshi (1812-1886), the eldest son of Totsuka Hidesumi, assumed leadership of the ryū as the ninth-generation headmaster after the death of his father in 1847. The school became known as Totsuka ha Yōshin Ryū under the leadership of Hidetoshi, who became legendary as a genius in both jūjutsu and teaching. Thus, the Shiba Akabane Dōjō steadily flourished. Thanks to a reputation for excellence, Hidetoshi was hired in 1860 to instruct military conscripts in jūjutsu at the Bakufu Kōbusho (Tokugawa shogunate Military Academy). After several months of such employment, the Kōbusho awarded Hidetoshi the title of Kōbusho Shihan (chief instructor/expert). However, jūjutsu was not a priority at the Kōbusho and it was taught only six times a month. Regardless, increased prestige for Hidetoshi resulted in increased enrollment at the Shiba Akabane Dōjō and in 1861 Hidetoshi closed the Akabane dōjō to open a much larger dōjō in Shiba Atogayama. This dōjō became the largest jūjutsu school in Edo with over 3,000 registered students. In 1862, the Bakufu Kōbushō ceased jūjutsu training as part of its curriculum and Hidetoshi resigned his Kōbushō Shihan title.

The Meiji Restoration in 1868 forced Hidetoshi to close the Shiba Atogayama Dōjō but in 1870, he opened a new dōjō in Chiba, southeast of Edo (renamed Tōkyō in 1868), where most of his students were police officers. There, he was approached at some point during the 1870s by the prestigious German physician, Dr. Erwin Baelz, about teaching jūjutsu classes at Tōkyō Imperial University. However, Dr. Baelz failed to convince the university authorities of the physical benefits jūjutsu could offer the university students. Years later, Dr. Baelz witnessed Hidetoshi's students participate in the first jūjutsu challenge match where the Totsuka ha Yōshin Ryū students soundly defeated the Kōdōkan Jūdō students of the young Professor Kanō Jigorō from Tōkyō Imperial University.

Nishimura Teisuke Hisatakashi (1848-1906), with his son. Teisuke was one of the Totsuka ha Yōshin Ryū Chiba dōjō's strongest jūjutsuka.
(Collection of the Takamura ha Shindō Yōshin Kai.)

Totsuka Hikokuro Hideyoshi (Hidemi) (1840-1908), the 10th- generation headmaster, assumed responsibility for continuing Totsuka ha Yōshin Ryū after his father's death in 1886. Hideyoshi is present in the famous photo of the Butokukai jūjutsu conclave where he is seated next to Professor Kanō Jigorō. Sadly, the Totsuka ha Yōshin Ryū familial line ended with the death of Totsuka Hideyoshi in 1908. Thereafter, Totsuka ha Yōshin Ryū became known as Yōshin Koryū. The Yōshin Koryū line of Miura Yōshin Ryū was led by a contemporary and senpai of Hideyoshi named Imada Masayoshi (1838-1909), who had been taught by Totsuka Hidetoshi. Imada Masayoshi received a Menkyo Kaiden, thus preserving the school. He in turn taught an exemplary student, Kanaya Motoyoshi (1843-1904), whose son Kanaya Motoo (1897-1964) also received a Menkyo Kaiden and opened his own dōjō in Tōkyō in 1913. Around 1916, an enthusiastic student of jūjutsu named Ōtsuka Hironori (1892-1982), who would become the shodai (founder) of Wadō Ryū karate, entered the Kanaya dōjō. His friend Konishi Kōsuke (1893-1983), the founder of Shindō Jinen Ryū karate, would also join this dojo.

Kanaya Motoo taught many notable early 20th century budō practitioners, including Sugino Yoshio (1904-1998), the famed student of jūdō, aikidō and Tenshinshō-den Katori Shintō Ryū. Sugino Yoshio achieved the rank of kyōshi in Yōshin Koryū around 1939, but never received a license of full transmission.

With the death of Kanaya Motoo in 1964, Yōshin Koryū lost transmission and most of the remaining students of Yōshin Koryū were officially accepted into Shindō Yōshin Ryū. Today, some of the teachings originating in Miura Yōshin Ryū can be found in Kōdōkan Jūdō, Shindō Yōshin Ryū, and Shintō Rikugō Ryū. Shintō Rikugō Ryū is a Meiji era jūjutsu school founded by Noguchi Senryūken and his brother Noguchi Seihachiro. As far as the authors know, the only person maintaining Shintō Rikugō Ryū is Shiigi Munenori, as taught to him by his father, Shiigi Keibun.

The Technical Legacy of Miura Yōshin Ryū (Totsuka ha Yōshin Ryū / Yōshin Koryū)

A densho held by the Takamura ha Shindō Yōshin Kai shows the official jūjutsu curriculum of Totsuka ha Yōshin Ryū comprises 112 kata, which is similar in size and focus to the Akiyama line of Yōshin Ryū jūjutsu. Both lines even share some kata names, but these similarities are not necessarily reflected in pedagogy or technical execution of the art. According to Takamura Yukiyoshi, the Akiyama Yōshin Ryū and the Totsuka ha Yōshin Ryū represented very different expressions of budō, with the Akiyama lineage embracing a more classical approach to training.

Totsuka ha Yōshin Ryū Shinbukan Dōjō members in the early 20th century. Kawakami Chū, a good friend of Shindō Yōshin Ryū's Obata Shigeta sits in the middle row, far right. Besides becoming a Yōshin Ryū shihan, he also became a prominent student of Kanō Jigorō and Kōdōkan Jūdō ninth dan. (Collection of the Takamura ha Shindō Yōshin Kai.)

Shindō Yōshin Ryū

Ōtake Moriyoshi (1852-1930), famed Totsuka ha Yōshin Ryū shihan and member of the Numazu Clan.

Kawakami Chū at his Horikoshi Dōjō. In addition to jūdō, Kawakami Chū studied both Totsuka ha Yōshin Ryū and Akiyama Yōshin Ryū.
(Collection of the Takamura ha Shindō Yōshin Kai.)

Even though the school was competitively dominant in the late Edo and early Meiji periods, little is known about the specific kuden (verbally-transmitted wisdom), or gokui (secrets) of Totsuka ha Yōshin Ryū. Other than what survives in Shindō Yōshin Ryū, Shintō Rikugō Ryū, and Kōdōkan Jūdō, the defining technical characteristics of the school remain speculative. That the curriculum originally reflected a sōgō bujutsu is confirmed, but by the mid-Edo period, and under the leadership of the seventh headmaster, Egami Taketsune, taijutsu became the dominant focus of the school. Evidence indicates Egami Taketsune revived a school in decline, and the study of classical weaponry, although included in the school curriculum, was not significantly emphasized during that revival.

The Miura/Totsuka-ha Yōshin Ryū probably would have remained one of many ubiquitous jūjutsu schools of the Edo period but for the eighth headmaster, Totsuka Hidesumi (1772-1847). Under his leadership, Miura/Totsuka ha Yōshin Ryū appeared to have evolved by the 1830s to embrace a more contemporary approach to jūjutsu, with a focus on freestyle application of waza and competitive shiai. Exactly how much the art originally focused on armed combat remains unknown, but the study of weapons seems to have been significantly abandoned under Totsuka Hidesumi. By the 1850s, the offensive use of classical Japanese weaponry was no longer pursued, and only cursory training in defence against such weaponry was still being taught. By the time Hidetoshi (1812-1886), the son of Hidesumi, had assumed control of the school, Totsuka ha Yōshin Ryū had become a competitive juggernaut within the jūjutsu community. This paradigm shift the Totsuka family brought to Miura Yōshin Ryū fundamentally changed not only the focus and pedagogy of Miura Yōshin Ryū, but also influenced many other conservative schools in the jūjutsu community. Furthermore, the popularity of the Totsuka school with police officers of the Edo period indicates unarmed force-on-force freestyle training had migrated outside competitive applications and into the arena of civil defense, supplementing the traditional training methods that focused on kata execution.

By the mid-1860s, a stable of talented fighters, mostly robust police officers who trained at the Totsuka ha Yōshin Ryū dōjō in Chiba, had established a reputation for being virtually unbeatable in competition, dominating all challengers in freestyle unarmed grappling. Some of the

History And Technique

top students of the Chiba dōjō included Terushima Tarō, Nishimura Teisuke, Katayama Takayoshi, Ōtake Moriyoshi, Yamamoto Kinsaku, Tsuzuki Hiroshi and Tadatsu Shingai.

Totsuka grave sites, Chiba City, Chiba Prefecture.

Ninth headmaster, Totsuka Hikosuke Hidetoshi (right).
Tenth headmaster, Totsuka Hikokuro Hideyoshi (left).

Shintō Rikugō Ryū

Shintō Rikugō Ryū jūjutsu was founded in the Meiji era by two brothers, Noguchi Senryūken and Noguchi Seihachirō. The school's technical foundation is Totsuka ha Yōshin Ryū, but it also includes influences from Shin no Shindō Ryū, Shinkage Ryū, Kiraku Ryū, Kitō Ryū, Musō Ryū, and Munen Ryū. The school is of historical interest because it was the first jūjutsu school to attempt to teach via correspondence courses. Comprehensive books illustrating the kata by way of photos and detailed written descriptions were published for school members so they could learn outside direct instruction. Below are some of the hundreds of photographs from the book titled Jūjutsu Kyōjusho/Shintō Rikugō Ryū published in 1913. Shintō Rikugō Ryū is today maintained by Shiigi Munenori in Tōkyō, Japan.

Noguchi Senryūken

Noguchi Seihachirō

Shindō Yōshin Ryū

Kakei (Lineage) / Miura Yōshin Ryū

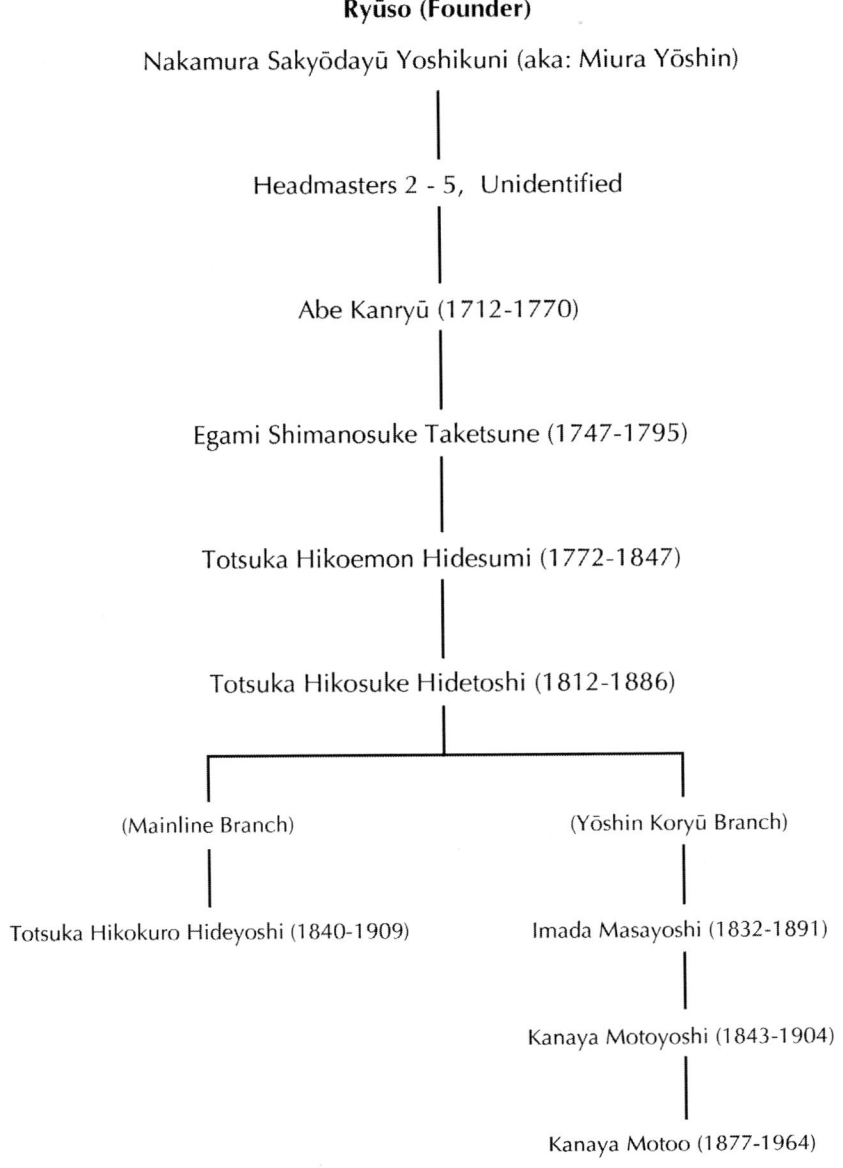

Miura Yōshin Ryū (Totsuka Line) Jūjutsu Curriculum*

Iai (22)

Yubi Dori	Zō Oshi	Gen Seki
Te Guruma	Obi Guruma	Kabezoe
Ai Dori	Kosode Gaeshi	Tōkyō Kushaku-1
Sode Guruma	Hiki Mawashi	Tōkyō Kushaku-2
Ude Guruma	Ōgoroshi	Tōkyō Kushaku-3
Obi Hiki	Matsuba Goroshi	Shin Guruma
Imon Kuzure	Kō Mawari	
Kō Mawashi	Fushi Shika	

Yukiai (29)

Koate	Waki Yamakage	Hiki Mawashi
Kogaeshi	Mukō Yamakage	Kohiza Mawashi
Kōyōno Midare	Ushiro Yamakage	Gohen-1
Monshū	Kenno Kurai-1	Gohen-2
Sotogake	Kenno Kurai-2	Gohen-3
Uchigake	Kenno Kurai-3	Isonami
Tsuki Tsuke	Urakaze	Kō Guruma
Ōate	Ryūhizen	Tsukimi
Torabashiri	Sekitome	Shimo Fuji
Taki Otoshi	Denkō	

Idori (21)

Shin no Kurai	Tsuri Gatame	Kan Dome
Mutō Wakare	Kō Mawashi	Shōkai
Sode Guruma	Uchikomi	Shōkai Deki
Zen Goshi	Enkō	Tsukiko
Shaken	Ō Gatame	Katana Shibari
Nukimi no Metsuke	Kan	Kō Guruma
Ō Dachi	Tama Kasumi	Ryūko

Miwake Gata (5) - Kuden

Kōjōzu Gata (7) - Chūmen Kyo, Kuden

Sappō (20) - Kuden

Kappō (8) - Kuden

Menkyo - Kuden

* The authors have been unable to locate a Miura Yōshin Ryū densho reflecting the original ryūha's comprehensive syllabus, which is said to have included the study of weaponry, but without proof, the extent of the school's study of weaponry remains speculative. The authors hypothesize that if a Miura Yōshin Ryū mokuroku including a weapons syllabus was located, this study would likely mimic that of Akiyama Yōshin Ryū as the preponderance of evidence suggests an early technical connection between the Miura and Akiyama schools.

"Historical material is scarce and unknowns are many, so dreams and legends have spread"

- Murata Noaki, Kōdōkan archivist

Professor Kanō Jigorō (1860-1938) Japanese educator and founder of Kōdōkan Jūdō. Kanō originally studied Tenjin Shinyō Ryū and Kitō Ryū jūjutsu. Kanō, an innovator, feared jūjutsu would be lost to history so he founded the Kōdōkan to preserve and modernize what he believed were the principal aspects of jūjutsu.

Jūdō vs. Jūjutsu: Fact or fantasy?

A myth was created during the early 20th century to promote and enhance the reputation of Kōdōkan Jūdō that was growing under the leadership of Kanō Jigorō. The myth comprises the story of a great competition between the Yōshin Ryū jūjutsu of Totsuka Hidesumi and Kōdōkan Jūdō. The result of the mythical competition was a decisive victory for the Kōdōkan, which proved the superiority of jūdō over the older schools of jūjutsu. The origins of this myth are published in a book titled, "Jigorō Kanō, Chosakushū, Vol #3" and it is recounted here:

> "In 1888, a tournament was organized for between 14-15 representatives from the Kōdōkan, and 14-15 representatives from the Totsuka jūjutsu school. Two teams of 10 men competed. In addition, individuals contested against jūjutsu men of other schools.
>
> Among those who represented the Totsuka school were two of their most able men, Tarō Terushima, an excellent tactician, and Teisuke Nishimura. Terushima fought Yoshiaki Yamashita, Nishimura fought Satō, and Kawai fought against Katayama. Apart from two or three draws, surprisingly all the remaining matches were won by the Kōdōkan representatives."

This myth was further augmented by the book entitled, "Sugata Sanshirō: The Jūdō Saga" written by Tomita Tsuneo (1904-1967), the son of Tomita Tsunejirō (1865-1937), Kanō Jigorō's first student. Two popular movies of the same title directed by the famed Kurosawa Akira (1910-1998) firmly established the mythical victory of Kanō Jigorō's Jūdō over the older classical jūjutsu schools as historical fact.

An Unbiased Third Person Account

The actual story is more credible and less sensational. Jūjutsu experienced an extreme decline in popularity around the time of the Meiji Restoration (1868). A highly-educated jūjutsu exponent of both Tenjin Shinyō Ryū and Kitō Ryū, fearing his beloved jūjutsu would be lost to future generations, sought to modernize and re-popularize the art. This jūjutsu advocate was a young Professor at Tōkyō Imperial University, Kanō Jigorō. He decided to confront the potential demise of jūjutsu by combining what he considered to be the best attributes of all the jūjutsu schools under one organization called the Kōdōkan (School to Study the Way). He also

History And Technique

Dr. Erwin Baelz (1849-1913), personal friend of Totsuka Hidetoshi, physician to the Japanese nobility, and Meiji era advocate of Japanese budō as an effective form of physical exercise. It is of note that this obscure German doctor who undertook the study of Japanese Kenjutsu may have played an important role in ensuring the survival of many koryū traditions.

sought to take a more scientific approach to teaching jūjutsu, which adhered to the current understanding of physical education and physiology. To this end, Professor Kanō invited a legendary jūjutsu teacher from nearby Chiba to visit Tōkyō Medical School for a friendly jūjutsu competition. The jūjutsu teacher was the famed Totsuka Hidetoshi, headmaster of the Totsuka ha Yōshin Ryū, and he was accompanied by some of the most competitively dominant jūjutsu practitioners in Japan. Professor Kanō was unaware Totsuka Hidetoshi had befriended Dr. Erwin Baelz, a prominent German doctor working at the same university, with close social connections to Japanese nobility. Like Professor Kanō, Dr. Baelz was a keen advocate for the promotion and preservation of Japanese martial arts, including jūjutsu. Fortuitously for historians, Dr. Baelz recorded a detailed account of the martial arts environment, and the first competition between the students of the Totsuka ha Yōshin Ryū and the university students who studied Kōdōkan Jūdō with Professor Kanō Jigorō. Dr. Baelz's eyewitness account stands in stark contrast to the myth promoted by the Kōdōkan some 25 years later. His account is published in his book entitled, "Awakening Japan, Diary of a German Doctor".

"In the 1870s at the outset of the modern era, Japan went through a strange period in which she felt contempt for her own native achievements. Their own history, their own religion, their own art, did not seem to the Japanese worth talking about, and were even regarded as matters to be ashamed of. The native methods of bodily exercise, Japanese fencing, jiujitsu, and the like, were placed under a ban. The older generation would not teach and the younger generation would not learn anything but European science. The students at the Imperial University of Tōkyō were badly nourished and overworked youths, who would often sit at their books all night, and took no bodily exercise, so when examinations were at hand they often broke down and sometimes actually died of exhaustion.

I did all I could in those early days to bring about a change for the better, but was unable to persuade the authorities to provide a gymnasium or an exercise ground for the students. Recognizing that kenjitsu, the old Japanese sword-fencing was an excellent gymnastic method, I recommended its revival, but it was discountenanced as a rough and even dangerous sport. Not until, in order to overcome this prejudice, I myself took lessons from the most famous fencing master of the day, Sakakibara, and secured a little publicity for the fact in the newspapers, did interest in this old method of fencing revive. It was felt that, if a foreigner, and, what was more, a professor of medicine at what was then the only university in the country, was studying this art, it was impossible to suppose Westerners could regard it as barbarous or dangerous.

It was about the same date that I first made acquaintance with jiujitsu. This was when I was visiting the provincial capital of Chiba. Talking to the governor about modern education, I complained about how little interest of sport of any kind was shown by well-to-do youths of the upper classes, though their health was poor, and vigorous exercise would do them a lot of good. The governor was quite of my way of thinking, and expressed his strong regret that jiujitsu, as a splendid method of physical training formerly much practiced in Japan, should have gone so completely out of use. It was, in fact, still practiced in his own town, where an old teacher of the art, Totsuka by name, instructed the police in it. The results had been marvelous, and his men found it of the greatest value in making arrests. Next day he asked me to attend a gathering where Totsuka, a man over 70 years of age, gave a demonstration of the principles of jiujitsu and showed the various grips. Then I watched dozens of jiujitsu contests, and was extremely impressed with the results. I saw what I should have expected to be neck-breaking trips and movements and throws executed without causing the least injury to the contestants; and I said to myself this would be an ideal form of gymnastics for my students.

Still I had no success with the matter in Tōkyō. The director of the medical school and the other leading Japanese at the university and in the Ministry for Education would not hear a word of my proposal to summon the jiujitsu expert from Chiba to give a demonstration in Tōkyō. The students, they said, had come to the university to do mental work. There had been some sense in jiujitsu in the old days, when people had to protect themselves against armed men, but that was all over now. My insistence that I was concerned only with jiujitsu as a means of bodily training, as a matter of health, had no effect. Then it occurred to me to do what I had done in the case of the Japanese sword-fencing and to arouse interest by studying jiujitsu for myself. Unfortunately, I could not find any teacher willing to accept me as a pupil, for they all said it is necessary to begin in boyhood, and that I, being 30, might easily do myself serious harm.

Meanwhile, however, some of the students and ex-students of the university had taken on jiujitsu. The young professor Kanō was especially active in the matter, and to him the renewed popularization of the old sport is especially due. He and his comrades were at length successful in inducing the university authorities to summon the jiujitsu expert from Chiba and a great jiujitsu contest took place. This made it clear how much training is needed to learn the art, for all the young men who had been working at it in Tōkyō, not one, not even Kanō could cope with the police officers who had been trained by Totsuka in Chiba. Next day old Totsuka, accompanied by his best student Satō, came to call on me and to thank me for my exertions in the matter. I can still see him in my imagi-

> *nation, this venerable old man, as, with tears running down his cheeks, he begged for my photograph that he said he would treasure to the end of his life. As a Japanese, he declared, it made him blush that a foreigner should have had to tell his fellow countrymen that it was incumbent upon them to revive jiujitsu; but now, when he knew that his beloved art would come into honour once more, he could die in peace."*

This passage by Dr Baelz is fascinating on many levels. It highlights how much the Meiji Restoration disrupted the foundations of Japanese national identity, causing the average Japanese citizen to see anything foreign as superior to their own time-honored traditions. It also illustrates the cultural insecurities that persisted into the 20th century. In the view of many Japanese, the westernization of traditional Japanese pursuits was essential if they were to be perceived as worthy of study. The cultural loss due to this homogenization of Japanese and western ideals is incalculable.

A further observation related to the jūjutsu versus jūdō controversy was imparted by Takamura Yukiyoshi to his student, Tobin Threadgill, the kaicho of Takamura ha Shindō Yōshin Ryū. According to Obata Shigeta (Takamura's grandfather) everyone was aware of the dominance of the Totsuka jūjutsu practitioners in unarmed shiai. When the myth of a jūdō victory over the Totsuka fighters was created around 1916, Totsuka Hideyoshi had been dead for almost a decade and no one saw much reason to contradict the politically powerful myth creator, Yamashita Yoshiaki. Here, Threadgill recalls a conversation with his teacher, Takamura Sensei:

> *"I once alluded to the Kurosawa movie, 'Sugata Sanshirō: The Jūdō Saga' over dinner with Takamura Sensei and he bristled at any suggestion of accuracy. He said the story was a myth created during the early 20th century by Yamashita Yoshiaki to bolster the reputation of the Kōdōkan. He said Totsuka Hidemi (Hideyoshi) had died a decade earlier and since most of his students had since joined the Kōdōkan, no one felt compelled to contradict Kanō's powerful senior student Yamashita's assertions. Takamura Sensei further stated one great jūjutsu competition never existed anyway, but rather numerous informal contests of various magnitudes occurred over two decades, starting in the late 1880s. Kanō's students were easily defeated in the earlier contests, particularly by the large and experienced police officers training with Totsuka in Chiba. However, the skills of the Kōdōkan students gradually improved to the point where they were accepted as equals among the older and more experienced koryū jūjutsuka. By the early 1900s, Kanō had acquired great public prestige and was able to convince most of the top jūjutsu practitioners to support his efforts to preserve jūjutsu under the umbrella of the Kōdōkan. Although this account seems more likely than the stirring Jūdō Saga, I still assumed this version of history recounted by Takamura Sensei was acrimony, until I read the eyewitness account diarized by Dr. Erwin Baelz. Now, I perceive this story in a different light, as it does seem to be more historically accurate. It just rings true to me in a way the melodramatic 'Jūdō Saga' does not."*

Shindō Yōshin Ryū

Historical Background of Tenjin Shinyō Ryū

Tenjin Shinyō Ryū demonstration at Meiji Jingū, 2015.
(Photo courtesy of S.F. Radzikowski.)

Tenjin Shinyō Ryū is a 19th-century development of Akiyama Yōshin Ryū, which was founded by Okuyama Hachiroji Masatari. Founding dates for the school are inconsistently represented between the various lines and surviving documentation. One document in the Takamura ha Shindō Yōshin Kai archive identifies the birth year of Okuyama as 1788 and the year of his death as 1863, at the age of 76. Aside from the dates, Okuyama was born in Ise Matsuzaka, in present day Mie Prefecture, to a samurai family living within the Kishū Domain. According to the Tenjin Shinyō Ryū Tai-i Roku, written by a first-generation disciple of the founder, Okuyama traveled to Kyōto to seek tutelage in Akiyama Yōshin Ryū under Hitotsu Yanagi Oribei in 1802, and studied until Hitotsu's death in 1809. At this point, Okuyama sought training under Honma Jōuemon Masatō, a first-generation disciple of Yamamoto Minzaemon Hidehaya (1716-1798), the founder of Shin no Shindō Ryū. Yamamoto was a dōshin torimono (Edo period police/constable), who studied Akiyama Yōshin Ryū under the second headmaster, Ōe Senbei. In creating Shin no Shindō Ryū, Yamamoto greatly abbreviated the Akiyama Yōshin Ryū curriculum for police applications, focusing on striking, grappling, and strangulation. Surviving documentation indicates the Shin no Shindō Ryū curriculum included 86 techniques. After six years of training under Honma, Okuyama received an okugi (inner secrets) license and

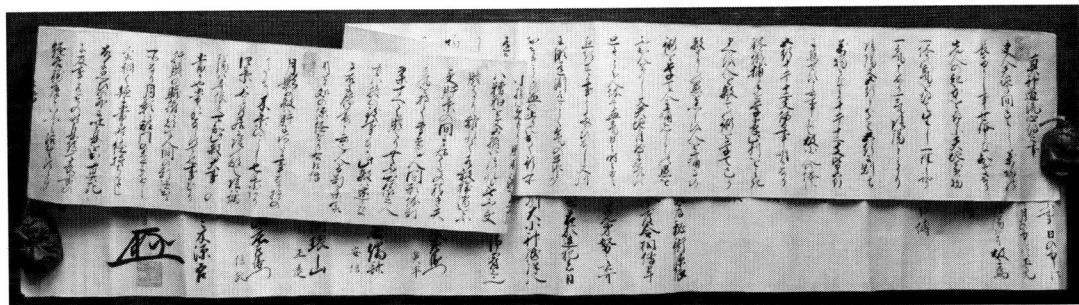

Shin no Shindō Ryū jūjutsu densho, issued by fifth-generation instructor, Sasaki Nobuyoshi.
(Collection of the Takamura ha Shindō Yōshin Kai.)

undertook a musha shugyō (warrior pilgrimage), visiting other jūjutsu schools throughout Japan. Legend holds Okuyama assumed the pseudonym Ryūkansai during his travels, and was never defeated in combat. During these travels, he and student Nishimura Tokinosuke were allegedly invited to teach jūjutsu in Kusatsu, Shiga Prefecture. They remained in Shiga for three years, where they cultivated many talented students. A tale of this period describes Ryūkansai and Nishimura becoming embroiled in an altercation in which they defended a man against a great number of adversaries. Atemi waza proved effective in this encounter, and became an area of study Ryūkansai would investigate in depth.

Ryūkansai adopted the name Kuriyama Mataemon after departing Shiga Prefecture for Tōkyō, where he established his own jūjutsu school called Tenjin Shinyō Ryū. The Japanese kanji characters chosen for Tenjin (天神; heavenly) implies the knowledge he acquired was divinely inspired, while the kanji characters chosen for Shinyō (真楊; true willow) pays homage to the earthly schools of its origin, Shin no Shindō Ryū and Akiyama Yōshin Ryū.

During his first few years of residence in Tōkyō, Ryūkansai/Kuriyama Mataemon married into the Iso family, of which he became the male inheritor, thus creating yet another identity change as he assumed the name Iso Mataemon Minamoto no Masatari.

Mataemon established a Tenjin Shinyō Ryū dōjō in Otamagaike (Kanda, Tōkyō) around 1820, which rapidly flourished, doubtless due to the impressive skills of Mataemon. The dōjō allegedly enrolled over 5,000 students between 1848 and 1864. The Otamagaike dōjō was located near the Hokushin Ittō Ryū/Genbukan dōjō and led by Chiba Shūsaku (1798-1856). Many students studied in both dōjō, which forged a link between Tenjin Shinyō Ryū and Hokushin Ittō Ryū. Notably, the founder of Shindō Yōshin Ryū, Matsuoka Katsunosuke studied in both these dōjō.

Legendary Tenjin Shinyō Ryū shihan Tobari Takisaburō was a student of Inoue Keitarō. Takisaburō's wife, Tobari Kazu led this line as well as a line of Shin no Shindō Ryū in Ōsaka. Until her death she maintained one of the three surviving lines of Tenjin Shinyō Ryū. Sadly, with her passing, the Tobari line lost transmission as no successor was appointed.

(Collection of the Takamura ha Shindō Yōshin Kai.)

Sometime after 1860, Mataemon was selected as a jūjutsu instructor to the Bakufu Kōbusho. During the dark days of public disinterest in classical martial arts after the collapse of the Tokugawa Shogunate in 1867, young Kanō Jigorō entered the Tenjin Shinyō Ryū dōjō of Fukuda Hichinosuke. Fukuda died 11 years later and Kanō Jigorō sought to train under Iso Mataemon Masatomo, third headmaster of Tenjin Shinyō Ryū.

Shindō Yōshin Ryū

Kitō Ryū and Tenjin Shinyō Ryū comprised the foundation of the understanding of jūjutsu acquired by Kanō, and to his eventual creation, Kōdōkan Jūdō. The Itsutsu no Kata of jūdō was based on the esoteric teachings of Tenjin Shinyō Ryū, whereas the Kime no Kata are reportedly representative of Tenjin Shinyō Ryū combat tactics. Offshoots of Tenjin Shinyō Ryū include Ito ha Shinyō Ryū, Ryūshin Katchū Ryū, Ishiguro Ryū, Iga Ryūha Katsushin Ryū, and Shindō Yōshin Ryū.

Tenjin Shinyō Ryū is still in existence today, and is frequently demonstrated at koryū embu throughout Japan. Although it is no longer led by the Iso family, two branches maintain the school's legacy. The Sakamoto Fusatarō line is led by Kubota Nobuhiro and the other line that descended through Miyamoto Hanzō, is led by Shibata Kōichi. Until recently, there was a third line, descended through Tobari Tokisaburō, which was maintained by his wife, Tobari Kazu, but this line lost transmission when she died without appointing a successor.

Technical Legacy of Tenjin Shinyō Ryū

The curriculum of Tenjin Shinyō Ryū comprises 124 techniques plus kuden (oral teachings), shiai-hō (freestyle application), and kappō (resuscitation); and is organized into nine categories. The first three sets, Te Hodoki (12 forms), Shodan Idori (10 forms), and Shodan Tachiai (10 forms), constitute the Shoden Mokuroku. These represent the basic and foundational teachings of the school. Completion of these categories confers eligibility to receive a Shoden Kirigami license.

The fourth and fifth sets are identified as Chudan Idori (14 forms) and Chudan Tachiai (14 forms), and are teachings that reflect a more combative approach to training, as well as a more practical application of the fundamental principles of the school. Completion of these categories confers eligibility to receive a Chūden Kirigami license.

The next category of study is Nagesute (20 forms), teachings, which take the combative approach to training further, and includes scenarios that address surprise attacks and multiple attackers. Completion of the Nagesute confers eligibility to receive the first mokuroku, which is identified as the Jūjutsu Chi no Maki (Scroll of Earth). Included on this scroll are the Chudan Idori, the Chudan Tachiai, the Goko no Den (five principles) and the Nanako no Den (seven principles).

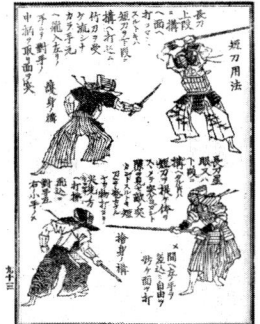

These illustrations are from Inoguchi Matsunosuke's Jūjutsu Ken-Bō Zukai Hiketsu, published in 1887. It includes jūjutsu kata from Tenjin Shinyō Ryū and other technques from various schools of jūjutsu, bōjutsu & kenjutsu. During the Meiji period, books outlining numerous koryū schools and their once secretive teachings first became available.

(Collection of the Takamura ha Shindō Yōshin Kai.)

History And Technique

 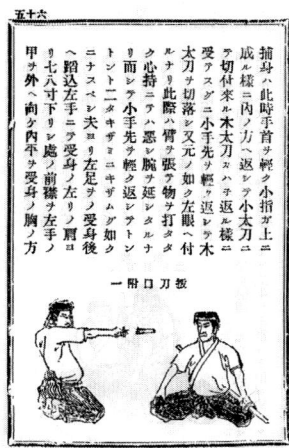 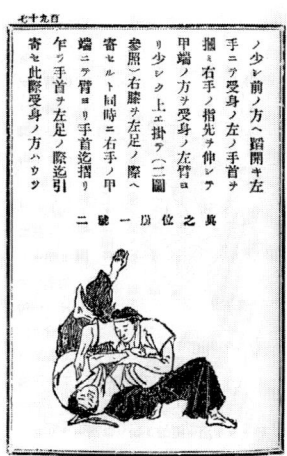

These illustrations are from Iso Mataemon Masayuki and Yoshida Chiharu's Jūjutsu Gokui Kyōju Zukai, published in 1893. The book illustrates 124 Tenjin Shinyō Ryū techniques and includes a foreword written by Kanō Jigorō. Illustrated from left to right are the techniques, Tsuki Kake, Nukimi no Metsuke and Shin no Kurai Kuzushi.

(Collection of the Takamura ha Shindō Yoshin Kai.)

Training in the different branches of Tenjin Shinyō Ryū can diverge above the chudan level, particularly in the exact order and progression of instruction. Generally speaking, the Shiai Ura, the Gokui Jōdan Tachiai, and the Gokui Jōdan Idori are taught in that order. The Shiai Ura, usually taught first, are best described as force-on-force pressure testing where kaeshi-waza (counter techniques) and the various forms of sente (initiative) are investigated so they can be applied in an actual combative context. The Gokui Jōdan Tachiai and the Gokui Jōdan Idori, which are then taught, are sophisticated studies in the application of intent, combat flexibility

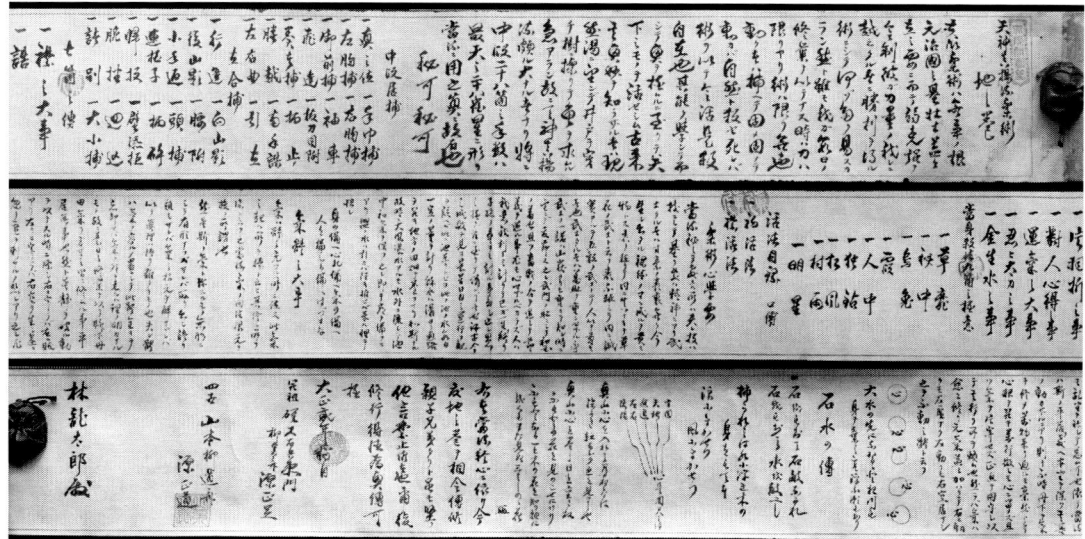

This is a Tenjin Shinyō Ryū jūjutsu Chi no Maki issued in November, 1913 by fourth-generation instructor, Yamamoto Ryūdōsai Minamoto no Masamichi. It was issued to Hayashi Ryūtarō. This unusual mokuroku includes an extensive amount of information along with didactic aids not commonly found on other Tenjin Shinyō Ryū densho of its type. Typical of Meiji era densho, the quality of the paper and calligraphy is much lower than those of previous periods.

(Collection of the Takamura ha Shindō Yoshin Kai.)

Shindō Yōshin Ryū

Kakei (Lineage) / Tenjin Shinyō Ryū

**Ryusō (Founder)
Iso Mataemon Minamoto no Masatari (1788-1863)**

Iso Mataichirō Masamitsu (1820?-1855)

Itō Ryūeisai
(Founder)
Itō-ha Shinyō Ryū

Iso Mataemon Masatomo (1818-1881)

Matsuoka Katsunosuke
(Founder)
Shindō Yōshin Ryū
1836-1898)

Inoue Keitarō

Iso Mataemon Masanobu

Yagi Torajirō
(1865-1946)

Fukuda Hachinosuke
(1828-1879)

Tobari Takisaburō

Miyamoto Hanzō

Iso Mataemon Masayuki

Sakamoto Fusatarō

Kanō Jigorō
(Founder)
Kōdōkan Jūdō
(1860-1938)

Tobari Kazu

Satō Masayoshi

Aimiya Wasaburō

Kubota Toshishiro
(1937-2013)

Shibata Kōichi
(Miyamoto Line)

Kubota Nobuhiro
(Sakamoto Line)

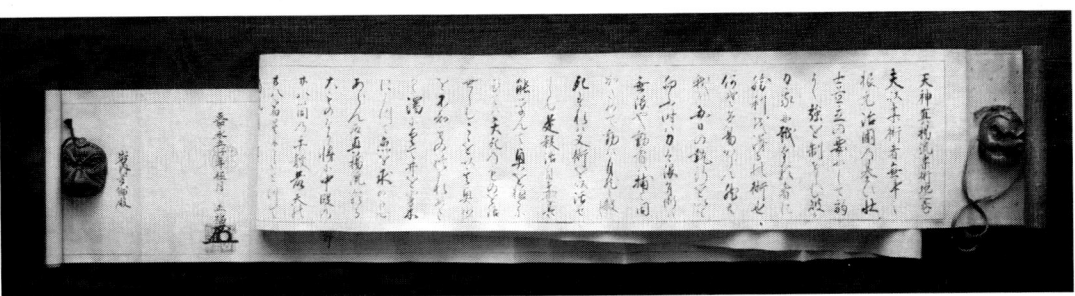

Tenjin Shinyō Ryū jūjutsu Chi no Maki issued in December 1852 by Nishi Kengorō to Iwauchi Tasetsu.
(Colletion of the Takamura ha Shindō Yōshin Kai.)

History And Technique

Tenjin Shinyō Ryū demonstration at Meiji Jingū, 2015.
(Photo courtesy of S.F. Radzikowski)

and psychological pressure. Completion of these sets of kata confers eligibility to receive a menkyo, in the form of a makimono identified as the Jūjutsu Keiraku Jin no Maki (Scroll of Man).

Further gokui level teachings are included in the Ten no Maki (Scroll of Heaven). They include sa-kappō (resuscitation), randori-hō (freestyle training) and the generation and application of ki. The Tenjin Shinyō Ryū hiden (innermost mysteries) are concerned with spiritual and mystical matters, which include visualization, vocalizations, and methods of calling on the spirit world for divination, moral courage, and prescience. In some branches, these teachings are contained in the Inyō no Maki (Positive and Negative Scroll). In other branches, they are also included in the Ten no Maki. Either way, a student reaching this level of training is eligible to be awarded a Menkyo Kaiden, a license symbolizing the complete transmission of the school's techniques, principles, and ethos.

Unlike its parent art Akiyama Yōshin Ryū, Tenjin Shinyō Ryū does not reflect the characteristics of a combatively oriented sōgō bujutsu. It is very much an art of its era. It places little emphasis on employing classical Japanese weaponry in an environment of warfare and the use of weapons in Tenjin Shinyō Ryū is purposely simple and straightforward. This illustrates that as the Edo period continued, arts like Shin no Shindō Ryū and its descendant, Tenjin Shinyō Ryū, evolved and adapted to a civilian environment. When Tenjin Shinyō Ryū was conceived by Iso Mataemon, Japan was relatively peaceful and free of military conflict.

"Shinkiryoku goitsu fuji no myō"

A unique and magnificent strength is born when resolve, spirit and power are unified.

- *Tenjin Shinyō Ryū koka*

Tenjin Shinyō Ryū and Shishin Takuma Kyūdai Kennichi Ryū

A notable historical detail confirmed by documentation in the Takamura ha Shindō Yōshin Kai archives relates to a connection between the jūjutsu schools of Tenjin Shinyō Ryū and Shishin Takuma Kyūdai Kennichi Ryū. Two densho in the Takamura ha Shindō Yōshin Kai collection are issued by the same instructor to the same student, but in different styles of jūjutsu. These densho further confirm several of the most prestigious shihan in Tenjin Shinyō Ryū were also shihan in Shishin Takuma Kyūdai Kennichi Ryū. The following high-level instructors are named on both of the makimono illustrated below:

1) Yoshida Naoshige
2) Takano Sadaie
3) Takao Kiyoshige
4) Yoshida Denzaemon Naoyoshi
5) Itō Kōzeamon Tadamoto

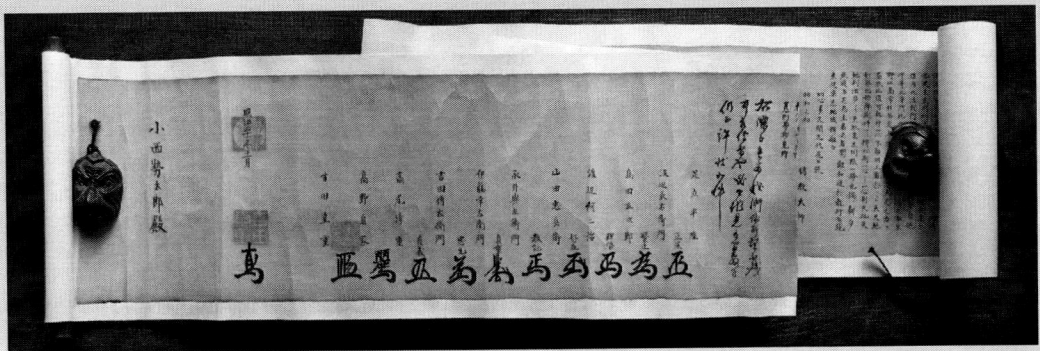

Shishin Takuma Kyudai Kennichi Ryū jūjutsu mokuroku, issued to Konishi Seitaro in 1898 by Yoshida Naoshige.
(Collection of the Takamura ha Shindō Yōshin Kai.)

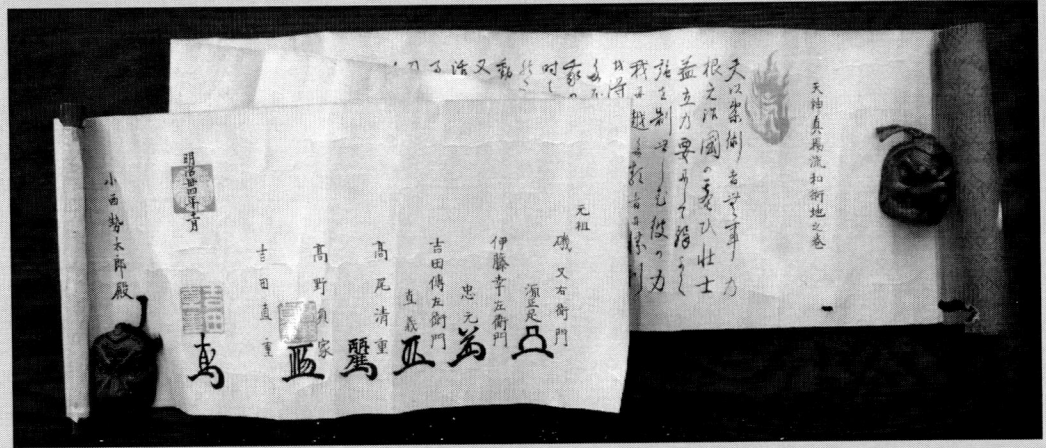

Tenjin Shinyō Ryū Wajutsu Chi no Maki, issued to Konishi Seitarō in 1891 by Yoshida Naoshige.
(Collection of the Takamura ha Shindō Yōshin Kai.)

Tenjin Shinyō Ryū Jūjutsu Curriculum (Iso Lineage)

Te Hodoki (12)
- Oni Kobushi
- Furi Hodoki
- Gyaku De
- Gyaku Yubi
- Kata Muna Dori
- Ryō Muna Dori
- Kote Gaeshi
- Ryōte Dori
- Ki Dori
- Tento
- Mogi Dori
- Uchi Dori

Shodan Idori (10)
- Shin no Kurai
- Soe Dori
- Gozen Dori
- Sode Guruma
- Tobi Chigai
- Nukimi Metsuke
- Kojiri Gaeshi
- Ryōte Dori
- Kabe Zoe
- Ushiro Dori

Shodan Tachiai (10)
- Yuki Chigai
- Tsuki Kake
- Hiki Otoshi
- Ryō Muna Dori
- Tsure Byōshi
- Tomo Guruma
- Kinu Katsugi
- Eri Nage
- Tamusa Dori
- Ushiro Dori

Chūdan Idori (14)
- Shin no Kurai
- Shikin Tori
- Hidari Muna Dori
- Migi Muna Dori
- Gozen Dori
- Sode Guruma
- Tobi Chigai
- Nukimi Metsuke
- Sosha Dori
- Tsuka Dome
- Zen Goshi
- Ryōte Zume
- Sayu no Kyoku
- Hiki Tate

Chūdan Tachiai (14)
- Yuki Chigai
- Mukō Yamakage
- Ushiro Yamakage
- Koshi Tsuki
- Kote Gaeshi
- Zu Dori
- Tsure Byoshi
- Mawari Komi
- Tsuka Kudaki
- Kaeri Nage
- Kabezoe Fusegi
- Ude Hishigi
- Sho Betsu
- Daisho Dori

Nagesute (20)
- Shumoku
- Karisute
- Kuchiki Taoshi
- Koshi Guruma
- Yoko Guruma
- Kata Muna Dori
- Tamusa Dori
- Kogusoku
- Koshigari Sute
- Dokko
- Kote Gaeshi
- Hiki Otoshi
- Taguri
- Sutemi
- Sagari Fuji
- Ude Garami
- Yahazu
- Ryōte Dori
- Ryō Tsuka Dori
- Ushiro Dori

Shiai Ura (24 kata, plus 18 waza)
- Shiai Guchi (3)
- Yoko Guruma Kuzushi (3)
- Tsukkomi Kuzushi (3)
- Betsure Kuzushi (3)
- Shin no Kurai Kuzushi (3)
- Ibetsu Kuzushi (3)
- Sode Guruma Kuzushi (3)
- Ratai Dori (3)

Jōden Tachiai (Gokui-10)
- Ke Kaeshi
- Omokage
- Morote Kudaki
- Sugi Taoshi
- Ōgoroshi
- Nami Wake
- Enkō Tsukemi
- Tegate Tori
- Ryōhi
- Tengu Shō

Jōden Idori (Gokui-10)
- Ushiro Kasugai
- Waki Kusagai
- Ushiro Dori
- Kataha Chijimi
- Yahazu
- Tsukikake
- Muni Ken
- Mitō Kyoku
- Ryūko
- Zanshin Metsuke

Shindō Yōshin Ryū

Kakei (Lineage) / Shindō Yōshin Ryū

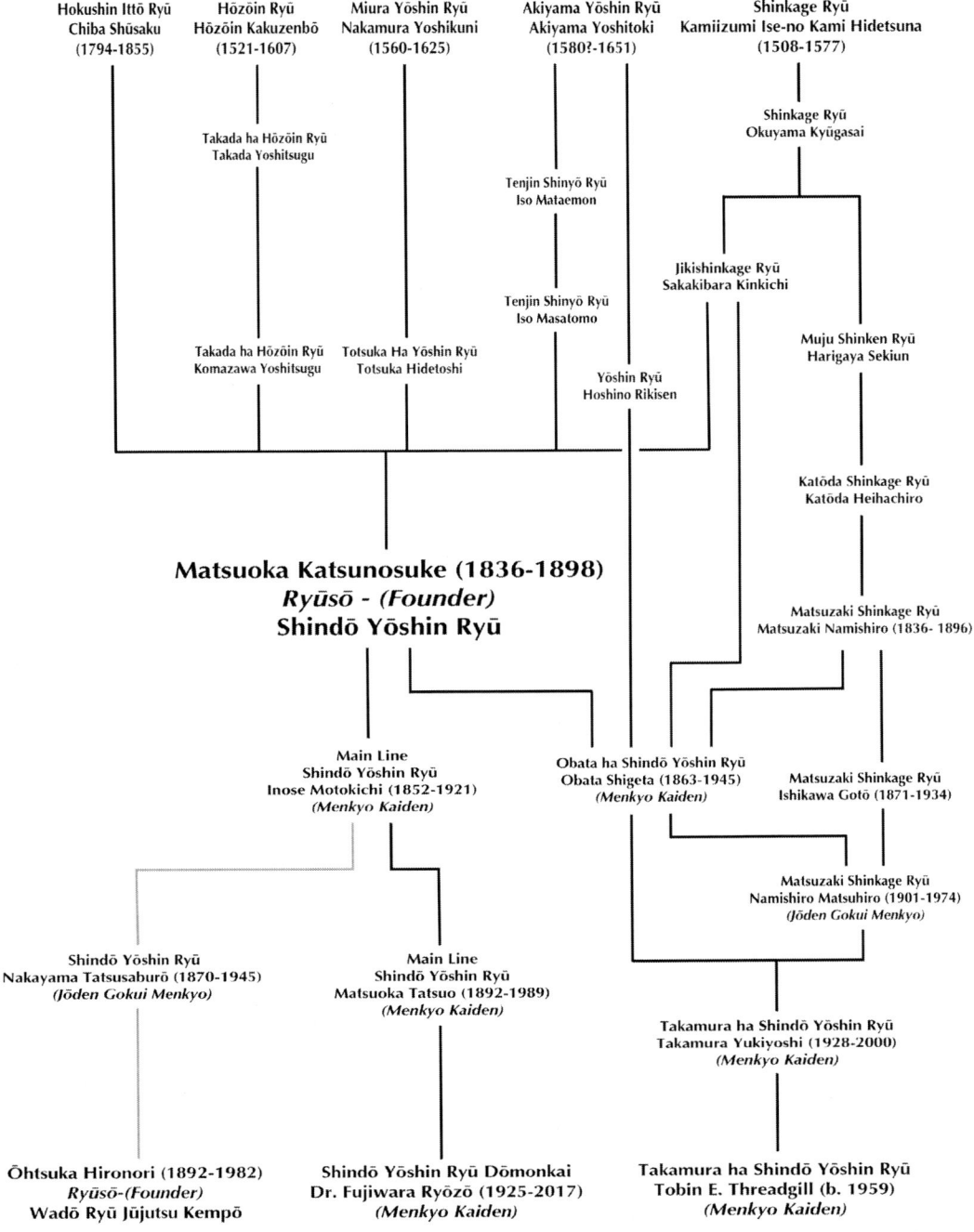

History And Technique

The History of Shindō Yōshin Ryū

Shindō Yōshin Ryū founder, Matsuoka Katsunosuke Hisachika (1836-1898).

During Japan's Edo period, hundreds of jūjutsu schools existed. Among those schools, the Yōshin Ryū schools were legendary. Sadly, most of the Yōshin Ryū lineage schools are no longer extant. One of the few Yōshin Ryū lineage schools that survived is Shindō Yōshin Ryū. The Ryūso (founder), Matsuoka Katsunosuke (1836-1898), established Shindō Yōshin Ryū in 1864, based on his expertise in Tenjin Shinyō Ryū jūjutsu, Totsuka ha Yōshin Ryū jūjutsu, Jikishinkage Ryū kenjutsu, Hokushin Ittō Ryū kenjutsu, and Hōzōin Ryū sōjutsu. In 1870, Matsuoka built a dōjō for both kendō (kenjutsu) and jūdō (jūjutsu) next to his medical clinic in Ueno, Hitachi (present day Ibaraki), which is northeast of Edo. Shindō Yōshin Ryū was conceived as a sōgō bujutsu. Its primary theory is the application of non-resistance and efficient natural movement, principles deeply studied and employed in the Yōshin Ryū lineages of jūjutsu.

Shindō Yōshin Ryū

The Historical Background of Shindō Yōshin Ryū Jūjutsu
Three Shindō Yōshin Ryū Lineages

1. Matsuoka (Main line)

Matsuoka Katsunosuke (1836-1898)

The founder of Shindō Yōshin Ryū, Matsuoka Katsunosuke, was a samurai born into the Kuroda clan during the late Edo period. He was an accomplished swordsman and jūjutsuka. In 1862, Matsuoka moved to Ueno, north of Tōkyō, and married. He established a medical clinic and dōjō in Ueno, teaching Shindō Yōshin Ryū, a comprehensive martial art he conceived. He fought on the side of the Tokugawa Shōgun in the battles of Toba-Fushimi and Ueno during the Boshin Wars and following the Tokugawa defeat, Matsuoka returned to Ueno and continued developing Shindō Yōshin Ryū. The main line passed through four generations with its last representative, Dr. Fujiwara Ryōzō. Fujiwara died in 2017 without appointing a successor to carry on the main line.

2. Nakayama (Wadō Ryū line)

Nakayama Tatsusaburō (1870-1945)

The Nakayama line of Shindō Yōshin Ryū is unofficial, but had a strong influence on Japanese budō. Nakayama Tatsusaburō was a student of the second headmaster of the main line, Inose Motokichi and Nakayama received his Shindō Yōshin Ryū Jōden Gokui Menkyo in 1895. In 1907, Nakayama was hired as the budō instructor at Shimotsuma Middle School, where he met a young and talented student, Ōtsuka Kō. Documentation indicates Ōtsuka went on to study Shindō Yōshin Ryū with Nakayama at his Genbukan Dōjō through 1910. In 1934-35, Ōtsuka combined his knowledge of Shindō Yōshin Ryū and Okinawan karate to create an innovative expression of Nihon budō initially associated with the Dai Nippon Karate Shinko Club, and eventually named Wadō Ryū karate.

3. Takamura (Obata Line)

Obata Shigeta (1863-1945)

The Obata line of Shindō Yōshin Ryū originated with Obata Shigeta, born in Kyōto in 1863. Obata was an accomplished budō practitioner when he met Matsuoka and asked to become his student. In 1895, Obata was awarded a Menkyo Kaiden and allowed to lead his own branch of Shindō Yōshin Ryū in Asakusa, Tōkyō. During the turbulent years of World War II, Obata officially selected his grandson, Obata (later Takamura) Yukiyoshi, born in 1928, as his inheritor. Thus, Takamura became the custodian of the art and three of his students eventually received Menkyo Kaiden. Tobin E. Threadgill is the current leader of the ryūha and the honbu dōjō is located in Evergreen, Colorado, United States. At the time of this writing, over 200 students in 12 countries are active in this line of Shindō Yōshin Ryū.

Shindō Yōshin Ryū and Its Evolving Name

Shin	Dō	Yō	Shin	Ryū	Jū	Jutsu
新	道	楊	心	流	柔	術
New	Way	Willow Tree	Soul/Heart	Path/Style	Flexible	Method
神	道	揚	心	流	柔	術
Divine/Deity	Way	Raising	Soul/Heart	Path/Style	Flexible	Method

Due to the complexities of the Japanese language, and its pictographic and ideographic writing system riddled with homophones, a symbolic change in a name can often be made without changing the way a name is pronounced. Among the koryū, such spelling alterations could be common, with words like musō (無双), meaning unequalled, evolving into musō (夢想), meaning dream. Alterations in the name of a koryū could represent a breakaway line, a change in leadership, or a newly-embraced underlying theory.

Yō 楊 (Willow) or Yō 揚 (Raising)

Documents, including scrolls, published books, and other materials, confirm two similar kanji characters pronounced "yō" have been frequently interchanged in writing Shindō Yōshin Ryū during its history. One is for willow tree (楊), while the other is for raising (揚). Considerable speculation surrounds the use of these characters and how they came to be interchanged. The fact they are differentiated by only a single brush stroke has led to conjecture the difference is a simple scrivener's error. However, Fujiwara Ryōzō of the Shindō Yōshin Ryū Dōmonkai has suggested the change from willow tree to raising might have been intentional. He has proposed that the raising character symbolized an upward evolution of the school as it continued development.

The kanji for "raising" has origins in China, where it is used to reference the Yángtze river (揚子江). Some speculate the origins of the kanji for willow tree are associated with the raising character, as a type of willow tree with upswept branches was commonly found on the banks of the Yángtze. It is also known as a school of martial arts, Yangzhou Quan (揚州拳/Japanese: Yōshūken), which originated in Yangzhou, which is located on the north bank of the Yángtze river. Some historians speculate the founder of Akiyama Yōshin Ryū was exposed to Yangzhou Quan during his travels in China. However, no convincing evidence supports this rather romantic notion beyond the common usage of these characters.

Shin 新 (New) or Shin 神 (Divine)

According to Obata, via his grandson Takamura, when Shindō Yōshin Ryū was founded, the kanji Matsuoka chose for his new martial arts system originally meant "New Way Willow Spirit School" (新道楊心流). This is reasonable as Matsuoka was creating a new school of jūjutsu by merging the teachings of Tenjin Shinyō Ryū and Totsuka ha Yōshin Ryū. After recovery from sustaining a gunshot wound in the back during the Battle of Ueno, Matsuoka allegedly changed the original kanji, shin (新) for new, to the kanji, shin (神) for divine, which did not change the way the name of the new school was pronounced (神道楊心流). An acknowledgement of divine intervention related to his survival and destiny appears to have been the rationale behind the decision of Matsuoka to change the kanji.

Takamura, the headmaster of the Obata line of Shindō Yōshin Ryū, altered the syllabus of the school in 1968 by adding a goshinjutsu curriculum, categorized as betsuden (separate teachings). In the early 1970s, Takamura chose to return to using the original kanji of the school and renamed the line the Takamura ha Shindō Yōshin Ryū (高村派新道楊心流).

Shindō Yōshin Ryū main line

Ryūsō - Matsuoka Katsunosuke
(Image Courtesy of Matsuoka Masahiro.)

Matsuoka Katsunosuke Hisachika (1836-1898)

The Matsuoka family name can be traced back to Ōtomo Sōrin, a Christian daimyō who ruled Matsuoka kyo (present day Ōita City) in Ōita gun, Bungo no kuni. During the Tokugawa Bakufu, the Matsuoka family achieved samurai status and came to be associated with medicine as well as martial arts. Matsuoka Dōrin, Katsunosuke's grandfather, was a samurai and medical doctor in Chikuzen Province, Fukuoka. His son Matsuoka Katsuharu Dōrin, Katsunosuke's father, also became a doctor of Chinese medicine. Family oral tradition says Katsuharu held Menkyo Kaiden in both Hōzōin Ryū sōjutsu and Miura Yōshin Ryū jūjutsu but the authors have not been able to document this claim. Katsuharu was stationed in Edo, where his son, Katsunosuke, was born on December 26th in the Edo-Hantei (Tōkyō headquarters) of the Kuroda clan in Kasumigaseki. The Kuroda clan opened its first school for their children in the Edo-Hantei in 1784, followed by a martial arts school in 1797. Katsunosuke grew up in Edo, where his family saw that he was educated in both medicine and martial arts. During this period, children of powerful clans could study at both clan schools and popular private martial arts schools.

Matsuoka Katsunosuke started training in Hōzōin Ryū under Komazawa Yoshitsugu in 1842, and Jikishinkage Ryū kenjutsu under Odani Nobutomo in 1846. In 1851, Matsuoka began the study of Chinese medicine at Kanda Hitotsubashi under Ogawa Yozaemon. He received a teaching license in Hōzōin Ryū 1852, and a teaching license in Jikishinkage Ryū in 1853. In January 1853, he entered the Otamagaike Dōjō in Kanda, where he studied Tenjin Shinyō Ryū jūjutsu under the third headmaster, Iso Mataemon Masatomo. In September 1855 at the age of 19, he received a Menkyo Kaiden from Iso and became an assistant instructor at the Iso Dōjō. Matsuoka was known as "The fierce tiger of the Iso Dōjō" because he accepted all challenges initiated there, and remained undefeated.

History And Technique

Matsuoka also trained briefly in Hokushin Ittō Ryū kenjutsu during this period, at the Genbukan Dōjō of Chiba Shūsaku (1793-1855). By 1858 when he was 22 years old, he was permitted to open his own Tenjin Shinyō Ryū dōjō adjacent to the Kannonji Temple in Asakusa, Edo. He was quickly recognized as an elite practitioner of martial arts, so the Kuroda Clan ordered him to enter the Bakufu Kōbusho as a trainee in 1860. At the Kōbusho, Matsuoka continued studying Jikishinkage Ryū kenjutsu under Sakakibara Kenkichi and began studying Totsuka ha Yōshin Ryū jūjutsu under Totsuka Hikosuke Hidetoshi. At this time, jūjutsu training was not a priority at the Kōbusho, so it was practiced only six days a month, on days 2, 7, 12, 17, 22 and 27. However, Matsuoka was very dedicated to jūjutsu, so he also trained at Totsuka's private dōjō in Atagoyama. Matsuoka became an assistant jūjutsu instructor at the Kōbusho in April 1862, but was released from teaching duties there in October 1862, when jūjutsu was dropped from the Kōbusho curriculum.

Matsuoka Shindōkan Dōjō in Ueno, early Meiji period. From Ueno Sonshi (History of Ueno Village, 1954.)

Following his release from the Kōbusho, Matsuoka moved to Ueno, a small village north of Tōkyō. However, his gravestone in the village states he moved there in 1861. He married Ishijima Yoshi (1840-1881), a daughter of the village mayor and was promoted to inspector of shogunate possessions in Shimotsuke and Hitachi, and in December 1862 opened a medical clinic in Ueno. Matsuoka received a Menkyo Kaiden in Jikishinkage Ryū in 1864 from Sakakibara Kenkichi, and afterwards decided to create a comprehensive system of bujutsu based on all the disciplines he had studied. On May 1st, 1864, he christened this system Shindō Yōshin Ryū (New/Willow Spirit/School). Shindō Yōshin Ryū is, therefore, a system of sōgō bujutsu founded on Matsuoka's knowledge of Hōzōin Ryū sōjutsu, Tenjin Shinyō Ryū jūjutsu, Totsuka ha Yōshin Ryū jūjutsu, Jikishinkage Ryū kenjutsu and Hokushin Ittō Ryū kenjutsu.

In 1866, the Bakufu gave Matsuoka an assignment to calm unrest in Hitachi and Shimofusa (present day Ibaraki and Chiba prefectures). He completed this task in February 1867 and was then ordered to present himself at Edo Castle, where he received orders to go to Kyōto, along with other former Kōbusho trainees, in May 1867. His task was to function as a bodyguard to the new Shōgun, Tokugawa Yoshinobu (1837-1913). On November 9th, 1867, Tokugawa was compelled to sign an agreement returning political and military control of Japan to the emperor, referred to in Japanese history as Taisei Hōkan (returning the emperor to power). The political forces compelling the Shōgun to do this were samurai from Chōshū (present day Yamaguchi prefecture), and Satsuma (present day Kagoshima prefecture) who were further supported by samurai from the Tosa

Matsuoka Katsunosuke
(Image Courtesy of Matsuoka Masahiro.)

Shindō Yōshin Ryū

and Hizen regions (present day Kōchi and Saga prefectures, respectively). The Bakufu regarded these groups as rebels and thus the political and military situation remained tense despite the signed Taisei Hōkan. Tokugawa returned to Edo in January 1868 with his entourage, including Matsuoka. Matsuoka was placed among the Seieitai, troops with a mandate to protect the Shōgun. Although the surrender of Edo was negotiated, violence erupted near Edo Castle at the Battle of Ueno (Tōkyō). The Seieitai lost to the new Kangun (government forces) on May 15th, 1868. Matsuoka was shot in the back while fighting several adversaries. Unable to continue fighting, he fled towards the Tone River where he tended his wounds. Local farmers later informed him the Aizu Clan had surrendered. He finally arrived in Ueno (Hitachi) in September 1868 and recovered from his injuries.

Matsuoka Teisaburō (1870-1914).
(Image Courtesy of Matsuoka Masahiro.)

Matsuoka continued running his medical clinic in Ueno (Hitachi) after regaining his health. Initially he taught Shindō Yōshin Ryū in an adjoining open courtyard but due to the harsh winters, in 1870 he constructed a 50-mat dōjō next to his medical clinic named the Shindōkan. Around this time he changed the kanji for "shin" of Shindō Yōshin Ryū from 新 for new, to 神 for divine, altering the name to mean "Divine Willow Spirit School". Matsuoka was formally regarded as a fugitive by the new imperial government and thus assumed his wife's family name, Ishijima, to obscure his true identity. The new Meiji government gradually became more tolerant and stopped pursuing many supporters who fought for the Bakufu. In fact, many members of the overthrown Bakufu were later employed by the new Meiji government and given positions of authority. Among these were: Yamaoka Tesshū (1836-1888) of Ono ha Ittō Ryū kenjutsu and Ittō Shōden Mutō Ryū; Enomoto Takeaki (1836-1908), samurai and admiral; and Katsu Kaishū (1823-1899) of Jikishinkage Ryū kenjutsu. The Meiji government officially permitted Matsuoka to run his medical clinic around 1878 and the Ministry of Home Affairs officially licensed him in 1884. At this time, only three people were permitted to run medical clinics in Ibaraki prefecture: Matsuoka in Ueno, and a father and son with the surname Ueno in Mito City. These facts indicate the new government must have perceived Matsuoka as a valuable medical practitioner. He was officially pardoned in 1887, which allowed him to revert to his original name, Matsuoka. The Meiji government's increasing tolerance, allowed him to travel freely and visit Tōkyō during the 1880s, where he met Obata Shigeta (1863-1945) around 1885 at the Totsuka ha Yōshin Ryū dōjō in Atagoyama.

Matsuoka had three daughters and a son:

> Matsu (1863-1927): married Ryōtarō, (1865-1904); mother of Matsuoka Tatsuo.
> Chiyo (1867-1887): died without children.
> Chau (1878-1914): married Hoshino Gen-ichi (1879-1934).
> Teisaburō (1870-1914): father of Matsuoka Nobuatsu.

Teisaburō, Katsunosuke's only son, was not interested in martial arts and became a successful bonesetter. According to the Matsuoka family, Ōtake Nobu, who worked for Katsunosuke, mentioned to Tatsuo and Hoshino Hisashi (cousin of Tatsuo and also a doctor) in 1932 that Katsunosuke frequently told his son Teisaburō:

"I have been training since the age of seven years old in horse riding, spear, jūjutsu and swimming. You should be motivated to train your body using your own will power."

Matsuoka's wife, Yoshi, died in 1881, when their eldest daughter, Matsu, was 18 years old and she was left to care for her brother Teisaburō, and sisters Chiyo and Chau. Soon after her mother's death, Matsu married Ryōtarō (1865-1904), who was the journalist son of a friend of Katsunosuke's, living in Tōkyō. After the marriage, Ryōtarō, who was originally from Ōtahara, (about 75 km north of Ueno), assumed the name Matsuoka because it was a prestigious samurai family name, which was a fairly common practice at the time, and moved to Ueno. There, he distinguished himself as a successful entrepreneur by establishing several textile factories, as well as a post office in 1902. Nothing indicates Ryōtarō ever practiced jūjutsu.

Matsu and Ryōtarō had three sons and a daughter:

Tatsuo (1892-1989)
Takeyasu (1896-1984)
Nagao (1900-1924)
Kiku (1903-1923)

By the 1880s, Matsuoka had become legendary as both a jūjutsu and kenjutsu practitioner, and leader of one of the most popular dōjō north of Tōkyō. Students on musha shugyō frequently visited this dōjō and by the mid-1890s, over 3,000 students had passed through the Matsuoka Shindōkan Dōjō in Ueno, two of the more talented receiving Menkyo Kaiden. One of these students was Obata Shigeta, a robust jūjutsu and kenjutsu practitioner who had trained in Yōshin Ryū and Jikishinkage Ryū, a background that closely mirrored that of Matsuoka. In 1895, a personal conflict between assistant instructor, Inose Motokichi and Obata Shigeta drove a wedge between the ryuha's two seniors and, as a result, Matsuoka issued Obata a document authorizing him to separate from the main line.

Upon the unexpected death of Shindō Yōshin Ryū's founder, on April 25th, 1898, age of 63, the Matsuoka family arranged a meeting among the senior students in the Matsuoka Shindōkan. At this meeting, it was decided Inose (1852-1921), the current shihan dai (assistant instructor) of the Shindōkan, would temporarily lead the school. In 1900, the Matsuoka family, honoring a common two-year delay, named Inose the second

Grave site of Shindō Yōshin Ryū founder Matsuoka Katsunosuke in present day Chukusei City, Ibaraki prefecture.

headmaster of Shindō Yōshin Ryū, with the understanding that a Matsuoka heir would become the third headmaster.

Katsunosuke might have expected his grandson Tatsuo to inherit Shindō Yōshin Ryū jūjutsu, but at the time of his passing in 1898, Tatsuo was only six years old and his other two grandsons, Takeyasu and Nobuatsu (born to Teisaburō in 1896), were both two years old. Takeyasu never showed any interest in budō, but in the ensuing years, Tatsuo and Nobuatsu both followed the family tradition by studying martial arts and medicine in Tōkyō.

Inose Motokichi (1852-1921)

Inose, the son of an Akeno farmer, was a physically powerful rural wrestler with a reputation as "The Beast of Tsukuba". Inose met Matsuoka in 1870 when he and a friend visited the recently-constructed Matsuoka Shindōkan Dōjō. Matsuoka easily dispatched the young wrestler and Inose enthusiastically petitioned Matsuoka to undertake jūjutsu training in his dōjō. Inose quickly emerged as a talented jūjutsu practitioner under Matsuoka and eventually ascended to the positions of kanjichō (secretary general) and shihan dai in the Matsuoka Shindōkan. Inose received Shindō Yōshin Ryū Shoden Kirigami, Chūden Mokuroku and Jōden Gokui Menkyo licenses in 1873, 1874, and 1877, respectively, followed by a Menkyo Kaiden in 1878.

Inose Motokichi, the second headmaster of Shindō Yōshin Ryū. Inose, a powerful jūjutsuka, transitioned the Shindō Yōshin Ryū mainline away from its roots as a sōgō bujutsu into a more contemporary school of jūjutsu/jūdō.

Inose was less skilled in kenjutsu than in jūjutsu, and thus jūjutsu training became dominant after Matsuoka's death in what was by then the Shindōkan Dōjō. With the increasing popularity of Kōdōkan Jūdō and his innate jūjutsu talent, it should not be surprising Inose decided to follow a path that had become popular among many classical jūjutsu schools of the era. Inose taught contemporary jūdō-like randori with jūdō rules as well as classical Shindō Yōshin Ryū jūjutsu kata. By 1910, the Shindōkan Dōjō was becoming a driving force in the jūjutsu and jūdō community as most of the competitive jūdō practitioners in Ibaraki prefecture were training under Inose at the Shindōkan Dōjō.

Monument dedicated to Inose in Akeno, Ibaraki.

The transposition of the words "jūdō" and "jūjutsu" can seem confusing, particularly since they were used interchangeably during the late 19th and early 20th centuries.

History And Technique

With the growing political power and prestige of Kōdōkan Jūdō, many jūjutsu schools simply appropriated the term jūdō due to its popular appeal. Notably, the Kōdōkan was not the first school to use the term jūdō. Jikishin Ryū, a school descended from Midare Kitō Ryū, used the term as early as 1724. Shindō Yōshin Ryū licenses commonly used the term jūdō instead of jūjutsu under the leadership of Inose.

The original weapons curriculum created by Matsuoka was mostly abandoned at the Shindōkan Dōjō after 1900, with only a few Kashima Shinden Jikishinkage Ryū weapons kata surviving as part of the official mokuroku. After 1910, the only swordsmanship taught in main line Shindō Yōshin Ryū was significantly influenced by Ittō Ryū and kendo as taught by Nakayama Tatsusaburō at his Genbukan Dōjō and at Shimotsuma Middle School.

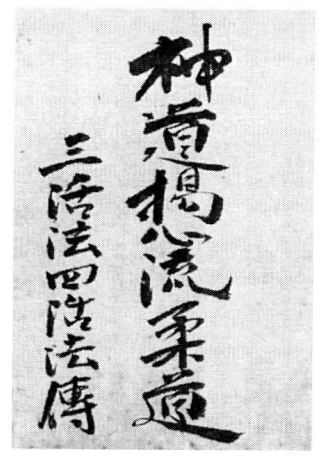
Shindō Yōshin Ryū "Jūdō"

According to the Shimotsuma Middle School archives, Nakayama Tatsusaburō received Shoden Kirigami, Chūden Mokuroku and Jōden Gokui Menkyo licenses from Inose in 1890, 1892 and 1895, respectively. Since Matsuoka was still alive and dōjōchō at this time, Nakayama's promotions indicate Inose, as kanjichō, held important teaching and administrative responsibilities at the Matsuoka Shindōkan Dōjō in Ueno.

In 1940, a granite monument honoring Inose Motokichi was erected by his friends and past students on the grounds of the Inose family ancestral home in Akeno, Ibaraki Prefecture. The text visible on the monument was composed by Matsuoka Tatsuo, the grandson of Matsuoka Katsunosuke and states the following.

> "Inose Sensei trained in Shindō Yōshin Ryū jūdō under Matsuoka Katsunosuke Sensei and received a license to teach from him. His students numbered several thousands in the three prefectures of, Ibaraki, Tochigi and Gunma. He served the nation by teaching budō and passed away in March, 1921."

Grave site of Shindō Yōshin Ryū's, second headmaster, Inose Motokichi in Chukusei City, Ibaraki prefecture.

Martial art history of Inose Motokichi:

    1870   Entered Matsuoka Shindōkan Dōjō
    1873   Shoden Kirigami (first level license)
    1874   Chūden Mokuroku (middle level license)

Shindō Yōshin Ryū

    1877   Jōden Gokui Menkyo (high level secrets license)
    1878   Menkyo Kaiden (full transmission license)
    1881   Shihan dai at Matsuoka Shindōkan Dōjō.
    1900   Authorized by the Matsuoka family as second headmaster of Shindō Yōshin Ryū two years after Matsuoka Katsunosuke's death.

Matsuoka Tatsuo (1892-1989)

Tatsuo, grandson of the founder, and third-generation main line headmaster of Shindō Yōshin Ryū.

Matsuoka Tatsuo performing Shindō Yōshin Ryū Idori kata.
(Collection of the Takamura ha Shindō Yōshin Kai.)

The third headmaster of Shindō Yōshin Ryū jūjutsu was Matsuoka Tatsuo, born in Ueno in 1892 to Matsu and Ryōtarō. Tatsuo was Katsunosuke's eldest grandson. Tatsuo started training in Shindō Yōshin Ryū at the age of seven under Inose. In 1904, his father, Ryōtarō died suddenly at the age of 39, and Tatsuo, his brother and sister were sent to live with their aunt Haru in nearby Nikkō. How consistently Tatsuo continued his training in Shindō Yōshin Ryū during this period of his life remains speculative, but he received a shoden kirigami certificate in 1910 at the age of 18. He moved to Tōkyō in the same year to pursue a career in bookkeeping, but in 1911 decided to follow the Matsuoka family tradition of pursuing a career in medicine, and entered Nippon Medical School (Nippon Igaku), Tōkyō. Tatsuo received a Shindō Yōshin Ryū Chūden Mokuroku license from Inose in 1911. In 1914, Tatsuo joined the Kōdōkan and started to study jūdō. He returned to Ueno in 1915, resumed training in Shindō Yōshin Ryū, and opened a medical clinic. Inose honored his promise to the Matsuoka family and issued Tatsuo a Shindō Yōshin Ryū Menkyo Kaiden in 1917, an event that returned leadership of Shindō Yōshin Ryū to the Matsuoka family. On January 3rd, 1918, most of the senior students studying Shindō Yōshin Ryū (about 200, including his cousin Matsuoka Nobuatsu) pledged loyalty to Tatsuo as the new headmaster by taking a kishōmon (oath) and keppan (signing the student register book in their blood). As the Shindō Yōshin Ryū main line headmaster he would also receive honorary teaching licenses in Kiraku Ryū jūjutsu and Asayama Ichiden Ryū jūjutsu.

Following Inose's death in 1921, Tatsuo changed the name of the dōjō to Shindōkan Matsuoka

History And Technique

Tatsuo with student victors of a youth jūdō tournament. Tatsuo is in the front row, third from the left.
(Collection of the Takamura ha Shindō Yōshin Kai.)

Dōjō, and instituted rules that were very similar to those of the Kōdōkan. He discarded the attire associated with the samurai, namely kimono and hakama, and instead changed the training attire to a keikogi (training jacket) identical to that used in jūdō.

Matsuoka Nobuatsu, son of Teisaburō, grandson of Katsunosuke, and cousin of Tatsuo, returned home to Ueno after completing his medical studies in Tōkyō and opened a medical clinic there in 1920. Around the same time Tatsuo left Ueno and moved to nearby Shimodate,

Tatsuo with his jūdō students at the Shimodate police station dōjō.

Tatsuo teaching jūdō class at the Shimodate police station dōjō in 1935.

where he opened a new medical clinic. Tatsuo was also the school doctor and jūdō instructor at Shimotsuma Middle School for a short period. Although Tatsuo had a background in koryū jūjutsu and responsibility for preserving Shindō Yōshin Ryū, records indicate he was also very devoted to Kōdōkan Jūdō. He actively trained in jūdō, gaining sixth dan in 1956 and later, seventh dan. Tatsuo enthusiastically dedicated himself to the preservation of budō. One example

Shindō Yōshin Ryū

of this was his involvement in the construction of the Shimodate Budōkan Dōjō in 1970.

Tatsuo was socially adept, a quality that served him well as a doctor and martial arts teacher. Almost by chance he found himself involved in local politics during the difficult years leading up to World War II and he became the mayor of Shimodate Town in 1940, and in 1956 he was elected Mayor of Shimodate City. Tatsuo was such a competent leader and manager that he was elected mayor of Shimodate for four terms, until 1972, when he had reached the age of 81. Tatsuo was greatly admired in circles as diverse as medicine, budō, and politics. He passed away in Shimodate in 1989, at the age of 98.

Matsuoka Tatsuo in Ibaraki Prefecture with notable political figures of the 1930s: Tōyama Mitsuru (1855-1944) and Tamamizu Kaichi (1859-1949). Tōyama was an enigmatic ultra-nationalist and founder of the Genyōsha, a controversial right-wing espionage organization. Tamamizu was a kendō instructor and influential right-wing political figure residing in Ibaraki. Both these men held powerful sway in the politics of Ibaraki. Their influence convinced Matsuoka Tatsuo to pursue a life in politics and public service.

Grave site of Tatsuo in Chukusei City, Ibaraki Prefecture.

Matsuoka Nobuatsu (1896 -1976)

Nobuatsu was the younger cousin of the third Shindō Yōshin Ryū headmaster, Tatsuo. He was of stocky build and excelled at jūdō and jūjutsu. He attended Shimotsuma Middle School between 1908 and 1913 and was also was a member of the school jūdō club along with Ōtsuka Hironori, the founder of Wadō Ryū karate/jūjutsu kempō. Nobuatsu is listed among a group of students who lived in the Shimotsuma Middle School dormitory. He is recorded as one among more than 200 students who declared their loyalty to Tatsuo by taking keppan, and signing the dōjō register book in blood in 1918. In the same year, Nobuatsu became one of the first graduates of Tōkyō Medical School (Tōkyō Igakkō). He opened a medical clinic in Ueno in 1920, and became the school doctor at Ueno Primary School in 1923.

Matsuoka Takeshi, son of Nobuatsu, with author, Ohgami Shingo, 2007.

History And Technique

Nobuatsu achieved the rank of fifth dan in Kōdōkan Jūdō and re-opened Matsuoka's original honbu dōjō in Ueno in 1937. He taught classes in Kōdōkan Jūdō and Shindō Yōshin Ryū there for over 26 years, finally retiring in 1963. In 2007, the authors of this book traveled to Ueno, renamed Chikusei City, in Ibaraki prefecture, and recorded an interview with Matsuoka Takeshi (b. 1930), Nobuatsu's son. Takeshi trained in Kōdōkan Jūdō and Shindō Yōshin Ryū at his father's dōjō and described classes that were mostly attended by students interested in Kōdōkan Jūdō. Takeshi noted that a few of the students stayed after jūdō training to practice Shindō Yōshin Ryū kata.

The Ueno Honbu Dōjō was destroyed in a fire during the mid-1970s and the Matsuoka Orthopedic Clinic now occupies the site. A monument including a bronze bust of Nobuatsu is displayed in front of the clinic, honoring his life and his dedication to the preservation of budō.

Monument dedicated to Matsuoka Nobuatsu at the Matsuoka Orthopedic Clinic in Chikusei City.

Visiting the Matsuoka family at the Ishijima/Matsuoka homestead in Chikusei City, July 12, 2007.

From left: Matsuoka Nobuatsu's son, Matsuoka Takeshi; Matsuoka Masahiro, owner of the Matsuoka Orthopedic Clinic; Tobin Threadgill; Ohgami Shingo; and Saitō Takao/former teacher at Shimotsuma High School. At this meeting, a discussion of family and budō history took place which clarified many historical inconsistencies existing in earlier written records. One such inconsistency was Matsuoka Katsunosuke's maternal family name. In most Japanese sources this name has been rendered Ishizuma. Threadgill, on the other hand, presented Ishijima as the correct name. The Matsuoka family members confirmed Threadgill to be correct. The residence where this photo was taken is the Ishijima homestead, which was located adjacent to the Ueno Shindōkan Matsuoka Dōjō.

Shindō Yōshin Ryū

Fujiwara Ryōzō (1925-2017)

The Nippon Kobudō Sōran (A Survey of Japanese Kobudō, 1989) lists Shindō Yōshin Ryū jūjutsu with Matsuoka Tatsuo as the third-generation headmaster of the main line, and Fujiwara Ryōzō as its technical representative. Fujiwara had a close personal connection with Tatsuo, professed a sincere wish to preserve Shindō Yōshin Ryū and was awarded a Menkyo Kaiden by Tatsuo in May 1975. Following Tatsuo's death, Fujiwara organized the Shindō Yōshin Ryū Dōmonkai (Same Gate Group) in an attempt to promote interest in preserving the school and its legacy. The Shindō Yōshin Ryū Dōmonkai remained registered with the Nippon Kobudō Kyōkai for many years, but was eventually dropped due to its inactivity.

The book entitled, "*History and Techniques in Shindō Yōshin Ryū, Sōzō 1983*", includes a conversation between Tatsuo and Fujiwara about Shindō Yōshin Ryū and Katsunosuke. In this conversation, Tatsuo mentions he is too old to preserve Shindō Yōshin Ryū jūjutsu, and is depending on Fujiwara to undertake this responsibility. Unfortunately this never came to pass, so Fujiwara Ryōzō was the last fully licensed representative of the Shindō Yōshin Ryū main line. He died in 2017 without passing mainline Shindō Yōshin Ryū to a successor.

In 2007, Ohgami and Threadgill traveled to Tōkyō and met with Tatsuno Yorihisa and Fujiwara Ryōzō. This was the first meeting between representatives of the remaining lines of Shindō Yōshin Ryū since a 1970 meeting between Matsuoka Tatsuo and Takamura Yukiyoshi.

Threadgill (Takamura ha Shindō Yōshin Kai), Fujiwara (Shindō Yōshin Ryū Dōmonkai), Tatsuno Yorihisa (Wadō Ryū), and Ohgami Shingo (Wadō Ryū) in Tōkyō, 2007.

Fujiwara and Threadgill inspecting a Jikishinkage Ryū kenjutsu densho issued by Sakakibara Kenkichi. Both Fujiwara and Threadgill have extensive densho collections.

Fujiwara was a researcher and author of several works, some of which are listed below:

- *Nippon Budō Taikei, Dōhōsha, 1982*
- *Nippon no Budō, 1983*
- *History and Techniques of Shindō Yōshin Ryū, Sōzō, 1983*
- *Discussion about the Modern History of Karate, Baseball Magazine, 1986*
- *History of Martial Arts, Baseball Magazine, 1990*
- *Thoughts of Shu-Ha-Ri, Baseball Magazine, 1993*
- *A Collection of Bujutsu Talks, Tōyō Shoin, 2001*
- *Horse Wine and Bone Cup, Sōzō, 2001*
- *History and Thoughts in Zen, Sōzō, 2001*
- *Movements of Stalin, Sōzō, 2006*
- *The History of Karate, Nippon Budō Taikei, Volume 8, 1982*
- *Nippon no Budō (Budō of Japan, 16 volumes, Kōdansha)*
- *History of Wadō Ryū Karate (Wadōkai World Cup Program, 1994)*

Nakayama Line

Nakayama Tatsusaburō

Nakayama Tatsusaburō (1870-1945)

Nakayama was born into a farming family in Kuramochi, Ibaraki Prefecture in 1870. As a youth he trained in Shindō Yōshin Ryū at the Matsuoka Akeno Dōjō near Kuramochi. Nakayama received a Shoden Kirigami license in March 1890 at the age of 20. He went on to receive a Chūden Mokuroku in March 1892 at the age of 22, and by the age of 25 had received a Jōden Menkyo from his principal teacher Inose, symbolizing successful initiation into the upper level curriculum of Shindō Yōshin Ryū.

Second headmaster Inose was less of a swordsman than a jūdō/jūjutsu practitioner and as noted previously, focused his teaching more on jūjustu, greatly diminishing the influence of kenjutsu during his stewardship of the Shindō Yōshin Ryū main line. However, Nakayama was very interested in swordsmanship and consequently sought out kendō/kenjutsu training in Ono-ha Ittō Ryū and Jikishinkage Ryū. According to "A History of Shimotsuma City", a dōjō named the Genbukan was built in front of Sandōchi Fudōsan, near Shimotsuma Middle School in 1905. The kanchō (administrative leader of the dōjō) was Hakomori Yosaburō, a sensei of Jikishinkage Ryū Kenjutsu. Hakomori asked Nakayama to accept the position of Genbukan dōjōchō (technical leader). Nakayama accepted the position, and provided instruction in kendō classes at the dōjō. Nakayama also committed himself to the study of Ono-ha Ittō Ryū kenjutsu and received a Kendō Tokugyō Shōsho (certificate of achievement) from Takano Sasaburō of Ono ha Ittō Ryū in 1906.

Nakayama accepted employment as a physical education teacher at Shimotsuma Middle School in 1907, and taught jūdō and kendō as after-school club activities. A Shimotsuma Middle School bulletin states the jūdō club trained on Tuesdays, Thursdays, and Saturdays and the kendō club trained on Mondays, Wednesdays, and Fridays. Nakayama also taught classes at the Genbukan Dōjō after teaching at Shimotsuma Middle School and he became involved

Shindō Yōshin Ryū

*Nakayama, a Butokukai Renshi, (center-front) with kendō students at Shimotsuma Middle School, 1931.
(Photo courtesy of Saitō Takao and Shimotsuma Daiichi High School, formerly Shimotsuma Middle School.)*

in the Dai Nippon Butokukai, a martial arts preservation organization. A Butokushi (Butokukai bulletin 4-2, 1909), states Nakayama demonstrated jūjutsu and kenjutsu on December 20th, 1908, at a Butokukai event. He demonstrated jūjutsu with Inose Kansuke, won a jūjutsu shiai against Ōtaki Toyokichi and fought to a draw in a kenjutsu shiai against Watabiki Torajirō. Nakayama was awarded a Butokukai Renshi license in 1913.

Nakayama began renting space in the Matsuoka Dōjō in Akeno in 1916 to teach kendō. In 1919, he ostensibly re-entered the Matsuoka Dōjō as a member in pursuit of a Jitsugi Shōmeisho, a legal certificate confirming his practical skills in bonesetting related to jūjutsu, and in 1920 he secured a bonesetting license with the authority granted by this certificate.

Kendo fifth dan certificate issued to Nakayama Tatsusaburō by the Dai Nippon Butokukai on February, 17th, 1939.

Nakayama received second dan in kendō in 1919, and fourth dan in 1923. Later the same year, the Ibaraki branch of the Nippon Butokukai awarded Nakayama a Kendō Seirenshō recognizing his dedication to kendō. In 1932 Nakayama retired from teaching at the Shimotsuma Middle School, but he continued running his bonesetting clinic and teaching kendō classes at the Genbukan Dōjō for over a decade. Nakayama received his fifth dan in kendō from the Butokukai president, Hayashi Senjūrō, on February 17th, 1939. Nakayama passed away on March 2nd, 1945, at the age of 76.

History And Technique

In 1973, Nakayama's students raised a monument in his memory near the Genbukan Dōjō. The monument states he trained in Shindō Yōshin Ryū jūjutsu at the Matsuoka Dōjō and identifies the Genbukan as a kendō dōjō. In 1974, another monument was raised in his memory by his kendō students at his family home in Kuramochi, where his descendants still live and his kendō fifth dan certificate is preserved.

Nakayama is an important person in Shindō Yōshin Ryū history because his most famous student was Ōtsuka Hironori, the founder of Wadō Ryū karate/jūjutsu kempō.

The Genbukan Dōjō Monument - Nakayama Tatsusaburō

"Sensei was born in Kuramochi in Meiji 3 (1870), as the oldest son of Nakayama Kenzaburō. During his youth he practiced budō. He studied Yōshin Ryū jūjutsu at the Matsuoka Dōjō and held the highest license. Furthermore, he studied kendō under Takano Sasaburō. When Hakomori Yosaburō from Sekidate built the Genbukan kendō dōjō in Shimotsuma, he entrusted Nakayama Sensei with its administration. Since then, at this place, he engaged himself in educating students. He was also appointed to be a teacher of bujutsu at Shimotsuma Middle School, and for more than 30 years he trained students there. Sensei was indifferent to worldly gain, and to his personal appearance. He was a person, who purely and whole-heartedly, served the nation through teaching kendō. Those who studied under him numbered several thousand. Some of his students hereby raise a monument to thank our teacher, and honor his memory. Showa 48 (1973), 1st of April, edited by Matsumoto Gengo, calligraphy by Mori Yoshitsugu."

On the reverse side the monument are names of 119 people who contributed to the monument including politician Akagi Munenori (1904-1993), Matsuoka Tatsuo, and Matsuoka Nobuatsu. Ōtsuka Hironori's name is not included.

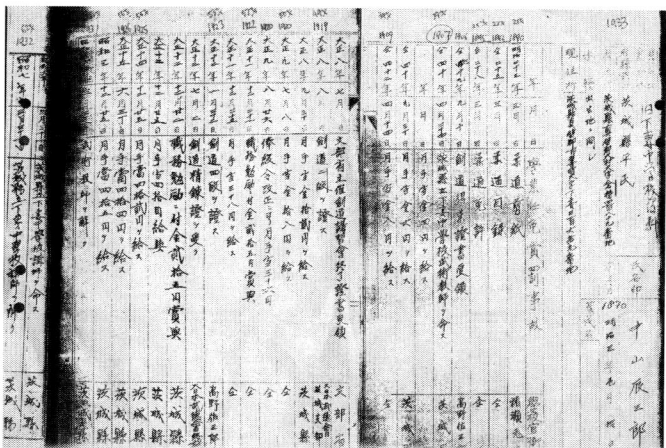

One of many important documents obtained by Ohgami from Shimotsuma Daiichi High School. This document confirms dates and teaching licenses issued to Nakayama Tatsusaburō. There have been lingering questions related to the highest level of teaching authorization Nakayama received from second headmaster, Inose Motokichi. This document is confirmation Nakayama received a Jōden Gokui Menkyo, the highest technical license, from Inose in 1895, but there is no mention of a Menkyo Kaiden. As previously agreed upon, in 1900, Inose Matakichi formally transferred the headmastership of the Shindō Yōshin Ryū main line back to the Matsuoka family by way of Matsuoka Tatsuo in 1917.

The Akeno Nakayama Tatsusaburō Monument

"The owner of the Genbukan, Nakayama Tatsusaburō received his license in Jikishinkage Ryū (kenjutsu) from Hakomori Yosaburō. A group of his students raised a monument for him in Sandōchi Fudōsan in Shimotsuma in 1973. We now celebrate the 30th anniversary of his death and raise this monument to him. We wish him eternal peace, March 3, 1974."

Shindō Yōshin Ryū

Sei Kotsu Shi (Bonesetter)

Bonesetting in Japan is officially called Jūdō Sei Fuku Shi (sei, to correct; fuku, to recover), but generally, it is called Sei Kotsu Shi or Seku Kotsu Shi. Students study at specialty bonesetting schools, or at colleges teaching bonesetting courses. About 100 bonesetting schools currently exist in Japan, and they offer services similar to physiotherapists at hospitals. The Matsuoka Clinic in Shimodate, Ibaraki employs four bonesetters together with other types of physiotherapists. Bonesetters in Japan have the right to open private clinics, whereas other types of physiotherapists do not.

Japanese bonesetters have a long historical connection with jūjutsu and jūdō. Individuals highly licensed in jūjutsu ryūha, particularly Yōshin Ryū jūjutsu, were not required to take a practical examination to become licensed as professional bonesetters during the Meiji and Taishō periods. Yōshin Ryū was thus a very attractive martial art to study as it could provide a jūjutsu master with the opportunity to pursue a secondary occupation.

Nakayama Tatsusaburō 1870-1933 or 1945?

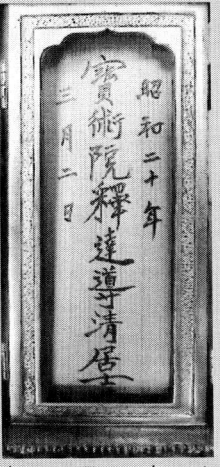

Left: A group photo of the Shimotsuma Middle School staff from a school album. Nakayama Tatsusaburō is standing at the far right of the second row. Right: Buddhist ihai (mortuary tablet) preserved at the Nakayama family homestead identifying Nakayama Tatsusaburō's date of death as March 2, 1945.

(Photo left, courtesy of Saitō Takao, Shimotsuma Daiichi High School. Photo right, the collection of Ohgami Shingo.)

Some of the most pressing historical questions confronted by the authors of this book concerned Nakayama Tatsusaburō, a Shindō Yōshin Ryū shihan frequently misidentified as the third-generation main line headmaster. In addition to questions surrounding his licensing within Shindō Yōshin Ryū, there are questions surrounding his date of death. In most sources it has been cited as 1933.

In 2005, co-author Ohgami Shingo traveled to Kuramochi, Ibaraki, and located a monument dedicated to Nakayama Tatsuburō at the Nakayama family homestead. Nakayama descendants still live at the residence, and relative, Nakayama Tsuyuko, was kind enough to allow Ohgami to photograph Nakayama Tatsusaburō's kendō godan certificate, which is preserved in the home. Ohgami initially assumed the rank was issued posthumously as it was dated February 17, 1939, however, Nakayama Tsuyuko presented Ohgami with an ihai (Buddhist mortuary tablet) confirming Nakayama Tatsusaburō's date of death as March 2, 1945. This evidence confirms family claims that after retiring from his teaching position at Shimotsuma Middle School, Nakayama continued teaching at the Genbukan Dōjō and running his bonesetting clinic for over a decade.

History And Technique

Ōtsuka Hironori

Ōtsuka Hironori (1892-1982)

Ōtsuka Kō was born on June 1st, 1892, in Shimodate, Ibaraki Prefecture, to Ōtsuka Tokujirō and his wife, Satō. He started training in Asayama Ichiden Ryū jūjutsu at the age of six, under his maternal great uncle, Ebashi Chōjirō. Chōjirō, a member of the Tsuchiura Clan was also trained in Jikishinkage Ryū kenjutsu. Between 1905 and 1910 Ōtsuka attended Shimotsuma Middle School (Shimotsuma Daiichi High School), one of only two middle schools in Ibaraki Prefecture, which was located 18 km from where Ōtsuka lived in Shimodate.

Shimotsuma Middle School was unique among schools of the era in that it started publishing a school bulletin in 1902 called Iō. In this bulletin, the authors have found the names Ōtsuka Kō, Matsuoka Nobuatsu and Nakayama Tatsusaburō. Iō issue #15 (1907) states that Nakayama was hired as a kōshi (part-time) physical education and martial arts instructor teaching jūdō (likely Shindō Yōshin Ryū) and kendō. Shimotsuma Middle School opened a dormitory in 1903 to accommodate students living too far from the school for daily travel. Iō issue #33 (1908) names the 64 students living in the dormitory, among whom was Nobuatsu, but not Ōtsuka. This implies that Ōtsuka likely had other living arrangements in the Shimotsuma area.

Co-author, Ohgami Shingo between Inose Katsuei, principal and Saitō Takao, ex-teacher, Shimotsuma Daiichi High School, 2005.

Ōtsuka, third row, center, with members of the Shimotsuma jūdō club, 1909.

Shindō Yōshin Ryū

Ōtsuka Hironori, 1916

Ōtsuka Kō is listed as a member of the school jūdō club. Iō issue #36 (1909) identifies Ōtsuka Kō and Matsuoka Nobuatsu as participants in a jūdō kangeiko (winter training session). Ōtsuka in particular, is noted for having an excellent oinage and was recognized as one of five individuals with a promising future in jūdō. Iō issue #37 (1909) states Ōtsuka Kō received a jūdō third kyu and Matsuoka Nobuatsu a jūdō fifth kyu. Iō issue #49 (1910) presents the future plans of the 50 students who would soon graduate. Ōtsuka is listed as one of six students who intended to enroll at Kōtō Kōgyō Gakkō, currently, Tōkyō Kōgyō Daigaku (Tōkyō Institute of Technology). For reasons unknown this did not come to pass. It appears Ōtsuka not only trained in jūdō with Nakayama during his years at Shimotsuma Middle School, but also attended the Genbukan Dōjō after school and trained in Shindō Yōshin Ryū. His training at the Genbukan Dōjō most likely continued through March of 1910.

As confirmed in a personal letter with Ohgami Shingo, in 1911, Ōtsuka was accepted for enrollment at Sodai (Waseda University) in Tōkyō. Tragically, Ōtsuka's father passed away in 1912, and sometime after his father's death, Ōtsuka ended his study at the university but continued his study of jūjutsu. He volunteered for military service in 1914 and was stationed in nearby Mito where he served for one year. After ending military service, he ostensibly secured a job at Kawasaki Bank and continued his study of jūjutsu. In personal letters to Ohgami, he states he trained in several styles of jūjutsu between 1911 and 1914, but never identified which styles. However, according to Ōtsuka's son Jirō, his father trained in Tenjin Shinyō Ryū, and Kitō Ryū during this period. According to Noguchi Kiyoshi of the Japanese Budo Academy, in 1916, Ōtsuka joined Kanaya Motoo's Azabu Dōjō, which taught Yōshin Koryū jūjustu.

An entry in Obata Shigeta's diary, indicates around 1917, Ōtsuka had a chance encounter with his old sensei, Nakayama Tatsusaburō during a visit to the Kōdōkan. During this meeting Ōtsuka explained he was frustrated with his clerical job at the bank. Nakayama suggested he obtain a bonesetter's license and open a bonesetting clinic as this career change would allow Ōtsuka to leave his clerical job at the bank and devote more time to his study of jūjutsu. According to Fujiwara Ryōzō, Konishi Yasuhiro (1893-1983), the founder of Shindō Jinen Ryū karatejutsu joined Kanaya Motoo's Azabu Dōjō in 1919, and was similarly interested in pursuing

Karateka in Tōkyō, circa 1930s. Left to right are Toyama Kanken, Ōtsuka Hironori, Shimoda Takeshi, Funakoshi Gichin, Motobu Chōki, Mabuni Kenwa, Nakasone Genwa, and Taira Shinken.

an occupation in bonesetting. Kanaya Motoo held powerful sway in the bonesetting community as he was the president of the Tōkyō Bonesetters Association. In the Taishō period, Yōshin Ryū shihan such as Kanaya Motoo were considered experts in bonesetting and could issue a document called a Jitsugi Shōmeisho. This document could substitute for the practical examination required to become a professional bonesetter. For Ōtsuka to realize this change in occupation he would need the assistance of his teacher, Kanaya Motoo.

Chūō University Karate Club, training camp, 1939.

Apparently, Kanaya Motoo initially agreed to assist both Konishi and Ōtsuka in their pursuit of establishing careers in bonesetting, and around 1920 issued both Konishi and Ōtsuka a Jitsugi Shōmeisho. It seems a later misunderstanding over the terms of the arrangement with Ōtsuka soured his relationship with Kanaya. Due to this misunderstanding, Ōtsuka left the Azabu Dōjō and postponed opening his new bonesetting clinic. Konishi however opened a clinic in Shibaura, Tōkyō, sometime around 1921. Frustrated, Ōtsuka again approached Nakayama who invited him to return to training in Shindō Yōshin Ryū at the Genbukan Dōjō. Ōtsuka did so, and Nakayama assisted him in finally obtaining a bonesetting license. Although the following claim is controversial, in a personal letter to Ohgami Shingo, Ōtsuka claimed Nakayama issued a Shindō Yōshin Ryū Menkyo Kaiden to him on his 29th birthday (30th by the old Japanese method of calculating age) on June 1st, 1921. Ōtsuka then finally opened his bonesetting clinic sometime in 1921 or 1922 under the name Nakura Seikotsuin.

Ōtsuka learned about Okinawan karate in 1922 from a friend, Itō Kazuo, a jūdō fifth dan. According to Ōtsuka Jirō, his father also heard about a tōde (karate) demonstration performed for Crown Prince Hirohito in Shuri, Okinawa. Curious about this Okinawan martial art, Ōtsuka visited an Okinawan karate master, Funakoshi Gichin, who was teaching the art at the Okinawan Meishōjuku dormitory in Suidōbashi, Tōkyō. Ōtsuka visited Funakoshi in Suidōbashi, inquired about training, and was enthusiastically accepted as a student. Ōtsuka trained diligently, receiving a shodan from Funakoshi in 1924. Soon afterwards, he became Funakoshi's assistant instructor at the Tōdai (Tōkyō University) Karate Club. Ōtsuka also assisted Funakoshi when teaching at Keiō University. Thus, these two institutions became a nexus for the early growth of Funakoshi's karate instruction in Japan.

Funakoshi Gichin and Ōtsuka Hironori at Nihon Ikadai (Nippon Medical College, 1940-41).

Shindō Yōshin Ryū

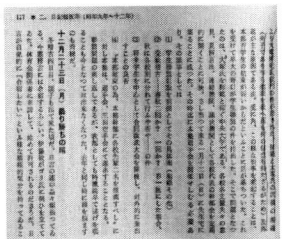

The Keio Diagaku Karatebu/Keio University Karate Club, 50 Year Anniversary Journal (1974). This journal includes entries from the karate club meeting documenting Otsuka Hironori's hamon (expulsion) from the Funakoshi Dōjō on December 21, 1935.

Ōtsuka Hironori training with Shimizu Toshiyuki (1899-1980), in 1939.

It is important to note Ōtsuka Hironori never operated a Shindō Yōshin Ryū dōjō, or awarded any Shindō Yōshin Ryū licenses before becoming a student of Funakoshi Gichin. After becoming involved in the study of karate, Ōtsuka steadfastly dedicated himself to the analysis and promotion of the Okinawan art introduced to him by Funakoshi. A desire for further knowledge later led him to study karate under Motobu Chōki (1870-1944), who arrived in Japan from Okinawa in 1921, and in Tōkyō in 1927, and also Mabuni Kenwa (1889-1952), who arrived in Japan from Okinawa in 1928.

Ōtsuka slowly started to follow a different technical path from Funakoshi, particularly in relation to soft application of jūjutsu waza, the implementation of paired forms, and the adoption of freestyle competition. These technical innovations introduced by Ōtsuka caused a rift to slowly deepen between the traditionally-minded Okinawan karate community and the more progressive approach to budō training pioneered by Ōtsuka. Funakoshi Gichin resigned from Tōkyō University Karate Club in 1929, reportedly in response to the desire of the club to add a competitive dimension to their training.

The Dai Nippon Karate Shinkō Club was founded in March 1934, with Ōtsuka Hironori listed as the shihan and Kawakami Daisaburō as the secretary general. This was the first time Ōtsuka presented himself as a karate shihan.

Funakoshi Yoshitaka, Funakoshi Gichin's son, announced to the Keiō University Karate Club membership on December, 21st, 1935, that Ōtsuka Hironori had been released from the Funakoshi Dōjō. The reason given was that Ōtsuka was no longer teaching the same style of karate as Funakoshi. A plausible argument can be made that this gesture severed Ōtsuka from the technical authority of Funakoshi and signaled the emergence of Wadō Ryū as an independent and uniquely Japanese (not Okinawan) style of karate.

Tantōdori, (identified as Tankendori-Omote: Nanahon), Kata Hiki Tate, from Nakasone Genwa's Karate-dō Taikan, 1938. The seven kata in this text are sourced to the Nakayama line of Shindō Yōshin Ryū.

By 1935, Ōtsuka had chosen to abandon koryū jūjutsu, dedicating his future to developing a new hybrid form of jūjutsu and karate that would initially be named Shinshū Wadō Ryū Karatejutsu. Ōtsuka became the shihan of the karate clubs at Tōkyō Nōgyō Daigaku (Tōkyō Agricultural University, Nōdai) and Tōkyō University (Tōdai) in 1935 and 1936, respectively.

Ōtsuka was invited to become the karate instructor at Meiji University in 1937. The Dai Nippon Karate Shinbukai was founded in 1938 with Ōtsuka Hironori as shihan, and Eriguchi Eiichi as its chairman. Eriguchi eventually became the most important political operative during the early history of Wadō Ryū. Having Eriguchi advocate for Wadō Ryū among the elite of the Japanese kobudō community resulted in Wadō Ryū gaining entry into several politically important budō organizations, which other karate styles had not yet successfully penetrated.

In 1938, Ōtsuka rented space to teach karate in the dōjō of Kubo Gihachirō (1889-1949), who was a Tokushima clan instructor of Yagyū Shinkage Ryū. Gihachirō suggested that Ōtsuka simplify the name of his new art to Wadō Ryū, explaining that "Shinshū" and "Wa" could both be interpreted to mean "Japan", so the name could be construed as redundant. Some people have suggested Ōtsuka sought training under Kubo while sharing the dōjō with him, and that Kubo's teachings influenced Wadō Ryū. The suggestion that Ōtsuka sought training in swordsmanship from Kubo seems rather fanciful to the authors as Ōtsuka was already quite familiar with swordsmanship via Nakayama who was licensed in Jikishinkage ryū and Ono ha Ittō ryū.

In 1939, The Dai Nippon Butokukai officially announced that karate was now eligible for membership in this conservative budō organization, and Ōtsuka, with the help of Eriguchi, petitioned for its acceptance of Wadō Ryū. Ōtsuka downplayed Wadō Ryū's Okinawan roots and emphasized its connection to Shindō Yōshin Ryū jūjutsu to increase the chances of acceptance into an association dominated by koryū schools. Ōtsuka identified the founder of Wadō Ryū, not as himself, but the legendary Akiyama Shirōbei Yoshitoki of Yōshin Ryū jūjutsu. Ōtsuka also listed a significant number of Shindō Yōshin Ryū kata as part of Wadō Ryū's official syllabus. Most of the Shindō Yōshin Ryū kata listed on the application to the Butokukai were never intended to be practiced as part of Wadō Ryū, as they were essentially technical padding to render the art more similar to a Japanese jūjutsu school than an Okinawan karate school. This adept tactical move, intended to emphasize Shindō Yōshin Ryū's influence, elevated Wadō Ryū and Ōtsuka into a class of martial arts associated with the samurai.

Ohgami Shingo, Eriguchi Eiichi, Ōtsuka Hironori and Suzuki Tatsuo in Sweden, 1970. *(Collection of Ohgami Shingo.)*

Ōtsuka Jirō, Ōtsuka Hironori and Ohgami Shingo in Gothenburg, Sweden, 1976. *(Collection of Ohgami Shingo.)*

Shindō Yōshin Ryū

Fujita Seiko (Kōga Ryū), Ōtsuka Hironori (Wadō Ryū) and Shimizu Takaji (Shintō Musō Ryū), at Ogasawara Kiyonobu's home during a Nihon Kobudō Shinkōkai party on June 27th, 1962.

Wadō Ryū became one of the most popular styles of Japanese karate in the world and was eventually accepted into the Nippon Kobudō Kyōkai and the Nippon Kobudō Shinkōkai, organizations that are both classical martial arts preservation societies. Ōtsuka was one of the founding members of the Kokusai Budōin (International Martial Arts Federation), along with other budō notables such as Mifune Kyūzō (1883-1965) of jūdō, Ueshiba Kisshōmaru (1921-1999) of aikidō, and Nakayama Hakudō (1872-1958) of kendō. In 1964, Wadō Ryū was accepted as one of the four founding styles of karate represented in the prestigious Japan Karatedō Federation. On April 29th, 1966, the Japanese government honored Ōtsuka Hironori with a medal (Sōkō Gyokujitsushō), in recognition of his dedication to teaching and promoting Japanese karate. The president of the Kokusai Budōin, Crown Prince Higashi Kuni no Miya, conferred the title of "Meijin" (person of excellence in a specific field) upon Ōtsuka in 1972.

A political disagreement between Ōtsuka Hironori and the JKF Wadōkai Board of Directors in early 1981 resulted in his resignation as head of the association. Ōtsuka Hironori then founded a private organization named Wadō Ryū Karatedō Renmei on April 1st, 1981. This schism effectively split Wadō Ryū into two independent organizations. Ōtsuka Hironori transferred leadership of Wadō Ryū Karatedō Renmei to his son Ōtsuka Jirō in December of 1981, and passed away at the age of 89 on January 29th, 1982.

Today, the Wadō Ryū Karatedō Renmei operates under the direction of Ōtsuka Hironori's grandson, Ōtsuka Kazutaka, and is headquartered in Nerima Ku (Ward), Tōkyō. The JKF Wadōkai board of directors oversees its global operations from its headquarters in Nishi Shinbashi, Tōkyō. A third Wadō Ryū organization, Wadō International Karate Federation, founded by Suzuki Tatsuo shihan in London, England, is presently under the leadership of Jon Wicks.

Tobin Threadgill, headmaster of Takamura ha Shindō Yōshin Ryū, distinguishes Ōtsuka Hironori as an innovator who pushed the boundaries of creativity in the karate world.

"Ōtsuka embraced the art of Okinawan Te and, through his genius, imbued it with the principles and body mechanics of koryū jūjutsu. This was a revolutionary idea, and is one reason Wadō Ryū has thrived and spread around the world. The appeal of Wadō Ryū has been essential to the survival of Shindō Yōshin Ryū, for without this historical connection, Shindō Yōshin Ryū, like many other koryū jūjutsu schools, might have slipped into obscurity. Although his desire to create a modern and uniquely Japanese style of karate led Ōtsuka to abandon a future in koryū jūjutsu, this decision likely ensured the survival of Shindō Yōshin Ryū for future generations."

Shindō Yōshin Ryū engenders significant interest in practitioners among all three major Wadō Ryū organizations, and many are experienced, highly ranked, and enthusiastically dedicated to the study and preservation of Takamura ha Shindō Yōshin Ryū. This synergy benefits and strengthens both Wadō Ryū and Shindō Yōshin Ryū. Wadō Ryū benefits by gaining deeper insights into its curriculum from a vibrant connection to its progenitor art, while Shindō Yōshin Ryū benefits from exposure to a large and talented multinational pool of budō practitioners with an interest in helping preserve this unique Japanese cultural treasure.

Ōtsuka Hironori and Ōtsuka Jiro demonstrating Kotenage in Berlin, 1970. (Photo by Ludwig Binder, courtesy of Andreas Sparmann/Nippon Berlin.)

Ōtsuka Jirō demonstrating the Wadō Ryū kata Kotenage at the Meiji Jingū Embu, 1990.
(Photo by Miles Kessler.)

Shindō Yōshin Ryū

Ōtsuka Hironori and Ōtsuka Jirō demonstrating the Wadō Ryū Shinken Shirahadori kata in Berlin, Germany, 1970.
(Photo by Ludwig Binder, courtesy of Andreas Sparmann/Nippon Berlin.)

Ōtsuka Hironori demonstrating Wadō Ryū in Berlin, 1970.
(Photo by Ludwig Binder, courtesy of Andreas Sparmann/Nippon Berlin.)

Ohgami with Ōtsuka Hironori in Sweden, 1970.
(Collection of Ohgami Shingo.)

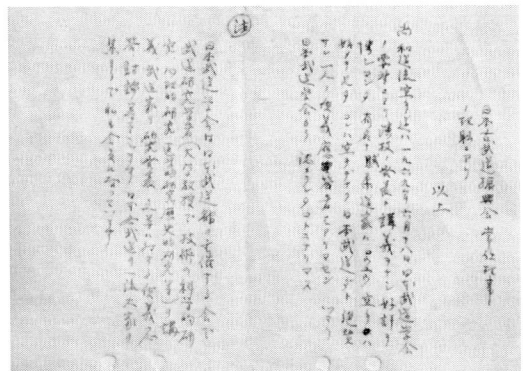
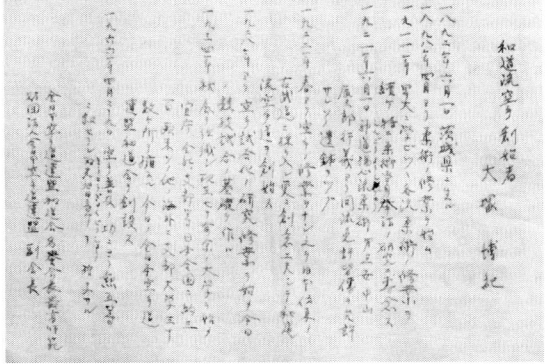
A letter on Wadō History by Ōtsuka Hironori to co-author Ohgami Shingo. Ohgami possesses over 30 personal letters received from Ōtsuka following his move to Gothenburg, Sweden. These are now preserved in his personal library.
(Collection of Ohgami Shingo.)

Translation of Letter

The Founder of Wadō Ryū karate, Ōtsuka Hironori.

1892,   June 1st, born in Ibaraki prefecture.

1898,   In April, started training in jūjutsu.

1911,   Initiated study at Sōdai (Waseda University). Continued training in various styles of jūjutsu, especially engaged in researching jūjutsu atemi kenpō.

1921,   June 1st, awarded Menkyo Kaiden by Nakayama Tatsusaburō Yukiyoshi, the third generation of Shindō Yōshin Ryū and succeeded his position.

1922,   Beginning in the spring, I started training in karate. Combining karate with traditional Japanese Kobudō led me to conceive of and create Wadō Ryū karate.

1928,   Initiated research and practice to create karate competition and build a foundation to devise the present-day competition games.

1934,   In autumn, I organized the kai. Today we have around 70 universities, offices, companies, and branches totaling about 300 all over Japan. We also have some 30 branches and universities abroad in Europe and America. We also started the present Zen Nippon Karatedō Renmei Wadōkai.

1966,   On April 29th, because of my contribution to the promotion of karate, placed to Kun Gotō and given Sōkō Gyokujitsushō.

Honorary president and Saikō Shihan of Zen Nippon Karatedō Renmei Wadōkai.

Vice-president of the foundation Zen Nippon Karatedō Renmei.

Standing executive at Nippon Kobudō Shinkōkai.

By the way of Wadō Ryū Karatedō, I performed a demonstration and lecture at the request of the Japanese Budō Academy on June 18th, 1969, and gained their favor. A famous Jūdōka stated this was the first time he had ever seen such karate. He further stated what he observed was not only karate but a Japanese budō. Not a single member asked any questions. This confirmed we are recognized by the Japanese Budō Academy.

The Japanese Budō Academy is an organization run by the Nippon Budōkan. It conducts lectures by budō researchers (professors at universities who make scientific research of the techniques, psychological research, medical research, historical research, etc). It presents the research, allows questions, answers, and discussions about budō. It is a society of top-class grand masters of each school of Japanese budō, and I am a member there.

Shindō Yōshin Ryū

Technical System of Wadō Ryū Karate/Jūjutsu Kempō
Seiteigata - Kakutōgi no Reikishi (1990)

(Despite decades of investigation by co-author Ohgami Shingo, the original Wadō Ryū technical curriculum as compiled in 1939 by Ōtsuka Hironori, and presented to the Dai Nippon Butokukai has been impossible to verify with any original documentation. Fujiwara Ryōzō presents different versions in 'Shindō Yōshin Ryū no Rekishi to Gihō' (1983), 'Kakutōgi no Rekishi' (1990), and the 'Wadōkai 60 Years Anniversary Program' (1994). Here, we would like to present the version from 'Kakutōgi no Rekishi' by Fujiwara Ryōzō, published in 1990. An interesting difference is seen in the Yakusoku Kumite (today it is called more commonly Kihon Kumite). In Fujiwara's 1983 version, it was included in the Ōyō Gata (10 techniques), and in 1994 in the Yakusoku Kumite Gata (10 techniques-present Yakusoku Kumite Gata), but it is completely omitted in his 1990 version.

When were the Yakusoku Kumite (Kihon Kumite) actually created? According to Ishizuka Akira (graduate of Tōkyō University, karate club member 1950-1954, and General Secretary of JKF Wadōkai in 1954), kata 1-5 were created around 1948-1949, and kata 6-10 created around 1949-1950 (See: Kenpō Kaihō No.53, 1995).

Tandoku Enrengata - 16 (Kata without an opponent)

Pinan Shodan - Godan (5 Kata)
Kushankū
Seishan
Naihanchi
Chintō
Wanshū

Passai
Jitte
Jion
Niseishi
Rōhai
Sūparinpei

Kihon Kumitegata - 36

Jōdan Uke (10) Omote-Ura
Chūdan Uke (10) Omote-Ura
Gedan Uke (6) Harai, Nagashi, Sabaki, Tori, Hasami
Nidan Henka (6) Omote-Ura, 3 each
Sandan Henka (4) Omote-Ura, 2 each

Idorigata - 6 (Sitting Defense)

Mae Dori-4
Ushiro Dori-2

Tachiaigata - 10 (Standing Body Throws)

Ude Otoshi (variation of Ōsoto Gari)
Sei Otoshi (Ushiro Otoshi)
Eri Otoshi (variation of Ōsoto Gari)
Sode Otoshi (variation of Ōsoto Gari)
Ashi Guruma (variation of Kouchi Gari)

Kōshi Guruma
Kata Guruma
Hiki Otoshi (Tekubi Hineri)
Karisute (variation of Butsudan Gaeshi)
Kinukuguri (variation of Seoinage)

Ōyogata - 10

Simplified kata from Shindō Yōshin Ryū Shoden Idori, Tachiai, and Nagekaeshi

History And Technique

Tantō Dori - 7 (Knife Defense)* - *Simplified from Shindō Yōshin Ryū Jūjutsu Omote Ura 14-7*

Ude Garami Dori
Kote Nage Dori
Unga Dori   * *(No technique of this type or name is included in the official Shindō Yōshin Ryū mokuroku - Author.)*
Eri Nage Dori
Zu Dori
Hiki Tate Dori
Hiki Otoshi Dori

Tachi Dori Gata - 7 (Sword Defense) - *from Shindō Yōshin Ryū*

Jōdan
Kesa (Left and Right)
Dō
Tsuki
Kote
Nagi

Kassatsu Jizai Gata - 7 (Saving and Killing Techniques) - *Shindō Yōshin Ryū Kappō*

San Kappō (3)
Yon Kappō (4)

Ratai Dori - 3 (Naked Techniques) - *from Shindō Yōshin Ryū*

Mae Dori
Yoko Dori
Ushiro Dori

Keisatsu Taihojutsu - 14 (Arrest Techniques for Police) - *from Shindō Yōshin Ryū*

Te Hodoki   *(14 waza in 4 categories - Author.)*
Kansetsu Waza
Nage Waza
Osae Waza

Joshi Goshinjutsu - 14 (Self-Defense Techniques for Women)

Mae Sabaki
Yoko Wake (Left and Right)
Daki Wake (Left and Right)
Ushiro Sabaki
Ude Otoshi
Gyaku Yubi

Kote Gaeshi
Ashi Fumi
Tsuri Gane
Mizo Ochi
Jin Chū
Ryō Gan

(Note: At present, the Kihon Kumite Gata, Tachiai Gata, Kassatsu Jizai Gata, Ratai Dori, Taihojutsu and Joshi Goshinjutsu are not practiced. The names of the Tachiai Waza (Nage Waza) have been changed and reorganized to 20 techniques, but are not practiced as a matter of fact: and nine Tandoku Enrengata are practiced, but not Passai, Wanshū, Jitte, Jion, Nīseishi, Rōhai and Sūparinpei.- Fujiwara Ryōzō)

Nakayama Tatsusaburō, Ōtsuka Hironori, and Issues of Succession

Questions about teaching licenses and the succession of administrative authority in Shindō Yōshin Ryū have been a subject of discussion between many budō historians. Frequently these questions also concern Ōtsuka Hironori's impression, or claim, that he was the fourth-generation headmaster of Shindō Yōshin Ryū.

Each koryū maintains its own dictates related to the transmission of knowledge and authority. In some ryūha, a Menkyo Kaiden represents ultimate administrative authority, symbolizing headmastership of the school. In other ryūha, holding a Menkyo Kaiden represents technical authority, but in and of itself, brings with it no administrative mandate. In this respect Shindō Yōshin Ryū reflects a rather orthodox policy, one where possession of a Jōden Menkyo represents full mastery of the technical curriculum, while possession of a Menkyo Kaiden represents technical authority, but does not necessarily represent headmastership or administrative authority. In this case there can be multiple shihan possessing a Menkyo Kaiden but operating under the administrative authority of a ryūha's headmaster. This policy in relationship to Shindō Yōshin Ryū is confirmed by Matsuoka Katsunosuke issuing a Menkyo Kaiden to Inose Motokichi in 1878, and also issuing a Menkyo Kaiden to Obata Shigeta in 1895. The sudden death of Matsuoka Katsunosuke, in 1898, left the headmastership of Shindō Yōshin Ryū undecided until 1900, when the Matsuoka family formally selected shihan dai, Inose Motokichi, as the second-generation headmaster. According to Fujiwara Ryōzō and Obata Shigeta's diary, an implied condition of Inose's appointment to headmaster was the intent to return control of Shindō Yōshin Ryū to the Matsuoka family when a suitable male family member reached adulthood. Previously unknown to the Matsuoka family, in addition to Obata's Menkyo Kaiden was a special letter issued in 1895 giving him the option to separate from the main line school and lead his own independent line of Shindō Yōshin Ryū. Following the recognition of Inose as the second-generation headmaster, Obata presented this letter to the Matsuoka family, which they viewed as an act of good will and authenticated. This was an honorable and wise thing for Obata to do. It provided Obata and his dōjō with autonomy while separating the only other holder of a Menkyo Kaiden from the main line. This reaffirmed Inose's status as the undisputed second-generation headmaster of the Shindō Yōshin Ryū main line.

The relationship between Shindō Yōshin Ryū shihan, Nakayama Tatsusaburō, and the Matsuoka family was clearly one of mutual respect. Logically, if Nakayama had tried to usurp the third-generation headmastership of Shindō Yōshin Ryū from Matsuoka Tatsuo, this would not have been the case. In fact, there is no indication Nakayama ever claimed to be the third-generation headmaster of Shindō Yōshin Ryū. This can be confirmed through various avenues of research.

In 1917, second headmaster Inose Motokichi honored his promise to the Matsuoka family by returning the headmastership of Shindō Yōshin Ryū to the founding family by way of Katsunosuke's grandson, Matsuoka Tatsuo. On January 3rd, 1918, over 200 students, including Matsuoka Tatsuo's cousin, Matsuoka Nobuatsu, pledged loyalty to Tatsuo as the third-generation headmaster by taking a kishōmon (oath) and signing the student register book in their blood (keppan). A list of the names of these students is found in the book *Shiawase to Heiwazukuri, Matsuoka Tatsuoshi no Ayumi (1987)*. Furthermore, employment records at Shimotsuma Middle School log the issuance of all Nakayama's budō licenses. The highest level license connected to Nakayama in relationship to jūdō/jūjutsu is dated 1895 and is identified as a Jōden Menkyo. With each new budō license awarded to Nakayama after his employment, came an associated increase in salary also logged in the school records. All salary increases related to budō are linked to Nakayama's promotions but there is no reference in the school's logs recording an increase in salary related to the issuance of a jūdō/jūjutsu Menkyo Kaiden to Nakayama Tatsusaburō.

Budō historian Noguchi Kiyoshi, of the Japanese Budō Academy's/Karate-Dō Kenkyūkai made a presentation at the third Karate-Dō Kenkyukai workshop in March, 2002, titled *"History of*

Modern Karate - Concerning Wadō Ryū". In this presentation, Noguchi wrote "It does not seem like it is historically true that Ōtsuka took over the fourth generation of Shindō Yōshin Ryū. There is no trace of Nakayama being active as a jūjutsuka. He is more involved in kendō." Although Nakayama would still teach budō at Shimotsuma Middle School for another 15 years, in 1909, Kōdōkan jūdō and kendō had become official school subjects.

According to Matsuoka Tatsuo, around 1916 he invited Nakayama to start teaching kendō in the Matsuoka Dōjō. In 1919, Nakayama formally rejoined the Matsuoka Dōjō as a member for a short period of time, but this appears to be related to his desire to obtain a Jitsugi Shōmeisho license so he could become a seikotsushi (bonesetter). After 1919, there is no record or indication of Nakayama being significantly involved in jūjutsu training of any kind.

Further proof of Nakayama's friendly relations with the Matsuoka family is evidenced by the fact both Matsuoka Tatsuo and Nobuatsu contributed funds to finance two stone memorial monuments recognizing Nakayama's contributions to budō, one in 1973, and the other in 1974. If Nakayama had been publicly claiming headmastership of Shindō Yōshin Ryū, would relations with the Matsuoka family have remained so cordial that they would have contributed financially to Nakayama's memorial monuments? This seems unlikely.

Exactly how Ōtsuka came to believe Nakayama was the third-generation headmaster of Shindō Yōshin Ryū remains speculative. Was he simply unaware Inose had passed the third-generation to Matsuoka Tatsuo in 1917? Was his acquisition of a Jitsugi Shōmeisho with Nakayama's help misinterpreted to indicate headmastership? Or, did he assume that because Matsuoka Tatsuo was deeply involved in jūdō, he had abandoned Shindō Yōshin Ryū to Nakayama? There is circumstantial evidence supporting this last option. In a letter to co-author Ohgami Shingo (see page: 98), Ōtsuka uses the term "I hatsu" usually spelled 衣鉢, meaning "assuming a master's mantle". Instead, Ōtsuka writes it thusly 遺鉢, inferring death or abandonment. Inferring death is unlikely as Nakayama did not pass away until 1945 and Matsuoka Tatsuo outlived Ōtsuka. Did Ōtsuka mistakenly assume the Shindō Yōshin Ryū main line had been abandoned?

Regardless, it's a verifiable fact of history that Matsuoka Tatsuo was awarded the third-generation headmastership of Shindō Yōshin Ryū in 1917 by Inose Motokichi, and this event was formalized by 200 witnesses on January, 3rd, 1918. It is also a fact of history that Ōtsuka Hironori was a dedicated and experienced jūjutsuka with many years of intense training behind him when he founded Wado Ryū. There have been cases where an unauthorized instructor stepped in as a de facto headmaster when the actual heir was either unable or unwilling to maintain the ryūha. Was a related misunderstanding the reason behind Ōtsuka's claim? The authors of this book prefer to give Ōtsuka the benefit of the doubt and reject any inference of malice on Otsuka's part because there is no way to determine his precise motivations. Furthermore, that Ōtsuka went on to found Wadō Ryū and never pursued a career in koryū jūjutsu ultimately makes his claim of headmaster irrelevant because Shindō Yoshin Ryu survived via two other verifiable lineages.

Over a century after its founding, the accurate history and legacy of Shindō Yōshin Ryū is important to preserve. In 1999, Tobin Threadgill took a blood oath to protect the denki (historical legacy) of Shindō Yōshin Ryū, something he is honor-bound to do. However, it is also true that any historical contradictions evidenced in the pages of this book have little technical bearing on contemporary Wadō Ryū or Takamura ha Shindō Yōshin Ryū. These two historically-connected schools of budō represent a unique and exclusive legacy with roots in China, Okinawa, and Japan. Wadō Ryū and Shindō Yōshin Ryū were founded by budō giants with a unique and evolutionary vision. In the 21st century, when so many traditional martial arts are at risk of being lost, these two arts find themselves in a symbiotic relationship where their legacies and historical connections strengthen one another. They both look to their past to understand the present. This mindset is represented in the Japanese term *keiko shōkon*.

Bakumatsu no Sanshu/幕末の三舟

At the end of the Bakumatsu period, three esteemed samurai/statesmen were also revered as exceptional calligraphers. They were Takahashi Deishū (Jitokuin Ryū), Katsu Kaishū (Jikishinkage Ryū) and Yamaoka Tesshū (Jikishinkage Ryū and Ittō Shōden Mutō Ryū). Since all their given names ended in the character shū (舟) they were known as Sanshū (the Three Shū).

As a young man training in the Jikishinkage Ryū Honbu Dōjō, Obata Shigeta had the opportunity to meet one of the famed exponents of the school, Katsu Kaishū. In time, Obata was also introduced to the legendary Yamaoka Tesshū. The progressive exploits of these samurai during the Meiji Restoration had such a profound impact on Obata that he impressed their example of duty, self-sacrifice, and philosophy upon his grandson Takamura Yukiyoshi. As Takamura grew into a man, he amassed a large collection of calligraphic works brushed by these and other samurai/artisans from the Bakumatsu period. Today, hanging scrolls from Takamura Sensei's collection are displayed on a rotating basis in the Takamura ha Shindō Yōshin Ryū Honbu Dōjō.

Katsu Kaishū
(1823-1899)

Yamaoka Tesshū
(1836-1888)

Takahashi Deishū
(1835-1903)

(Collection of the Takamura ha Shindō Yōshin Kai.)

Obata Line

Obata Shigeta

<u>Obata Shigeta (1863-1945)</u>

According to his diary, Obata Shigeta was born in Kyōto in 1863 to a samurai family within the Asano clan. His father, Shibuharu, from Aki (present day Hiroshima), lived in the Kyōto residence of the Asano Clan and functioned as a bodyguard to an Asano Clan emissary. Renowned for his martial prowess, Shibuharu was licensed in Yōshin Ryū, Hōzōin Ryū, Takeda Ryū and Motsugai/Fusen Ryū. Shibuharu was particularly dedicated to the headmaster of Motsugai Ryū, Motsugai Zenji (1795-1867), who represented himself to be a ninth-generation descendant of the Takeda Clan. During the 1864 Hamaguri Rebellion in Kyōto, the Asano Clan residence was destroyed in a fire set by rebel forces attempting to kidnap the Emperor. Shibuharu reportedly fought and killed several rebel attackers before safely escorting the Asano Clan emissary to nearby Ōtsu. He eventually returned to Aki Prefecture in 1866, after he received permission from the Asano Clan to move his family to western Kyōto so he could live closer to the aging Motsugai Zenji, although regrettably, Motsugai Sensei passed away only a few months after their arrival. When the clan system was abolished in 1871, Shibuharu moved his family to Ōtsu on the shores of Lake Biwa where he became a respected maker of mitsudōgu (arresting weapons for use by police), and based on his previous training in Hōzōin Ryū and Yōshin Ryū, Shibuharu founded Obata Ryū, a school of hobakujutsu (arresting techniques).

Shibuharu's eldest son was Obata Shigeta. He was educated at Onjō-ji (Miidera) Temple and his father also taught him Takeda Ryū yabusame (mounted archery). At the age of 10, he was enrolled in the local Hoshino Yōshin Ryū dōjō, and received a mokuroku in Miura Yōshin Ryū jūjutsu and Akiyama Yōshin Ryū naginatajutsu/iaitachijutsu while still in his teens. At that time, both schools were simply called Yōshin Ryū with no real distinction made between the two different lines. After the death of his teacher, Hoshino Rikisen, in Ōtsu, the 20-year-old Obata traveled to Tōkyō in search of Totsuka Hideyoshi, the famed headmaster of Totsuka ha Yōshin Ryū. After starting classes at the Totsuka Atogayama Dōjō, Obata saw a demonstration of Kashima Shinden Jikishinkage Ryū by headmaster Sakakibara Kenkichi (1830-1894) and one

Shindō Yōshin Ryū

one of Matsuzaki Shinkage Ryū by Matsuzaki Namishiro (1833-1896). The audacious nature of these Shinkage Ryū schools appealed to him, so he immediately petitioned for enrollment in these schools. The longer he studied Shinkage Ryū, the more disillusioned he became with Totsuka ha Yōshin Ryū. The Totsuka school's reputation was impressive as it was quite dominant in the realm of competitive shiai, but Shigeta was a purist who realized jacket wrestling was a pursuit separate from authentic samurai bujutsu, so he searched for a comprehensive school of bujutsu that reflected a more classical approach to training.

Obata Shigeta teaching Yōshin Ryū bōjutsu in the dōjō of Kawakami Chū. Kawakami was a Yōshin Ryū shihan who would also become a famed Kōdōkan Jūdō ninth dan.
(Collection of the Takamura ha Shindō Yōshin Kai.)

In 1885 Obata encountered a man from Ueno village at Sakakibara Kenkichi's dōjō named Ishijima. Ishijima introduced Shigeta to a relative, Matsuoka Katsunosuke. Matsuoka made a positive impression on Obata at this meeting so Obata consulted Sakakibara Kenkichi about studying under Matsuoka in Shindō Yōshin Ryū. Matsuoka had received a Menkyo Kaiden from Sakakibara before the Boshin Wars and both men had remained cordial over the years. Sakakibara enthusiastically supported Obata's desire to pursue jūjutsu training at the Asakusa Shindōkan Dōjō. So, Obata decided to discontinue his study of Totsuka ha Yōshin Ryū and instead immersed himself in the study of Shindō Yōshin Ryū, feeling the school's training combined the intensity of Shinkage Ryū with the sophistication of Yōshin Ryū. Then, in 1895, after 10 years of training at the Asakusa Shindōkan dōjō, he received a Shindō Yōshin Ryū Menkyo Kaiden from Matsuoka. Thereafter, Obata became an assistant instructor in the Asakusa Shindōkan Dōjō.

Two years after receiving his Menkyo Kaiden, Obata was appointed dōjōchō over the Asakusa Shindōkan Dōjō in Tōkyō. During a visit by his senior, Inose Motokichi, a disagreement resulted in him being asked to stop visiting the Asakusa dōjō. Inose and Obata had never been on particularly good terms, and so, Inose reported the incident to headmaster Matsuoka requesting Obata be disciplined. Matsuoka refused this demand. He had been aware of tensions between his two senior practitioners for years, and as a political pressure relief valve, had provided Obata a letter with his Menkyo Kaiden authorizing him to start an independent line of Shindō Yōshin Ryū. Matsuoka passed away suddenly in 1898, and after a two-year period of uncertainty, the Matsuoka family appointed Inose as the second headmaster of Shindō Yōshin Ryū. Following this recognition, Obata presented his letter to the Matsuoka family, which they authenticated. This was an honorable thing for Obata to do, as it provided him with administrative autonomy over his dōjō while withdrawing himself from the main line. This diffused the tension that had been simmering during the two years the school was operating without a headmaster. With Obata's withdrawal, Inose became the undisputed headmaster of the Shindō Yōshin Ryū main line.

Following Obata's withdrawal from the main line he abandoned the Asakusa Shindōkan and established a new dōjō in Asakusa. Virtually all of the Asakusa Shindōkan Dōjō's students joined Obata in this effort, and the new dōjō was financed by student Hasegawa Shigemichi, a wealthy local merchant. The new dōjō, named the Obata Eibukan, opened in the Asakusa district of Tōkyō in 1901.

Shigeta was disappointed to learn Shindō Yōshin Ryū weapons training was being neglected in favor of a syllabus more similar to that of Kōdōkan Jūdō, and assumed this was because Inose lacked advanced swordsmanship skills. Although a recently-licensed classmate, Nakayama Tatsusaburō, stepped in to provide instruction in swordsmanship, Obata did not relent. He did not consider Nakayama fully versed in the Shindō Yōshin Ryū curriculum as envisioned by Matsuoka, and as a result, Obata further separated himself from main line Shindō Yōshin Ryū by designating the art he taught, "Obata ha Shindō Yōshin Ryū".

(Collection of the Takamura ha Shindō Yōshin Kai.)

A meeting of Yōshin Ryū, Miura Yōshin Ryū and Daitō Ryū shihan in Yūbetsu, Hokkaido, at the beginning of the Taishō era. This photo has engendered lively discussion about possible technical links existing between Yōshin Ryū and Daitō Ryū, but there is no solid evidence of such a technical connection. A cryptic astrological method (Kushiyo 駆使曜) was employed as a code to identify the individuals on the back of the photo, and it has only recently been fully deciphered. Japanese astrology and numerology codes are included in the Takamura ha Shindō Yōshin Ryū Gokui.

Front row left, Takeda Sōkaku (Daitō Ryū). Second from the left is Obata Shigeta (Shindō Yōshin Ryū). Left rear of Obata is Yoshida Kōtarō (Daitō Ryū). Also identified are Inazu Masamizu (Miura Yōshin Ryū), Hiratsuka Katsuta (Akiyama Yōshin Ryū), Hasegawa Shigemichi (Shindō Yōshin Ryū), Hoshino Kubo (Shiten Ryū & Yōshin Ryū) and Katayama Takayoshi (Akiyama Yōshin Ryū).

A meeting of budōka including Obata Shigeta (Shindō Yōshin Ryū). Recognized by Takamura in the group are brothers Saitō Takeshi and Saitō Shintarō (Akiyama Yōshin Ryū,) Ōmura Shinzō (Akiyama Yōshin Ryū) Sakabe Ryūzan (Miura Yoshin Ryū), and Yoshida Kōtarō (Daitō Ryū). The location, time, and circumstances of the meeting are unknown.

In 1992, this photo was presented as a personal gift to Takamura Yukiyoshi by Donald J. Angier. Angier was a student of Yoshida Kenji, the son of Yoshida Kōtarō.

(Collection of the Takamura ha Shindō Yōshin Kai.)

Shindō Yōshin Ryū

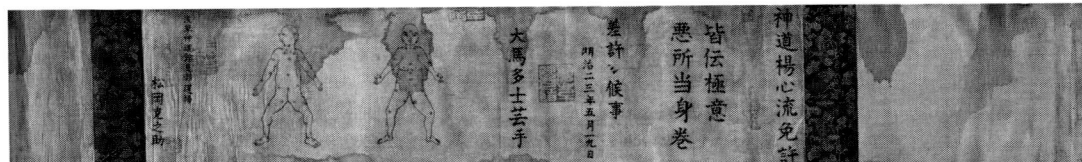

Shindō Yōshin Ryū Gokui, Akusho Atemi no Maki, issued to Obata Shigeta by Matsuoka Katsunosuke in Meiji 23 (1890). Shigeta Obata's name is represented in an unusual manner, written "many horses, expert hand". Japanese frequently changed their name to reference evolving life events, areas of expertise or marriage into a higher social class. These kanji characters likely acknowledge Shigeta's expertise in Takeda Ryū yabusame (mounted archery).
(Collection of the Takamura ha Shindō Yōshin Kai.)

In 1899 a son named Hideyoshi was born to Obata, who had decided to pursue a career as a newspaper reporter to support his family. His new job required frequent travel and provided Obata with the opportunity to visit many famous budō practitioners including Hiratsuka Katsuta and Katayama Takayoshi of Yōshin Ryū, Inazu Masamizu of Yōshin Koryū, Kanō Jigorō of Kōdōkan Jūdō, and Yoshida Kōtaro and Takeda Sōkaku of Daitō Ryū.

Obata began instructing his son Hideyoshi at the Obata Eibukan Dōjō in 1909, and as the years progressed, he asked his senior students to be hard on the young man to prepare him for proper shugyō (austere training). Hideyoshi and his best friend, Namishiro Matsuhiro, trained hard and thrived in this demanding environment under Obata's direction.

According to Obata's notes, Hideyoshi joined the military in 1918 and ascended through the ranks as a result of having excellent leadership skills, which Obata attributed to years of shugyō in classical budō. Following in his father's footsteps, Hideyoshi became the chief instructor of the Obata Eibukan Dōjō in 1925. Hideyoshi married and had a son, Obata Yukiyoshi (later Takamura Yukiyoshi), in 1928, but due to the demands of military duty Namishiro was appointed dōjōchō. Namishiro was injured during a training accident in the early 1930s while training in Matsuzaki Shinkage Ryū kenjutsu, and the injury left him blind in his left eye. While he recovered, Obata returned to Tōkyō to temporarily assume the position of dōjōchō at the Eibukan Dōjō and began providing his grandson Yukiyoshi with private instruction.

Obata was privy to details about the changing political situation in Japan through press connections, and recognized a rising demand for men of uncompromising character. He decided his grandson must become one of these men, and bujutsu would be the anvil on which his character would be forged. During an event that brought Namishiro and Hideyoshi back to the dōjō, Obata explained his vision concerning the future of his grandson, whose training was immediately intensified. Namishiro, honoring the wishes of his teacher, promised to personally assume responsibility for training young Yukiyoshi when Obata and Hideyoshi were absent.

Obata visited the dōjō often, being revered as the past master, and he was impressed with his students as they were serious, dedicated, and the training excellent. Despite his partial blindness, Namishiro had phenomenal skills, and what Shigeta witnessed was a proud validation of his obligation to his father and ancestors.

Namishiro Matsuhiro (1901-1974) left, with Ishikawa Goto of Matsuzaki Shinkage Ryū.

History And Technique

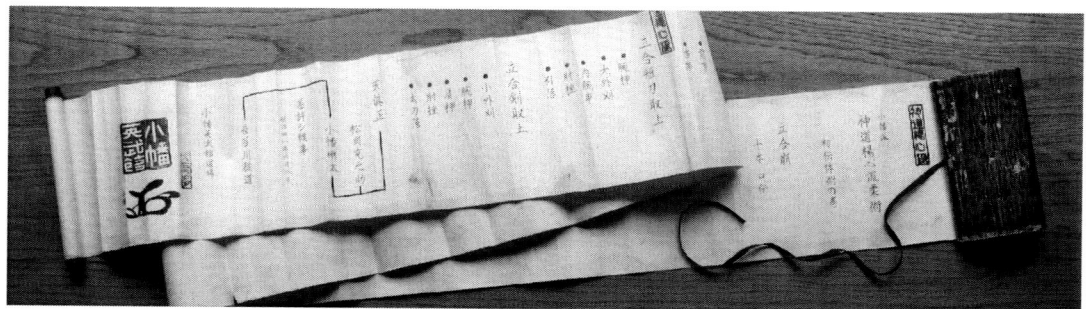

Obata ha Shindō Yōshin Ryū Shoden Taijustu no Maki issued by Obata Shigeta to Hasegawa Shigemichi on June 8th, 1908, at the Obata Eibukan Dōjō. (This license is reproduced in its entirety on page 131.)
(Collection of the Takamura ha Shindō Yōshin Kai.)

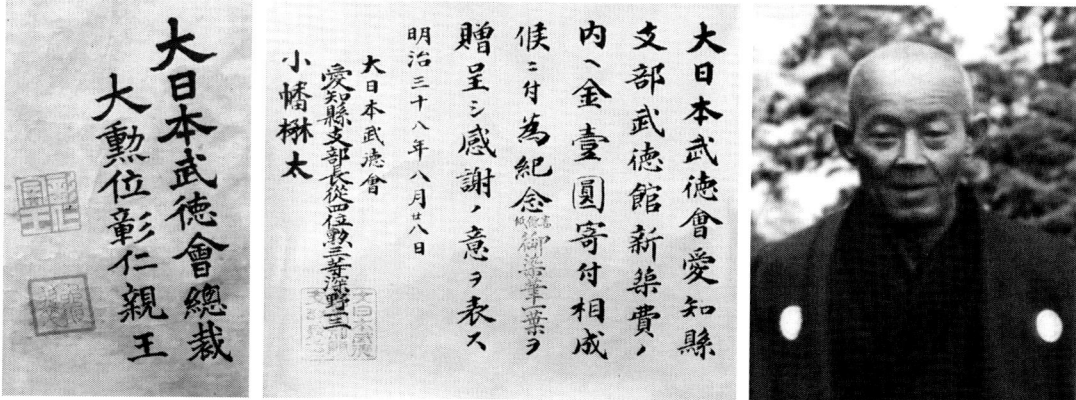

Left: Prince Komatsu no Miya Akihito brushed this banner given to Obata Shigeta for a donation to the Butokukai. Middle: A letter to Obata Shigeta thanking him for a one yen donation to build a new Budōkan in Aichi Prefecture. Right: Photo of Obata Shigeta dated Showa 19 (1944). *(Collection of the Takamura ha Shindō Yōshin Kai.)*

At the start of hostilities leading up to World War II, many students departed the dōjō for military service and Hideyoshi eventually left for the Pacific as an officer in a proud army. The Japanese assumed the war in China would be short and Japan would emerge victorious, but the war dragged on and many of the dōjō's finest students were lost to the war. By 1944, children accounted for most of the students, but chief instructor Namishiro, one of the few men of his age who were ineligible for military service due to his compromised vision, did not allow the training to suffer. Young Yukiyoshi continued to progress under Namishiro's guidance, thus Obata regarded his grandson as a worthy heir to his family legacy.

Journalistic work put Obata in contact with many politicians, members of the military and yakuza crime bosses. Informed of the true course of events in the Pacific, he used his wealth and political contacts to organize contingencies to ensure his grandson's survival. Obata was particularly concerned about a Russian invasion of Japan, given the embarrassing loss the Russians had suffered during the Russo-Japanese War in 1905.

News that Hideyoshi had died in battle was reported to Obata in September 1944. He broke this news to Yukiyoshi and his mother, Hanako, and explained the martial traditions of his ancestors were now Yukiyoshi's responsibility. Obata moved Yukiyoshi and Hanako to the countryside for safety before the fire-bombing of Tōkyō began in late 1944, as he was convinced the Americans and Russians would successfully invade Japan.

Shindō Yōshin Ryū

Takamura Yukiyoshi Tsugiso

Takamura Yukiyoshi Tsugiso (1928-2000)

Takamura Yukiyoshi was born Obata Yukiyoshi on April 1st, 1928, during a rare spring snow storm in Ono Village on the northern outskirts of Ōtsu, Japan. His father was Obata Hideyoshi, Obata Shigeta's only son. His mother, Fujita Hanako, was the daughter of a close friend of Shigeta's. Takamura was unusual because he was born with almost totally white eyes, and during his Oshichiya (Shintō naming ceremony), a priest at Ono no Takamura Shrine suggested the name "Yukiyoshi" (雪由) meaning favorable snow. White symbolizes purity in Shintō, so the unusual circumstances of his birth and the color of his eyes were seen as virtuous omens.

While Takamura was still very young, his father, Hideyoshi, chose to make his career in the Japanese military permanent, and spent extended periods away from home. Thus, little is known about Hideyoshi, and it appears he only had occasional contact with his family. Obata Shigeta, believing his grandson should have a strong role model, visited Ono Village frequently, and became a father-figure to the young boy. At around the age of six, Obata started teaching his grandson the basics of kenjutsu and jūjutsu during occasional visits to Tōkyō and Ono Village. Takamura demonstrated uncanny maturity for a boy of his age, so the kannushi (head priest) at Ono Shrine asked the seven-year-old with pure white eyes to assist him as a tōya (shrine attendant). This early introduction to Shintō and its embrace of symbolic ritual was foundational for Takamura, who developed an appreciation of budō sahō (formalities) and a deep interest in Shintō mythology. According to the dictates of Japanese numerology, Takamura was released from shrine duties one day before his ninth birthday, so Obata decided at the time to take his grandson on a pilgrimage to Mount Kurama, the home of Sōjōbō, king of the tengu. During this and subsequent pilgrimages to the summit of Mount Kurama, Obata regaled his grandson with stories of Shintō kami, brave samurai, and tales of Ushiwakimaru (Minamoto no Yoshitsune) and his adventures with the mountain tengu.

When Yukiyoshi was 10 years old, Obata convinced Hanako to move permanently to his Asakusa residence in Tōkyō, where young Yukiyoshi could receive a better education and be-

History And Technique

Takamura Yukiyoshi, a 12-year-old member of his school kendō club.
(Photo courtesy of Mariko Takamura-Thomas.)

Takamura Yukiyoshi in formal attire for Susu Harai in 1944. This Shintō event, held during the winter solstice, also celebrated his acceptance of a Menkyo Kaiden from his grandfather Obata Shigeta. This ceremony symbolized passing of the art to a new generation.
(Photo courtesy of Mariko Takamura-Thomas.)

gin budō training at the Eibukan Dōjō. She agreed and after arrival in Tōkyō, Takamura trained under the critical eyes of Obata and Namishiro Matsuhiro, the dōjō's senior instructor. He also had the opportunity to see his father on the rare occasion he visited. Prior to Takamura and his mother's arrival in Tōkyō, political tensions had increased with the Japanese invasion of China. After Japan entered the war against the United States, Obata became deeply concerned the war was a mistake and that Japan could not triumph. Upon learning Hideyoshi had died in September 1944, Obata began efforts to ensure his grandson's safety and the survival of Obata ha Shindō Yōshin Ryū. Obata moved Hanako to his summer house in rural Ono, and Namishiro escorted Yukiyoshi to Morioka, north of Tōkyō. A friend of Obata's who trained at the Shoshō Ryū Wajutsu Honbu Dōjō offered to shelter Takamura in the countryside, then in late December 1944, during the Shintō ceremony of Susu Harai, Obata and Namishiro traveled to Morioka and awarded a Menkyo Kaiden to Takamura Yukioshi. This designated him as the formal heir to Obata ha Shindō Yōshin Ryū at the age of 16. With this designation, Takamura received the name Tsugiso (次礎), which means "the next cornerstone".

Tragically, the Obata Eibukan Dōjō in Tōkyō was incinerated by an American firebombing campaign in March 1945. Obata was assumed to have been killed at that time, as he was known to be in the vicinity. Namishiro retrieved what he could from the ashes of the destroyed dōjō, recovering several sword blades and two scorched densho issued to Obata by Matsuoka. One of these densho remains in the possession of Takamura ha Shindō Yōshin Kai today (see page 107).

Namishiro retrieved Takamura from Morioka in the aftermath of the war and reunited him with his mother in Ōno Village. Namishiro was a carpenter by trade, and he found work in nearby Kyōto, one of the few cities that remained essentially unscathed by the allied bombing campaigns. He taught Takamura to be an assistant carpenter and they eked out a meager living. Although life was difficult, Namishiro demanded Takamura continue training in Shindō Yōshin Ryū. At the same time, Takamura was also taught the finer points of Matsuzaki Shinkage Ryū, a style of kenjutsu with common origins to the Jikishinkage Ryū that so strongly influenced Matsuoka's Shindō Yōshin Ryū.

In 1948 at age 20, Takamura married a young woman from Ōtsu named Yamada Kiyoko. Kiyoko was the daughter of a close family friend, Aiko. Ten months later, both Kiyoko and

Shindō Yōshin Ryū

Ono no Takamura Shrine in Shiga Prefecture.

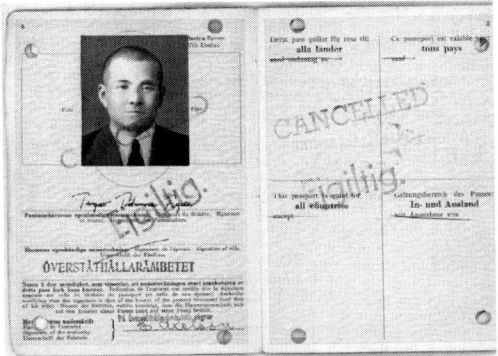
Swedish passport issued to Takamura in 1956.

Takamura's newborn son tragically died during complications of childbirth. Following the death of his young wife and son, Takamura spent extended periods of time training and meditating in Sōjōgatani, the valley of the high priest, on the slopes of Mount Kurama. During this time Takamura stated he experienced periods of spiritual transcendence where he came to grasp gōhō, the Shintō concept of destiny, reward and retribution. Gōhō would soon have a significant impact on Takamura's life.

In June 1952, an incident involving a physical assault resulted in a violent altercation between Takamura and a suitor rejected by his mother. The suitor was a respected and wealthy business owner with political connections in Ōtsu. The police were summoned, and when it was obvious justice would not be served, Namishiro approached several longtime and powerful friends of Obata's for advice. These men counseled Namishiro that given the political environment, and the fact the country had only recently regained its sovereignty, Takamura was in danger of being charged with a serious crime. Shigeta's friends were able to intervene and negotiate a settlement with the local authorities, but advised that Takamura would probably need to leave Japan for a time. Upon receiving this news, Takamura went to the Ono no Takamura Shrine, where he had been a shrine assistant as a young boy. He prayed to the kami for guidance in relation to gōhō, and during a vision, he claimed he was inspired to take the name Takamura in honor of the shrine's namesake. Thus, Obata Yukiyoshi Tsugiso became Takamura Yukiyoshi Tsugiso.

Obata's friends arranged for Takamura and his mother to leave Japan and settle with associates in Sweden, so on September 2nd, 1953, Takamura and his mother left Kōbe for Honolulu, Hawaii, on the SS President Cleveland. From there they travelled to Argentina. By 1954, Takamura and

Takamura, age 20, with mother-in-law, Yamada Aiko in Ōtsu, 1949.
(Photo courtesy of Mariko Takamura-Thomas.)

Argentinian identification document issued to Takamura's mother in 1953.
(Document courtesy of Mariko Takamura-Thomas.)

History And Technique

Takamura Yukiyoshi demonstrating Shindō Yōshin Ryū jūjutsu kata, Gyakute Gaeshi in the Japanese Friendship Gardens, San Jose, CA.,1978.
(Photo courtesy of David Maynard.)

his mother had arrived in Stockholm and started building a new life in Europe.

Takamura immersed himself into learning Swedish and within six months was conversant in the language, while his woodworking skills allowed him to find employment in furniture restoration. Hanako remained unable to speak Swedish and returned to Japan in 1959 where Namishiro assured her the incident in Ōtsu had been forgotten by the police during the ensuing years. Takamura, on the other hand, had cultivated a lucrative import/export business in the intervening years and was determined to make a life for himself outside Japan.

Namishiro visited Takamura in early 1960 and encouraged him to start teaching Shindō Yōshin Ryū in Sweden. To teach koryū outside Japan was a controversial decision, but Namishiro convinced Takamura the survival of the school was more important than the race or nationality of its students. Takamura located a jūdō dōjō in Stockholm named St. Erik's Budōklubb. He negotiated the rental of training space for Shindō Yōshin Ryū classes and agreed to assist in teaching jūdō for the dōjō. There he cultivated a small group of jūjutsu students, mostly comprising jūdōka and wrestlers. The first Shindō Yōshin Ryū instructor licensed outside Japan was a female jūdōka, Karin Andersson. Several years later, Takamura relocated to Uppsala, a college town 75km from Stockholm, and moved his dōjō there. This dōjō, named The Obata Budōkan, was successful, with 21 students, who are listed in the school's eimeiroku (student

Ships manifest for the SS President Cleveland. Takamura traveled first to Honolulu staying in public rooms available at the Kuakini Hospital. This hospital, originally Nihonjin Byoin, was a Japanese charity hospital, funded by the Japanese Government. During World War II it was seized and renamed. Following a short stay in Hawaii, Takamura traveled to Argentina, and later to Sweden.

Takamura Yukiyoshi demonstrating Matsuzaki Shinkage Ryū at a Japanese American Citizens League festival in San Jose, CA., 1978
(Photo courtesy of David Maynard.)

112

Shindō Yōshin Ryū

Takagi Iso, (1926-2005), Ryūsō, Takagi Hachihō Ryū & Menkyo Kaiden, Takamura ha Shindō Yōshin Ryū

Takamura Yukiyoshi demonstrating kenjutsu in San Jose, CA, at the Kelley Park Japanese Friendship Gardens during an embu in 1978.
(Photo courtesy of David Maynard)

register), becoming official deshi. Eventually, three of the students from the Uppsala Obata Budōkan received teaching licenses in Shindō Yōshin Ryū.

In 1962, a student from the old Eibukan Dōjō in Tōkyō contacted Namishiro Matsuhiro. Takagi Iso, a longtime training partner of Takamura's, had been teaching Shindō Yōshin Ryū, unaware Takamura or Namishiro had survived the war. He petitioned for membership in the Takamura ha Shindō Yōshin Ryu and was enthusiastically accepted.

The import/export business required Takamura to travel frequently. A passport possessed by the Takamura ha Shindō Yōshin Kai confirms his extensive global travel between 1956 and 1961. This travel frequently took Takamura through the United States, particularly San Francisco. During one trip through San Francisco, Takamura was introduced to a lovely Japanese-American woman named Michiko, who owned a Japanese antique store. A romance blossomed, and Takamura asked Michiko to marry. In 1964, Takamura started preparing to leave Sweden and upon arrival in the USA, Takamura moved to Hayward, California, to start a new life.

Martial arts were experiencing a boom in the United States when Takamura arrived, but most people had no idea what to make of koryū jūjutsu. The teaching methodology and strict dōjō environment was too rigid for the average American student to appreciate. To address this challenge, Takamura added a goshinjutsu (self-defense) curriculum to the regular Shindō Yōshin Ryū classes and called it Obata Jūdō Jūjutsu. This curriculum could be taught in a more spontaneous method, something more familiar to non-Japanese. These classes became popular with jūdō practitioners as well as students of the recently-introduced art of karate. Sometime after 1968, Takamura officially added the goshinjutsu curriculum to the Shindō Yōshin Ryū mokuroku as betsuden and in the early 1970s renamed the art Takamura ha Shindō Yōshin Ryū. None of the original koryū curriculum was abandoned during the evolution from Obata ha to Takamura ha, but some of the kata were rearranged within the syllabus in a manner Takamura believed was more logical and balanced.

History And Technique

During a trip to Japan in early 1970, Takamura arranged a meeting with Matsuoka Tatsuo, of the Shindō Yōshin Ryū main line and Tatsuo was surprised to learn Shindō Yōshin Ryū was being taught outside Japan. Tatsuo conveyed he was aware of Obata Shigeta, and knew him to be an exceptional Shindō Yōshin Ryū practitioner, but he was under the impression Obata had later in his life founded a completely different martial art instead of continuing the Obata ha Shindō Yōshin Ryū. Tatsuo was encouraged by the news of Obata ha Shindō Yōshin Ryū's survival, and believed the future of the school depended on a path more aligned with Kōdōkan Jūdō. He was convinced that kata training had to be integrated with a modern approach to budō, one which included sport competition.

This thinking can be traced back to the second-generation headmaster, Inose Motokichi, whose technical foundation was competitive wrestling. Takamura fundamentally disagreed with Tatsuo on this point, and explained that the place of Obata ha Shindō Yōshin Ryū in the 20th century budō world was decidedly different from an Olympic sport like Kōdōkan Jūdō. He felt any attempt to mix the two would marginalize both. To Takamura, Shindō Yōshin Ryū was a sacred trust placed in his care by his ancestors. It was an art of the samurai class that should be pursued with the spirit of humility and service, avoiding the risk of ego gratification that comes with sport competition. This exchange highlights a fundamental difference between the aims of modern budō and classical budō, one of personal and societal benefit versus historical preservation. As a gesture of respect to the Matsuoka family, Takamura traveled to Ueno and visited the Shindō Yōshin Ryū Honbu Dōjō. There he met Matsuoka Nobuatsu, who opened up the then empty dōjō. Prior to Takamura's arrival Nobuatsu had a plank removed from the side of the dōjō which he presented to Takamura, and asked him to use as a kanban (visual sign) on the California dōjō. On his return to the USA, Takamura had a sign cut from the plank, calligraphed with the name Takamura ha Shindō Yōshin Ryū and placed on the front of the Takamura ha Shindō Yōshin Ryū Honbu Dōjō in San Jose, California.

Between the mid-1970s and early 1980s, the quality of Takamura ha Shindō Yōshin Ryū training had reached a very high level in the United States and Europe. The first generation of non-Japanese students to receive teaching licenses were Karin Andersson (Sweden), David Maynard (United States), Henri Gembelliot (France), Annaue Yumoto (Sweden), Nanette Ōkura (United States), Karl Garrison (United States), David Montagne (France), Ronaldo Ermita (Philippines), Johan Vlacht (Belgium), and Louis Batton (France). Although the total number of Shindō Yōshin Ryū students remained fairly small, the quality of the teaching and training was building a solid foundation for the future.

In contrast, Shindō Yōshin Ryū in Japan was struggling. The main line tradition under Matsuoka Tatsuo had been so strongly influenced by sport jūdō that Shindō Yōshin Ryū started to lose its classical aspects. With the retirement of Matsuoka Nobuatsu and the closure of the Ueno Honbu Dōjō in 1963, the main line was left to a dwindling group of aging men. Without an influx of younger students, the main line would eventually be lost. It became obvious to Takamura that the future of the Shindō Yōshin Ryū practiced by Matsuoka had fallen solely to the Obata/Takamura lineage.

Now in his mid-40s, Takamura had matured into a excellent teacher and technician. According to his early students he became a demanding taskmaster, pushing his students very hard. Long-time student Karl Garrison holds the opinion Takamura was driven to push his students so hard because he saw Shindō Yōshin Ryū in Japan faltering. He was determined to see his

Shindō Yōshin Ryū

Kelley Park Japanese Friendship Garden, San Jose, CA.

The San Jose Japantown Takamura ha Shindō Yōshin Ryū Honbu Dōjō, 1989.

grandfather's legacy survive even if it had to do so outside Japan.

Namishiro passed away in 1974 at the age of 74, having carried the school through the bleak days following Obata's death, and the allied occupation at the close of World War II. To increase the chances the school would survive in Japan, Takamura issued a Menkyo Kaiden to his old training partner, Takagi Iso, reasoning that for Shindō Yōshin Ryū to survive in Japan, it would have to be under the guidance of Takagi Iso instead of the main line.

Takamura secured space for a dōjō in San Jose's Old Town when he moved to the South Bay area in 1978, and with the help of a local friend, Al Kawabata, regular training was expanded to the Japanese Friendship Garden in Kelley Park, San Jose. These outdoor classes on Sunday mornings proved very popular and attracted many new students. The growth in enrollment at the honbu dōjō resulted in overcrowding, as space in the original Old Town Dōjō was limited and in the mid-1980s, a larger dōjō of 48 mats was acquired near Japantown, San Jose. Thus, Takamura ha Shindō Yōshin Ryū expanded during this period as several instructors opened branch dōjō in the United States and Europe. David Maynard, senior student and assistant instructor at the honbu dōjō, introduced Tobin Threadgill and Daniel Nakamoto to Shindō Yōshin Ryū in 1985. Both would become senior-level instructors.

Takamura realized his mother was ailing during a trip to Japan in 1994, so he and his wife Michiko began to make frequent extended trips to Japan to support her. Takamura maintained his position as kaichō while David Maynard temporarily assumed the positions of honbuchō and shibuchō, taking over the day-to-day running of the organization. Just months after the death of Takamura's mother Hanako, Michiko unexpectedly passed away too.

On Takamura's return to the United States, he resumed his role as honbuchō of the dōjō in San Jose. In early 1996, Takamura was diagnosed with throat cancer and decided to return to Sweden for medical treatment. Before leaving for Sweden, he officially announced his temporary retirement from teaching, and organized a meeting of all the senior instructors in San Francisco, California. Present at that meeting were Takagi Iso (Japan), David Maynard (United States), Henri Gembelliot (France), Tobin Threadgill (United States), and Nanette Ōkura (United States). Takamura's vision for the future of Takamura ha Shindō Kai was discussed at the meeting and a revised draft of the organization's kaiki (bylaws) was formulated. Takamura

History And Technique

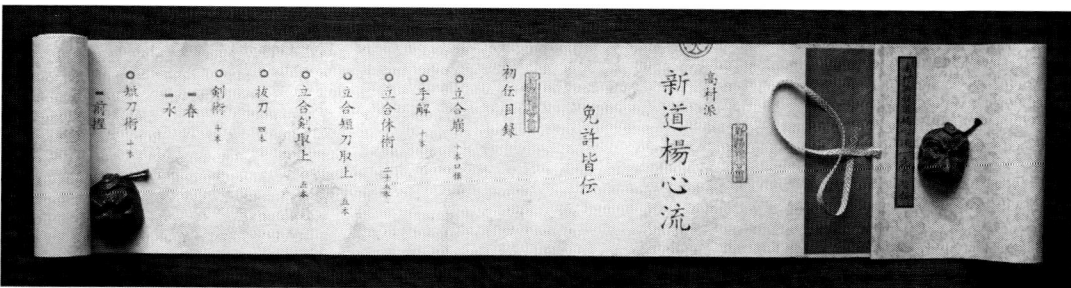

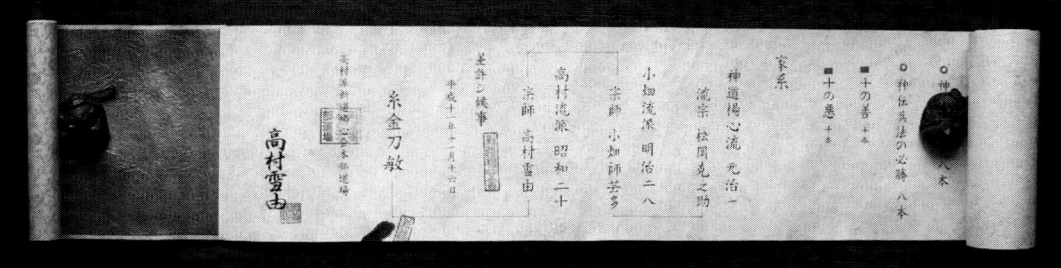

Takamura ha Shindō Yōshin Ryū Menkyo Kaiden issued to Tobin Threadgill by Takamura Yukiyoshi. When a student enters jōden level training they are given a Japanese name. This is the name used on all upper level teaching licenses. Tobin Threadgill's name in Japanese is rendered Itokane Tobin (糸金刀敏), meaning "golden thread, swift sword".

announced David Maynard would be issued a Menkyo Kaiden and designated honbuchō, Henri Gembelliot and Tobin Threadgill would both be issued Jōden Menkyo and designated European and American shibuchō (branch directors), respectively. Takamura also announced he would remain the kaichō of the Takamura ha Shindō Yōshin Kai.

Takamura's cancer went into remission within six months and he returned to the United States. He attended seminars and supervised teaching by his licensed instructors where he stressed the importance of cultivating superior teaching skills, as well as honing technical knowledge during this period. The cancer returned in early 1997, however, the prognosis was bleak. Takamura closed the honbu dōjō in San Jose, California, and decided to return to Sweden. He announced he would issue a Menkyo Kaiden to Tobin Threadgill, but specified it could not be formally recognized until 2001, when Threadgill reached the age of 42.

Takamura returned again to the United States in November 1997 to visit his daughter, Mariko. Tobin Threadgill, assisted by David Maynard, took several portraits during this visit which can be seen on the following page. It was the last time Takamura would accept social visits by any of his students.

Takamura was interviewed for a San Francisco Bay Area budō newsletter during the mid-1990s and the interview found its way to the publisher of a popular budō magazine called Aikidō Journal, published by Stan Pranin, who was impressed with the insights evident in the interview. Pranin contacted Takamura in 1998 by way of a common friend suggesting an expanded version of the interview for his magazine.

The interview with Takamura Yukiyoshi, of Shindō Yōshin Ryū jūjutsu was released in the 1999 summer (121), and autumn (122) editions. This book's co-author, Ohgami Shingo, who had subscribed to the Japanese version of Aikidō Journal for many years was surprised to see this

Shindō Yōshin Ryū

Takamura Yukiyoshi, 1997

interview and immediately sent a letter to the publisher. Pranin was kind enough to send the inquiry directly to Takamura, and Ohgami received a prompt answer from him. Much to his surprise, Ohgami discovered Takamura had lived in Sweden where Ohgami had lived since 1969. Takamura told Ohgami he could not demonstrate Shindō Yōshin Ryū due to his illness, but would contact a past Wadō Ryū student in the United States, Tobin Threadgill, who could demonstrate in his place. Subsequent correspondence between Ohgami and Threadgill revealed Threadgill held a Jōden Mokuroku, and could help Ohgami learn more about Shindō Yōshin Ryū. In a letter to Ohgami, Takamura wrote that in 1982 he had seen a demonstration of Wadō Ryū in Gothenburg, Sweden by Ohgami, who at the time was in charge of organizing the European Karate Federation (EKF) Championships. Ohgami was astounded to learn he and Takamura had come so close to meeting all those years ago.

By late 1999, Takamura's health started to deteriorate and he decided to refuse further cancer treatment. He continued communicating with his senior students, providing them with advice and counseling them on how to run the organization after his passing. In early 2000, his daughter Mariko, moved in with him to assist with daily chores and noted he continued to train in battō (sword drawing) every morning in a sun room at the back of the apartment. In March of 2000, Takamura quietly passed away while asleep after a daily walk in a nearby park. He was 72 years old.

"Anyone who calls himself a master, or allows his students to call him a master in his presence, isn't a master."

- Takamura Yukiyoshi

Matsuzaki Namishiro/Matsuzaki Shinkage Ryū

Matsuzaki Namishiro (1833-1896) was born in Kurume to a Kurume Clan samurai. He was introduced to Katōda Heihachirō, the headmaster of Katōda Shinkage Ryū hyōhō in 1844. Namishiro was also introduced to Okimono Morihei of Hōzōin Ryū sōjutsu later in the same year. He received his first license in Katōda Shinkage Ryū in 1848 and a license in Hōzōin Ryū in 1849. He received Menkyo Kaiden in Katōda Shinkage Ryū in 1854.

In 1855 at the age of 22, Matsuzaki left Kurume and traveled on a musha shugyō throughout northern Japan. During a contest held at the Oka Clan Edo headquarters, Matsuzaki impressively defeated the famous swordsmen Momoi Shunzō (Kyōshin Meichi Ryū) and Saitō Shintarō (Shintō Munen Ryū). He also fought the highly-respected Ueda Umanosuke (Kyōshin Meichi Ryū) to a draw. It was during this event he caught the attention of the legendary Yamaoka Tesshū. They would go on to become life-long friends.

In 1868, Matsuzaki participated in the Boshin Wars as a member of the Kurume Clan. He returned home in 1869, and in 1870 was ordered by the prefectural headquarters to serve as a shinan-yaku (official kenjutsu instructor). With this recognition came the title of Shizoku, one-generation samurai status. Tsuda Kyōshū of Tsuda/Asayama Ichiden Ryū, Imai Masaaki of Jikishinkage Ryū, and his own teacher, Katōda Heihachirō, were also named as Kurume Clan instructors at this time. These three styles were major arts in Kurume. Since Tsuda was only 21 years of age, Imai was 70, and Katōda was 60, Matsuzaki was asked to be the chief instructor. With this recognition, Matsuzaki founded his own branch of Shinkage Ryū, which came to be known as Matsuzaki Shinkage Ryū or Matsuzaki Ryū. This resulted in his fame spreading and he being referred to as Kyūshū Tatsujin (number one sword master of Kyūshū).

Following the Meiji Restoration, the samurai class was abolished and many samurai found themselves out of work. However, the Meiji government's desire to consolidate authority over the country led the government to recruit men educated in the use of arms and jūjutsu as police officers. In a very short period of time, ex-samurai from both sides of the conflict were being accepted back into society as policemen. This resulted in police-associated dōjō becoming a powerful force in kendō, a status that remains true today.

By 1882, Matsuzaki's friend, Yamaoka Tesshū, had become a famous statesman and chamberlain to Emperor Meiji. In 1883, Yamaoka contacted his friend Namishiro and invited him to visit and train in his Shunpūkan Dōjō in Tōkyō. Documents are discrepant, but it appears Matsuzaki arrived in Tōkyō in February 1884. During this visit, Matsuzaki had the opportunity to converse with many old friends and competitors from his past, including Ueda Umanosuke (Kyōshin Meichi Ryū), Yazaki Masakatsu (Hokushin Ittō Ryū) Watanabe Noboru (Shindō Munen Ryū), and Yoshida Takeshirō (Shindō Munen Ryū). Also during this visit, Sakakibara Kenkichi (Jikishinkage Ryū) introduced Matsuzaki to a young and eager Yōshin Ryū practitioner from Ōtsu named Obata Shigeta. Obata would go on to study kenjutsu under both Sakakibara and Matsuzaki.

Matsuzaki, a keen competitor, jumped into training at the Shunpūkan Dōjō with intense vigor despite his age of 52 years. During one visit, he asked to shiai with six of Yamaoka's senior students, most of them half his age. In these six contests, only one prevailed over Matsuzaki.

Shindō Yōshin Ryū

During recurring visits, Yamaoka became so impressed with Matsuzaki he encouraged Matsuzaki to accept a position as a shihan in the newly-formed Eizoku-sha, a budō preservation group. Others who were asked to join included Yoshida Takeshirō, Sakakibara Kenkichi, Ōhara Tokusaburō and Doi Toshiharu. The opening ceremony was held at a new dōjō next to the police headquarters in Ōhira-cho, Marunouchi, Tōkyō. Over 150 matches were held during the opening ceremonies. Jikishinkage Ryū kenjutsu was demonstrated by Yamaoka's senior student, Kominami Yasutomo, while Matsuzaki Shinkage Ryū iaijutsu was demonstrated by Matsuzaki.

Matsuzaki was said to be a man of sincere temperament and humble character. He was not known to drink heavily, smoke, or engage in gambling. Although he appreciated calligraphy due to his long friendship with Yamaoka and Katsu Kaishū, he had no deep passions outside of swordsmanship. It is said Matsuzaki loved nothing more than the discussion of swordsmanship and strategy with his budō companions. He remained an avid and respected competitor until his early 60s.

In 1885, Matsuzaki decided it was time to return home to his dōjō in Fukuoka. In 1888, he was again employed as a kenjutsu instructor for the Kyōto Prefectural Police. In 1895 Matsuzaki was selected as one of the first 15 Seirenshō award recipients at the Dai Nippon Butokukai's first Kyōto Taikai. On June 19th, 1896, Matsuzaki died at his home. He was 64 years old. He is remembered as one of the most skilled and humble samurai of the late Bakumatsu period.

One of the last fully-licensed instructors of Matsuzaki Shinkage Ryū was a student of Umezaki Yaichirō named Ishikawa Gotō. Gotō adopted a young and talented swordsman into his family and named him for his schools founder. This was Namishiro Ishikawa Matsuhiro. Namishiro would go on to be Takamura's principal instructor after his grandfather Obata's passing. It is through Namishiro the advanced teachings of Obata ha Shindō Yōshin Ryū and Matsuzaki Shinkage Ryū were passed to Takamura Yukiyoshi.

12 Seirenshō recipients from the Butokukai's first Kyōto Taikai in 1895. In the back row center is Matsuzaki Namishiro, founder of Matsuzaki Shinkage Ryū, and in the front right is Namishiro's student, Umezaki Yaichirō. Also present are five Jikishinkage Ryū shihan: Tokuno, Okumura, Takayama, Hagiwara, and Abe.

History And Technique

Tobin Threadgill

Tobin Threadgill (b. 1959)

Tobin (Toby) Threadgill was born in January, 1959, in Fort Worth, Texas, and grew up in a middle-class family. His father was a mechanical engineer, and his mother, a talented musician, taught piano. Threadgill graduated from high school with honors and then attended the Brooks Institute of Photography, located in Santa Barbara, California. He graduated from the Brooks Institute in 1980 with a major in advertising photography and a minor in color technology. Threadgill went on to become an award-winning advertising photographer with studios in Dallas, Texas, and Long Beach, California. He specialized in automotive, aviation, and special effects product advertising.

While attending college in Santa Barbara, California in 1978, Threadgill was able to pursue a longtime interest by seeking instruction in western swordsmanship under fencing maestro Capt. Hart Kait, United States Navy. After building a solid foundation in swordsmanship by studying foil, he was encouraged to undertake the study of épée and saber. Threadgill excelled in fencing, appreciating the art's physical subtlety and mental strategy. He placed seventh in foil and achieved gold in épée during his first regional competition.

Upon graduation from college, Threadgill moved to Dallas, Texas, to begin a career in advertising photography. Unable to locate fencing classes in Dallas that were up to the caliber he had experienced under Kait. Threadgill looked into other avenues of martial study. Initially, this led him to kendō, but a business associate studying Japanese karate suggested he watch a Wadō Ryū karate demonstration. Intrigued, Threadgill starting training in Wadō Ryū karate under J. Gerry Chau in the spring of 1981 and achieved shodan in 1986. Eventually, Threadgill became a partner with Chau, founding the Wadōkan Dōjō with other

Fencing maestro Capt. Hart Kait.

120

Wadō Ryū sensei, J. Gerry Chau, 1989

dōjō members Robert and Vickie Severns. Threadgill continued to study Wadō Ryū for over 12 years. He also studied Jeet Kune Do under Dan Inosanto, Muay Thai boxing under Surachai Sirasute, aikidō under Bryan Robbins and Yanagi Ryū under Don Angier. In 1989, Tobin and Bryan Robbins co-founded the Southern Methodist University Martial Arts Club in Dallas, Texas, a club that continues to operate on the SMU campus.

In 1986, Threadgill had a chance encounter with David Maynard, senior student of Takamura Yukiyoshi at the Wadōkan Dōjō. Some individuals in the Wadō Ryū community had led Threadgill to believe Shindō Yōshin Ryū was no longer extant, but David Maynard explained only the Nakayama line of Shindō Yōshin Ryū had ended with the founding of Wadō Ryū by Ōtsuka. The Matsuoka line of Shindō Yōshin Ryū was still extant and led by Matsuoka Tatsuo in Tōkyō, while Takamura in California led the Obata/Takamura line. Long-curious about Shindō Yōshin Ryū and its relationship to Wadō Ryū, Threadgill wrote to Takamura enquiring about the technical, and historical legacy of the school. Following several written exchanges, Threadgill arranged his business schedule to visit Takamura's San Jose dōjō. This first visit was a watershed event that left Threadgill deeply impressed, not only with the art of Shindō Yōshin Ryū, but with Takamura's sublime technical abilities. Threadgill immediately perceived the subtlety and effectiveness of his jūjutsu technique and the impressive mix of precision and aggressive power in his swordsmanship. Threadgill had not observed such exquisite swordsmanship since his days of training with Hart Kait, a fencer of legendary status. Curiosity piqued, Threadgill visited Takamura several times in the coming months and was given the opportunity in mid-1986 to join Takamura ha Shindō Yōshin Ryū as an official deshi. Adhering to proper protocol, Takamura Yukiyoshi contacted both J. Gerry Chau and Bryan Robbins, and

The first-generation instructors of the SMU Martial Arts Club. (L to R) Bryan Robbins, John Lewis, Dr. Thomas Barry and Tobin Threadgill. This club has operated on the Southern Methodist University Campus since 1986.

Tobin Threadgill with his Muay Thai coach Surachai Sirasute in Dallas, Texas, 1986.

Tobin Threadgill during a training session held at the Tsubaki Grand Shrine, 2009.
(Photo by Miyamoto Kozue.)

with their permission, Threadgill was initiated into Takamura ha Shindō Yōshin Ryū by taking the Takamura ha Shindō Yōshin Ryū kishomon/keppan (blood oath) in October 1986.

Studying authentic koryū was a new experience for Threadgill, and he realized Takamura was an uncompromising instructor who demanded the highest level of dedication to training and to the preservation of the art. The strict reigi (etiquette) in a koryū dōjō was also new to Threadgill and initially confusing, but in time he came to appreciate how the adherence to budō reigi was not just window dressing or a cultural affectation. Properly followed, koryū reigi facilitated a superior training regimen, allowing for intensity, safety and a level of predictability, which is frequently absent in modern schools of budō. Reigi also serves as a method of introducing unfamiliar Japanese cultural norms into the budō experience of non-Japanese students, something absolutely demanded in what is essentially a Japanese martial arts historical preservation society.

Takamura awarded Threadgill a Chūden Menkyo in 1990 and admonished him to start honing his teaching skills. Cultivating competent instructors was the only way the art entrusted to him by his ancestors would survive for future generations. Initially Threadgill started teaching Shindō Yōshin Ryū classes at the Wadōkan Dōjō, but soon realized he needed to further develop his understanding of the Takamura ha Shindō Yōshin Ryu riai-den (principle-based teaching methodology).

In 1991 Takamura Sensei asked Threadgill to enter into the school's advanced level training class, which required passing the Shinryoku Tanren, a proprietary test of spiritual and mental strength. Threadgill passed this test, and was asked to take the gokui (secret level teachings) keppan and affix a blood seal to a scroll containing the school's kishomon-dai (advanced level oath of initiation). Thus, Threadgill became an officially-recognized jōden level initiate.

After gaining a deeper understanding of the Takamura ha Shindō Yōshin Ryu teaching methodology, Threadgill completed his training in the Jōden Okugi and Gokui curricula in March 1995. Takamura issued Threadgill a Jōden Menkyo license on June 1st, 1995, officially giving Threadgill the authority to teach the entire Takamura ha Shindō Yōshin Ryu mokuroku, and identifying him as a senior level instructor. Later that year, Threadgill started construction of a Japanese dōjō at his home in Dallas, Texas. In December 1995, he officially opened it and in consultation with Takamura named it the Sōryūshin Dōjō (Twin Willow Training Hall). The name acknowledges the origins of Shindō Yōshin Ryū in both Akiyama and Miura Yōshin

Shindō Yōshin Ryū

Stan Pranin, Tobin Threadgill and Tony Alvarez at Threadgill's Menkyo Kaiden Zōteishiki, April, 7th, 2001

Ryū jūjutsu lineages. In 1996, the Sōryūshin Dōjō was selected as the American Takamura ha Shindō Yōshin Ryū Headquarters Dōjō and Threadgill as the North American Shibuchō. Takamura presented Threadgill with both Jōden Okugi and Gokui densho in March, 1996.

Takamura Sensei announced his decision to issue a Menkyo Kaiden to Threadgill in February 1999, the third recipient of this distinction. In 1995, during compilation of the Takamura ha Shindō Yōshin Ryū kaiki, Takamura decided that going forward, the minimum age to represent Takamura ha Shindō Yōshin Ryū as a Menkyo Kaiden recipient would be 42 years of age (Kazoedoshi-One year old at birth). This decision was based on the Shintō concept of kigaku (divination). Kigaku considers the age of 42 climactic and is called taiyaku (misfortune), whereas the following year is the inauspicious age atoyaku (ominous). Given these considerations related to Shintōism, the date of formal presentation to Threadgill had to fall after atoyaku, which translated to Jan 20th, 2001. In late 1999, with his health failing, Takamura contacted his friend Stan Pranin, the publisher of Aikidō Journal Magazine, and asked him to serve as his proxy by formally presenting the Menkyo Kaiden menjō and densho to Threadgill. On April 7th, 2001, a gathering of friends and martial artists convened at the Soryūshin Dōjō, where a group of esteemed budō adepts including Stan Pranin, J. Gerry Chau, Makio Nishida, Don Angier and Fred Ishii participated in the Menkyo Kaiden Zōteishiki (presentation ceremony). A 500-year-old katana that had belonged to Namishiro Matsuhiro and was in Takamura's possession, was presented to Threadgill during the ceremony.

This presentation meant by 2001 three people held Takamura ha Shindō Yōshin Ryū Menkyo Kaiden: Takagi Iso, David Maynard, and Tobin Threadgill. Takagi was suffering from health problems by early 2001, which would require his imminent retirement, and David Maynard could not realistically function as the honbuchō due to a career change and relocation to Europe. Thus, the recently constructed Sōryūshin Dōjō was selected as the interim Takamura ha Shindō Yōshin Ryū Honbu Dōjō and Threadgill was appointed interim honbuchō. David Maynard also decided Threadgill should function as the kanjichō (administrative head) of the honbu dōjō. David Maynard would maintain the position of chief instructor and assume the position of kaiden shihan, as outlined in the school's kaiki.

Tobin Threadgill executing Hiki Otoshi Nage on Ayman Nassar in London, UK 2014
(Photo by Jon Classick.)

David Maynard was involved in a tragic accident in 2003, which resulted in a debilitating back injury and by the middle of the year he realized his life of teaching Shindō Yōshin Ryū was over. In consultation with Takagi Iso, Maynard agreed Threadgill should ascend to the position of kaichō, which merges the technical and administrative positions of kaiden shihan (chief instructor) and kanjichō (general secretary), respectively. Initially Threadgill balked at the notion, feeling Maynard should allow himself more time to recover from his injury before making such an important decision. However, a meeting with him in late 2003 convinced Threadgill of the severity of Maynard's physical injuries, and he agreed to assume the position of kaichō. This change in status coincided with Threadgill moving from Dallas, Texas, to Evergreen, Colorado, and the construction of a new and larger dōjō. In April 2004, the new Sōryushin Dōjō was purified in a Shintō Ōharai, and designated the new Takamura ha Shindō Yōshin Ryū Honbu Dōjō.

Rev. Koichi Barrish at the honbu dōjō to perform a Shintō Koharae, 2018.

The school experienced slow but steady growth during the years after relocating Takamura ha Shindō Yōshin Ryū outside Japan. The 1999 interview with Takamura in Aikidō Journal Magazine resulted in a dramatic upsurge in visibility and in 2001, Maynard was approached by Oscar Recio-Coll from Palma de Mallorca, Spain, about teaching a seminar. Threadgill was dispatched to Spain where a series of successful annual seminars introduced Takamura ha Shindō Yōshin Ryū to a new generation of European budō practitioners.

In 2002, Pranin organized a martial arts event called the Aiki Expo, which brought together various prominent Japanese budō practitioners from around the world. In response to feedback and interest generated about Shindō Yōshin Ryū by the earlier Takamura interview in Aikidō Journal, Pranin asked Threadgill to participate in the event by demonstrating Takamura ha Shindō Yōshin Ryū. This event introduced Threadgill in a large public venue as the Takamura ha Shindō Yōshin Ryū Kaichō, the first non-Japanese instructor to become the undisputed headmaster of a koryū school. Threadgill would again be invited to teach and demonstrate at the Aiki Expo in 2004 and 2005.

Ohgami, this book's co-author and a senior JKF Wadōkai instructor, arranged to have Threadgill visit his Samurai Dōjō in Gothenburg, Sweden, to introduce his Wadō Ryū karate students to Shindō Yōshin Ryū jūjutsu in the spring of 2004. Subsequent visits to Gothenburg have occurred annually since that initial seminar, and the ensuing friendship between Ohgami and Threadgill led to collaborative research on the historical and technical connections between Shindō Yōshin Ryū and Wadō Ryū. Their research has culminated in this book.

Bob Nash, another JKF Wadōkai senior instructor, observed a seminar taught by Threadgill

Shindō Yōshin Ryū

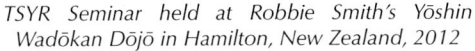

TSYR Seminar held at Robbie Smith's Yōshin Wadōkan Dōjō in Hamilton, New Zealand, 2012

TSYR Seminar held at Ohgami Shingo's Samurai Dōjō in Gothenburg, Sweden, on May 1st, 2004.

in Seattle, Washington, in July, 2004, which resulted in several invitations for Threadgill to teach cooperatively with other respected JKF Wadōkai instructors, including two JKF Wadōkai technical committee chairmen, Takagi Hideho and Arakawa Tōru. Nash also invited Threadgill to teach a cooperative seminar with him in Germany in 2005. That seminar initiated a public event that has continued annually in Berlin for over a decade.

Robbie Smith, sixth dan, JKF Wadōkai and chief instructor of the Yōshin Wadōkan Dōjō in Hamilton, New Zealand, traveled to the Takamura ha Shindō Yōshin Ryu Honbu Dōjō in Colorado in 2006. Robbie had been introduced to Shindō Yōshin Ryū during a 1994 seminar in London, England, taught by Takamura. Following Takamura's passing in 2000, Smith assumed his opportunity to learn more about Shindō Yōshin Ryū had passed. He learned several years later that Takamura ha Shindō Yōshin Ryū was operating under the leadership of Tobin Threadgill. Upon learning Threadgill would be teaching in Lakeland, Florida with Takagi Hideho, he attended the event to learn more about the art. Smith was greatly impressed with what he experienced during his time with Threadgill in Florida and upon returning home sought and received permission to start an official Shindō Yōshin Ryū study group at his Yōshin Wadōkan Dōjō in New Zealand. Smith organized the first Shindō Yōshin Ryū seminar to be taught in Oceania in 2007. This event led to bi-annual seminars in Hamilton, New Zealand, and eventually facilitated the spread of Shindō Yōshin Ryū within New Zealand and to Australia.

In 2005, Ohgami Shingo visited the Nakayama and Inose homesteads in Ibaraki prefecture. He also visited Shimotsuma Daiichi High School where he was given access to school records related to Nakayama Tatsusaburō. In 2007, Ohgami and Threadgill traveled to Chikusei City, Japan in response to an invitation from Matsuoka Masahiro and Matsuoka Takeshi. This meeting introduced Threadgill to Matsuoka Katsunosuke's descendants. The Matsuoka family, initially unaware the martial art founded by their ancestor was still being taught, was pleased with the revelation. The Matsuoka family generously took the time to participate in an extensive interview with the authors, answering questions about family history and their noted ancestor Katsunosuke. They also escorted Ohgami and Threadgill to

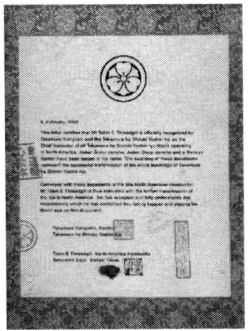

Left: Menkyo Kaiden menjō and densho in kiri box. Right: Letter certifying issuance of Jōden Gokui, Jōden Okugi and Menkyo Kaiden, dated February 5, 1999.

History And Technique

Tobin Threadgill with Matsuoka Takeshi at the grave of Matsuoka Katsunosuke in 2007.

two cemeteries where Matsuoka Katsunosuke, Inose Motokichi, and Matsuoka Tatsuo's remains reside. The interview provided the authors with previously unpublished information and photographs, and dispelled several oft-repeated myths surrounding the history of Shindō Yōshin Ryū. The meeting also rejuvenated the link between Takamura ha Shindō Yōshin Ryū and its founding family, a link that had been inactive since Takamura visited Matsuoka Nobuatsu in the 1970s.

By 2014, a decade after Threadgill assumed the position of Takamura ha Shindō Yōshin Ryū Kaichō, the school comprised over 30 dōjō and study groups in 11 countries. With so many koryū suffering from limited membership and meager interest, for a koryū to generate such enthusiasm is quite unusual. This success can be attributed, at least in part, to its historical link to a popular modern budō - Wadō Ryū karate. This link has attracted a significant number of Wadō Ryū students who are curious about Wadō Ryū's progenitor art. Another factor in the global growth and development of Shindō Yōshin Ryū is the training Threadgill received from a worldly and enlightened teacher who internalized the foundational principles of Shindō Yōshin Ryū and adeptly re-conceptualized them in a manner and pedagogy more familiar to non-Japanese. The theory underlying the curriculum of many koryū schools is often conveyed via obscure cultural metaphors, which can render the knowledge being imparted obscure or unintelligible for students from different cultures. After years of struggling to teach his western students as he was taught, Takamura created a new teaching method, which capitalized on the different learning styles in the west. Although theory-based teaching was foundational in Shindō Yōshin Ryū from its conception, the exact manner in which these theories were taught evolved over time. Threadgill reiterates that Takamura encouraged all licensed teachers to cultivate their own unique teaching style, as he felt teaching diversity was a strength, not a weakness. Takamura believed the strictly-defined curriculum of a koryū system did not extend to implementing a strictly-defined pedagogy. Different approaches to teaching allow the same knowledge to be more effectively passed on to a greater number of students. Threadgill explains the teaching philosophy of Takamura with this metaphor.

"Teaching in a koryū could be likened to the job of a symphony conductor. Generations ago the musicians and conductors were different, but they all worked from the same musical score used today. Every individual symphony has a unique musical quality and though all conductors will embrace their own personal interpretation of the composer's vision, the musical notes never change.

In consideration of a performance, all great conductors evaluate the strengths and weaknesses of each musician in the symphony, to

Tobin Threadgill executing Te Gaeshi Nage on Marco Pinto in London, UK 2014
(Photo by Jon Classick.)

Shindō Yōshin Ryū

Joint Shindō Yōshin Ryū & JKF Wadōkai seminar in Berlin, Germany, with Tobin Threadgill and Robbie Smith, 2014

create what they believe will be the best possible representation of the composer's inspiration. Consequently, no two symphonies or conductors will ever create an exact duplicate of a previous performance, but each remains unique in its beauty.

Now imagine the arrogance of a conductor who dislikes a melody in Paganini's Violin Concerto #1, and decides to just change it on a whim? This is unthinkable. Paganini cannot simply be rewritten to suit personal idiosyncrasies. Another composer might take inspiration from a previous Paganini composition and create a different musical work that is an homage (such as that done by Rachmaninoff), but that is quite different from rewriting an existing score. In a budō context, Shindō Yōshin Ryū is a specific entity inspired by its progenitors. It must remain true to its Japanese roots and founding principles, or it betrays its origins. No-one rewrites a Paganini Concerto, and no-one simply rewrites the Shindō Yōshin Ryū score."

Today, Threadgill embraces this philosophy in overseeing Takamura ha Shindō Yōshin Ryū. He seeks to fiercely maintain the tradition entrusted to him while allowing each student to cultivate an individual representation of the art that venerates the past while acknowledging the daunting challenges of the future. Koryū must remain true to its origins while thriving beyond the shores of Japan. The tradition must embrace the unique knowledge and cultural identity that is felt in the heart rather than represented by a uniform. There are some who dress like samurai while claiming to represent classical bujutsu but they are just faking it, imitating art. Centuries of wisdom cannot be contrived or pantomimed for show. The environment experienced in a real koryū dōjō is rare, culturally unique, and it can never be duplicated or faked.

Takamura Yukiyoshi with Tobin Threadgill, in Charlotte, North Carolina, 1997.

History And Technique

The Technical Legacy of Shindō Yōshin Ryū

Shinai-geiko training in the Takamura ha Shindō Yōshin Ryū Honbu Dōjō.

Shindō Yōshin Ryū is an unusual ryūha among those founded in the mid-to-late Edo period. Most Japanese budō traditions founded during the 19th century reflected a curriculum influenced by the Tokugawa era's extended years of peace. However, Shindō Yōshin Ryū's founder was born into a time when the pillars of the Tokugawa Shogunate's political stability were powerfully shaken. Matsuoka Katsunosuke recognized the samurai arts he had spent his life studying were more suited for self-defense in a civilian environment than actual military conflict. In the early 1860s, Matsuoka started reformulating the skills he had learned with the intention of creating a contemporary school of budō that was modeled on older sōgō bujutsu.

Shindō Yōshin Ryū

In 1864, Matsuoka Katsunosuke completed the task of organizing the school of bujutsu he named Shindō Yōshin Ryū. Initially, he drew from all the previous schools he had studied, including a significant influence from Jikishinkage Ryū swordsmanship and Hōzōin Ryū spearmanship. Four years later, in 1868, Japan was embroiled in a civil war, which convincingly demonstrated the superiority of western military technology over the traditional combat methods employed by the samurai. Matsuoka's personal experience in battle at Toba-Fushimi, and his severe wounding by firearms during the battle of Ueno forced him to reconsider the technical foundations of Shindō Yōshin Ryū. Although the samurai class had been abolished by the Meiji Restoration, and modern technology had proven itself superior on the battlefield, Matsuoka realized the classical tactics and strategies of warfare remained as vital as ever. He became convinced classical budō could still be used as a path to forge a contemporary samurai who could then provide superior leadership as part of a modernized imperial military.

From a technical standpoint, Matsuoka realized jūjutsu should be the dominant area of study in an art no longer directly tied to military capability. However, he understood kenjutsu was the technical, as well as spiritual wellspring from which all Japanese budō flowed. Consequently, sword work originating in Jikishinkage Ryū remained a vital area of study in Shindō Yōshin Ryū. From its inception, the tactics and combat mindset of Jikishinkage Ryū had been woven into the character of the jūjutsu techniques originating in Tenjin Shinyō Ryū and Totsuka ha Yōshin Ryū.

The exact number of kata and the technical composition of Matsuoka's original Shindō Yōshin Ryū curriculum has been impossible to ascertain, but documents in the possession of the Takamura ha Shindō Yōshin Kai, originating with Obata Shigeta, indicate the original curriculum comprised over 200 kata. Given the shock created by the defeat of the Tokugawa samurai, it is logical to assume Matsuoka didn't settle on a clearly defined-curriculum until the mid-1870s. Following Matsuoka's death in 1898, a schism occurred within Shindō Yōshin Ryū, which saw the second mainline headmaster, Inose Motokichi, embracing a technical direction influenced by Kanō Jigorō's emerging Kōdōkan jūdō. However, Obata took his independent branch of Shindō Yōshin Ryū down a path intended to represent the one envisaged by the founder, Matsuoka Katsunosuke.

The Shindō Yōshin Ryū main line under Inose Motokichi

As taught by Inose in the early 20th century, the Shindō Yōshin Ryū's abbreviated mainline curriculum comprised 86 kata plus an extensive study of kyūsho atemi, other kuden (oral teachings), shiai-hō (freestyle application), and kappō (resuscitation). The curriculum is organized into nine categories. The first four sets, Te Hodoki (10 forms), Nage Kaeshi (10 forms), Shoden Idori (10 forms), and Shoden Tachiai (10 forms) constitute the Shoden kata. Embedded in these kata are the shoden ura no waza (underlying fundamental principles) and the shoden no heihō (basic application strategies). Combined, these teachings represent the entire main line Shoden Mokuroku. Upon completion of these categories the student is eligible to receive a Shoden Kirigami license.

The fifth and sixth kata sets are identified as the Chūden Idori (14 forms) and Chūden Tachiai 14 forms). These teachings reflect a combative approach to training, as well as a more practical application of the school's fundamental principles. The Chūden Tachiai included scenarios that addressed surprise attacks and multiple attackers, both armed and unarmed. Embedded in these kata are the chūden ura no waza (underlying intermediate principles) and the chū-okuden (mid-level hidden teachings). Upon completion of these categories of study, the student is eligible to receive a Chūden Mokuroku license.

The seventh set is labeled Gokui. These teachings take the combative approach to training further, including force-on-force pressure-testing where kaeshi-waza (counter techniques) and the various forms of sente (initiative) are studied so they could be applied in an actual combative context. The Gokui teachings also addressed combat flexibility, psychological pressure and randori-hō (freestyle training).

The last two sets are Ratai Dori and Kappō. The Ratai Dori (three forms - naked captures) are jūjutsu applications that can be used combatively without depending on clothing like sleeves or collars. This category of study also includes an extensive study of atemi (striking) and kyūsho (vital points). The Kappō (four forms) are resuscitation techniques, employed when an unconscious person is in danger of expiring without intervention.

Further Shindō Yōshin Ryū Gokui level kuden teachings are concerned with spiritual and mystical matters, which include visualization, vocalizations, and methods of calling on the spirit world for divination, moral courage, and prescience. A student reaching this level of training is eligible to be awarded a Menkyo Kaiden, a license symbolizing the complete transmission of the school's techniques, principles, and ethos.

The Obata/Takamura ha Shindō Yōshin Ryū line.

The Obata/Takamura line, officially branching off from the main line in 1895, continued and even expanded upon the technical legacy envisaged by the school's founder, Matsuoka. While the mainline tradition turned abruptly towards modernity by eliminating a majority of the school's weapons study, the Obata line turned strongly towards a more classical approach, expanding its study of classical Japanese weaponry. Obata's previous experience in Jikishinkage Ryū, Matsuzaki Shinkage Ryū, and Akiyama Yōshin Ryū, led him to re-work and expand the original kenjutsu and battō/iaijutsu curriculum. By the time Obata re-named his line of Shindō Yōshin Ryū the Obata ha, the curriculum reflected approximately 350 kata.

As passed to the current headmaster, Threadgill, the Takamura ha Shindō Yōshin Ryū curriculum comprises 346 forms plus a fuzoku bugei (assimilated school) of bōjutsu called Takagi Hachihō Ryū, which includes an additional 32 forms. The Takamura ha Shindō Yōshin Ryū mokuroku as it is currently organized is divided among eight densho plus a Menkyo Kaiden.

- *Shoden Taijutsu no Maki*
- *Shoden Buki no Maki*
- *Chūden Taijutsu no Maki*
- *Chūden Buki no Maki*
- *Jōden Gokui Jin no Maki*
- *Jōden Gokui Ten no Maki*
- *Jōden Okugi Chi no Maki*
- *Jōden Okugi Tengu Tobi no Maki*
- *Menkyo Kaiden*

Shindō Yōshin Ryū

The Shoden Taijutsu no Maki comprises 60 jūjutsu kata and 19 goshinjutsu waza included as betsuden (auxiliary teachings). The kata are organized in seven sets: Tachiai Tedori Kuzushi (10 forms), Tachiai Taidori Kuzushi (10 forms), Tachiai Te Hodoki (10 forms), Idori Te Hodoki (10 forms), Idori (five forms), Tachiai Tainage (five forms), Tachiai Tantō Toriage (five forms), Tachiai Ken Toriage (five forms) and the Goshinjutsu Waza (19 techniques). Listed separately are the Shoden Ura no Waza (underlying basic principles) and the Shoden no Heihō (basic application strategies). The Shoden Buki no Maki comprises 29 kata. The kata are organized into four sets: Battō (four forms), Kenjutsu Kumitachi (10 forms), Tantōjutsu Kumitantō (10 forms), Battō Torikaeshi (five forms). Combined, these teachings represent the entire Takamua ha Shindō Yōshin Ryū Shoden Mokuroku.

An important aspect of the shoden level training is the subtlety demanded in the proper execution of the kata. The idea here is developing a high degree of sensitivity as the shoden level inculcates the technical skills required to minimize injuries during the more advanced levels of training. During the chūden and gokui levels of training, the risk of serious injuries increases due to the more aggressive and spontaneous application of force by the uchite (attacker).

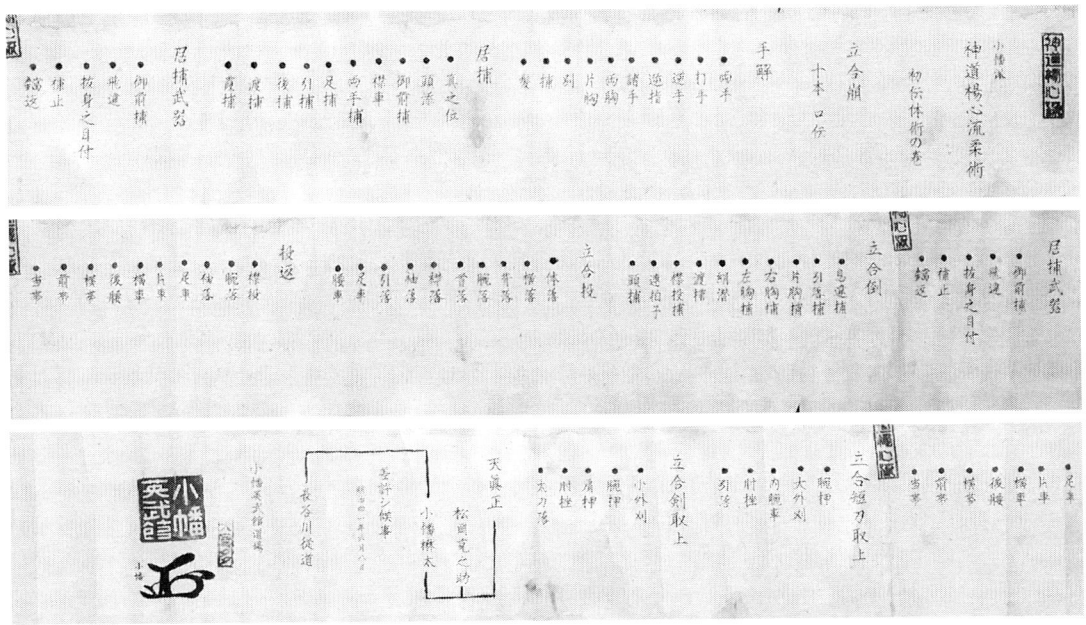

Obata ha Shindō Yōshin Ryū Shoden Taijustu no Maki issued by Obata Shigeta to Hasegawa Shigemichi on June 8th, 1908, at the Obata Eibukan Dōjō.
(Collection of the Takamura ha Shindō Yōshin Kai.)

Upon gaining a solid understanding of the studies listed on the Shoden Taijutsu no Maki and the Shoden Buki no Maki, a student is eligible to receive a Takamura ha Shindō Yōshin Ryū Shoden Kirigami teaching license.

The Chūden Taijutsu no Maki comprises 108 jūjutsu kata. The kata are organized in 12 sets: Idori (10 forms), Idori Buki (five forms), Idori Kogusoku (five forms), Tachiai Taoshi (15 forms), Tachiai Nage (19 forms), Nage Kaeshi (nine forms), Tachiai Kogusoku (five forms), Tachiai Tantō Toriage (five forms), Tachiai Ken Toriage (five forms), Tachiai Battō Toriage (10 forms) Kyūsho Atemi (10 forms) and Shime (10 forms). Listed separately are the Chūden Ura no

Waza (underlying intermediate principles) and the Chū-Okuden no Heihō (mid-level hidden teachings). The Chūden Buki no Maki comprises 66 kata. The kata are organized into four sets: Battō (six forms), Kenjutsu Kumitachi (35 forms), Hibuki (15 forms), and Battō Torikaeshi (10 forms). Combined, these teachings represent the entire Takamura ha Shindō Yōshin Ryū Chūden Mokuroku.

The chūden level teachings are the first time a student is introduced to a truly combative approach to training, as well as a more practical application of the school's combat principles. Chūden level training includes scenarios that address surprise attacks and multiple attackers. Both armed and unarmed situations are investigated and studied. As part of the Chūden Kenjutsu Kumitachi, special protective armor is worn. This training, identified as shinai geiko (training using a fukuro shinai) includes katchū kata (semi-freestyle forms) and shinai shiai (freestyle combat using fukuro shinai).

Upon internalizing the studies listed on the Chūden Taijutsu no Maki and the Chūden Buki no Maki, a student is eligible to receive a Takamura ha Shindō Yōshin Ryū Chūden Mokuroku teaching license.

The Jōden Gokui Jin no Maki (Scroll of Man) comprises 35 kata. The kata are organized in four sets: Battō (10 forms), Kenjutsu Kumitachi (15 forms), Ratai Dori (three forms), and Kappō (seven forms). Two additional sets of study are included on the Jin no Maki: Atemi (striking) and Myōden (mysterious teachings). Atemi includes the study of 72 vital points separated into three categories, while Myōden includes the study of advanced principles separated into two categories, physical and mental. This level of training introduces the student to kata that require merging high-level physical and mental dynamics into a unified expression of martial skills.

The Jōden Ten no Maki (Scroll of Heaven) comprises 16 kata included in two sets: Happō Shinden Nairiki no Gyō (eight forms) and Happō Shinden Misogi no Gyō (eight forms). Four other categories of study are included on the Jōden Ten no Maki. They are the Happō Shinden Heihō no Hisshō, Jū no Zen, Jū no Aku and Shintō Norito. The teachings included on the Jōden Ten no Maki integrate moral awareness, internal body training, methods of spiritual purification, and advanced strategies for defeating an adversary's malevolent mental and spiritual powers.

The subject of morality is of serious consideration during gokui level training and is particularly addressed on the Jōden Ten no Maki. Every practitioner at this level of training must understand the mental and physical powers gained through advanced level training require an acknowledgment of personal responsibility and self-sacrifice seldom demanded outside an endeavor such as koryū. A strict and benevolent moral code based on a Shintō ideal of service for the greater group must be cultivated. Personal considerations and desires of one's ego must not be allowed to dominate the benefit of the group.

The studies included on the two gokui densho, when combined, prepare an advanced student for the highest level of martial study. This level of study is included in the Jōden Okugi Chi no Maki (Scroll of Earth) and the Jōden Okugi Tengu Tobi no Maki (Flying Tengu Scroll). The okugi scrolls introduce 32 kata to the student, but the majority of the information identified on the okugi scrolls is kuden, orally-taught proprietary secrets. Consequently, the contents of these scrolls are naiden (internal teachings) and are not openly discussed outside the Takamura ha Shindō Yōshin Ryū membership.

Shindō Yoshin Ryū Curriculum (Main line)

(This Domonkai version of the Shindō Yōshin Ryū mokuroku, reflects the mainline (Matsuoka) curriculum as adjusted by Inose Motokichi in the early 20th century. Under Inose's leadership most of Matsuoka's original Buki no Mokuroku (weapons curriculum) was neglected. This decision to minimize weapons study was arrived at during a period when the popularity of Kōdōkan Jūdō was on the rise. The benefits of studying swordwork as a component of jūjutsu training was viewed as antiquated in a budō environment where competitive grappling was becoming a dominant aspect of training.

For those members who preferred to maintain Shindō Yōshin Ryū as a sōgō bujutsu, it was felt the study of Jikishinkage Ryū could replace the orginal Shindō Yōshin Ryū weapons curriculum as compiled by the art's founder, Matsoka Katsunosuke. Around 1905, a student of Inose Motokichi, Nakayama Tatsusabro started teaching Ono ha Ittō Ryū and Jikishinkage Ryū in his Genbukan Dōjō as adjunct study to the Shindō Yōshin Ryū Jūjutsu Mokuroku. Nakayama Tatsusaburō would go on to become Ōtsuka Hironori's, (founder of Wadō Ryū) Shindō Yōshin Ryū instructor.)

Kirigami Shoden (40)

Te Hodoki

Ryōte
Uchite
Gyaku Te
Gyaku Yubi
Morote

Ryōmune
Katamune
Wakare
Tori
Kami

Nage Kaeshi

Ude Otoshi
Sei Otoshi
Eri Otoshi
Sode Otoshi
Ashi Guruma

Koshi Guruma
Kata Guruma
Yoko Obi
Mae Obi
Ate Obi

Shoden Idori

Shin no Kurai
Soe Dori
Gozen Dori
Eri Guruma Dori
Tobi Chigai Dori

Nukimi no Metsuke Dori
Yoroi Gaeshi
Ryōte Dori
Heki Dori
Watari Dori

Shoden Tachiai

Iki Chigai Dori
Hiki Otoshi
Katamune Dori
Ryōte Dori
Ryōmune Dori

Kashu Dori
Kinukuguri
Eri Nage Dori
Te Kami Dori
Watari Dori

Shindō Yōshin Ryū Curriculum (Main line)

Chūden Mokuroku (28)

Chūden Idori

Shin no Kurai
Kanegi Dori
Hidare Mune Dori
Migi Mune Dori
Gozen Dori
Sode Guruma Dori
Tobi Chigai Dori

Nukimi no Metsuke Dori
Hosha Dori
Tsuka Dori
Mae Goshi Dori
Ryōte Dori
Migi Ate Dori
Hiki Tate

Chūden Tachiai

Iki Chigai Dori
Kanegi Dori
Migimune Dori
Koshi Tsuke Dori
Kogusoku Dori
Atama Dori
Ren Byōshi

Mune Ōbori Dori
Tsuka Dori
Kaeshi Nage
Koshi Guruma Dori
Ude Dori
Sutemi Dori
Daisho Dori

Jōden Menkyo (16/Kuden)

Gokui

Hassō
Ittō Ryōdan
Ryūbi (Left and Right)
Omokage (Left and Right)
Matsukaze
Hayafune
In no Kamae no Koto
Yō no Kamae no Koto

Soshin no Koto
Soshu no Koto
Gokui
Kito
Sotai
Kojō Gokui no Koto
Kiritsu no Sho
Jū Aku

Ratai Dori (3)

Mae Dori
Sayu Dori
Atemi (Kuden)

Kappō (Kuden)

Yu Kappō
Eri Kappō
San Kappō
Yon Kappō

Shindō Yōshin Ryū

Takamura ha Shindō Yōshin Ryū Curriculum

(This list represents the categories of study and number of kata in each category. It does not include the kata names, the betsuden waza, or the kata studied as part of the fuzoku bugei.)

Shoden Taijutsu **(60)**

    Tachiai Te Dori Kuzushi (10)

    Tachiai Tai Dori Kuzushi (10)

    Tachiai Te Hodoki (10)

    Idori Te Hodoki (10)

    Shoden Idori (5)

    Tachiai Tai Dori (5)

    Tachiai Tantō Toriage (5)

    Tachiai Ken Toriage (5)

Shoden Buki **(29)**

    Battō (4)

    Kenjutsu Kumitachi (10)

    Tantōjutsu Kumitantō (10)

    Battō Torikaeshi (5)

Chūden Taijutsu **(108)**

    Chūden Idori (10)

    Chūden Idori Buki (5)

    Chūden Idori Kogusoku (5)

    Tachiai Taoshi (15)

    Tachiai Tai Nage (19)

    Nage Kaeshi (9)

    Tachiai Kogusoku (5)

    Tachiai Tantō Toriage (5)

    Tachiai Ken Toriage (5)

    Tachiai Battō Toriage (10)

    Kyūsho Atemi (10)

    Shime (10)

Chūden Buki **(66)**

    Battō (6)

    Kenjutsu Kumitachi (35)

    Hibuki (15)

    Battō Torikaeshi (10)

Jōden Gokui Jin no Maki **(35)**

    Battō (10)

    Kenjutsu Kumitachi (15)

    Ratai Dori (3)

    Kappō (7)

Jōden Gokui Ten no Maki **(16)**

    Kuden

Jōden Okugi Chi no Maki **(32)**

    Kuden

Jōden Okugi Tengu Tobi no Maki **(Kuden)**

Menkyo Kaiden **(Kuden)**

History And Technique

Kenjutsu's Influence on Shindō Yōshin Ryū

Kashima Shinden Jikishinkage Ryū Kenjutsu

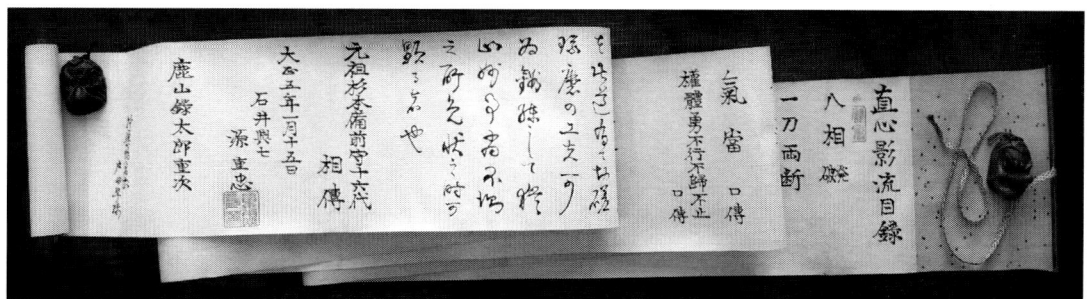

Jikishinkage Ryū kenjutsu Mokuroku, issued January 15th, 1916.
(Collection of the Takamura ha Shindō Yōshin Kai.)

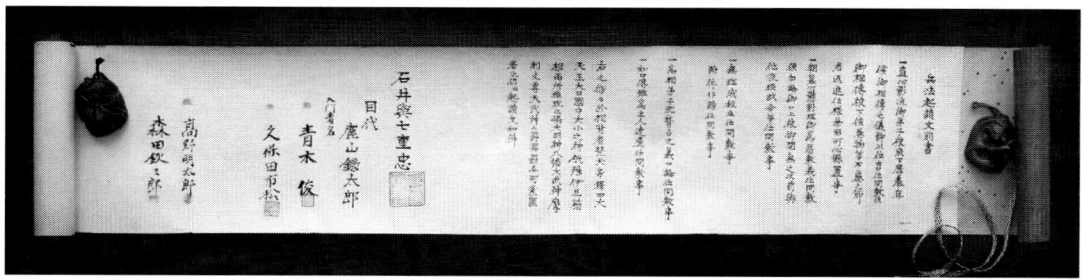

Jikishinkage Ryū kenjutsu Kirigami Kishōmon Maegaki.
(Collection of the Takamura ha Shindō Yōshin Kai.)

Kashima Shinden Jikishinkage Ryū is a descendent of the Shinkage Ryū line of kenjutsu founded by Kamiizumi Ise no Kami (1508-1577), which was descended from the Kashima Shinkage Ryū of Matsumoto Bizen no Kami (1467-1534). Jikishinkage Ryū was originally a sōgō bujutsu, which included the study of various combat systems including kenjutsu, sōjutsu, naginatajutsu, kusarigamajutsu, and yawara. The identity of the actual founder of Jikishinkage Ryū as a distinct branch of Shinkage Ryū is open to interpretation, but the name was first used by Yamada Heizaemon Ippūsai (1638-1716), a student who lived five generations after Kamiizumi Ise no Kami. According to Takamura, it was the Yamada Heizaemon Ippūsai lineage that most closely represented the two Shinkage Ryū lineage schools taught to his grandfather, Obata. The name Jikishinkage Ryū translates to "Proper or Correct-Mind Shadow School".

Matsuoka and Obata of Shindō Yōshin Ryū both trained in Jikishinkage Ryū under 14th-generation headmaster Sakakibara Kenkichi (1830-1894), a giant in the kenjutsu community during the Bakumatsu period, and a close associate of the Shōgun, Tokugawa Iemochi (1846-1866). Obata is said to have also trained in the Naganuma line but the extent of this training is unknown. Sakakibara and his teacher Odani Nobutomo were engaged to teach kenjutsu at the Bakufu Kōbusho in 1856. Notably, both Sakakibara and Matsuoka served as personal body guards to the Tokugawa Shōgun during the period leading up to the Meiji Restoration. According to Ryōzō Fujiwara, Matsuoka, the founder of Shindō Yōshin Ryū, functioned as the Jikishinkage Ryū honbuchō while Sakakibara was elsewhere protecting Tokugawa Iemochi. Following the Boshin Wars (1868-1869) and the fall of the Tokugawa Shogunate, Sakakibara promoted kenjutsu through a series of demonstrations called gekiken kōgyō, in which bamboo swords were used in shinai shiai (competition). These demonstrations proved very popular.

Shindō Yōshin Ryū

Sakakibara Kenkichi (1830-1894), 14th-generation headmaster of Kashima Shinden Jikishinkage Ryū. Shindō Yōshin Ryū founder, Matsuoka Katsunosuke, and Obata Shigeta both trained under Sakakibara Kenkichi.

Shindō Yōshin Ryū is significantly influenced by Kashima Shinden Jikishinkage Ryū. Like most schools descended from Shinkage Ryū, Jikishinkage Ryū is considered a positive (aggressive) school of swordsmanship, embracing a tactic called, "sen wo toru" (seizing initiative). A Jikishinkage Ryū practitioner strives to maintain an aggressive, intimidating pressure on an adversary, and aims to seize the initiative and control the outcome of an encounter.

In the grappling portion of the taijutsu syllabus of the Shindō Yōshin Ryū, the strategy of sen wo toru is supported through the application of advanced body dynamics that allow either subtle or aggressive execution within the same kata.

The application of constantly advancing physical and mental pressure is a foundational tactic in most Shindō Yōshin Ryū weapons kata. Such pressure manifests itself in four types of mental projections symbolized by the seasons. The intent of such unrelenting pressure is to totally overwhelm an adversary, forcing a withdrawal or the commission of a tactical error.

Hokushin Ittō Ryū Hyōhō

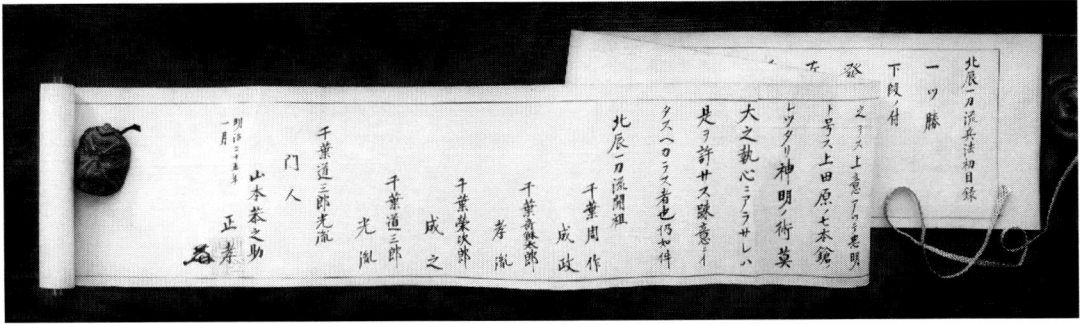

Hokushin Ittō Ryū Hatsu Mokuroku, issued 1892.
(Collection of the Takamura ha Shindō Yōshin Kai.)

Hokushin Ittō Ryū (Pole Star One Cut School) was founded by Chiba Shūsaku Narimasa (1783-1856) around 1820 and is derived from Hokushin Musō Ryū and Nakanishi ha Ittō Ryū. Matsuoka was training in the Tenjin Shinyō Ryū Kanda Otamagaike Dōjō of Iso Mataemon Masatomo during the 1850s. Notably, many Tenjin Shinyō Ryū jūjutsuka also trained in Hokushin Ittō Ryū because the Genbukan Dōjō of Chiba was located nearby.

The technical impact of Hokushin Ittō Ryū on the Shindō Yōshin Ryū of Matsuoka is relatively minimal and the Shindō Yōshin Ryū mokuroku do not indicate any significant influence. However, Chiba was a revolutionary in the realm of teaching pedagogy and adopted the notion of principle-based instruction early in his career. This type of instruction allowed the teaching concept of shu ha ri (See page 227) to realize its highest expression. Matsuoka is said to have based his own instructional methods on those of Chiba. Therefore, Hokushin Ittō Ryū directly influenced this aspect of Shindō Yōshin Ryū.

Katōda/Shin/Matsuzaki Shinkage Ryū Kenjutsu

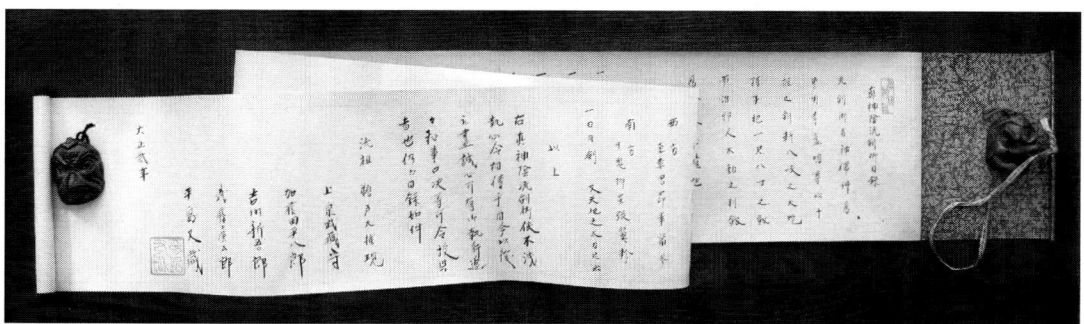

Shin Shinkage Ryū/Katōda Shinkage Ryū kenjutsu mokuroku, issued by Heijima Matazō in 1919.
(Collection of the Takamura ha Shindō Yōshin Kai.)

Katōda Shinkage Ryū, also called Shin Shinkage Ryū, descends mythologically from Udo Dai Gongen, the principle deity of Udo Shrine. The earthly reality is the school descends from Kamiizumi Ise no Kami Nobutsuna, through Okuyama Kyūgasai Kamishige (1526-1602) and then through Ogasawara Genshin Nagaharu (1574-1644). This is the same Shinkage Ryū line from which Kashima Shinden Jikishinkage Ryū originates. According to Takamura Yukiyoshi, the Okuyama line became significantly and technically divided between Kamiya Denshinsai Naomitsu (1582-1663) and Harigaya Sekiun (1592-1662), who were both students of Ogasawara. Legendary swordsmen Katōda Heihachiro and his student Matsuzaki Namishiro emerged through the Harigaya line, eventually leading their own branches of Shinkage Ryū. Consequently, both Matsuzaki Shinkage Ryū and Kashima Shinden Jikishinkage Ryū influenced the Takamura ha Shindō Yōshin Ryū, whereas the Matsuoka and Nakayama lines of Shindō Yōshin Ryū were almost solely influenced by Kashima Shinden Jikishinkage Ryū.

As taught to Namishirō by Ishikawa Gotō, the methods of Matsuzaki Shinkage Ryū body conditioning aimed to develop practitioners with maximal speed and precise targeting. Thus, seizing the initiative and precise targeting were preferential to the use of raw power. Traceable to Katōda Heihachiro, Matsuzaki Shinkage Ryū preferred the use of a tsuka (hilt) longer than commonly found in most other Shinkage Ryū descended schools of kenjutsu. This preference

Right: Kenjutsu instructors gathering for the first Butokukai Kyōto Taikai in 1895. The newly-formed Butokukai sought to preserve the martial traditions of Japan in an era when such traditions were waning in popularity. Fifth from the right, front row is Matsuzaki Namishirō (white beard), founder of Matsuzaki Shinkage Ryū. Matsuzaki was one of only 15 swordsmen in the first Kyōto Taikai issued "Butokukai Seirenshō", a certificate recognizing them as master level instructors.

allows for more precise control of the kissaki (tip) and the ability to apply a rapid parrying deflection with the mune (back edge) of a blade. The principle of forward pressure is consistent with most Shinkage Ryū descended kenjutsu schools. In Matsuzaki Shinkage Ryū this principle is called tō no mae (sword forward).

According to Ishikawa Gotō, Matsuzaki included a system of battō/iaijutsu in his teachings originating in Taisha Ryū. Some of these kata are included in the Takamura ha Shindō Yōshin Ryū mokuroku. These teachings were apparently passed via a licensed student of Marume Kurandonosuke Tessai (1540-1629) in Kyūshū named Okuyama and eventually to Matsuzaki. Another comprehensive set of kata listed in the Jōden Okugi Chi no Maki (Earth Scroll of Higher Level Secrets) is identified as Nitō Awase (Two Swords in Harmony). The Matsuzaki Shinkage Ryū mokuroku contains identical terminology, therefore Matsuzaki Shinkage Ryū is assumed to be the origin of the Takamura ha Shindō Yōshin Ryū Nitō Awase curriculum.

Anyone familiar with Shinkage Ryū who can evaluate the greater curriculum of Takamura ha Shindō Yōshin Ryū would quickly recognize the imprint on the system by the weapon arts descended from Kamiizumi Ise no Kami. This influence is perhaps even more obvious in the Obata/Takamura line of Shindō Yōshin Ryū, due to its comprehensive curriculum sourced from both Matsuzaki Shinkage Ryū and Jikishinkage Ryū. A formless projection of physical force and mental intent, characteristics fundamental in Shindō Yōshin Ryū, are tactics that were conceived and refined through centuries of application in combat, and reflect a strategic mindset called marobashi which originated in the Shinkage Ryū lineages of swordsmanship.

Akiyama Yōshin Ryū Iaitachijutsu/Kenjutsu

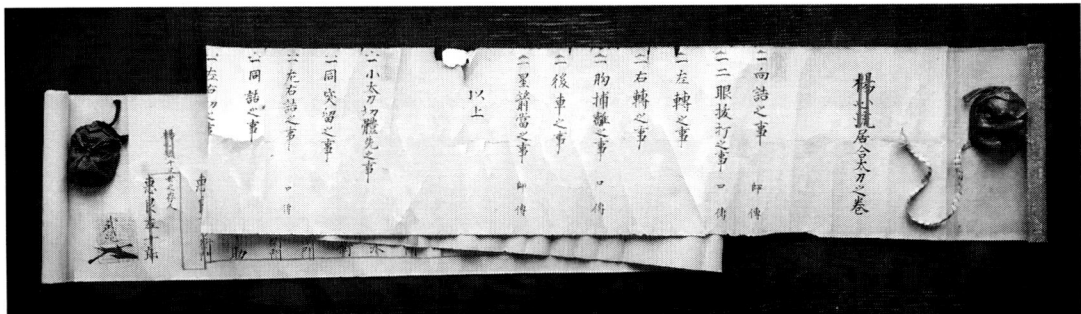

Yōshin Ryū, Iaitachijutsu no Mokuroku, issued 1868.
(Collection of the Takamura ha Shindō Yōshin Kai.)

As discussed previously, many origination theories surround the foundation of Akiyama Yōshin Ryū. The most widely accepted is Akiyama Shirōbei Yoshitoki established the school around 1651 in the port city of Nagasaki. Akiyama conceived this art as a sōgō bujutsu dominated by the study of heifuku kumiuchi (unarmored) combat, although the art does include some training in katchū kumiuichi (armored) combat. Akiyama Yōshin Ryū originally included iaitachijutsu and kenjutsu within its curriculum, but these sword-based arts are no longer extant as distinct areas of study. The only schools that seem to maintain any of these teachings are Yōshin Ryū Naginatajutsu, and to a lesser extent, Takamura ha Shindō Yōshin Ryū jūjutsu. Evidence possessed by the Takamura ha Shindō Yōshin Ryū confirms the study of weapons taught within Akiyama Yōshin Ryū influenced Obata when he created his line of Shindō Yōshin Ryū. However, the boundaries of such influence are difficult to determine given the powerful influences from the Shinkage Ryū kenjutsu schools.

History And Technique

Shibuharu, Shigeta's father, was licensed in Akiyama Yōshin Ryū and enrolled Shigeta in Miura Yōshin Ryū taijustsu and Akiyama Yōshin Ryū kenjutsu/iaitachijutsu around 1875. The instructor of these arts was a family relative named Hoshino Rikisen, who managed a dōjō in Ōtsu, Shiga Prefecture. Documents held by Takamura ha Shindō Yōshin Ryū indicate Hoshino made little distinction between these two arts as both were simply referred to as Yōshin Ryū. Shigeta received a Yōshin Ryū menkyo from Hoshino and was an assistant instructor in the Hoshino Dōjō by the age of 18. Hoshino Rikisen passed away in 1883. Thereafter, Shigeta traveled to Tōkyō to study under the renowned jūjutsu instructor, Totsuka Hideyoshi.

Owing to its creation by a physician, Akiyama Yōshin Ryū combat theory is based upon a comprehensive understanding of anatomy, muscular dynamics and body articulation. Takamura described the nature of engagement espoused by Yōshin Ryū kenjutsu as neutral, unlike the positive tactics of Shinkage Ryū. By embracing a highly-refined form of go-no-sen (reactive initiative), Akiyama Yōshin Ryū swordsmen were considered superior bodyguards who would not provoke hostility. The technical execution of Akiyama Yōshin Ryū kenjutsu was reportedly fluid and subtle, as well as rapid and effortless, due to smooth, masterful footwork. The mental dynamics of Akiyama Yōshin Ryū were similar, reflecting flexibility through the embrace of a highly-refined expression of reactive initiative. Adepts of Akiyama Yōshin Ryū could effortlessly and lethally adapt to any circumstance, such as evading a cut while delivering a cut. Successful Akiyama Yōshin Ryū swordsmen thus mastered mushin, a state of mind reflecting a potent mental discipline that allows intuitive flow through combat unhindered by conscious thought or fear.

The direct influence of Yōshin Ryū weapons study can be identified in the Takamura Shindō Yōshin Ryū mokuroku. Several battō kata and kumitachi kata listed in the Shindō Yōshin Ryū Chūden Buki no Maki and the Jōden Okugi Chi no Maki imply considerable influence from Akiyama Yōshin Ryū. Other kata are directly sourced from the teachings of Akiyama. The curriculum of Obata ha Shindō Yōshin Ryū originally included several Yōshin Ryū naginata kata. However, these kata have been lost and are no longer taught as part of Takamura ha Shindō Yōshin Ryū.

Takamura ha Shindō Yōshin Ryū instructor, Kathryn Douglass, manifesting the mental state of mushin (no mind). In a state of mushin, the adept practitioner experiences hyper-awareness, devoid of consciousness or ego. There is no fear or desire for victory. The disciplined and trained mind, intuitive and engaged, takes control.

Although the neutral mental/psychological aspects of Akiyama Yōshin Ryū combat tactics are essential teachings of the school, they do not play the dominant role. Both Matsuoka Katsunosuke and Obata Shigeta preferred the more aggressive positive mental dynamics associated with the Shinkage Ryū schools of kenjutsu.

Shindō Yōshin Ryū

The Takamura ha Shindō Yōshin Ryū Mokuroku

The following section of this book represents a limited portion of the Takamura ha Shindō Yōshin Ryū mokuroku (catalog of techniques). It should be viewed as general reference only. Represented in the photographs are orthodox examples of the Takamura ha Shindō Yōshin Ryū omote kata, omote waza, as well as henka (variations) and embu (demonstration) versions. Some techniques are also represented in an incomplete manner with vital details altered or omitted. This is done as a precaution against the unscrupulous misrepresentation of the school's lineage and teachings. In the past, individuals without access to authorized instruction and/or teaching certification have attempted to fraudulently represent koryū schools and their legacy by mimicking publicly-available photos. An art as intricate and technically-nuanced as Takamura ha Shindō Yōshin Ryū cannot be learned by way of mere visual reference. Only by way of hands-on instruction from a licensed instructor can an art like Takamura ha Shindō Yōshin Ryū be properly studied, internalized and finally mastered.

History And Technique

Te Hodoki

手解

The Shindō Yōshin Ryū Te Hodoki kata are forms where an adversary's grab is used against him to gain tactical superiority. Along with the kuzushi no kata, the te hodoki are considered foundational for the taijutsu curriculum, embodying the most important basic principles of Shindō Yōshin Ryū. When properly internalized and mastered, the concepts of jūnan na shin-tai (maintaining a flexible body) and chūshin wo tadasu (maintaining proper body structure) can be employed. These skills allow the practitioner of Shindō Yōshin Ryū to be tranquil in body and mind, able to respond without hesitation to any threat, freely and intuitively.

Ryōte

Idori Te Hodoki

The kata begins with uchite (attacker) and shite (defender) facing one another in heiza (seated) torima (grasping distance).

1

Uchite shifts upward into kiza (seated position on the balls of the feet), while firmly securing shite's wrists.

2

Shite rotates her right hand around uchite's forearm in a forward clockwise spiraling motion until her own palm is face up.

3

居捕手解 両手

Shite next drives her right elbow forward under uchite's arm compromising the strength of uchite's grip.

4

Shite now pushes her right hand forward and across her seichusen (centerline) with her palm facing her cheek. This results in a te hokodi (hand release).

5

Shite executes a tegatana ate (hand sword strike) with her right hand to uchite's jaw, while driving her left elbow backwards. This has the effect of drawing uchite's body forward into the strike.

6

Shindō Yōshin Ryū

Uchite

Idori Te Hodoki

The kata begins with uchite and shite facing one another in heiza torima.

1

In an example of sen sen no sen (preemptive attack), shite acts by executing a right tegatana ate to the face of uchite.

2

Uchite responds by blocking with his right hand and aligning his body structure to intercept the strike.

3

居捕手解　　　　　　　　　　　打手

History And Technique

Shite tightens his body core drawing power up through his structure and into uchite, compromising his posture. This destroys uchite's ability to resist the effects of the strike.

4

Shite grasps uchite's wrist and continues pressing into uchite's body, achieving kuzushi (off-balancing) and toppling him to the right.

5

With uchite's body structure totally compromised, shite pins uchite's wrist to the tatami.

6

Shindō Yōshin Ryū

Morote

Idori Te Hodoki

The kata begins with uchite and shite facing one another in heiza torima.

1

Uchite shifts up and forward into kiza grasping shite's right arm with both hands, left hand on shite's elbow and right hand on shite's wrist.

2

Uchite shifts back trying to draw shite forward into kuzushi so an elbow control can be applied. Simultaneously, shite rotates her forearm clockwise while executing a hokote ate (spear hand) to uchite's abdomen. Uchite suddenly tenses her arms to resist the threat.

3

居捕手解　　　　　　　　　　　諸手

History And Technique

Shite, taking advantage of uchite's tension, thrusts her elbow backwards drawing uchite forward. Shite next reaches forward with her left hand to block uchite's attempt to step forward with her right leg.

4

Shite shifts her body forward driving uchite into left kuzushi.

5

Shite twists clockwise causing uchite to fall to her left.

6

Shindō Yōshin Ryū

Ryōmune

Idori Te Hodoki

The kata begins with uchite and shite facing one another in heiza torima.

1

Uchite shifts up and forward into kiza grasping shite in ryōmune (both lapels), right hand on top.

2

As uchite tries to drive shite backwards, shite extends his right arm over and across uchite's left elbow in the direction of uchite's right hip. This intercepts uchite's attack by twisting his body and compromising his structure.

3

居捕手解   両胸

History And Technique

Shite grasps uchite's right lapel with his left hand and slides his grip up to the collar behind uchite's neck.

4

Maintaining a strong connection to uchite, shite drives his body up and forward, forcing uchite back onto his toes.

5

Shite rotates clockwise by raising his right knee. Uchite, unable to resist, falls to his left. Shite applies a kyūsho ate (vital point strike) to the neck of uchite with his left hand.

6

Shindō Yōshin Ryū

Kami / Tamusa

Idori Te Hodoki

The kata begins with uchite and shite facing one another in heiza torima.

1

Uchite steps forward with her right leg and attempts to bear hug shite. Shite responds by stepping to the right with her right leg and extending her left arm, little finger up, under uchite's left armpit.

2

Shite rotates her left arm, palm up.

3

居捕手解　　　　　　　　　　　　　髪

History And Technique

4

Shite next twists her body counter-clockwise, rotating her hips. Simultaneously, she draws uchite's elbow into the space between them with her left hand. This rotates uchite, clockwise allowing shite to secure uchite's hair with her right hand.

5

Shite twists back to the right while extending her right arm. This drives uchite's head to the rear compromising her body structure.

6

Shite drops her right arm to the tatami outside her right leg, allowing uchite to fall backwards with shite's shin across uchite's shoulder. Shite finishes the kata by executing uraken ate (backfist) to a kyusho point on uchite.

Shindō Yōshin Ryū

Age Nuki

Tachiai Te Hodoki

The kata begins with uchite and shite facing one another in gyaku-hanmi shinkiritsu torima (open, upright stance, grasping distance).

1

Uchite steps forward and seizes shite's right wrist with his left hand in an attempt to restrain his arm.

2

Shite bends his knees, pulling his body forward and down as he places his fist below uchite's wrist. Shite simultaneously feeds his elbow forward until his forearm is vertical, compromising uchite's grip.

3

History And Technique

立合手解　　　　　　　　　　　　　　　　　　上抜

Shite then drives his body up with his legs, breaking uchite's grip.

4

Shite rotates his fist clockwise to tateken (vertical fist) position.

5

Shite executes tateken ate to uchite's jaw.

6

Shindō Yōshin Ryū

Sode Nuki

Tachiai Te Hodoki

The kata begins with uchite and shite facing one another in gyaku-hanmi shinkiritsu torima.

1

Uchite steps forward and seizes shite's right wrist with his left hand in an attempt to restrain his arm.

2

Shite bends his knees, pulling his body his forward and down. He simultaneously feeds his elbow forward until his forearm is vertical. The outside edge of the hand is facing uchite during this motion.

3

History And Technique

立合手解　　　　　　　　　　　　　　　　袖抜

As shite's elbow continues moving forward, uchite's wrist flexion is compromised resulting in rearward kuzushi.

4

With uchite's wrist locked, shite continues the pressure on the wrist by pulling his body forward with his front leg. Uchite's structure becomes totally compromised.

5

Unable to release the pressure on his wrist, uchite is driven away from shite.

6

Shindō Yōshin Ryū

Te Gaeshi

Tachiai Te Hodoki

The kata begins with uchite and shite facing one another in gyaku-hanmi shinkiritsu torima.

1

Uchite steps forward and seizes shite's right wrist with his right hand in an attempt to restrain his arm.

2

Shite lowers his elbow rotating vertical axis created by uchite's grip.

3

立合手解　　　　　　　　　　　　　　　　　　　　手返

Shite continues rotating his forearm and slightly lowers his body, which finally releases uchite's grip on shite's forearm. Shite's forearm should be aligned and in contact with the back of uchite's hand.

4

Shite extends his arm bending uchite's wrist and folding his palm backwards and outside his own forearm.

5

With shite's arm fully extended and applying pressure to the back of uchite's hand, the wrist eventually locks. Continued pressure on the wrist joint compromises uchite's body structure gaining kuzushi.

6

Shindō Yōshin Ryū

Ude Kujiki

Tachiai Te Hodoki

The kata begins with uchite and shite facing one another in gyaku-hanmi shinkiritsu torima.

1

Uchite steps forward and seizes shite's right wrist with his left hand in an attempt to restrain his arm.

2

Shite reaches across with his left hand placing it on the back side of uchite's left elbow.

3

History And Technique

立合手解　　　　　　　　　　　　　　　　腕挫

4

With both arms, shite feeds uchite's arm up and into the rear of the shoulder socket.

5

Shite slightly rotates his body in a counter-clockwise arc in a manner that feeds uchite's shoulder forward achieving an evenly-weighted forward kuzushi.

6

When shite feels uchite's weight shift onto his right wrist, shite drops slightly by bending both knees abruptly allowing uchite to fall forward.

Note: Shite should never pull on uchite's left elbow with his left hand.

Shindō Yōshin Ryū

Ushiro Kubishimi

Tachiai Te Hodoki

The kata begins with uchite and shite facing the same direction, uchite behind shite in shinkiritsu torima.

1

Uchite seizes shite's neck attempting to apply ushiro kubishime (rear neck choke).

2

As uchite tightens the choke, shite raises his right shoulder tightly trapping uchite's right hand.

3

立合手解 後首締

Shite cross-steps laterally backwards with his left leg, rotating counterclockwise while drawing his right hand into striking position.

4

Shite pivots on the balls of his feet, rotating counterclockwise while maintaining an uchiude garami (inside arm coil lock) on uchite.

5

Shite executes a tateken ate to uchite's suigetsu (xiphoid process).

6

On Kata

"The kata given to me by my ancestors represents theory, not real fighting. The kata were created by the theory only. Because many people misunderstand kata, they believe kata are useless, but I don't think so. Properly understood, kata leads us to another world." - Kuroda Tetsuzan, Soke, Kuroda Ryūgi

In most koryū, prearranged combative forms executed between partners constitute the primary teaching methodology. These forms are called kata (形). Kata first appeared in the Kamakura period (1185-1333) and were created by warriors who instructed their colleagues on the most successful tactics and lessons they acquired in battle. As kata evolved, they started to represent layers of knowledge beyond those of physical combat. Mind and body unification, as well as the effects of psycho-chemical stress were addressed. By the early Edo period, kata training influenced by the previous centuries of prolonged warfare represented a sophisticated level of internalized combat knowledge that included highly-polished cognitive responses and combative intuition.

Generally, kata function as a vessel that contain the riai, or underlying principles at the heart of effective combat. Most often, the movements in a kata are not intended to replicate real fighting but instead constitute an idealized version of conflict embodying multiple layers of knowledge ensconced in predetermined movements. Kata were conceived to be a teaching tool that accentuated specific aspects of conflict so these aspects could be evaluated, internalized and then refined. These aspects include body dynamics, timing, distance, initiative, tactics, strategy, cognition, mindset and intuitive responses.

In Shindō Yōshin Ryū, kata are divided into these three categories:

Omote (理合/Riai-Theory)

Omote kata function as the orthodox teaching form. The skills and principles taught in an omote kata are foundational, and are purposely structured to complement other skills and principles taught in other kata which are part of a larger but related area of study and training. In every dimension, the omote kata are strictly adhered to with little variation tolerated, as any variation risks altering the foundational wisdom and riai embedded in the forms.

Ura (解説/Kaisetsu-Explanation)

Ura kata operate on the principle of kaisetsu, frequently reflecting deeper and more sophisticated investigation of the principles embedded in the omote kata. In Shindō Yōshin Ryū, the ura kata can be executed in a less structured and more spontaneous manner, which encourages the development of combat flexibility and the refinement of intuitive combat skills. Ura kata should not be taught until the omote version of a kata is thoroughly internalized.

Henka (発展/Hatten-Development)

Henka kata are a variation created by an individual practitioner based on a specific omote kata. These kata represent the application of specific combat principles influenced by the strengths and limitations of the individual practitioner. For instance, a person of much smaller stature may need to investigate and internalize various adjustments required when engaging a stronger or larger adversary. Henka represent an enlightened evolution of kata and should only be developed after the omote and ura versions of a kata are thoroughly internalized.

History And Technique

Tachiai Kuzushi

立合崩

The Shindō Yōshin Ryū kuzushi no kata are forms where an adversary's strike or grab is used to physically off-balance him. They are separated into two sets, 10 executed by manipulating the arms (手取: tedori) and 10 while manipulating the entire body structure (体取: taidori). Even though they are part of the shoden curriculum, they were considered secret teachings at the time of the school's founding. The principle of off-balancing an opponent before executing a throw was not something commonly taught in most of the koryū jūjutsu schools. Prior to the emergence of the Akiyama Yōshin Ryū and Kitō Ryū, kuzushi was rarely utilized, but it became a subject of intense study by Kanō Jigorō, the founder of Kōdōkan Jūdō.

Shindō Yōshin Ryū

Ude Osae

Tachiai Kuzushi/Te Dori

The kata begins with uchite and shite facing one another in aihanmi shinkiritsu torima (closed, upright stance, grasping distance).

1

Uchite and shite raise their arms into awase (crossed wrists).

2

As uchite attempts tegatana ate to shite's face with his right hand, shite intercepts the strike with his right hand, deflecting the strike towards uchite's fuantehō (weak line).

3

立合崩／手取 腕押

4

Shite continues applying pressure to uchite's attacking arm by using his left hand on the elbow to further deflect uchite's attack towards his fuantehō.

5

Shite extends his arms while opening his hips clockwise by stepping to the right with his front foot. This continues driving uchite further off balance.

6

Kuzushi achieved, shitachi releases uchite and they both return to awase.

Shindō Yōshin Ryū

Kubi Osae/Oshi

Tachiai Kuzushi/Te Dori

The kata begins with uchite and shite facing one another in aihanmi shinkiritsu torima.

1

Uchite and shite raise their arms crossing wrists into awase.

2

As uchite attempts tegatana ate to shite's face with his right hand, shite intercepts the strike with a cross capture, right hand over left, deflecting it to uchite's fuantehō while stepping diagonally forward with his right foot.

3

立合崩/手取　　　　　　　　　　　　　　　　首押

4

Shite uncrosses his wrists as he shifts his body into uchite's fuantehō. Simultaneously, shite parries uchite's right hand with his left hand, while placing his right palm on the lower part of uchite's throat.

5

Shite pulls his body forward with his front leg and then drops vertically, achieving rearward kuzushi on uchite.

6

Kuzushi achieved, shitachi releases uchite and they both return to awase.

Shindō Yōshin Ryū

Atama Osae

Tachiai Kuzushi/Te Dori

The kata begins with uchite and shite facing one another in aihanmi shinkiritsu torima.

1

Uchite and shite raise their arms crossing wrists into awase.

2

As uchite attempts tegatana ate to shite's face with his right hand, shite covers with his right hand and disengages stepping in and to his left, simultaneously blinding uchite by placing his palm over uchite's eyes.

3

立合崩/手取　　　　　　　　　　　　頭押

History And Technique

4

Shite next pulls his body forward with his front leg while lifting and then tipping uchite's head rearward.

5

Shite rotates clockwise behind uchite while placing the back of his left wrist into uchite's lower back gaining kuzushi.

6

Kuzushi achieved, shite releases uchite who spins clockwise and they both return to awase.

Shindō Yōshin Ryū

Mae Kata Osae

Tachiai Kuzushi/Te Dori

The kata begins with uchite and shite facing one another in gyaku-hanmi shinkiritsu torima.

1

Uchite and shite raise their arms crossing wrists into awase.

2

As uchite attempts tegatana ate to shite's face with his right hand, shite covers his entry with his right hand and disengages, stepping in and to his left. Continuing to cover uchite's right hand with his left, shite rotates clockwise sliding his left arm over uchite's right arm.

3

History And Technique

立合崩/手取　　　　前肩押

4

Shite slides his left arm farther forward placing his left elbow over uchite's seichusen.

5

Shite drops his body by abruptly bending both knees, gaining kuzushi and driving uchite to the rear.

6

Kuzushi achieved, shite releases uchite and they both return to awase.

Shindō Yōshin Ryū

Hiji Otoshi

Tachiai Kuzushi/Te Dori

The kata begins with uchite and shite facing one another in aihanmi shinkiritsu torima.

1

Uchite and shite raise their arms crossing wrists into awase.

2

As uchite attempts tegatana ate to shite's face with his right hand, shite intercepts the strike deflecting it to uchite's fuantehō. Shite next intercepts uchite's attacking arm at the elbow.

3

立合崩/手取　　　　　　　　　　　　肘落

Shite first extends his right arm and then pulls his body forward with his right leg.

4

As uchite's balance shifts rearward, shite drops vertically by bending both knees, driving uchite back into kuzushi.

5

Kuzushi achieved, shite releases uchite and they both return to awase.

6

Sōdansha - Kai Advisors

The Takamura ha Shindō Yōshin Kai has had the benefit of a first-class membership from the time it was founded. As an organization created to preserve the arts of Shindō Yōshin Ryū jūjutsu and Takagi Hachihō Ryū bōjutsu, its members have not only devoted enormous resources to this task, but have also become valued resources themselves. When an instructor possessing unique capabilities chooses to retire from teaching he may be asked to function as a Sōdansha (internal advisor) to the Takamura ha Shindō Yōshin Ryū Honbu Dōjō.

David Maynard

David Maynard holds a Menkyo Kaiden in Takamura ha Shindō Yōshin Ryū and is the student who trained with Takamura Yukiyoshi the longest. David started his budō journey in 1966 at the San Francisco Jūdō Institute under Mitsuho (Mits) Kimura. Curious about jūjutsu as the progenitor art of jūdō, he was introduced to Takamura Yukiyoshi in 1967 and soon realized the jūjutsu Takamura Sensei taught was very different from the sport jūdō he had been studying and asked permission to become a formal student. He trained in Takamura ha Shindō Yōshin Ryū for 37 years, and after Takamura Sensei passed away in 2000, was designated as the senior instructor of the Takamura ha Shindō Yōshin Kai.

Serious injuries suffered in an automobile accident in 2003 forced him to retire from active teaching and today he is the senior advisor to the TSYR Honbu Dōjō, with historical, curricular and administrative responsibilities.

Karl Garrison

Karl Garrison holds a Chūden Mokuroku in Takamura ha Shindō Yōshin Ryū and maintains the rank of fourth dan in Kōdōkan Jūdō. He started his martial arts journey in 1966, when he took up boxing while in the U.S. Marine Corps. After being introduced to jūdō, he recognized his natural aptitude for grappling and devoted himself to pursuing this new Olympic sport and trained in jūdō in Europe and Japan during the 1960s and 1970s.

He first met Takamura Yukiyoshi in Hayward, CA in 1968 and joined Takamura ha Shindō Yōshin Ryū jūjutsu as an official deshi in 1971, quickly distinguished himself, becoming one the organization's top instructors.

Now a licensed physical therapist, he donates his time helping military veterans through various charitable organizations. He continues to serve Takamura ha Shindō Yōshin Ryū as a respected advisor on body conditioning, recuperative health and as a valuable counsel on administrative affairs to the honbu dōjō.

History And Technique

Idori

居捕

The Shindō Yōshin Ryū Idori kata are forms where both the shite and uchite are kneeling. Thirty of the kata are performed from heiza no kamae while five are performed from hira no kamae. Many of these kata assume a politically-hostile environment where negotiations between adversaries are in progress. Consequently they represent both assassination attempts and assassination interventions. These kata are multi-layered studies in appearance, psychology and sophisticated body dynamics, which reflect the depth of both the technical and tactical study included in the Shindō Yōshin Ryū mokuroku.

Shindō Yōshin Ryū

Eri Guruma/Kinsha Dori

Idori

1

The kata starts in heiza kōshōma (negotiation distance) equaling a full tatami apart. In this kata it is assumed that uchite has threatened shite resulting in a physical response.

2

Shite pivots left, lifts his left knee and prepares to stand.

3

Shite starts to walk past uchite's right side.

4

When torima is reached, shite uses his right hand to distract uchite to his left.

5

This distraction allows shite to secure uchite's left collar with his left hand, placing his forearm across uchite's throat.

6

Shite cross-steps right leg in front of left and seizes uchite's upper left sleeve with his right hand, passing it across the back of uchite's neck.

History And Technique

居捕 襟車/襟捨

7

Shite then steps directly behind uchite with an eri guruma (collar wheel) secured.

8

Shite uses his leg strength to lift and drop uchite to the rear while stepping back and kneeling on his left knee.

9

Shite allows uchite to fall deeply on his back while maintaining the eri guruma.

10

Shite then drives uchite forward and places his right knee against uchite's spine while tightening the choke. Uchite attempts to strike rearwards at shite but his head is placed low on uchite's spine, out of range.

(*Note:* The choke executed during this kata is quite dangerous and can damage or collapse the trachea. Open communication between uchite and shite should be maintained at all times.)

11

Uchite claps his hands together loudly to signal submission and the end of the kata.

Shindō Yōshin Ryū

Gozen Dori

Idori

1

This kata starts with uchite and shite side by side seated in heiza.

2

Shite, perceiving an impending threat, employes sen sen no sen and seizes the initiative by grasping and securing uchite's right wrist.

3

Shite steps in front of uchite placing his right shin in front of uchite's seichusen. Simultaneously, he grasps uchite's left hand and presses his left elbow into uchite's sternum.

4

Shite rises and cross-steps with his left leg in front of his right. Simultaneously, he applies tekubigiri (wrist cut lock) to uchite's left wrist and pivots counter-clockwise.

5

Shite finishes his pivot facing uchite with his right leg back and uchite's left arm controlled.

6

Shite executes a powerful maegiri (front kick) to uchite's lower left ribs.

History And Technique

居捕 　　　　　　　　　　　　　　　　　　　　御前捕

7

Shite pivots counter-clockwise maintaining tekubi kiri and a hiji kujiki (elbow strain lock). Simultaneously, he brings his feet together and aligns his body structure.

8

Shite drops his body structure abruptly and steps forward with his left leg, driving uchite forward into his fuantehō.

9

Shite kneels forward on his left knee just outside uchite's wrist while pinning his elbow to the tatami (mat). He maintains the hiji kujiki and the tekubi kujiki.

10

Shite pivots right, stretches his right leg back and then executes a maegiri to uchite's ribs.

11

Shite shifts his weight forward applying increasing pressure to the tekubi kujiki. Uchite taps the tatami to indicate submission.

Shindō Yōshin Ryū

Ashi Dori

Idori

1

The kata begins with uchite and shite facing one another in heiza torima.

2

Uchite steps in with his right leg and seizes shite's wrists, restraining him.

3

Shite drops his right shoulder and raises his right hand up uchite's seichusen, placing his palm on uchite's throat.

4

Shite pivots slightly clockwise and seizes uchite's right ankle just above the foot while maintaining pressure on uchite's throat achieving kuzushi.

5

Shite reverses direction, pivoting counter-clockwise and abruptly dropping his right palm while simultaneously sweeping uchite's foot forward.

6

Shite continues applying pressure to uchite's throat resulting in his fall to the rear.

History And Technique

居捕　　　　　　　　　　　　　　　　　　　　足捕

7

Shite places his hand right hand behind uchite's right knee.

8

Shite then pushes the knee up towards the hip and then across to the right, pinning it to the tatami.

9

Shite folds uchite's left lower leg up and across his right thigh.

10

Shite next folds the right lower leg over the left, crossing uchite's ankles. Next, he slides his right knee forward, pinning the crossed ankles together.

11

Shite finally grabs uchite's collar with his right hand pulling up powerfully before executing a strike to uchite's spine.

Shindō Yōshin Ryū

Zu Soe

Idori

1

The kata begins with uchite and shite facing one another in heiza torima.

2

Uchite steps forward deeply attempting a mae jujijime (front crossed-arm choke).

3

The instant uchite seizes shite's collar, but before he can apply the choke, shite tightens his body core and begins pulling his body forward.

4

As shite rises by continuing to pull forward with his legs, he cuts in and forward into uchite's right elbow with a left tegatana.

5

Immediately following the attack on uchite's right elbow, shite executes a nakadaka ate (middle knuckle strike) to uchite's suigetsu.

6

Shite releases uchite's elbow and slides his left arm under uchite's right arm. Shite seizes uchite's chin with his left hand and his head with the right hand in a twisting motion.

History And Technique

居捕　　　　　　　　　　　　　　　　　　　　頭添

7

Shite pivots clockwise and continues feeding uchite's body structure in a downward spiral.

8

As uchite finally up-ends, shite secures uchite's right hand preventing him from releasing shite's lapel.

9

Uchite falls with shite's knee pressing into his body between his neck and shoulder.

10

Shite presses harder into uchite with his knee and raises his right hand in preparation for an atemi.

11

Shite executes an uraken ate to uchite's kasumi (temple), finishing the kata.

Shindō Yōshin Ryū

Kasumi Dori

Idori

1

The kata begins with uchite and shite facing one another in heiza torima.

2

As uchite steps forward with his right leg and attempts a strike with his right fist. Simultaneously, shite also steps right and deflects the attempted strike.

3

Shite follows by immediately striking uchite's kasumi with a tegatana ate.

4

Shite next switches hands, striking uchite's suigetsu with a tateken ate while covering uchite's right hand with his left palm.

5

Shite stands and spirals his right arm around uchite's right arm, deflecting him towards his fuantehō.

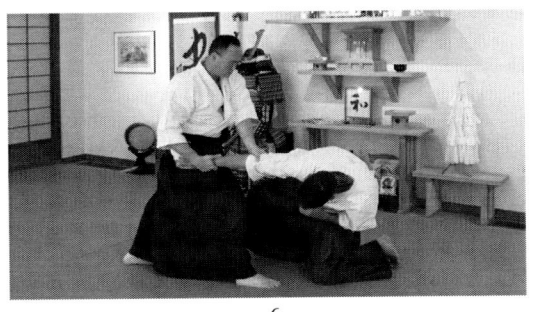

6

Shite secures uchite's left arm and applies a hiji kujiki for control.

History And Technique

居捕   霞捕

7

Shite pivots left and steps forward driving uchite's arm further towards his fuantehō and achieving kuzushi.

8

Increasing pressure on uchite's elbow drives his body to the tatami.

9

Shite pins uchite's elbow to the mat with his left hand and then pivots left bending uchite's arm at the elbow, 90 degrees.

10

Shite switches his feet in place pinning the forearm to the tatami

11

Shite stands, rocks uchite's forearm forward locking the elbow and draws his tantō securing him.

Shindō Yōshin Ryū

Hiki Dori

Idori

1

The kata begins with uchite and shite facing one another in heiza torima.

2

Uchite steps in with his right leg and seizes shite's wrists, restraining him.

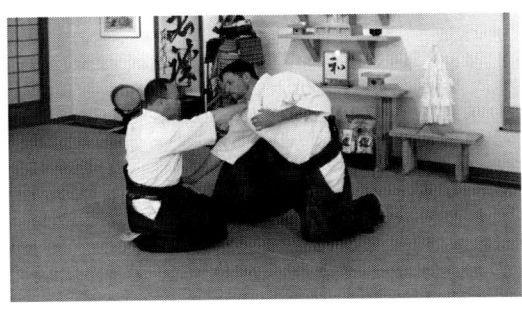

3

Shite executes an age nuki (rising escape) te hodoki with his right hand and grabs uchite's right upper sleeve.

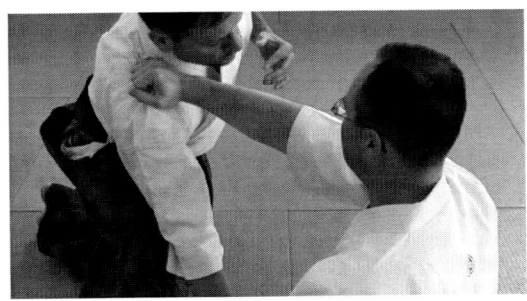

4
(Reverse angle detail)

5

Shite rises to his knees driving uchite up and backwards.

6

Shite executes a maegiri to uchite's abdomen.

History And Technique

居捕   引捕

7
As shite retracts the kicking leg he opens his hips to the right driving uchite towards his fuantehō with his right hand.

8
As uchite falls, shite coils his left arm around uchite's right arm, securing a hebimaki dori (snake coiling capture).

9
Shite continues driving uchite forward to the tatami with his right arm.

10
Shite folds uchite's arm behind his lower back.

11
Shite pivots clockwise driving his left leg against uchite's elbow. Shite releases the grip on uchite's shoulder and places his right fist on uchite's spine.

188

Shindō Yōshin Ryū

Gyakute Dori

Idori

1

The kata begins with uchite and shite facing one another in heiza torima.

2

Uchite shifts forward into kiza and seizes shite's wrists in an attempt to restrain him.

3

Utilizing a connected shisei (body structure), shite begins to rise driving uchite backwards and onto the balls of his feet.

4

As shite rises to his knees, he crosses his forearms right over left and secures a grip on uchite's left hand/thumb with his left hand.

5

Uchite tries to escape but shite holds on securely and executes a maegiri to uchite's abdomen.

6

Shite withdraws the kick and executes a gyakute gaeshi (opposite hand, reversed lock) on uchite's left wrist achieving kuzushi.

History And Technique

居捕　　　　　　　　　　　　　　　　　　　逆手捕

7

Shite continues to apply pressure to the gyakute gaeshi eventually upending uchite.

8

When uchite lands, shite continues to apply pressure to the wrist lock.

9

Shite steps forward and places the ball of his foot on the collar bone of uchite, pinning his right shoulder to the tatami.

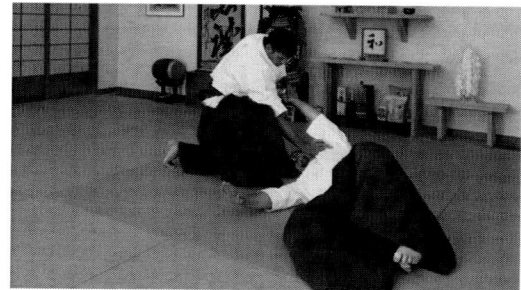

10

Shite executes a tegatana to uchite's jaw.

11

Shite withdraws his strike finishing the kata.

Shindō Yōshin Ryū

Ryote Dori

Idori

1

The kata begins with uchite and shite facing one another in heiza torima.

2

Uchite shifts forward into kiza and seizes shite's wrists in an attempt to restrain him.

3

As shite rises to his knees he feeds his right hand under uchite's right elbow applying upward pressure. Uchite rises to his feet.

4

Shite executes a te hodoki and then sweeps his left hand over uchite's right arm.

5

Shite seizes uchite's right hand and drops it into his fuantehō achieving kuzushi.

6

As uchite tries to regain his balance shite applies an upward tekubi kujiki to uchite's right hand.

History And Technique

居捕 　　　　　　　　　　　　　　　　　両手捕

7

Shite rolls uchite's left hand palm downward and left, dropping it abruptly towards the tatami.

8

Uchite up-ends, falling in shite's antehō (strong line).

9

With the fall, shite maintains pressure on uchite's wrist.

10

Next, shite pivots to the left 90 degrees, straightens uchite's right arm and prepares to execute an atemi.

11

Shite secures uchite's right arm and executes a tegatana to a kyūsho on uchite's face.

Shindō Yōshin Ryū

Kanegi Dori/Shumoku Dori

Idori

1

This kata starts with uchite and shite seated side by side in heiza. In this kata it is assumed that uchite has threatened shite, resulting in a physical response.

2

Shite pivots left stepping behind uchite with his left foot. Simultaneously, shite executes a tegatana to a kyūsho on uchite's face.

3

Shite secures uchite's right wrist with his right hand and his right collar with his left hand.

4

Uchite reaches up in an attempt to apply a kubishime (neck choke) on shite.

5

Shite dives forward executing a sutemi nage (sacrifice throw) into uchite's fuantehō.

6

Shite rolls clockwise onto his back driving uchite forward and across his body.

History And Technique

居捕 鐘木捕

7

Shite continues to roll, driving uchite onto his left side.

8

Shite stops the roll by placing uchite's left wrist on the tatami.

9

Shite drives both of his knees forward into uchite's back and then tightens the collar, applying a choke to uchite's throat.

10

Shite drives uchite's right arm up over his head, locking the right shoulder.

11

Shite feeds uchite's arm back across his own thigh and then applies downward pressure on the wrist. He finishes the kata applying both a hiji kujiki and a kubishime.

Shindō Yōshin Ryū

Ushiro Dori

Idori

1
The kata starts with shite in heiza with uchite to his rear.

2
Uchite steps in, slides his right arm under shite's chin grabbing his left collar. He simultaneously places his left hand on shite's head forcing it forward to apply erijime.

3
Shite shifts forward at the waist drawing uchite to his toes. Next, he traps uchite's right arm against his chest and secures a grip on uchite's right shoulder with his right arm.

4
Shite rises up to his knees keeping uchite's weight forward gaining kuzushi.

5
Shite drops his body abruptly while kicking his left leg out to the side.

6
Shite then drives his hips back and his shoulders forward, finishing with his back parallel to the tatami, up-ending uchite.

History And Technique

居捕 後捕

7
As uchite falls forward over shite's right shoulder, shite raises his body.

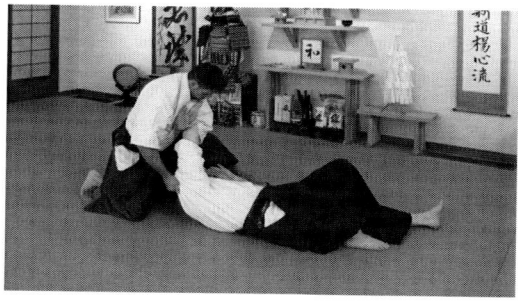

8
As uchite lands on the tatami, shite places his left hand inside uchite's collar grip with his right hand.

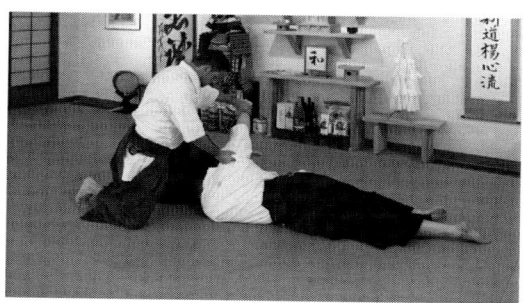

9
Shite breaks uchite's grip on his collar with his left hand and then drives uchite's body clockwise to a face down position.

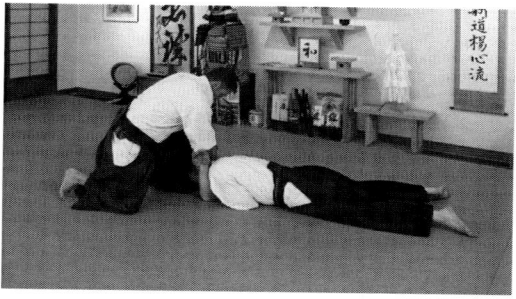

10
Shite folds uchite's right forearm across his throat to arrive in a ushiro jujijime (rear cross choke).

11
Shite forces his hips back, allowing his body weight to drive his forearms down and into the back of uchite's neck increasing the force of the jujijime.

Shindō Yōshin Ryū

Tobi Chigai Dori

Idori Buki

1
The kata begins with uchite and shite facing one another in heiza torima.

2
Uchite begins to draw a tessen (iron fan) from his obi.

3
Uchite steps in with his right leg and attempts a kasumi ate with the tessen to shite's left temple.

4
Shite steps forward with his right leg, intercepts the kasumi ate with his left hand and places his right palm on uchite's throat.

5
Shite twists his hips to the left gaining kuzushi.

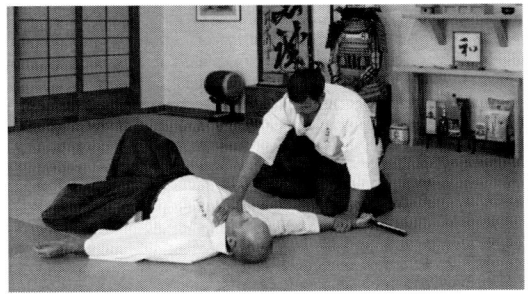

6
Uchite falls and is driven onto his back. Shite secures uchite's right wrist to the tatami.

History And Technique

居捕武器　　　　　　　　　　　　　　　　飛違捕

7

Shite leaps into the air posting off his left arm.

8

Shite drops his knee into uchite's torso.

9

He then applies pressure to uchite's throat.

10

Shite brings his left foot up and disarms uchite.

11

Increased pressure to uchite's throat results in uchite tapping the tatami in submission.

Shindō Yōshin Ryū

Nukimi no Metsuke

Idori Buki

1

The kata starts in heiza kōshōma.

2

Uchite reaches for his shōtō (short sword) and simultaneously shite reaches for his tessen.

3

Uchite and shite sweep both weapons in a horizontal arc, left to right.

4

Uchite raises his shōtō in preparation for a tenchigiri (heaven to earth cut). Simultaneously, shite raises his tessen into a deflecting position.

5

As uchite attacks, shite deflects the blade towards his fuantehō.

6

Shite stands and strikes downward with the tessen, striking uchite's hand.

居捕武器　　　　　　　　　　　　　　　　　抜身之目付

7

Shite throws the tessen towards uchite's face as a distraction.

8

Shite immediately reaches forward, securing a grip on uchite's left collar.

9

Shite steps around to uchite's right side maintaining the grip on the collar.

10

Shite continues to pivot clockwise and across uchite's leg.

11

Shite turns an additional 90 degrees and kneels backwards dragging uchite against his right knee while simultaneously applying a erijime with uchite's left collar.

Shindō Yōshin Ryū

Jogensha - Outside Kai Advisors

When Takamura Yukiyoshi founded the Takamura ha Shindō Yōshin Kai he felt a koryū ryūha as comprehensive as Shindō Yōshin Ryū would benefit from partnering with individuals of unique skills for advice and counsel. Past advisors have included highly-licensed instructors who are historically linked to Shindō Yōshin Ryū, as well as individuals with unique language and administrative skills. Although Jogensha have no administrative or technical authority within the organization, their advisory role is considered valuable to the overall health and vitality of the organization.

The individuals listed below are expert budōka with extensive experience in Kōdōkan Jūdō. They retain the title TSYR Jogensha and have participated in classes that explore our technical foundations and provide insights into the contemporary application of the TSYR mokuroku.

Piotr Chelstowski

Piotr Chelstowski, fourth dan IJF, is a professional European martial arts trainer who graduated from the Polish Academy of Sport and Physical Education and holds a Masters Degree, with a specialization in jūdō. As a competitor and a martial arts instructor, he has studied several hand-to-hand combat systems including jūdō, jūjutsu, sambo, kick-boxing and aikijūjutsu.

He is a former assistant coach for the Polish National and Olympic jūdō teams and his trainee-competitors have won 12 medals in Continental and World University Games. He has over 40 years of experience in jūdō and other martial arts and has been coaching professionally for the past 38 years in Poland, Sweden, Germany, Belgium and the United States.

Aaron Clark

Aaron R. Clark, seventh dan Jiyushinkai aikibudō, third dan jūdō, is a seasoned budōka with four decades of experience and as a youngster won numerous state and national level jūdō championships. His principle teachers are Chuck. E. Clark and Karl Geis. He has also studied Shintō Musō Ryū jōjutsu (gomokuroku) and Tenshinsho-den Katori Shintō Ryū kenjutsu under Phil Relnick Sensei.

Aaron Clark served in the U.S. Navy as a Hospital Corpsman and currently works as a senior clinical systems analyst for the University of Washington Medical Centers. He is the dōjōchō of the Jiyushinkan Dōjō near Monroe, WA.

History And Technique

Tachiai Taijutsu

立合体術

The Shindō Yōshin Ryū tachiai taijutsu kata (standing unarmed grappling forms), make up the core of the unarmed jūjutsu curriculum listed in the shoden and chūden taijutsu mokuroku. These forms generally represent four overlapping categories of study, kansetsu (joint-lock throws and takedowns), tainage (body throws), shime (chokes) and kyūsho atemi (vital-point strikes). Unarmed grappling was originally ancillary to the study of weaponry, consequently most tachiai taijutsu kata have their origins in either the offensive use of weaponry or in defense against weaponry. The tachiai taijutsu kata are further divided into three categories of study, the omote version, the ura version and henka waza.

Shindō Yōshin Ryū

Hiki Tate

Tachiai Taijutsu

The kata begins with uchite and shite facing one another in gyakuhanmi shinkiritsu torima.

Uchite steps in with the left leg, secures shite's left wrist with his left hand and prepares to strike with his right hand.

Before uchite can strike, shite counters with a right teishō ate (palm heel strike) to uchite's jaw.

Shite rotates his left palm flat drawing uchite's face forward into the strike.

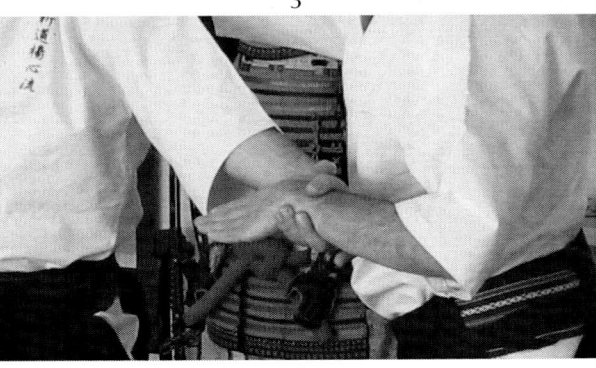

History and Technique

立合体術　　　　　　　　　　　　　　　　　　　引立

5

Shite now reaches over uchite's arm and under his elbow. Simultaneously, shite executes a te hodoki and secures uchite's left wrist.

6

Shite extends uchite's left arm to completely straighten it.

7

Shite then presses down on the secured wrist applying a hiji kujiki. Uchite taps shite's right shoulder to indicate submission.

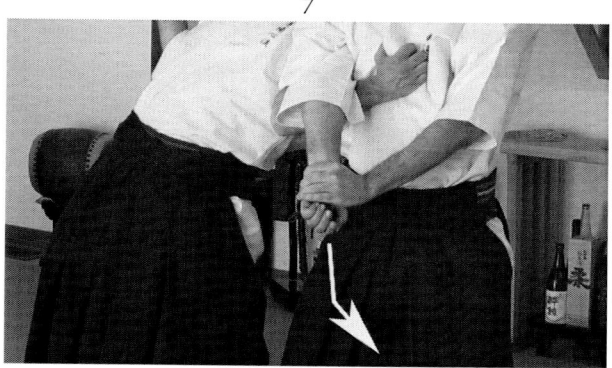
8

(Close-up detail)

Shindō Yōshin Ryū

Soto Ude Otoshi

Tachiai Taijutsu

The kata begins with uchite and shite facing one another in gyakuhanmi shinkiritsu torima.

Uchite grabs shite's left wrist with his left hand in preparation for a tateken strike with his right hand. Shite swings his left arm out towards uchite's fuantehō. Shite simultaneously places his right hand on the inside of uchite's left elbow.

Shite pivots counter-clockwise bending uchite's arm, driving the elbow into uchite's fuantehō, gaining kuzushi.

Shite collapses abruptly dropping uchite's elbow straight to the tatami.

History and Technique

立合体術　　　　　　　　　　　外腕落

The abruptness of the drop up-ends uchite.

As uchite lands, shite presses his elbow to the mat and pivots 90 degrees counter-clockwise, placing his left ankle against uchite's ribs and his knee above, but not resting on uchite's shoulder. Next shite bends uchite's arm 90 degrees upward over his head.

Shite then raises uchite's forearm while sliding his shin forward over the shoulder/rotator cuff. Uchite taps the tatami to indicate submission.

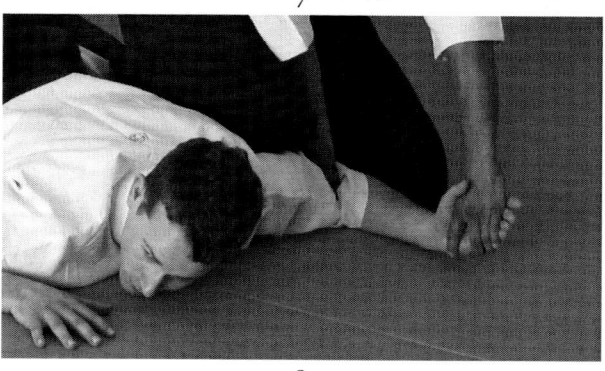

(Close-up detail)

Shindō Yōshin Ryū

Kinukuguri

Tachiai Taijutsu

The kata begins with uchite and shite facing one another in aihanmi shinkiritsu torima.

1

Uchite initiates a right tetsui ate (iron fist strike).

2

As uchite strikes, shite parries the strike, steps forward with his right leg and grasps uchite's collar.

3

Shite pivots his body clockwise while rotating his gripping hand counter-clockwise, gaining kuzushi.

4

立合体術　　　　　絹潜（きぬくぐり）

5

Shite pivots 180 degrees clockwise on his left leg and kneels. During the pivot, shite keeps extending his right arm up and forward. Simultaneously, he places his left arm on the inside of uchite's left leg.

6

Shite abruptly shifts his body back while extending his right arm up and forward. As shite's hip shifts backwards it locks uchite's knee. Shite's arm prevents uchite from stepping forward with his left leg. Uchite up-ends.

7

It is important that as uchite falls, shite pulls back with his right hand permitting uchite's body to rotate cleanly, preventing him from striking his head on the tatami.

8

Uchite should complete the fall in shite's antehō with his feet pointing away.

(Note: Kinukuguri is the inspiration for Wadō ryu's Kihon Kumite #10.)

Shindō Yōshin Ryū

Kinukatsugi

Tachiai Taijutsu

The kata begins with uchite and shite facing one another in aihanmi shinkiritsu torima. Uchite then prepares to strike.

1

Uchite steps in with his right foot and executes a tateken ate with his right hand. Shite parries the strike to the right.

2

Shite grasps the bottom of uchite's sleeve and presses it forward towards his fuantehō.

3

Shite seizes uchite's hand in gyakute, steps forward with his left leg locking uchite's shoulder and gaining kuzushi.

4

History and Technique

立合体術

絹担

5

Shite passes under uchite's arm, pivots clockwise on his left leg and kneels. During the pivot, shite draws uchite's sleeve downward.

6

Shite applies pressure to the gyakute gaeshi upending uchite. Shite's leg blocks an attempt by uchite to step forward.

7

As uchite falls, shite pulls on the controlled sleeve allowing his body to rotate facilitating a safe fall.

8

Uchite completes his fall in shite's antehō.

Shindō Yōshin Ryū

Kinumoguri

Tachiai Taijutsu

The kata begins with uchite and shite facing one another in aihanmi shinkiritsu torima.

Uchite initiates a right tetsui ate.

As uchite strikes, shite parries the strike, steps forward with his right leg and grasps uchite's collar.

Shite passes uchite's right arm in front and towards his fuantehō.

History and Technique

立合体術　　　　　絹潜（きぬもぐり）

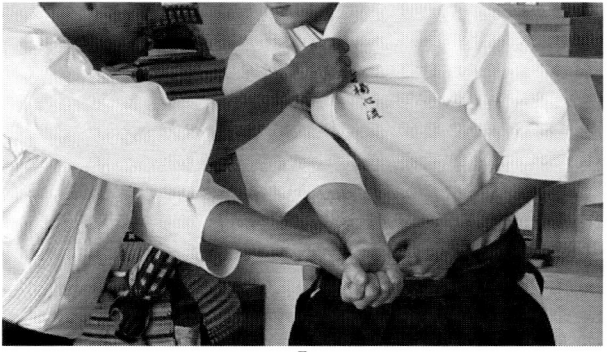
5

(Close-up detail)

6

Shite steps in with his left leg and pivots clockwise 180 degrees and kneels. During the pivot, shite draws uchite downward applying pressure to his elbow increasing kuzushi.

7

Shite pulls back on uchite's wrist up-ending him.

8

Uchite completes his fall in shite's antehō, feet pointed away.

Shindō Yōshin Ryū

Gyakute Gaeshi
Tachiai Taijutsu

1

The kata begins with uchite and shite facing one another in aihanmi shinkiritsu torima.

2

Uchite grabs shite's left wrist with his right arm in preparation for a tateken ate with his left hand.

3

Shite rotates counter-clockwise, immediately striking uchite's ribs with a right tateken ate.

4

Shite rotates clockwise, executing a yoko nuki (horizontal hand release) and then secures a hiji kujiki to uchite's right arm with a gyakute hand grip.

5

Shite cross-steps with her right leg in front of uchite passing under his right arm. Shite maintains the hiji kujiki with her shoulder.

6

Shite executes a hiji ate (elbow strike) to uchite's suigetsu.

立合体術　　　　　　　　　　　　　　　　　逆手返

7

Shite pivots clockwise with her right leg forward and secures a gyakute gaeshi on uchite's right arm.

8

Shite kneels, driving uchite's locked wrist towards the tatami.

9

Uchite upends.

10

Shite pins uchite's wrist to the tatami.

11

Shite pivots counter-clockwise and applies a hiji kujiki to uchite's right elbow with her right knee. Uchite taps the tatami to indicate submission.

Shindō Yōshin Ryū

Hidare Mune Dori

Tachiai Taijutsu

1

The kata begins with uchite and shite facing one another in aihanmi shinkiritsu torima.

2

Uchite steps in with his right leg, grasps shite's collar and attempts a tetsui ate to uchite's kasumi.

3

Shite slides to the right and applies a strike to uchite's jaw.

4

Shite slides in and farther to the right, spiraling his right arm counter-clockwise around uchite's left arm and securing his keikogi in the mid-back.

5
(Close-up detail)

6

Shite slides deeper to the right increasing kuzushi on uchite.

立合体術　　　　　　　　　　　　　　　　　左胸捕

7

Shite drops abruptly while powerfully sweeping uchite's left leg upward with his left arm.

8

Uchite is up-ended.

9

Uchite lands flat on his back.

10

Following uchite's fall, shite breaks uchite's grip on his lapel with a right tegatana cutting upward.

11

Shite feeds uchite's left hand over his head and pins it to the tatami with his right foot. He finishes the kata with a nakadaka ate to uchite's left eye socket.

Shindō Yōshin Ryū

Soto Ude Garami

Tachiai Taijutsu

1

The kata begins with uchite and shite facing one another in aihanmi shinkiritsu torima.

2

Uchite initiates a right tateken ate.

3

Shite intercepts and parries uchite's strike with his right hand while simultaneously responding with a left tateken ate to uchite's jaw.

4

Following his strike, shite cuts back into uchite's right elbow with his left hand bending the arm. Simultaneously, shite flexes uchite's right wrist to the inside.

5

(Close-up detail)

6

Shite steps in deep with his right foot, pivoting counter-clockwise and spiraling uchite's elbow into his fuantehō.

立合体術　　　　　　　　　　　　　　　　　外腕絡

7

Shite continues to pivot counter-clockwise 180 degrees, achieving kuzushi. The grip should be very light and uchite's forearm near vertical.

8

Shite kneels abruptly, dropping uchite's elbow into his fuantehō, up-ending uchite.

9

When uchite hits the tatami, shite slides forward placing his shin behind uchite's back.

10

Shite straightens uchite's arm in preparation for a strike.

11

Shite executes a tegatana to a kyūsho on uchite's face, finishing the kata.

Shindō Yōshin Ryū

Ranshō

Tachiai Taijutsu

The waza begins with uchite and shite facing one another in aihanmi.

1

Uchite attempts a migi munedori (right hand lapel grab). Shite parries uchite's attempted grab feeding the arm towards his fuantehō.

2

Shite captures uchite's hand with both his hands, successfully gaining kuzushi. Shite next swings uchite's right arm in an arc to the left driving uchite's weight to his right leg.

3

Shite steps with his left foot placing it outside uchite's right foot. Shite continues driving his body forward placing his head under uchite's right armpit while simultaneously grabbing uchite's thigh from the inside with his right arm.

4

History and Technique

立合体術　　　　　　　　　　　　　　　　　　乱勝

5

Shite slides his left foot forward and behind uchite, landing on his left hip. Shite having firmly secured uchite's arm and leg, uchite begins to fall in an arc over shite's right shoulder.

6

Shite straightens his back placing his left shoulder blade onto the tatami, totally upending uchite.

7

Uchite lands on the tatami, shite's throw successfully executed.

8

Shite rotates his head and shoulder around to the back of uchite's right arm and applies a hiji kujiki with his shoulder.

Shindō Yōshin Ryū

Koshi Nage

Tachiai Taijutsu

The waza begins with uchite and shite facing one another in gyaku-hanmi.

1

Uchite executes migi munedori with her right hand and attempts a strike to shite's face with her left hand.

2

Shite immediately responds by seizing uchite's sleeve just outside the elbow and rotating his forearm clockwise to tighten the sleeve. Next he rotates his body left drawing uchite's balance forward achieving kuzushi.

3

As uchite strikes, shite steps with his right foot pointed to uchite's right foot. Simultaneously, shite jams uchite's strike with the right arm and then reaches around uchite's back. Firmly securing uchite, shite then cross-steps to the rear with his left foot, placing his heel just inside uchite's left heel.

4

History and Technique

立合体術　　　　　　　　　　　　　　腰投

5

Shite next rotates counter-clockwise on the balls of his feet with his hips slightly rotated to the right. Next, he starts bending his legs and lowering his hips so uchite tips onto his lower back.

6

With uchite's torso now resting on shite's hip and lower back, uchite is elevated and effortlessly supported by shite's body. Shite should be in a stable and balanced position.

7

Shite next rotates his hips and torso counter-clockwise, dropping uchite to the right and onto the tatami at his feet.

8

Shite finishes the waza by quickly straightening his back and aligning his body structure so he has control of uchite and cannot be pulled to the mat.

Shindō Yōshin Ryū

Harai Goshi

Tachiai Taijutsu

The waza begins with uchite and shite facing one another in aihanmi.

1

Uchite grabs shite's collar with his right hand and attempts a strike with his left hand. Shite steps in right foot pointing to uchite's right foot, while securing uchite's right arm from the inside.

2

Shite begins twisting her body to the left drawing uchite's body forward to his right foot to achieve kuzushi. Simultaneously shite reaches around uchite's back.

3

Shite now steps back and across with her left leg continuing to draw uchite's body forward. Shite shifts her weight to her left foot.

4

History and Technique

立合体術　　　　　　　　　　　　　　　　　払腰

Shite raises her right thigh parallel to the tatami.

5

Shite drives her leg backwards sweeping uchite's hips, lifting him.

6

Uchite's body rotates over shite's hips, falling to the tatami.

7

Shite finishes the waza by quickly pulling her right leg forward, straightening her back and aligning her body structure so she has control of uchite and cannot be pulled to the tatami.

8

Shindō Yōshin Ryū

Yoko Otoshi

Tachiai Taijutsu

The waza begins with uchite and shite facing one another in aihanmi.

1

Uchite grabs shite's collar with the right hand and attempts a tateken ate to her face with his left hand. Shite responds by seizing uchite's left sleeve and parrying his strike to the outside right.

2

Shite shifts back and to the left achieving kuzushi and weighting uchite forward and onto his right leg.

3

立合体術　　　　　　　　　　　　　　　　横落

Shite twists to the left extending both her arms, driving uchite to the right rear.

4

Shite keeps extending her arms as she slides her left leg foward, dropping the left side of her body to the tatami. Uchite, with his right foot blocked by shite's leg, up-ends.

5

Shite continues to extend her arms, driving uchite away from her position.

6

On Teaching

A common misconception in Japanese budō culture is the idea that technical skills and teaching skills are cultivated simultaneously; that a talented technician will likewise be a talented teacher. In fact, technical skills and teaching skills are only loosely connected. Teaching, like all instructional skills, requires the cultivation and development of proper pedagogical methods.

In Takamura ha Shindō Yōshin Ryū there is no technical ranking system similar to the dan-i system employed in modern budō schools. Densho (teaching licenses) are issued based on teaching ability related to technical understanding, not necessarily a predetermined level of technical execution. When a student achieves a certain level of technical familiarity with the curriculum, he is gradually introduced into instructional training. Koryū survival depends on cultivating competent teachers, so developing superior teaching skills is of primary importance to the ryūha, and mandatory for a member's continued progress through the school's curriculum.

Three stages of technical development are traditionally recognized in koryū martial arts systems. They are identified as shu-ha-ri. As a part of Takamura ha Shindō Yōshin Ryū, shu-ha-ri was described in great detail by Takamura Yukiyoshi in his essay entitled *"Teaching and Shu-Ha-Ri"*, and expanded upon further during his cultivation of advanced level instructors.

Shu 守 (Embracing the Kata)

Shu requires the student to become immersed in the omote kata and follow his teacher's instructions as precisely as possible. The student should do everything in his power to become an exact technical duplicate of his seniors, and not allow any deviation to the ryūha's standard to manifest itself during his execution of technique. Because the omote kata is a koryū's technical foundation, the school's most direct expression of its kihon (basics) and riai (theory), no deviation should be allowed by the teacher. At the later stages of shu, the student should be a competent representation of technical orthodoxy.

Ha 破 (Diverging from the Kata)

Ha assumes the student has embraced the omote kata with such discipline that the body mechanics and theories underlying the forms are merging unconsciously in the student's execution of technique. It is time to let the student start to explore the deeper lessons of the kata and coax the deeper wisdom out of them. During ha, many students' innate capabilities demonstrate themselves powerfully for the first time. This is a training period of delicate balance as the student should be encouraged to pursue kaisetsu (investigation), while being reminded of the deeper riai, something all too easily missed. The student must be reminded of the core theories of the school or he risks proceeding in a technical direction unintended by the founder of the art.

Ri 離 (Discarding the Kata).

Ri is mastery. It is not so much taught, as it is arrived at. At the level of ri, the riai of the kata is so intuitively ingrained in the practitioner's movement that the outer shell of the kata fades away leaving a state of mind we call marobashi. The kata has done its job. Every movement becomes a masterful representation of the ryuha's foundational theories. Conscious thought, something mostly overcome during the later stages of ha, is completely erased at ri. Observation, cognition and response times merge into movement, which has become so efficient and natural that to an outside observer the practitioner seems psychic, able to acknowledge and engage potential threats before they come to fruition. This level of mastery is formless and elusive, and may never be achieved by even the most dedicated student.

History And Technique

Tantō Toriage

短刀取上

Tantō Toriage is combat where an unarmed defender is forced to engage and disarm a knife-wielding attacker. For a defender to prevail against a competent practitioner of tantōjutsu, extreme skill and superior tactics are required. In Shindō Yōshin Ryū success hinges on seizing the initiative by utilizing superior hyōshi (timing), creating mental and physical disruption through the application of atemi, dominating the adversaries seichūsen (center line), and aggressive control of maai (distance).

Shindō Yōshin Ryū

Te Gaeshi

Tantō Toriage

1

The kata begins with uchite and shite facing one another in aihanmi shinkiritsu uchima (striking distance). Uchite draws her tantō and obscures its view behind her hakama.

2

Uchite steps in with her right leg and attacks shite's torso with a thrust. Shite responds by parrying the attack and striking uchite's kasumi with an uraken.

3

Shite seizes uchite's right wrist, steps in with his right leg and presses uchite's arm down to gain kuzushi.

4

Uchite attempts to recover her balance by straightening up. As uchite rises, shite pivots counter-clockwise and shifts forward rotating the tantō towards uchite.

5

Shite raises his right knee in preparation to attack uchite's structure.

6

Shite extends his leg driving uchite's hips back while feeding the tantō forward. This is not a kick in the typical sense, but a leg thrust intended to achieve kuzushi.

短刀取上　　　　　　　　　　　　　　　　　　　　　　　　　　　　手返

7
(Close-up detail)

8
As uchite starts to fall, shite drops vertically and pulls slightly on the secured arm pivoting uchite's body to the side.

9
Shite steps forward placing both feet under uchite's shoulder, one on each side of the arm. Uchite's arm should be secured against shite's legs with the knees behind the elbow.

10
Shite drops by slightly bending his knees. This applies increasing pressure on uchite's elbow. Simultaneously, shite feeds the tantō downward, releasing it from ucihite's grip.

11
Shite steps back with his right leg but maintains pressure on uchite's elbow until she taps the tatami indicating submission.

Shindō Yōshin Ryū

Soto Ude Garami — Tantō Toriage

1

The kata begins with uchite and shite facing one another in aihanmi shinkiritsu uchima. Uchite draws a tantō from his obi and obscures its view behind his hakama.

2

Uchite steps in with his right leg and attacks shite's throat with a thrust. Shite responds by parrying the attack to the outside.

3

Shite executes a glancing strike to uchite's ribs with his right hand.

4

Shite turns his right palm vertical and raises his elbow up to the bottom of uchite's arm. Simultaneously, he secures uchite's right wrist with his left hand.

5

Shite cuts backward powerfully with his right hand while feeding uchite's right wrist up and back with his left hand, bending the arm.

6

Shite reaches forward with his right hand, grabbing uchite's right wrist while placing his left palm on uchite's right elbow, securing a soto ude garami (outside arm coil).

History And Technique

短刀取上　　　　　　　　　　　　　　外腕絡

7

Shite presses his right hand forward raising his elbow and locking his shoulder.

8

Shite continues pressing forward gaining kuzushi, while raising his right thigh parallel to the tatami.

9

Shite executes an ōsoto gari (large outside reap) to uchite's right leg.

10

As uchite hits the ground, shite pins his elbow and shoulder to the tatami with his left hand. Shite prepares to strike with his right hand.

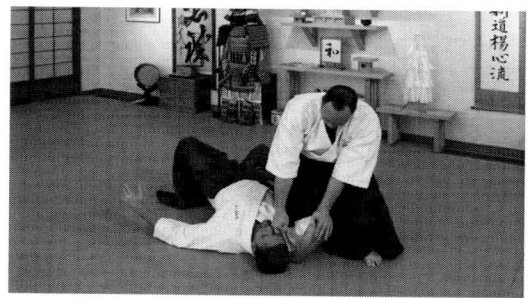

11

Shite executes a nakadaka ate to uchite's eye socket.

Shindō Yōshin Ryū

Hiji Kujiki — Tantō Toriage

1

The kata begins with uchite and shite facing one another in gyakuhanmi shinkiritsu uchima. Uchite draws a tantō from his obi and obscures its view behind his hakama.

2

Uchite steps in with his right leg and attacks shite's throat with a thrust. Shite quickly rotates his shoulders counter-clockwise and shifts his body off the line of attack.

3

Shite raises both his arms and begins to parry the attack towards uchite's fuantehō with his right forearm.

4

Shite steps in with his right leg and powerfully opens his hips and drives forward, executing a double strike to uchite's face and ribs.

5

Shite secures uchite's right arm with both hands.

6

(Reverse view)

History And Technique

短刀取上　　　　　　　　　　　　　　　　肘挫

7

Shite slides forward with his right foot towards uchite's fuantehō while applying an upward hiji kujiki.

8

Shite abruptly drops uchite's wrist while levering pressure against his elbow.

9

Uchite is up-ended and thrown forward.

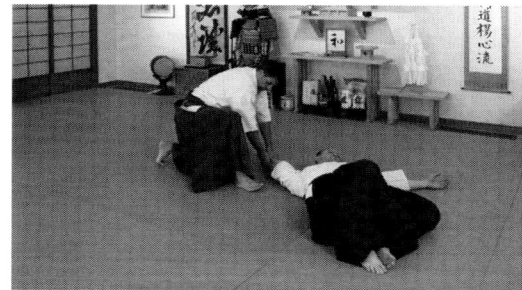

10

As uchite lands on the tatami, shite secures uchite's elbow with his right arm and disarms him with his left.

11

Shite switches the tantō from his left hand to his right hand, pins uchite's elbow to the tatami with his right foot and places the edge of the tantō over uchite's tricep, securing him.

Shindō Yōshin Ryū

Uchi Ude Garami

Tantō Toriage

The kata begins with uchite and shite facing one another in gyakuhanmi shinkiritsu uchima. Uchite draws a tantō from his obi with his right hand and obscures its view behind his hakama.

1

Uchite steps in with his right leg and attacks shite's throat with a tantō thrust. Shite responds by parrying the attack to his left.

2

Shite immediately attacks uchite's eyes with a right-handed yubi ate (finger rake strike).

3

Shite captures uchite's right arm with his right hand on top and his left hand underneath the elbow.

4

History and Technique

短刀取上　　　　　　　　　　　　　　　内腕絡

5

Shite whips uchite's right arm over the top of his head by powerfully rotating his body clockwise and stepping in with his left leg.

6

As shite gains kuzushi on uchite, he releases the wrist with his left hand and traps uchite's forearm in an elbow restraint against his body. With his right hand, shite applies an uchi ude garami (inside arm coil).

7

Shite disarms uchite by applying pressure to the tantō's mune (back edge) and driving it forward.

8

Roles reversed, uchite, trapped by the elbow restraint, cannot prevent shite from thrusting the captured tantō to his abdomen.

Shindō Yōshin Ryū

Age Nagashi

Tantō Toriage

The kata begins with uchite and shite facing one another in aihanmi shinkiritsu uchima. Uchite draws a tantō from his obi with his right hand and obscures its view behind his hakama.

1

Uchite steps in with the right leg and attacks shite's chest with a tantō thrust. Shite responds by rotating clockwise and executing a parrying tateken ate with her right hand to uchite's ribs.

2

Shite quickly traps uchite's arm and applies a hiji kujiki to his right elbow by rotating slightly clockwise. The arm control must be soft but secure.

3

Shite places her right hand over the mune of the tantō blade, securing its control.

4

History and Technique

短刀取上　　　　　　　　　　　上流

Shite drives the tantō down forcing its release from uchite's grip.

5

Shite steps straight back with her left leg, pivots powerfully counter-clockwise, sweeping uchite's right arm to his rear, gaining kuzushi.

6

Shite steps through with her right leg and cuts uchite's neck with the tantō in her right hand.

7

Uchite and shite both pivot counter-clockwise to finish the kata.

8

Adam Coleman, Kaji / Japanese Bladesmith

Many koryū formed partnerships with, or directly recruited members into their ranks with unique skills or knowledge. This included artisans like shoka (calligraphers), ekaki (painters), yoroisei (armorers) and kaji (swordsmiths). The Takamura ha Shindō Yōshin Kai is fortunate to have in its ranks its own in-house kaji.

Kaji Adam Coleman learned the craft of forging and mounting Japanese swords under his kaji sensei, Michael Bell, owner of Dragonfly Forge and himself an apprentice of famed kaji Nakajima Muneyoshi. In 2005, Adam started his life as an apprentice, a relationship he still maintains today. Following construction his own forge, Michael Bell suggested Adam use the name "Yama Kuni", meaning "mountainous land."

Adam is rare among those in the sword-making community. He has been trained to traditionally make a sword under one roof. From forging the blade, creating all the furniture, and mounting the blade, Adam can produce a sword from conception to completion.

His obsessive attention to detail and his innate sense of shibusa is evident not only in his work but also his surroundings. His traditional kajiya and Takamura ha Shindō Yōshin Ryū dōjō, both adorned in hinoki, adjoined by a beautiful Japanese garden, are testaments to his unique level of dedication in maintaining these rare Japanese traditions.

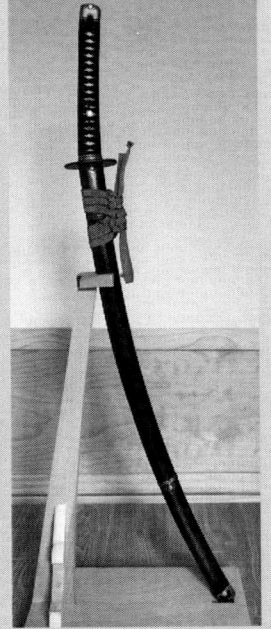

History And Technique

Ken Toriage

剣取上

Ken Toriage is combat where an unarmed or very lightly-armed defender is forced to engage and disarm a sword-wielding attacker. For a defender to prevail against a competent swordsman, almost super-human skill and superior tactics are required. In Shindō Yōshin Ryū, success hinges on seizing the initiative by creating mental disruption through the deployment of a projectile weapon called a shuriken (metal dart), while exposing only discretely armored targets to the attacker. During training a small leather bag filled with sand, simulating a shuriken, is thrown at the attacker at a critical moment, disrupting the attacker's timing and allowing the defender to enter into grappling distance.

Shindō Yōshin Ryū

Iri Sumigaeshi

Ken Toriage

The kata begins with uchite and shite facing one another in gyakuhanmi shinkiritsu uchima. Uchite draws his sword to jōdan (high position) in preparation for a kirioroshi (downward cut).

1

Shite steps in with his left leg and quickly pivots clockwise evading the sword cut, deploying a shuriken and applying tateken ate.

2

Shite drops his hands over the mune of the sword. The left hand is in the middle of the tsuka (hilt) and the right hand is in the middle of the blade.

3

Shite cross-steps with his right foot. He pivots his body in an arc determined by a rotational axis located at uchite's front hand.

4

History and Technique

剣取上　　　　　入隅返

5

Shite then steps in with his left leg displacing uchite's hips. Next, shite rotates his hips in a upward tilt disrupting uchite's body structure.

6

Shite abruptly tilts his left hip downward removing his support of uchite's body structure and gaining kuzushi.

7

Shite relaxes his arms and begins a rotating downward cut with the sword. This rotation removes uchite's structural support and he is up-ended.

8

As uchite falls to the mat, shite finishes the rotating downward cut, targeting uchite's face, which he protects with his left forearm.

Shindō Yōshin Ryū

Te Gaeshi

Ken Toriage

The kata begins with uchite and shite facing one another in aihanmi shinkiritsu uchima. Uchite draws his sword to jōdan in preparation for a kirioroshi.

1

Shite deploys a shuriken with her right hand, steps in with her left leg and quickly pivots her body clockwise evading the sword cut. She captures uchite's right hand in te gaeshi grip with her left hand.

2

Shite applies an uraken ate to uchite's face with her right hand while pressing the sword towards uchite's fuantehō.

3

Shite grabs the center of the sword tsuka with her right hand and steps deep with her right leg achieving kuzushi.

4

History and Technique

剣取上　　　　　　　　　　　　　　　　　　　手返

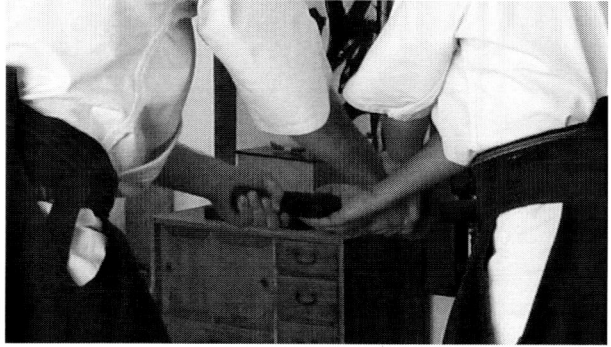
5

(Close-up detail)

6

As uchite attempts to regain his balance, shite pivots counter-clockwise driving the sword directly into uchite's rear fuantehō.

7

At the first sign of resistance from uchite, shite drives the sword left by pivoting farther counter-clockwise. Next, shite abruptly drops the sword in an arc, edge upwards, to the mat by applying te gaeshi, up-ending uchite.

8

With uchite's hand trapped on the sword he falls onto the edge of the blade with the back of his neck.

Shindō Yōshin Ryū

Kosoto Gari

Ken Toriage

The kata begins with uchite and shite facing one another in aihanmi shinkiritsu uchima. Uchite draws his sword to jōdan in preparation for a kirioroshi.

1

Shite deploys a shuriken with his right hand, steps in with his left leg and pivots his body clockwise, evading the sword cut and applying a tegatana ate to uchite's face.

2

Shite captures the sword blade with his right hand and the sword tsuka with his left hand by reaching over uchite's right arm.

3

Shite pivots counter-clockwise driving the sword tsuka over uchite's right forearm and the sword blade against his abdomen.

4

History and Technique

剣取上　　　　　　　　　　　　　　　小外刈

5

Shite pulls his body forward with his left leg and places his right leg behind uchite's right leg.

6

Shite executes a kosoto gari (small outside reap) to uchite while continuing to apply pressure to his abdomen with the sword blade.

7

As uchite falls, shite steps forward with his right leg and continues cutting uchite's abdomen.

8

When uchite hits the tatami, shite has the sword tip pointed at uchite's chest in a right leading forward stance.

Shindō Yōshin Ryū

Tachi Otoshi

Ken Toriage

The kata begins with uchite and shite facing one another in aihanmi shinkiritsu uchima. Uchite draws his sword to jōdan in preparation for a kirioroshi.

1

Shite deploys a shuriken with his right hand, steps in with his left leg and pivots his body clockwise, evading the sword cut and applying a kyūshō ate to uchite's torso.

2

(Close-up detail)

3

Shite captures the mune with his right hand and the tsuka with his left by reaching under uchite's right arm.

4

History and Technique

剣取上　　　　　　　　　　　　　　　　　　太刀落

Shite steps forward with his right leg driving the sword forward and uchite's arms toward his front fuantehō, gaining kuzushi.

Shite kneels and abruptly drops the sword towards the tatami.

Uchite, up-ends and rolls away.

Shite draws the blade in an overhead arc and cuts to uchite's face which he defends with his left forearm.

Shinai-geiko / Katchu, and Shinai Shiai

In the mid-1500s a practice weapon made of bamboo strips covered in a leather sheath was developed by Shinkage Ryū's founder, Kamiizumi Ise no Kami Nobutsuna. The weapon was conceived to prevent severe impact injuries during vigorous training and is referred to as a fukuro shinai (sleeved bamboo sword). Despite the success of the fukuro shinai in preventing injuries, during the mid-Edo period bōgu (protective armor) was developed to safely allow for even more aggressive training. By the late Edo period the armor included face, hand, and torso protection. In the early Meiji period, Sakakibara Kenkichi, the 14th headmaster of Jikishinkage Ryū popularized shinai-geiko (training with shinai) through a series of public events between various swordsmen called gekiken (aggressive sword). Gekiken would evolve during the Meiji and Taisho eras into the modern budō-sports of Kendō and Atarashi Naginata.

The roots of kenjutsu training in Takamura ha Shindō Yōshin Ryū can be traced to Jikishikage Ryū and Matsuzaki Shinkage Ryū, schools which included extensive shinai-geiko. In Takamura ha Shindō Yōshin Ryū, shinai-geiko is divided into two categories. Katchū (armor and helmet) refers to specialized kata performed in armor and executed in a semi-freestyle manner that allows the student to develop superior combat intuition, flexibility, distance and timing. Shinai shiai (bamboo sword contests) refers to the actual freestyle application of combative waza (technique) and riai (theory).

It was Takamura Yukiyoshi's opinion that kata training alone cannot refine practical combat skills to their highest level without some method of freestyle engagement. He believed sharpening effective combat skills when confronted by constant changes in distance, timing, and mental inertia

demanded a type of spontaneity only available in shiai. However, shiai carries with it many pitfalls. All too often shiai degenerates into a contrivance where effective combat waza is supplanted by dubious methods of execution. In these situations shiai becomes an impediment to developing genuine combat ability by creating only the illusion of practical engagement. Shiai must be strictly managed by a competent instructor so the student can internalize the benefits of such essential training without falling prey to the numerous stumbling blocks that can accompany such practice.

History And Technique

Kenjutsu

剣術

Kenjutsu is the art of combat between two sword-wielding adversaries. In Shindō Yōshin Ryū this encompasses combat between swordsmen wielding weapons including daitō (long swords), shōtō (short swords) and tantō (daggers). The majority of kenjutsu kata are practiced with bokken (wooden swords) and require fine control to prevent hard contact and injury. A smaller part of the kata curriculum is performed as shinai-geiko (bamboo sword training) and identified as katchū kenjutsu (armor and helmet). Katchū kenjutsu utilizes specialized body armor that reduces the risk of serious injury. This method of training allows for a more aggressive and spontaneous application of combat technique.

Shindō Yōshin Ryū

Issoku no Tsume

Kenjutsu (Kumitachi)

1

The kata starts with uchitachi and shitachi in shizentai (natural stance) tōma (sword distance). They perform gehanen reigi (lower half circle salutation) and move into aihanmi kyōtōgamae (threatening sword stance).

2

Uchitachi and shitachi both step forward with their right legs executing erigiri (collar cut) and stopping on contact, with no pressure exerted on their adversaries' blades.

3

After a pause, uchitachi and shitachi withdraw their right legs and retreat again to kyōtōgamae.

4

Uchitachi and shitachi again both step forward with their right legs and execute erigiri.

5

On contact, uchitachi disengages and attempts a cut to shitachi's right leg. Shitachi responds by blocking uchitachi's ha (edge) with the shinogi (side) of her sword.

6

Using nairiki (internal strength), shitachi overpowers uchitachi capturing her seichusen and driving her blade towards her front fuantehō.

History And Technique

剣術（組太刀）

一足の詰

7
Shitachi leaps in the air switching her stance and cutting to uchitachi's leg. Instantly, uchitachi responds in kind, blocking while moving her leg out of range.

8
Uchitachi and shitachi land in jūtō (crossed swords) with the blades shinogi to shinogi.

9
After a pause, uchitachi and shitachi withdraw to kyōtōgamae with shitachi slightly elevating her elbow.

10
Uchitachi steps forward and right preparing to cut kirioroshi to shitachi's exposed elbow.

11
Shitachi drops her elbow and shifts forward dominating uchitachi's exposed fuantehō. She presses her blade forward, parrying uchitachi's blade and threatening her throat.

Shindō Yōshin Ryū

Gyaku Aku/Nigiri

Kenjutsu (Kumitachi)

1

The kata starts with uchitachi and shitachi facing one another in shizentai tōma. They perform gehanen reigi and place their swords in teitō (at their sides).

2

Uchitachi and shitachi proceed to walk past one another, passing on the right.

3

As shitachi comes into uchima, uchitachi draws his sword and attempts to cut shitachi's lower leg.

4

Shitachi raises his leg, letting the cut pass under his foot while drawing his sword in gyaku aku (reverse grip).

5

Shitachi whips his sword's kissaki (tip) clockwise towards uchitachi's neck, driving him back.

6

Shitachi and uchitachi pause in aihanmi uchima. Uchitachi is in kyōtogamae, shitachi in gyaku aku kyōtōgamae.

History And Technique

剣術（組太刀）　　　　　　　　　　　　　　　　　逆握

7

Uchitachi steps in initiating an erigiri. Shitachi responds by dominating uchitachi's seichusen with his superior body structure; the swords are in jūtō.

8

Employing nairiki, shitachi snaps uchitachi's blade to the left completely seizing the seichusen.

9

Shitachi slides forward placing his sword's ha on uchitachi's left shoulder.

10

Shitachi lowers the tsuka down, trapping uchitachi's sword against his body and then pulls himself forward achieving kuzushi.

11
(Close-up detail)

Shindō Yōshin Ryū

Kurabatsu

Kenjutsu (Kumitachi)

The kata starts with uchitachi and shitachi facing one another in shizentai tōma. They draw their weapons and perform gehanen reigi. Uchitachi takes up gyakuhanmi jōdangamae (overhead stance) and shitachi, seigangamae (eye height stance).

1

Uchitachi steps in with his right leg and cuts kirioroshi, attempting to deflect shitachi's sword downwards. Shitachi avoids the cut by stepping right and raising his sword into tate kyōtō (vertical threatening sword).

2

Shitachi now cuts kirioroshi, trying to deflect uchitachi's sword downwards. Uchitachi avoids this cut by circling his blade left and under shitachi's blade and then raising his sword to jōdan.

3

Uchitachi cuts kirioroshi at shitachi's exposed right forearm. Shitachi pivots clockwise, snaps his blade in a right upward angle deflecting uchitachi's blade with a muneuchi (rear edge strike) and instantly continuing to jōdan.

4

剣術（組太刀）

暗伐

5

Despite uchitachi being momentarily in kuzushi due to his blade being deflected into his front fuantehō, he attempts to cut yokogiri (horizontal cut) across shitachi's abdomen.

6

Shitachi shifts his body slightly backward out of range, reaches out to the right and drops his blade's shinogi onto uchitachi's shinogi in a parrying motion.

7

Shitachi now scoops uchitachi's yoko-giri downward and harmlessly across his seichusen.

8

Shitachi now steps forward and drops his body, pivoting his sword upward under uchitachi's arms and thrusting into his abdomen.

Shindō Yōshin Ryū

Nebari (Shōtō)

Kenjutsu (Kumitachi)

The kata starts with uchitachi and shitachi facing one another in shizentai tōma. They draw their weapons, perform gehanen reigi and place their swords in aihanmi seigan.

1

Uchitachi advances on shitachi and attempts a yoko ate (horizontal strike) to press shitachi's shōtō to her right.

2

As uchitachi disengages and attempts a thrust towards shitachi's torso, shitachi blends, deflecting uchitachi's sword to her left.

3

Shitachi shifts slightly back feeding uchitachi's sword across her seichusen and to her right.

4

History and Technique

剣術（組太刀） 粘（小刀）

5

As uchitachi's sword continues on an arc to her left she reverses the blade's edge and attempts chitengiri (earth to sky cut).

6

Shitachi performs okuriashi (sliding step), advancing forward while whipping uchitachi's blade in and down.

7

In desperation, uchitachi attempts to withdraw the sword and apply a yoko giri to shitachi's abdomen, but shitachi closes to torima, seizes the tsuka of uchitachi's sword and presses her shōtō towards uchitachi's throat.

8

Shitachi presses the blade of the shōtō farther forward forcing uchitachi to submit by releasing her sword to shitachi's control and retreating.

Shindō Yōshin Ryū

Ate

Kenjutsu (Katchū)

1
The kata starts with uchitachi and shitachi in shizentai tōma. They draw their weapons, perform gehanen reigi and place their swords in aihanmi kyōtōgamae.

2
Uchitachi stalks shitachi, eventually attempting an attack with erigiri. Shitachi baits uchitachi by closing and pointing his kissaki towards uchitachi's face.

3
As uchitachi attempts to beat shitachi's sword and take the seichusen, shitachi disengages and strikes uchitachi's men with his sword's kashira.

4
Shitachi hooks uchitachi's right arm with the tsuka of his sword.

5
Shitachi traps uchitachi's arm and cuts across his torso immobilizing his sword.

6
Shitachi's draws himself forward to his left leg and raises his right thigh parallel to the tatami.

History And Technique

剣術（甲冑）

当

7

Shitachi execute's an ōsoto gari (outside leg reap).

8

As uchitachi falls to the tatami, shitachi drives his shins into uchitachi's back, forcing him on to his left side.

9

Shitachi drops his bodyweight on to uchitachi's left side, pinning him.

10

Shitachi thrusts his sword into uchitachi's unprotected armpit.

11

Shitachi finishes by inverting the blade and executing a circular atemi to uchitachi's torso with the mune of his sword.

(Note: The katchu kata are performed in a semi-freestyle manner allowing much more flexibility in execution. Uchitachi is free to kiai, stalk, feint, circle or rush shitachi, but the first attack is always directed at the predetermined target.)

Shindō Yōshin Ryū

Saegiri
Kenjutsu (Katchū)

1

The kata starts with uchitachi and shitachi in shizentai tōma. They draw their weapons, perform gehanen reigi and place their swords in aihanmi kyōtōgamae.

2

Uchitachi stalks shitachi, eventually attempting an attack with erigiri. Shitachi baits uchitachi by pointing his sword's kissaki towards the uchitachi's face.

3

As uchitachi attempts to beat shitachi's sword and take the seichusen, shitachi disengages by thrusting the sword handle forward and stepping in deeply with his left leg.

4

As shitachi rushes past uchitachi, he slices to the lightly protected underarm and arm pit.

5

As uchitachi rotates clockwise to cut yokogiri, shitachi rotates counter-clockwise dropping his sword's kissaki.

6

Facing uchitachi with his right leg forward, shitachi presses his sword forward, intercepting uchitachi's yokogiri near the tsuba (hand guard).

History And Technique

剣術（甲冑） 遮

7

Shitachi executes a mae fumikomigeri (front thrusting kick) with his left leg to uchitachi's hip while rotating his sword counter-clockwise.

8

Uchitachi's structure compromised, his sword passes his center line to his right side.

9

As uchitachi falls backwards, shitachi steps forward dominating the seichusen.

10

As uchitachi hits the tatami, he attempts to defend his seichusen but his sword has been driven to the right.

11

Shitachi charges in, stepping with his right leg and driving his sword into uchitachi's chest, pinning him to the tatami.

Tameshigiri/Test Cutting

Tobin Threadgill performing tameshigiri in the Dallas, Texas Soryūshin Dōjō, 1997.

Tameshigiri is the practice of test-cutting with a Japanese sword. It is properly performed on rolled and water-soaked tatami omote (rice straw mats), or recently-harvested takenoko (bamboo). It is an important endeavor for anyone undergoing proper kenjutsu or battō training, but extreme care must be taken in its execution. The risks associated with tameshigiri, both spiritual and physical are frequently underappreciated. In Takamura ha Shindō Yōshin Ryū every tameshigiri session must be overseen by an instructor holding a Jōden no Maki or Menkyo Kaiden.

All swords used for tameshigiri during a Takamura ha Shindō Yōshin Ryū training session must be inspected by a qualified licensed instructor prior to use. In particular, the mekugi (bamboo peg) securing the tsuka (hilt) to the nakago (tang) must be inspected for its condition and proper fit. If the peg shows signs of wear or an improper fit, it must be replaced prior to the sword's use. Any visible flaw or crack in the sword, particularly near the munemachi or hamachi will disqualify a sword from use.

Before a Takamura ha Shindō Yōshin Ryū tameshigiri session begins, all the swords and the training area where the session will proceed must be purified in a Shintō ritual called harai, where salt is liberally scattered and protective prayers are recited. During the session all participants must stand quietly behind the individual performing the cutting. As each participant approaches and withdraws from the target they must perform the appropriate reigi. Between each individual cutting session the area must be cleaned so no debris remains on the ground. Following the tameshigiri session, the swords and training area must again be properly cleaned and a Shintō closing purification ritual performed.

Tameshigiri is a necessary part of kenjutsu training as a means to an end. That end is a confirmation of proper cutting dynamics and mental focus. Beyond the confirmation of proper technique, tameshigiri serves no further purpose. All too often tameshigiri is treated as if it is a game or a spectacle. It is not. Tameshigiri is a sacred and potentially corrupting practice. It is the simulation of the cutting down of another human being with a sword. To let ego or pride enter into such practice is an example of moral corruption. Ego and pride has no place during such training as its influence compromises one of the most important moral precepts of Shinkage Ryū, Setsunintō/Katsujiken (the life taking sword/the life giving sword).

History And Technique

Battōjutsu / Iaijutsu

抜刀術／居合術

Battōjutsu (standing sword-drawing) and iaijutsu (kneeling sword-drawing) are arts that teach the exponent to quickly draw and cut with a sword in one motion. The origins of battōjutsu are found in the environment of battlefield combat, when a warrior utilizing a yari (spear) or naginata (glaive) found an adversary inside the combat distance of his pole arm and was forced to quickly draw his sword. In the Edo period, battōjutsu and iaijutsu gained more importance among the samurai as arts of civilian self defense. The Takamura ha Shindō Yōshin Ryū battō/iai curriculum includes drawing daitō (long swords - 25 kata) and shōtō (short swords - five kata). Each daitō kata is performed in both standing and kneeling versions.

Shindō Yōshin Ryū

Seishi   # Battōjutsu

1

The kata begins in shinkiritsu tachigamae (upright sword stance).

2

The swordsman advances in jujiashi (cross-step) while reaching for the tsuka.

3

He initiates the nuki (sword drawing) with sayaoshi (pushing the scabbard forward), pressing the saya up at a 45 degree angle.

4

Next, he executes sayabiki (pulling the scabbard back) as he continues drawing the sword forward and up.

5

As the sword's kissaki clears the koiguchi (mouth of the saya) the swordsman abruptly drops his elbow and body allowing the sword to rotate on its center of gravity.

6

As the sword nears chūdan (middle position), the swordsman secures the sword's tsuka, stopping its cut.

History And Technique

抜刀術   生死

7

The swordsman now inverts the sword by raising his left hand and rotating blade so the shinogi faces upwards.

8

As the swordsman steps forward with his left leg he drives the blade to jōdan.

9

The swordsman executes a kirioroshi.

10

Stepping forward with his right leg he stops the cut at sagamae (hanging forward).

11

The swordsman raises the sword to seigan and slides forward executing a tsuki (thrust).

12

After a moment of zanshin (focused stillness), the swordsman lowers the sword to chūdan.

Seishi

Battōjutsu

13

The swordsman performs chiburi (blood cleansing), snapping his hips clockwise and the sword horizontal to the right.

14

The swordsman initiates the nōtō (re-sheathing) by snapping the sword up and at an angle across his body.

15

As he retreats with his right leg, he lines the sword's mune up with the koiguchi.

16

As he shifts his weight backwards, he feeds the tsuka down while pulling the koiguchi back.

17

When the kissaki reaches the koiguchi, the swordsman pushes the saya down, re-sheathing the blade between 30 to 45 degrees across the body.

18

The swordsman continues retreating until he is evenly weighted and the tsuba meets the saya.

History And Technique

抜刀術   生死

19

The swordsman rotates his body counter-clockwise

20

The swordsman executes sakura reigi (ritual of re-seating the sword in the saya).

21

The swordsman now draws his rear foot forward, returning to shinkrirtsu tachigamae and finishing the kata.

Shindō Yōshin Ryū

Men

Iaijutsu

1
The kata starts in ihiragamae (kneeling half-open stance).

2
The swordsman steps up with his right leg.

3
The swordsman rises and advances in juji-ashi. He initiates the nuki performing say-aoshi, pressing the saya up at a 45 degree angle.

4
He next executes sayabiki pushing the saya back as he continues pushing the sword forward and up, out of the saya.

5
The swordsman rotates his body clockwise placing the sword with his right hand in front of his upper body, angled down, right to left.

6
The swordsman next rotates and raises the sword to jōdan.

History And Technique

居合術　　　　　　　　　　　　　　　　　　　　　　　　　　面

7

The swordsman then executes a kirioroshi.

8

As the sword nears chūdan, the swordsman drops his body by sliding his right foot forward and stops the cut.

9

The swordsman now steps right raising the sword into tate kyōtō.

10

The swordsman shifts his body behind his sword and cuts mengiri (face cut) while dropping into manjigamae (90 degree stance).

11

The swordsman finishes his cut at seigan.

12

After a moment of zanshin, the swordsman lowers the sword to chūdan.

Shindō Yōshin Ryū

Men

Iaijutsu

13

The swordsman performs chiburi, snapping his hips clockwise and the sword horizontal to the right.

14

The swordsman retreats by rising up. Simultaneously he initiates the nōtō by snapping the sword up and at an angle across his body.

15

As he shifts his weight further backwards to his left leg, he lines the sword's mune up with the koiguchi.

16

While stepping back with the right leg he feeds the tsuka down while pulling the koiguchi back.

17

When the kissaki reaches the koiguchi, the swordsman pushes the saya down, re-sheathing the blade between 30 to 45 degrees across the body.

18

The swordsman retreats into a kneeling position. Simultaneously with his left knee touching the tatami, the tsuba should meet the koiguchi.

History And Technique

居合術

19
The swordsman now rotates his left shin counter-clockwise placing his ankle under his hips.

20
He executes sakura reigi.

21
The swordsman now settles into his base and returns to ihiragamae.

Richard Elias / Tsukamaki-shi

Richard Elias, a licensed instructor in the Takamura ha Shindō Yōshin Ryū Kenshinyokan Dōjō, is a tsukamaki-shi, an adept craftsman whose speciality is making and wrapping the handles of Japanese swords. Handle wrapping is a tedious and exacting process that demands extreme patience and an obsessive attention to detail. All training swords eventually require the services of a tsukamaki-shi as the silk, cotton, or leather tsuka-ito (handle cord) wears, and eventually loosens.

Tightly wrapped tsuka-ito (handle cord) is indispensable for a training sword as any looseness compromises the connection between the swordsman and his weapon. Before wrapping, the tsuka-ito must be soaked and pre-stretched so it will not loosen after being tightly wrapped around the handle core. The most traditional style of wrapping is called hinerimaki (twisting wrap). Each time the tsuka-ito is wrapped around the handle core it is twisted and crossed. At the juncture, a hishigami (small paper triangle) is inserted into the folded over ito. This stabilizes the juncture of the parallel strips of ito and raises it from the samegawa (stingray skin) covered handle core to allow for a more secure grip.

It was common for Nihon koryū to recruit craftsmen and artisans into their ranks to help support the ryūha. The Takamura ha Shindō Yōshin Ryū is fortunate to have within its membership several skilled craftsmen who can serve as a resource for advice and services related to the creation, maintenance and repair of classical Japanese weaponry.

History And Technique
Battō Torikaeshi

Battō Torikaeshi is the study of weapon retention. In these kata an attacker quickly approaches a swordsman whose sword is in his saya (scabbard) and attempts to disarm him. The swordsman utilizes sophisticated body dynamics to take the initiative from his attacker and successfully draw his sword. Although these kata are technically part of the weapons curriculum, they have a great deal in common with taijutsu as they essentially represent armed grappling. The principles of jūnan na shintai (maintaining a flexible body) and shintai no chūshin tadasu (maintaining proper body structure) must manifest themselves at a very high level in these kata for consistent success.

Shindō Yōshin Ryū

Saya Oshi

Battō Torikaeshi

The kata begins with uchitachi and shitachi facing one another in aihanmi torima.

1

Uchitachi steps forward attempting to seize shitachi's sword tsuka and push it across his body.

2

Shitachi steps in deep with his right leg, cutting off uchitachi's attempt to cross his seichusen. Shitachi next pivots counterclockwise feeding the sword up and forward in an arc, striking uchitachi on the left side of his face with the tsuka.

3

History And Technique

抜刀取返　　　　　　　　　　　　　　　　　鞘押

Uchitachi is thrown with shitachi's tsuka ate to the face.

4

As uchitachi lands on the tatami, shitachi steps forward with his right foot and draws his blade.

5

He then executes seishi, cutting to uchitachi's right forearm.

6

Shindō Yōshin Ryū

Hiji Kujiki

Battō Torikaeshi

The kata begins with uchitachi and shitachi facing one another in gyaku hanmi torima.

1

As uchitachi steps forward attempting to seize shitachi's tsuka with his right arm, shitachi executes an atemi to uchitachi's jaw.

2

Shitachi steps left and grasps the tsuka of his sword with his right arm while locking uchitachi's right elbow.

3

History And Technique

抜刀取返 肘挫

4

Shitachi executes hiji kujiki and pivots clockwise gaining kuzushi.

5

Shitachi lowers his hips and continues rotating clockwise by pulling with his right leg. Uchitachi, up-ended, rolls away.

6

Shitachi executes yokogiri and then covers uchitachi in hokogamae (spear cover position).

Shindō Yōshin Ryū

Hiji Otoshi

Battō Torikaeshi

The kata begins with uchitachi and shitachi facing one another in gyaku hanmi torima.

1

Uchitachi steps forward with his right leg, secures shitchi's right elbow with his left hand and seizes the tsuka with his right hand.

2

As uchitachi attempts to disarm shitachi by drawing his sword, shitachi extends his arm, spiraling the sword tsuka counter-clockwise over uchitachi's forearm while advancing towards his rear.

3

Shitachi now rotates the sword clockwise, dropping uchitachi's elbow into his rear fuantehō and gaining kuzushi.

4

History and Technique

抜刀取返 　　　　　　　　　　　　　　　肘落

5

Shitachi abruptly collapses his body structure dropping uchitachi to his rear.

6

As uchitachi falls, shitachi thrusts the sword scabbard up and forward, breaking uchitachi's grip on the tsuka.

7

Shitachi continues this motion drawing his sword from the scabbard.

8

Shitachi executes seishi, cutting to uchitachi's mid-torso.

Shindō Yōshin Ryū

Tekubigiri

Battō Torikaeshi

The kata begins with uchitachi and shitachi facing one another in aihanmi torima.

1

Uchitachi slides forward with his right leg, grasping shitachi's right forearm with his right hand.

2

As uchitachi attempts to drive shitachi's sword across his seichusen, shitachi blends with the pressure and steps deeply to the right while raising his sword.

3

The sword is now directly in uchitachi's fuantehō. Shitachi pivots counter-clockwise facing uchitachi. Through this movement shitachi must maintain pressure into uchitachi's rear fuantehō.

4

抜刀取返　　　　　　　　　　　　　手首切

5

Shitachi pulls his body structure forward with his front leg while feeding the saya forward and out of his obi, gaining kuzushi.

6

Shitachi drops his body structure, collapsing uchitachi to his rear fuantehō.

7

Shitachi continues this motion, drawing his sword from the scabbard initiating seishi.

8

Shitachi finishes seishi cutting downward to uchitachi's inside thigh.

Shindō Yōshin Ryū

Shisei no Gyō

姿勢の行

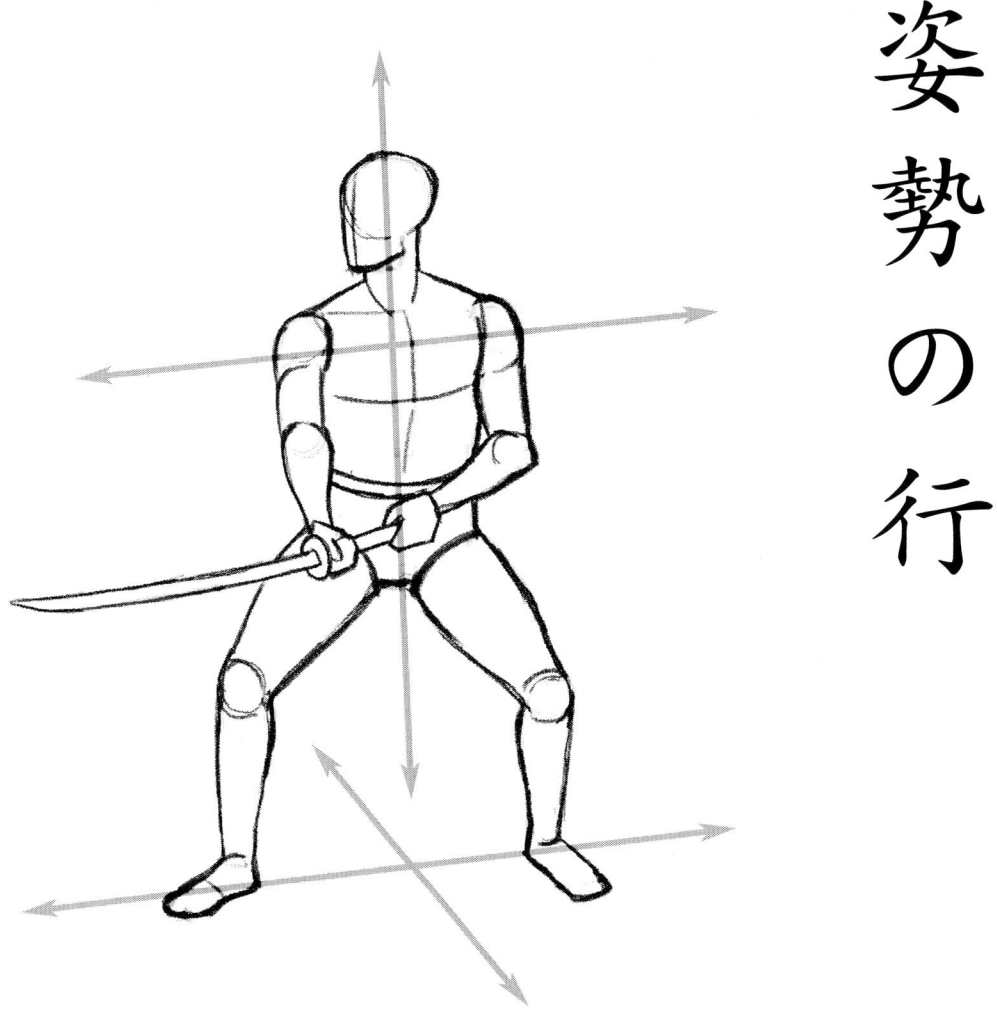

Shisei no Gyō translates as teaching of body structure. Sophisticated body mechanics and muscular articulation of the skeletal structure were areas of deep study in the Akiyama and Totsuka lines of Yōshin Ryū jūjutsu as well as Shinkage Ryū kenjutsu. Because the Yōshin Ryū schools were created by samurai with a background in medicine, a unique foundation on which to conceive a system of both armed and unarmed combat was forged. On the following pages are illustrations and detailed descriptions of 15 basic and intermediate physical principles utilized in Takamura ha Shindō Yōshin Ryū. In total, there are over 40 physical principles considered part of the school's riai (kata theory). The most advanced teachings, identified as myōden, are naiden and only taught to senior level members of Takamura ha Shindō Yōshin Ryū.

Seichūsen

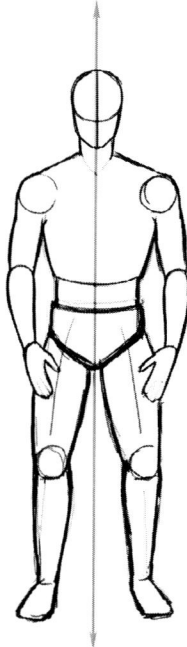 

Seichūsen (正中線) translates as correct center line. Understanding the seichūsen and its relation to maintaining proper body structure is foundational to an art like Shindō Yōshin Ryū. Being aware of, and controlling, the seichūsen is among the most fundamental requirements of performing efficient body locomotion and articulation.

Physically, the seichūsen represents a vertical line running from the center of the head, through the center of gravity of the body, and to a point representing the center of the structural base. The center of two vertical planes, this line separates the body left from right and front from back.

Tactically, using the seichūsen as an axis is critical to developing different forms of power generation. Rotating the body on the axis of the seichūsen is one of the easiest methods to generate a powerful strike, block, kick, parry, or sword cut. Using the legs to rotate the body on its center line allows the shoulder or hip to physically move towards a target. This allows the body to successfully generate power without changing the percentage of weight being supported by each foot.

The seichūsen is also a tactically important target. When a strike or sword cut connects with a point on the body located outside the seichūsen, that point can be easily moved away from the attacking weapon. Rotating on the axis of the seichūsen can dissipate any energy transfer to the target. However, when a strike or cut connects with a point on the body in alignment with seichūsen, no amount of rotation moves the target away from the attacking weapon. In such a situation, the only way to negate the energy transfer to the target is to tactically disengage by moving the seichūsen away from the attack.

Shindō Yōshin Ryū

Chūshin wo Tadasu

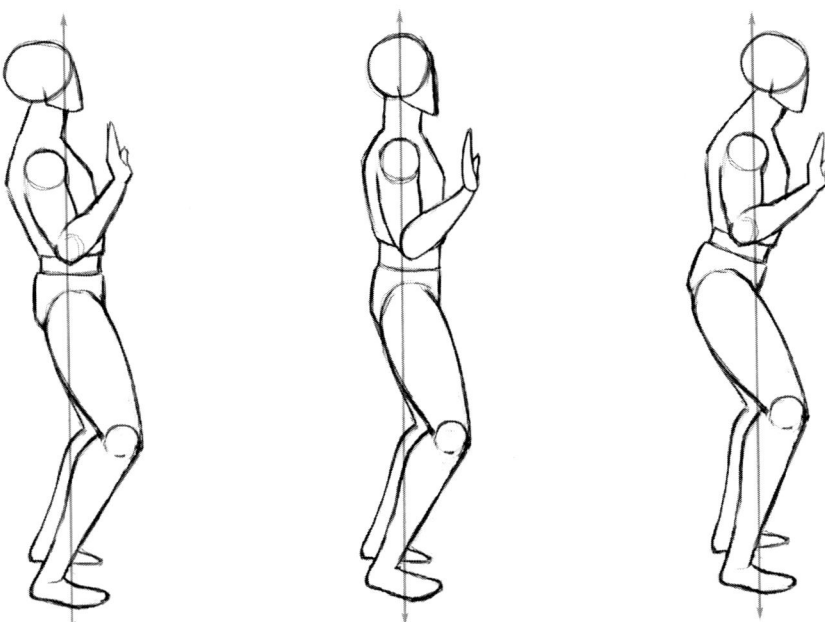

Chūshin wo Tadasu (中心を正す) translates as center correct. The term refers to the principle of maintaining proper body posture. Effective Shindō Yōshin Ryū technique requires flexible joints and a supple body, one free of muscular tension and stiffness. This can best be achieved by maintaining a properly-aligned skeletal structure.

Supporting the weight of the body always starts at the feet. The center of balance over the foot should align near the front of the shin as it enters the ankle. Regardless of the amount of bend in the knee, the hip socket should remain aligned over the center of the foot. The lower back should be slightly tucked in so the sacrum encourages a slight curve as the spine exits the pelvis and rises to the scapulothoracic joints. The center of the shoulder socket should rest over the hip socket with the neck and head erect while the chin is slightly tucked. In this position a minimal amount of muscular engagement is required to support an upright posture.

The most common flaw in body posture occurs when the head and shoulders are carried forward (stoop-shouldered), and the hips are shifted backwards in an attempt to counter the forward weight bias. This creates tension in the lower back, shoulder and neck. A less common flaw occurs when the head and shoulders are shifted in a backward position (swayback). This strains the lower back, hip flexors and thigh muscles.

When the body's skeletal framework is misaligned, muscles must engage through increasing contraction to keep the body upright. This wastes energy and creates tension that can migrate into the surrounding muscles. When muscles are tense, they are no longer available for locomotion or joint articulation, making budō technique slow, stiff and weak.

Antehō/Fuantehō

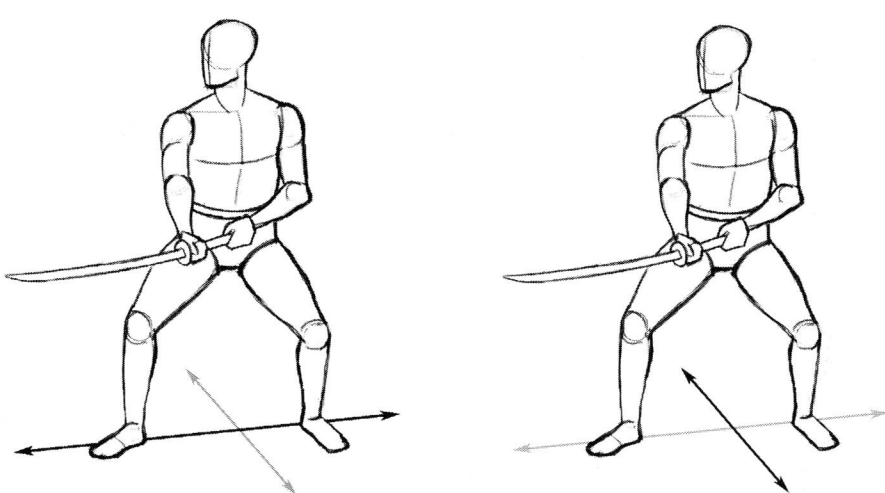

Antehō (安定方) translates as stable direction. The term references a line passing through the feet of a person's stance.

From a defensive point of view, a force projected onto a body structure along the antehō will encounter resistance related to the distance between the feet. This makes kuzushi along this line more difficult to achieve. A common tactic in Shindō Yōshin Ryū is to meet a threat by positioning the antehō through the seichūsen of an adversary.

From an offensive point of view, an attack projected along this line will benefit from the inherent stability of the stance in this dimension.

Fuantehō (不安定方) translates as unstable direction. The term references a line running 90 degrees perpendicular to the antehō.

From an offensive point of view, a force projected onto a body structure along the fuantehō line will encounter little resistance as an adversary has no significant structural support for resistance. Compromising an adversary's structure is most easily achieved along his fuantehō, so kuzushi is often attempted on this line. Counter-attacks, as well as blocks, along this line are also weaker due to the lack of structural support, so it is beneficial to attack and defend against an adversary along his fuantehō.

When an attacker positions his antehō through the seichūsen and fuantehō of his adversary, he gains significant tactical and structural advantage.

Mae Kado/Ushiro Kado

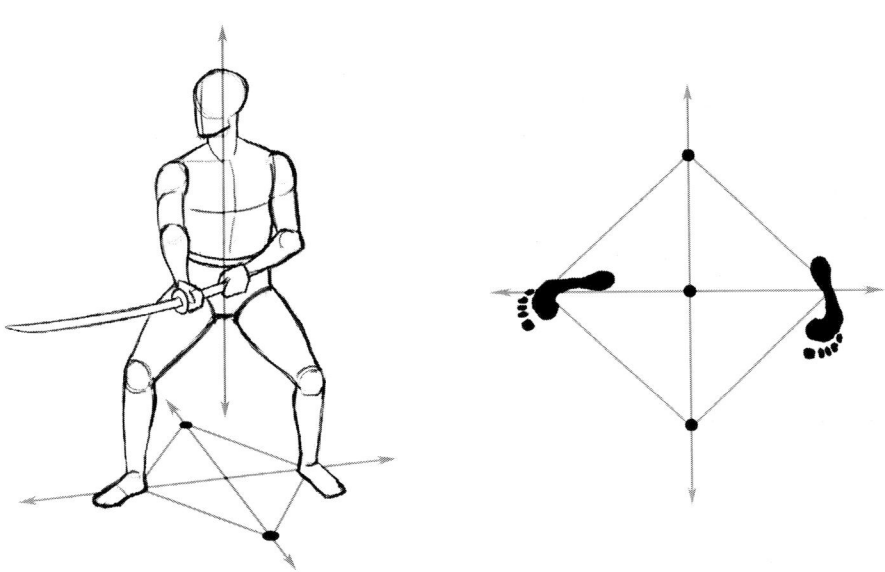

Mae Kado (前角) translates as front corner. The term references a forward point falling on the fuantehō, half the width of the base from the seichūsen.

From an offensive point of view, pressure directed to an adversary's mae kado evenly weights the balls of the feet, inhibiting his freedom of movement. Most commonly, a hand, elbow or shoulder is directed over the mae kado and lowered to achieve a weighted base. Dropped further, the adversary's structure can be broken forward at the hip or knees, achieving kuzushi and facilitating a throw or take-down.

Ushiro Kado (後角) translates as rear corner. The term references a rear point falling on the fuantehō, half the width of the base from the seichūsen. If you draw a line through the feet, the mae kado and the ushiro kado, you get a near perfect square.

Although it seems you would utilize these two points in the same manner, there are significant differences when you consider rearward and forward joint articulation. Our knees and hips in particular do not articulate backwards. We also have feet protruding forward but not backward. This means it is easier to achieve kuzushi on an adversary to his rear. Similar to the front, using a hand, elbow or shoulder, directed over the ushiro kado and lowered will achieve a weighted base, however, the amount of drop required to achieve kuzushi is smaller. Without the option of articulating the hip or knees, and no foot to offer resistance, the body structure will fall to the rear and behind the antehō more rapidly, and with less effort than towards the front.

Using these points to fix in place or off-balance a human body is a fundamental principle of combat dynamics in Shindō Yōshin Ryū.

History And Technique

Jūji

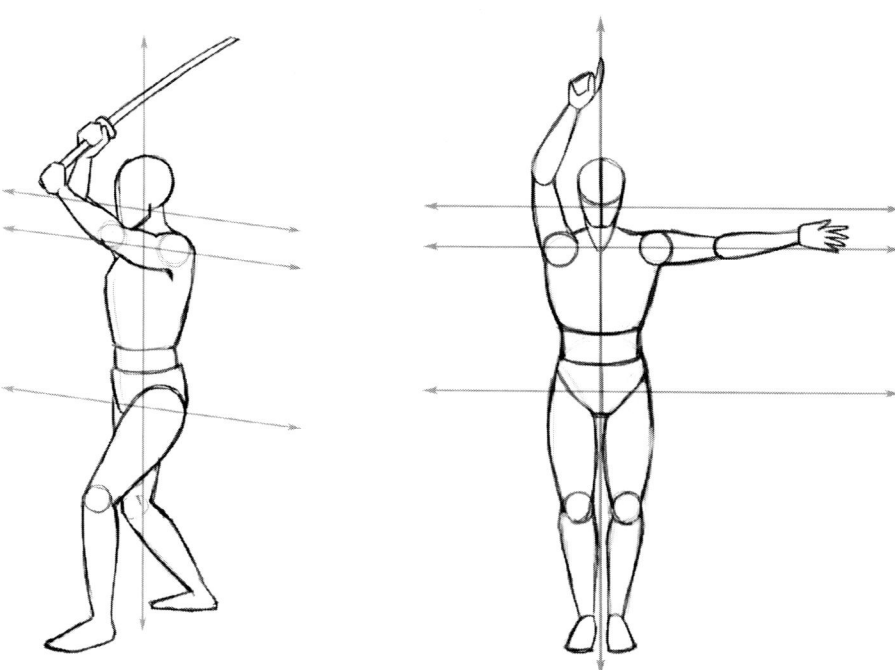

Jūji (十字) literally translates as cross. The term references the mandibular cross of the head passing horizontally through the jaw, the thoracic cross of the body passing horizontally through the shoulders, and the pelvic cross passing horizontally through the hip sockets. These structural crosses link the spine with the head, and the four limbs of the body.

With a properly aligned body structure, the upper line passing through the jaw joints, the middle line passing through the shoulder sockets, and the lower line passing through the hip sockets, all these lines are parallel to the ground. When one or more of these horizontal lines are not parallel to the ground, the spinal column must flex laterally, creating asymmetry. This asymmetry creates uneven loading of the shoulder, back and/or hip muscles, resulting in tension. Asymmetry can also affect the body's weight distribution, which creates more uneven loading of the musculature. When the musculature is unevenly loaded, the resulting tension in the upper and lower torso inhibits freedom of movement. This tension can also create a muscular connection in the body core that an adversary can exploit in combat.

To move quickly and efficiently, one should seek to employ the least amount of energy when resisting gravity and maintaining a standing position. By maintaining a more symmetrical and aligned body, the gravitational load is spread evenly throughout the bone structure. All the musculature needs to do is hold the bones in the proper alignment to maintain an upright position.

Tai Otoshi

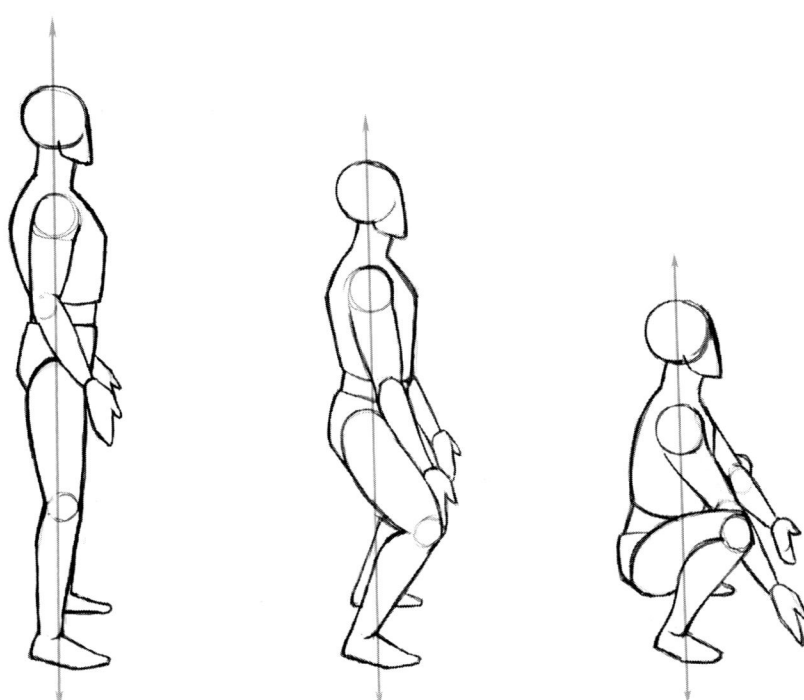

Tai Otoshi (体落とし) translates as body-drop. The term references lowering one's body with attention to maintaining an aligned but connected body structure. Keeping the feet, hips, shoulders and head all aligned while lowering or raising one's body requires superior joint flexibility, as well as muscular strength. It is another fundamental skill required in the execution of Shindō Yōshin Ryū techniques.

One form of power generation in Shindō Yōshin Ryū is based on utilizing tai otoshi. In kenjutsu, connecting one's center of gravity to a sword, and then dropping one's connected body structure utilizes weight and gravity to generate power for a cut. With this method of power generation, the musculature is free to focus on speed and targeting. Since the musculature is not overly concentrated on power generation, the body can remain supple and relaxed while still in a connected state.

In the realm of taijutsu, when musubi (connection) is created by an attacker attempting to control or restrain an adversary, energy can be generated by dropping one's connected body structure. This energy, properly channeled, can be projected into the attacker's body structure to create kuzushi or execute nagewaza. The amount of power generated is directly related to the weight and speed at which the body drops. Consequently, the body should be dropped as quickly as possible to generate the maximum amount of energy.

Koshi Otoshi

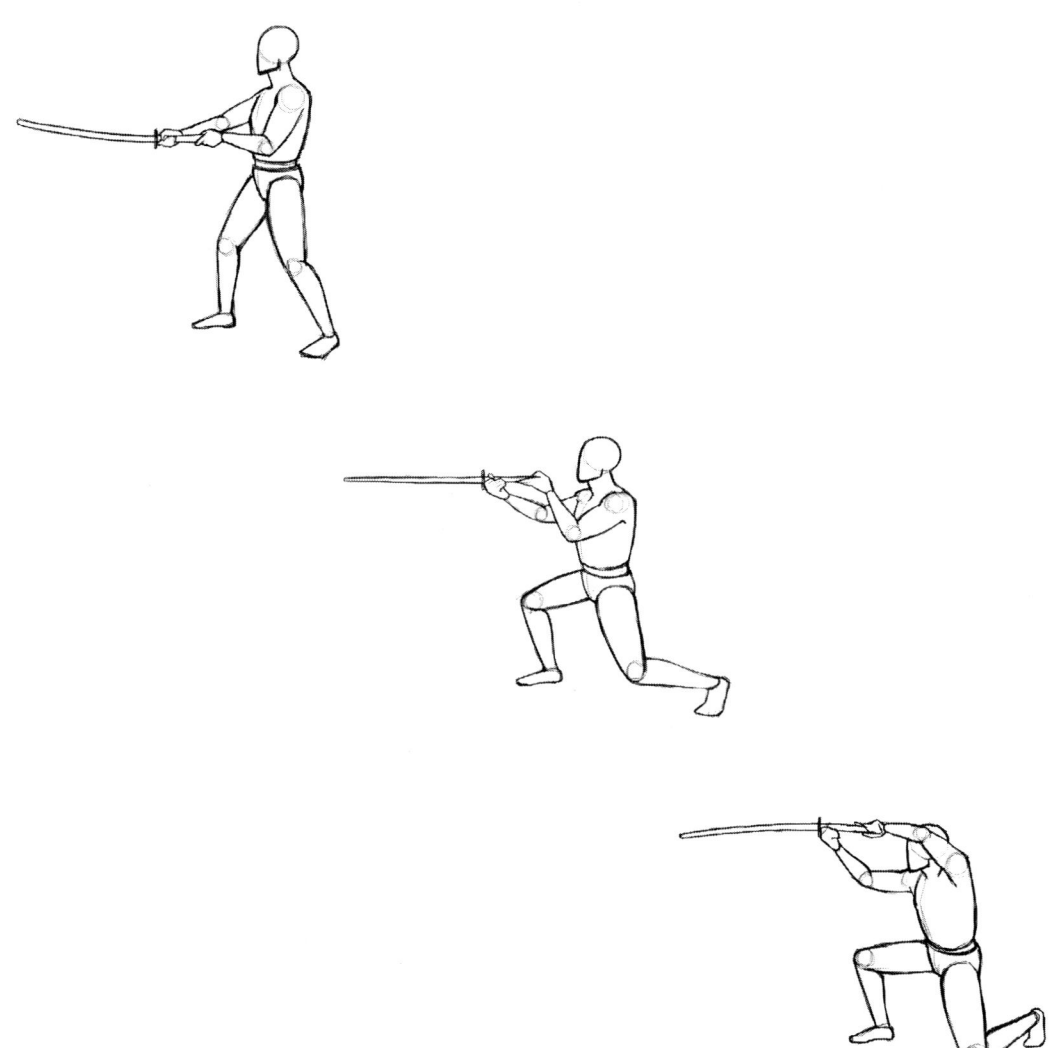

Koshi Otoshi (腰落とし) translates as hip-dropping. The term references the principle of dropping the body as a form of evasive taisabaki (body movement). In the context of kenjutsu, the principle is utilized in a manner that allows a weapon to essentially float in space, virtually weightless, while the swordsman drops beneath it. Because the body can drop more swiftly by using gravity than the musculature can raise a sword in opposition to gravity, it is a critical principle to master in the environment of bladed weapons.

In the realm of taijutsu, inasu (tactical evasion) can be achieved through the principle of koshi otoshi to swiftly avoid a strike while simultaneously achieving a position of advantage. Maintaining jūnan na shintai (a flexible body) and chūshin wo tadasu (properly aligned body structure) is crucial in the successful application of this physical principle.

Jiku

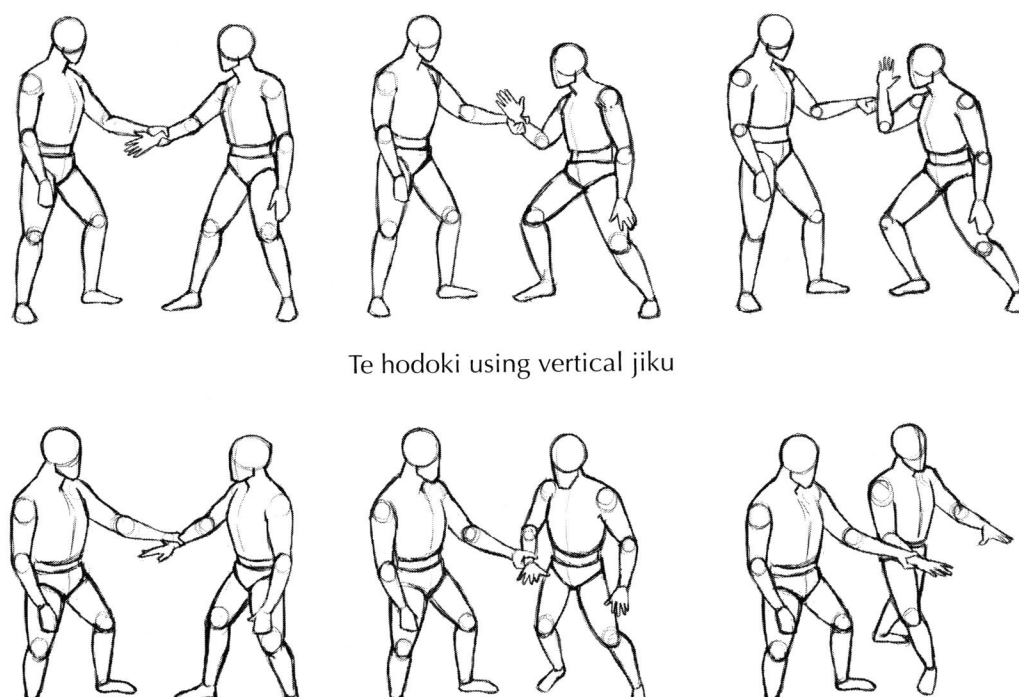

Te hodoki using vertical jiku

Taisabaki using horizontal jiku

Jiku (軸) translates as rotational axis. In the context of taijutsu, one application of the principle involves leaving any point on the body seized by an aggressor in place with the defender moving around that point. In this example, if the defender attempts even the slightest movement of the connection point it will create a muscular link between the aggressor and defender that can be exploited by the aggressor. To properly apply this principle in combat the defender must make their structure as pliable as possible without relaxing to the point of passivity. This will allow the defender to move freely so they can acquire a position of tactical superiority resulting in te hodoki or in kuzushi of the aggressor.

Another method of applying the principle of jiku in taijutsu is rotating along a linear axis in the manner of turning a spool. If an aggressor attempts to seize the adversary's limb, rotating the limb along its long axis can compromise the attackers body structure, reversing the roles of aggressor and defender. In this example, the act of attacking compromises the attacker at the instant of physical contact.

In the context of weapons combat, the principle of jiku is applied in so many diverse ways, it is beyond the scope of this book to intricately describe them. An astute understanding and application of rotational dynamics is a foundational principal in the arts descended from Akiyama Yōshin Ryū and Shinkage Ryū.

History And Technique

Mon

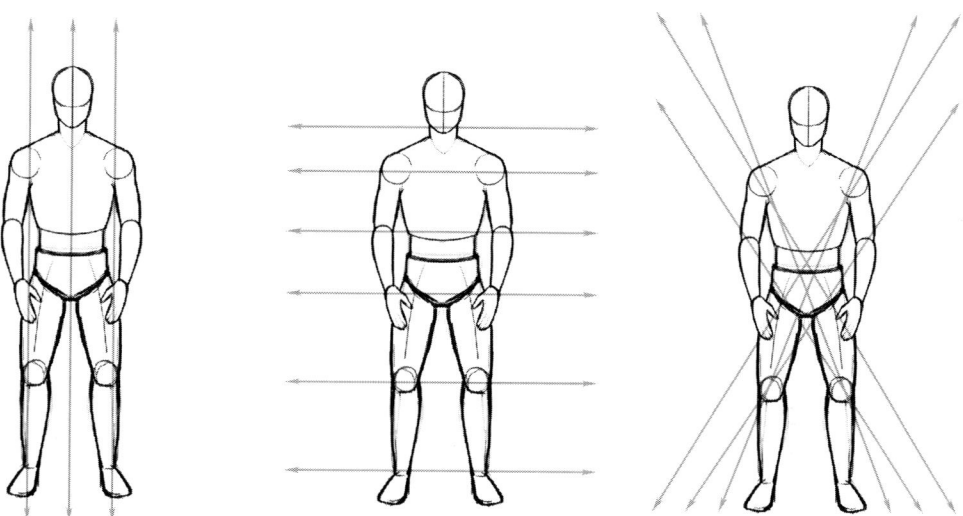

Mon (門) translates as gate, and is a further development of the principle jiku. The term references the principle of taking three points on the body structure, holding two of them stationary, and moving the third point in an arc perpendicular to an axis going through the two stationary points. The gate can be used offensively or defensively to project force, dissipate force, evade an attack, or be the target of one.

Vertical Gates

There are three primary vertical gates. The seichūsen is the gate most familiar to the average martial arts practitioner. The other two primary gates (kaimon) run from the foot, through the knee, and up through the shoulder.

Horizontal Gates

There are six primary horizontal gates. Five of the six primary horizontal gates run through joints located symmetrically on the body. These are the ankles, knees, hips, elbows, and shoulders. The sixth is the rotational axis where the neck enters the skull. This loosely equates with the mandibular joint.

Diagonal Gates

There are six primary diagonal gates and 10 secondary ones. An example of a primary diagonal gate is a rotational axis running from the left knee through the right shoulder. An example of a secondary diagonal gate would be a rotational axis running from the right ankle through the left elbow. Generally, horizontal and vertical gates affect the body structure symmetrically, while diagonal gates affect the body structure asymmetrically.

Kaimon

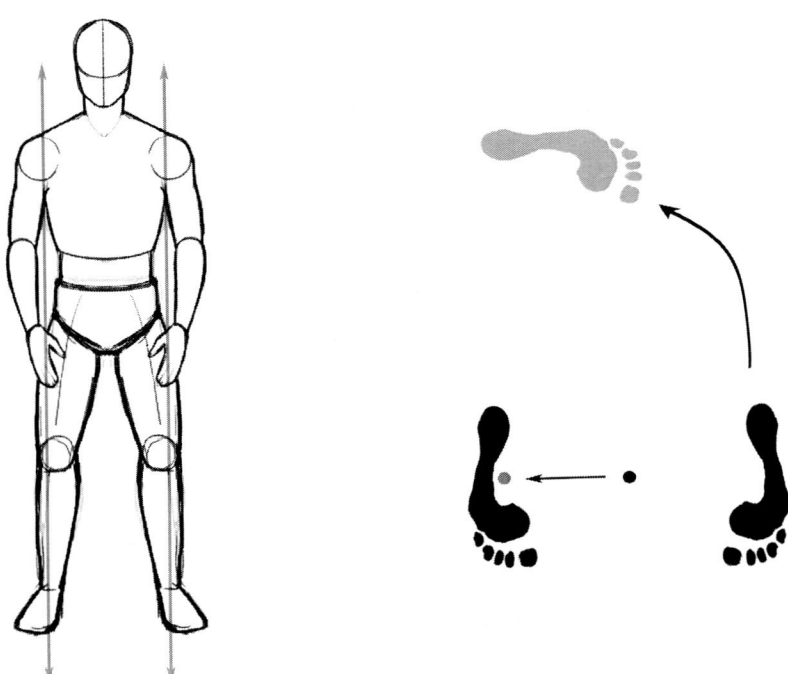

Kaimon (開門) translates as opening the gate and the term further expands on the mon principle (gate). By fixing one vertical gate and moving the gate in an arc perpendicular to the fixed gate, the body swings on the vertical axis of the stationary gate, as if opening a door.

A subtle but important feature of kaimon is as the body opens, the body's center of gravity must shift toward the vertical axis of the stationary gate, not to its seichūsen. This leaves the body in a position where most of its weight is near the stationary gate.

Kaimon is most often employed as a form of evasive taisabaki where the body moves out of the path of an attack without increasing its distance from the attacker. If an attacker closes the distance to the defender by supporting his structure through the use of his antehō, and the defender responds with kaimon, the attacker will find himself exposed and in a disadvantageous position. This is because the defender's weight is forward and his fuantehō has been converted into an antehō.

Kaimon can also be used to generate power in the execution of tachiai taoshi or nagewaza. Used in combination with the principle of tai otoshi, kaimon can create and steer its own energy while being supplemented by the additional energy of a dropping body structure. Although its application can be decisive in taijutsu, kaimon most powerfully demonstrates its tactical value in an environment where edged weapons are in play.

Tai no Kaiten

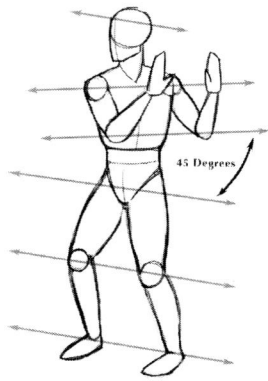 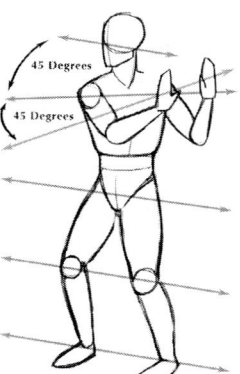 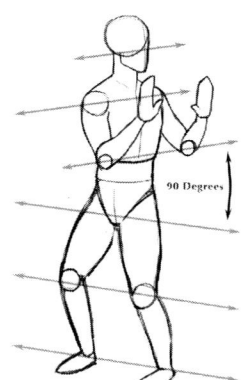

Tai no Kaiten (体の回転) translates as body rotation. The term references the principle of separating the body into stacked horizontal layers and rotating them either independently or connected to one another. This allows rotational deflection or projection of energy in a way that can be isolated in one layer or enhanced by another. Generally the body is separated into three stacked layers: the mandibular cross passing through the jaw, the thoracic cross passing through the shoulders, and the pelvic cross passing through the hip sockets. Additionally, the thoracic cross has what functions as a secondary layer created by the two arms.

The pelvic layer is the most powerful rotational layer due to its access to the largest muscles in the body. The driving power of the legs and the ability to lower the center of gravity by bending the knees gives the pelvic layer great rotational flexibility and considerable angular flexibility.

The thoracic layer, although less powerful than the pelvic layer, can still call upon strong muscles in the body core for rotation. The thoracic layer is the most versatile because the arms are attached to a shoulder cross, which can be horizontally rotated. If you add the articulation of the shoulder socket, with the rotation of the thoracic layer, you have a potent tool for the projection or deflection of energy in multiple directions.

The mandibular cross is of minimal use in power generation but it is extremely important in maintaining a relaxed body structure, balance, and situational awareness. When one's head droops forward or tilts to the side, it creates residual tension in the neck and shoulders.

Any adjacent layer of the body can be instantly connected and coordinated with another layer. Similarly, any layers that are connected can be immediately unconnected, so each layer can operate independently. Being able to connect or disconnect each layer adds flexibility in how to apply tai no musubi.

Offensively, tai no kaiten is fundamental in coordinating and connecting multiple body layers, which supports projecting energy through something as simple as a hand strike. Defensively, disconnecting the thoracic layer from the pelvic layer impedes a grapplers attempt to control a defenders body structure when he attacks only one layer.

Hiki Ashi

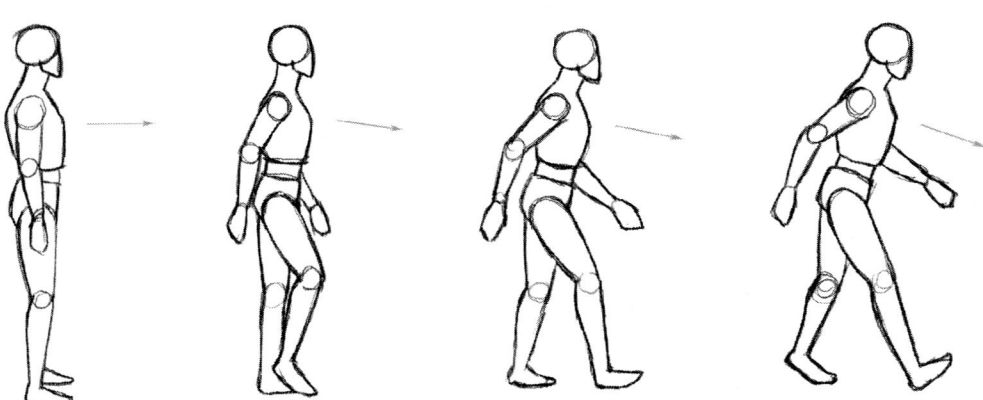

Hiki Ashi (引き足) literally translates as pulling foot. The term references the principle of pulling oneself forward with the front foot instead of pushing oneself forward with the rear foot.

In the above illustration the subject lifts the right knee while allowing his body to tilt forward. Next, he extends his right leg as he pushes off with his left leg and allows his body to fall farther forward. Finally, with his right leg fully extended his foot touches the ground stopping his fall. This common method of locomotion is inherently unstable because the body is constantly falling beyond its base and then catching itself.

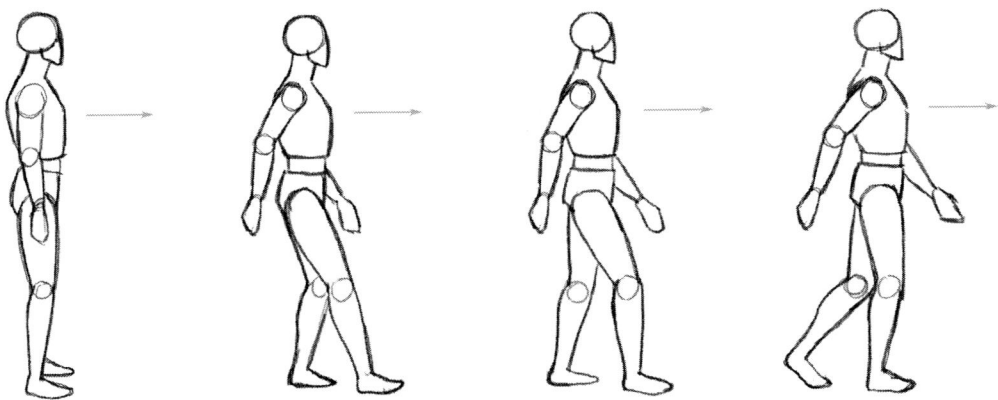

In this illustration the subject reaches forward with the right leg/foot as he lowers his body by bending the left leg. With the right foot connected to the ground he pulls his body forward with his right leg. As the weight transfers to the right foot, the left leg does not push forward. It only acts to support the weight of the body. Once the right foot has pulled the subject's center of gravity completely over the right foot, the left heel raises in preparation for taking a forward step. In this method of locomotion the body moves smoothly forward, never loosing its balance because its center of gravity remains inside the boundary of its base.

History And Technique

Oshi Te

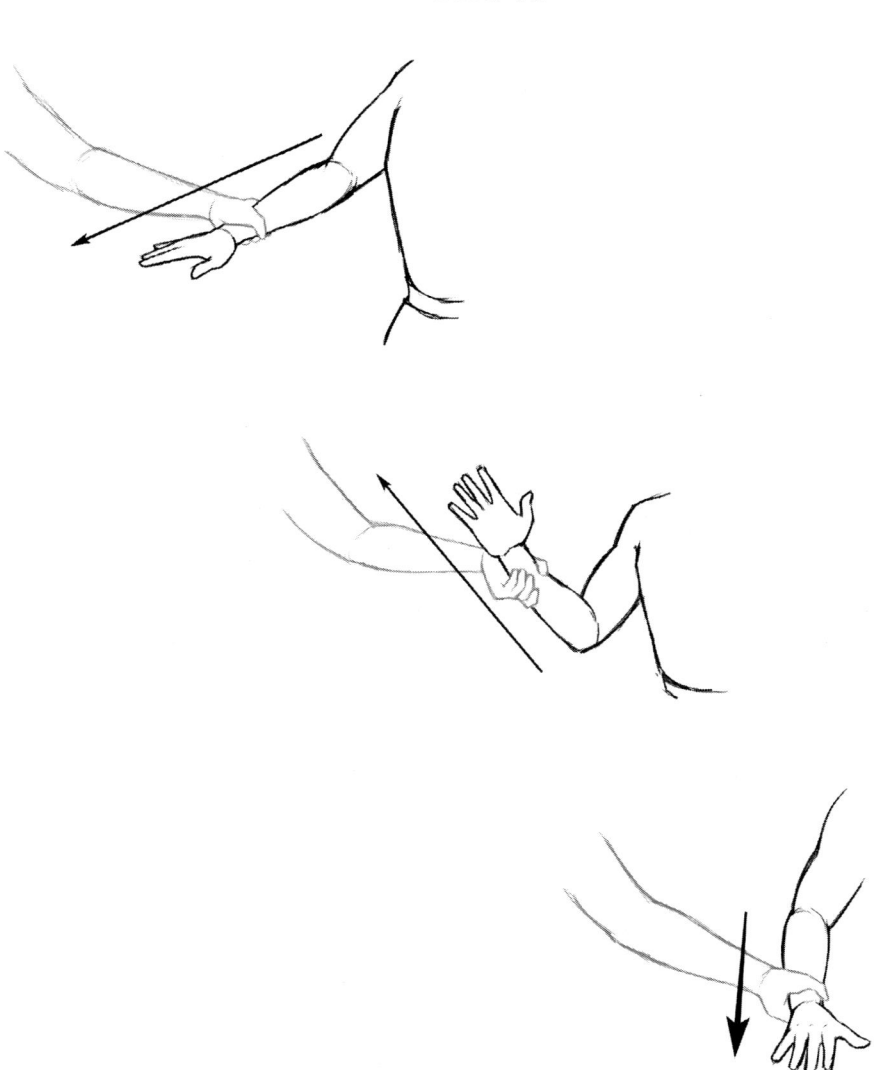

Oshi Te (押し手) translates as pushing hand. The term references the principle of extending one's hand by feeding the radius and ulna bones of the forearm linearly thorough an attacker's grip. When an attacker seizes a defender's forearm in an attempt to restrain or control him, he creates a dynamic connection to the defender's center of gravity. Feeding the defender's forearm through the grip of an attacker uses the attacker's strength against him. Reversing the connection can then be used by the defender to gain structural advantage over the attacker.

It is vitally important the pressure exerted by the forearm bones when grabbed travels in a linear fashion precisely through the grip, and does not resist any lateral pressures exerted by the attacker. If the defender resists any lateral pressure applied by the attacker's grip, it creates dynamic tension that can allow the aggressor to retain structural advantage over the defender.

Tanden Dori

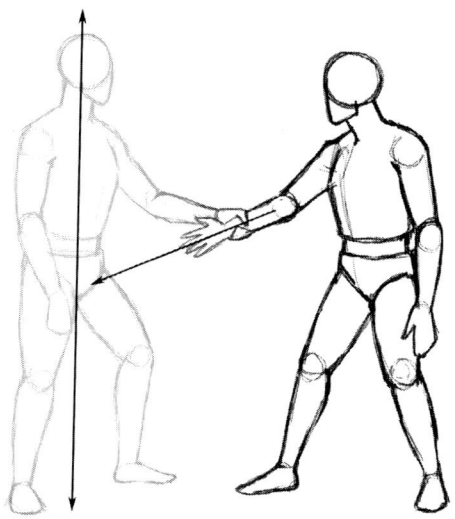

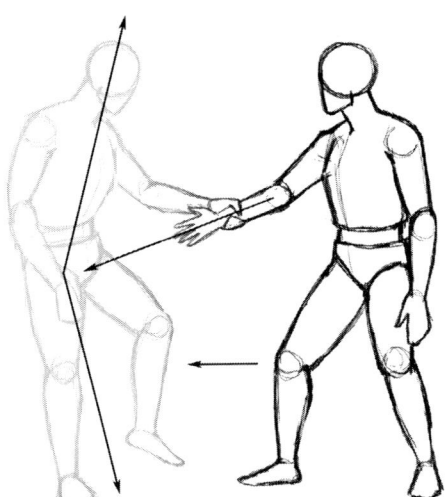

Tanden Dori(丹田取) translates as center capturing and the term references a tactic which expands on the principles of hiki ashi and oshi te.

The tanden is a point just below the navel that represents the body's physical center of gravity. Extending the hand/forearm directly towards the seichūsen just below the the attacker's navel creates a connection that directly threatens the attacker's structural integrity. Once the slack is taken out of the connection by the muscles of the arm, the body core and the leg's powerful muscles can be engaged to continue drawing the body forward. This continued irimi (entering) of the defender's body structure applies pressure into the attacker's tanden and base, which eventually compromises the attacker's structure, forcing collapse, retreat or disengagement.

Rasen no Tai

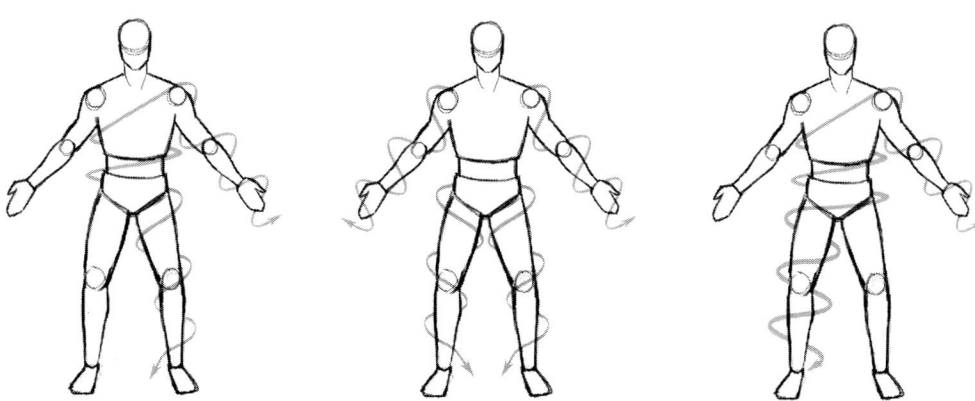

Rasen no Tai (螺旋の体) translates as spiraling body. The term references the principle of using a spiraling form of power generation to store or release energy. Rasen no tai is also a superior method of circumventing linear forms of resistance.

In a spiraling movement the body winds tissue much like a metal cable, giving it strength and stability, while maintaining flexibility. Rasen no tai is also related to developing tai no musubi (connected body). The act of twisting and extending the body simultaneously gathers and unifies the musculature in a collective effort that is supported by the fascial web. In this way, the body operates as a coordinated and connected whole.

Muscles used in body articulation only contract in a linear fashion; therefore, all projections of force and resistance of force originate in a linear contraction of muscle tissue. When the body moves in a linear fashion, the mind has a fairly simple job calculating the muscular contraction needed to execute the movement. When the body moves in curves and spirals, however, the mind must coordinate multiple muscles in a complex series of precisely-timed contractions. With practice these complex movements become amazingly precise, allowing us to intuitively operate in all three dimensions. Resisting movement is altogether different. Resisting linear movement is fairly simple because it is predictable and because the musculature contracts in a linear fashion. Resisting movement operating in multiple dimensions is virtually impossible because the mind cannot calculate where multi-dimensional movement is going, and if it could, all the attacker would need to do is alter the vector of the movement. For this reason it is exceptionally difficult for the human body to thwart movement operating in three dimensions without resorting to static resistance.

Effective resistance of an attack projected in three dimensions requires a more adept response in three dimensions. Spiraling the musculature of the body, sometimes in opposing directions, creates a uniform and connected body structure that can shift, twist and rotate in arcs or spiral projections, which compromise the structure of the attacker. No matter how they attack, their spirals are projected back into their structure, disconnecting their base from the ground. Because the thighs and abdominal core muscles are the largest and most powerful in the body, articulating the knees and femur heads in the pelvic girdle is particularly vital in effective spiraling.

Akiyama Lineage Internal Strength Training

Research confirms various forms of internal body training existed in many koryū schools, and these teachings have no apparent connection to China. In some koryū schools, particularly those dominated by the use of bladed weaponry, internal training supported development of extreme speed and accuracy as opposed to power. Given the benefits of speed and accuracy over power development in an environment where bladed weapons dominated, this makes pragmatic sense.

Sometime in the 17th century, internal body training to develop power, identified as nairiki, is said to have been introduced to Japan from China through the schools of Akiyama Yōshin Ryū and Kitō Ryū. These newly-introduced skills were considered secret knowledge and rarely described in writing beyond cryptic references appearing on high-level teaching scrolls. Because Akiyama Yōshin Ryū was so ubiquitous, its teachings spread among its various lines and evolved in divergent ways many other classical jūjutsu schools did not. Consequently, it is difficult to identify an orthodox pedagogy in the Akiyama Yōshin Ryū lineages that accurately outlines how these internal strength skills were passed forward. It appears in some lines of Akiyama Yōshin Ryū, nairiki training held important status and was assiduously pursued, while in other lines teaching related to internal strength was virtually ignored. Cryptically-referenced on one rare Akiyama lineage Yōshin Ryū Jōden Gokui no Maki possessed by densho collector Kobayashi Toshishiro, is a category of kuden (oral teachings) identified as Shinden Nairiki no Koto. Exactly what comprised this study remains speculative but it is tantalizing to imagine how these internal strength teachings were originally passed forward in Akiyama Yōshin Ryū. Without any surviving documentation that includes didactic aids, researchers are left with little evidence to support any definite conclusions. Traditional Nihon koryū pedagogy confirms that solo kata training has always been rare in Japan, so it is logical to assume most nairiki study was conducted through partner training. However, since nairiki training is said to have originated in China, where solo kata training was common, the possibility exists that the Nairiki no Gyō, as they survive today in Shindō Yōshin Ryū, might closely mimic those originally imported from China.

This emakimono illustrated in tonbo-e style (dragonfly) is from an Akiyama Yōshin Ryū Inyō Gokui no Maki. Densho like this one were not universally issued in all the lines of Yōshin Ryū as nairiki training was frequently taught only through oral transmission. This one was issued in Tenpō 4 (1833). It is unclear if the illustrations indicate kata or partner drills. Internal training drills with a partner are practiced in Takamura ha Shindō Yōshin Ryū as part of our nairiki kunren. Interestingly, a Shindō Yōshin Ryū Nairiki no Gyō solo kata utilizes the same name listed first on this densho, "Banjaku". The Shindō Yōshin Ryū "Banjaku" is illustrated on page 315.

(Photo of densho courtesy of Kobayashi Toshishiro)

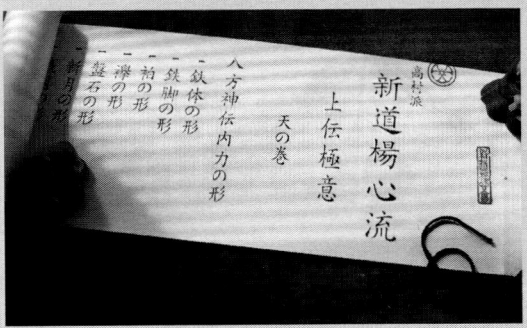

This is a Takamura ha Shindō Yōshin Ryū Jōden Gokui Ten no Maki densho issued to Tobin Threadgill in 1999. Listed on the densho is Happō Shinden Nairiki no Gyō (eight divinely transmitted internal power forms). These eight solo forms represent the foundation of the internal body training passed down in Shindō Yōshin Ryū. Originating in Akiyama lineage Yōshin Ryū, forms like these became ubiquitous in the jūjutsu schools of the Edo period. Sadly, many of these internal teachings have been neglected or lost during the last century.

History And Technique

Nairiki: Internal Power

内力

Shindō Yōshin Ryū, Internal Strength Training, Developing a Budō Body

The port of Nagasaki was the most important city in 17th century Japan, as exchange and trade with outside nations were allowed. This led to the arrival of a considerable amount of technological, medicinal and literary information in Japan during this period. Nagasaki was home to several schools of classical Japanese martial arts, one of the most famous being Akiyama Yōshin Ryū. The school's founder was allegedly a medical doctor named Akiyama Shirōbei Yoshitoki, who lived in Nagasaki, where he learned elements of an indigenous Chinese martial art system and medical techniques. Akiyama eventually settled in Nagasaki and developed a school of budō based on the Chinese sourced information he learned. Part of this training is said to have included sophisticated methods of internal body training (nairiki) and vital-point striking (kyūsho). These internal methods involved structural unification of the body, controlled breathing, muscle coordination and sophisticated joint articulation. Such merging of indigenous jūjutsu techniques with the internal body training introduced from China via Akiyama Yōshin Ryū resulted in Nihon koryū achieving a new level of sophistication.

From Akiyama Yōshin Ryū to Shindō Yōshin Ryū

These teachings and the Chinese-influenced legacy of Akiyama Yōshin Ryū survive today in Shindō Yōshin Ryū. Internal body training is transmitted via a series of forms identified as nairiki no gyō and partner drills identified as nairiki kunren. These exercises originated in Akiyama Yōshin Ryū, which included specific body skills related to efficient, relaxed and situationally-aware movement. Takamura ha Shindō Yōshin Ryū headmaster Takamura Yukiyoshi believed investing in these skills results in the development of what he called a budō body. By nature of a blood oath, I am only permitted to reveal certain aspects of the omote (overt/basic versions) of these forms to readers outside Takamura ha Shindō Yōshin Ryū (TSYR). Therefore, what follows is a glimpse of these methods, and how they are integrated into Shindō Yōshin Ryū.

The Budō Body

Nairiki kunren with force directed through the strong line (antehō) of shite by uchite. In this drill, shite employs internal deflection and rooting skills to compromise uchite's attempt to disrupt shite's body structure.

Nairiki study in TSYR comprises 16 nairiki no gyō, eight omote and eight ura (obscure/advanced), plus the nairiki kunren paired exercises. These forms initially focus on improving muscle strength, correct balance, and mind/body coordination, while further developing the relaxed application of the muscle dynamics that the school's diverse curriculum requires. As practitioners become adept at executing these forms, the study of nairiki fine-tunes physical skills, allowing them to develop a more connected mind/body structure. In this way, the internal skills of practitioners embrace an integrated type of mind/body sensitivity, as opposed to an uncoordinated being in whom the mind and individual body parts do not reflect the capabilities of a unified whole.

To begin the journey of achieving true internal body skills, the practitioner must first cultivate a heightened level of overall body sensitivity. This sensitivity must exist in overlapping structural/skeletal, external/tactile, internal/proprioceptive and dynamic/kinesthetic dimensions.

中心を正す Chūshin wo Tadasu (Skeletal-Posture)

The skeleton should be aligned in such a way that minimal muscular involvement is required to stand upright. Muscle strength must be increased to support an upright structure when the skeleton is improperly aligned and such increased muscular dependence has detrimental consequences for a jūjutsu practitioner. This is because muscles working to support a misaligned skeleton creates residual tension in the body core, most detrimentally in the upper shoulders and sacrum at the lower back. This wastes energy, causing fatigue and ultimately, even illness. Such misdirected use of muscles means they are unavailable during the execution of jūjutsu techniques.

Another issue arises when a body core muscle has a particular task and a related movement is required. In this situation, a less efficient muscle pathway must provide the desired movement. Such inefficient body articulation can result in overloading the musculature, which culminates in unnecessary energy expenditure. Consequently, movement becomes strained and increasingly ineffective.

Using core muscles to compensate for poor postural alignment radiates tension from the core through the extremities that a skilled adversary can exploit as a pathway to attack the center of gravity. Proper skeletal alignment releases the comprehensive core musculature for efficient execution of Shindō Yōshin Ryū techniques and avoids the formation of tension pathways.

外気覚 Gaikikaku (External/Tactile Sense)

Enhanced tactile sensitivity is indispensable for the execution of Shindō Yōshin Ryū technique. The ability to identify subtle pressure changes during body contact allows practitioners to accurately evaluate and appropriately respond to threats. The slightest pressure against the skin of practitioners with properly developed tactile sensitivity can alert them to the direction, speed, and power of an attack before the body can be structurally compromised.

The nairiki kunren, paired contact exercises, introduce Shindō Yōshin Ryū practitioners to tactile sensitivity drills with increasing complexity and difficulty. Practitioners who internalize these drills, develop the foundational dexterity required for successful internal body training.

内気覚 Naikikaku (Internal/Proprioceptive Sense)

Proprioception is the culmination of sensory integration, namely, the awareness of the position of all parts of the body in three-dimensional space without the need for visual orientation. Balance, joint position, and body articulation are all major components of proprioceptive ability. Highly-developed proprioceptive awareness is indispensable in any complex physical activity such as gymnastics, dance or martial arts.

Proprioception is supported by proprioceptors in muscles, tendons, joint capsules and neurons of the inner ear. Training in nairiki no gyō engages and heightens proprioceptive skills through skeletal alignment challenges, force vectors and balance disruption. Executing nairiki no gyō exercises blindfolded or with eyes closed is one of many methods that enhance proprioceptive cognition.

Physiologists have only recently started to study internal tactile sensitivity or interoception (awareness of internal status of one's body) as an adjunct to proprioception (unconscious perception of movement and spatial orientation arising from internal stimuli detected by nerves within the body and semicircular canals of the inner ear) and nociception (response of sensory nervous system's response to harmful or potentially harmful stimuli). This nascent field of science is confirming the validity of the centuries-old practice of nairiki. The goal of nairiki training is to help practitioners expand proprioceptive skills beyond general internal awareness to include the ability to redirect specific forces passing through the body structure. Being able to feel and control with precision how the pelvis rests on top of the femur heads is one example of internal tactile sensitivity. The perception of the power and direction of forces entering a joint, such as the shoulder or elbow, is essential for applying subtle energy deflection to protect structural integrity. The nairiki kunren help develop this sensitivity. Internal tactile sensitivity realized through joints and bone structures support the precise projection of force into the body structure of an adversary for offensive applications. Such internal tactile sensitivity allows increasingly effective direction of energy through a specific pathway.

動気覚 Dokikaku (Dynamic-Kinesthetic)

All muscles used for articulated movement and skeletal support contract in a linear fashion. Because of this physiological characteristic, complex movement requires the highly-coordinated action of several muscles. As training progresses, certain voluntary muscle movements begin to assume the characteristics of involuntary movement. This is sometimes referred to as muscle memory. Muscle memory becomes a beneficial result of proper dynamic training when correctly ingrained. However, muscle memory can become inefficient; muscles that provide oppositional movement can involuntarily engage at the wrong moment. Such muscle incoordination creates dynamic muscle tension that wastes energy and leads to slower and weaker movement. On a more advanced level, dynamic tension creates a pathway that can be exploited to attack and compromise the body structure of an adversary.

Nairiki training teaches the Shindō Yōshin Ryū practitioner to retrain and upgrade muscle coordination, replacing inefficient movement with more efficient and budō-appropriate movement. With increasing proprioceptive awareness, the practitioner can begin to identify individual muscles and the movements they create. Once practitioners can identify individual muscle movements, they can develop the conscious ability to engage and disengage the individual muscles involved. Practitioners who achieve this level of kinesthetic awareness can identify oppositional tension as it begins and disengage the oppositional muscles. This results in a relaxed and powerful expression of fluid movement, devoid of dynamic tension.

Through these four integrated dimensions of body sensitivity and awareness, Shindō Yōshin Ryū practitioners seek to acquire and increase their ability to detect the natural physiological status within their own bodies. They learn to precisely perceive how their own structure rests on the ground in relation to gravity, how the bones are placed in relation to one another, how their muscles individually contract and relax to create movement, and how contact with another body results in force vectors that affect their structure and musculature. Once practitioners can sense their bodies in these many dimensions, nairiki training can progress to develop a more sophisticated level of skills referred to as "ten chi jin" (heaven, earth, and man).

天地人 Ten Chi Jin (Heaven, Earth, Man)

Ten chi jin, the foundational nairiki kunren (internal strength drill) where uchite exerts a force directly through shite's unsupported weak line (fuanteho). Ten chi jin is one of the primary exercises upon which the Takamura ha Shindō Yōshin Ryū internal body principles are investigated, internalized, and expanded for martial application.

Imagine a person standing with feet side by side, shoulder-width apart, arms slightly bent and extended forwards in front of the shoulders. Further imagine the legs slightly bent, feet naturally facing forwards planted on the earth, while the head, supported by a straight back, is just touching the heavens. This position is called ten chi jin in Shindō Yōshin Ryū.

Now imagine a lateral force entering through the arms in an attempt to topple the person towards the rear. Now visualize that person splitting the force entering the body through the arms, and directing half of it down towards the earth through the feet and the other half overhead through the hands into the heavens. Although metaphorical, this is an accurate depiction of an actual physical skill that is cultivated in Shindō Yōshin Ryū. A person's ability to receive forces that act upon the body structure and redirect them through numerous skeletal and/or muscular pathways is the foundation of Shindō Yōshin Ryū nairiki skills. These skills are the result of nairiki training and can be applied to martial combat.

So what advanced skills must the practitioner cultivate to manifest ten chi jin?

体の結び Tai no Musubi (Connected Body)

One important application of Shindō Yōshin Ryū nairiki skills is to make musubi (connection) a one-way event. If one person in combat can identify and affect the center of gravity of a second, such that the second becomes helpless to reverse the connection, then the second person becomes relieved of all possible means of defense or any other strategy to avoid domination by the first.

A connected body offers the advantages of being flexible but truly unified when required to move. The total amount of strength in a body is available for action at any time when this state is realized. Different muscles attempt to generate power independently of other supporting structures in an unconnected body. The most misunderstood of these structures is the muscle fasciae.

The fasciae are bands or sheets of connective tissue below the skin that, like ligaments and tendons, mainly comprise collagen. They attach, stabilize, enclose and separate muscles as well as other internal organs and structures. Three layers of fascia are recognized. They are superficial, deep, and visceral or parietal fascia, according to function and anatomical location. Like ligaments, aponeuroses, and tendons, the fibrous connective tissues of the fasciae contain closely-packed bundles of collagen fibers oriented in waves parallel to the direction of pull. Fasciae are thus flexible, and resistant to large unidirectional tension forces to the point where the waves of fibers are straightened by the pulling force.

The popular view until recently was that fasciae were simply an assortment of individual, passive structures that transmit tension and reduce fric-

1

2

3

Right - Nairiki kunren with force directed through shite's unsupported weak line. (Fig. 1) Shite starts lowering his body while maintaining proper skeletal alignment and muscular dynamics. The slightest skeletal misalignment or creation of muscular tension will result in the loss of his body structure. (Fig. 2) Dropping into a full squat with proper skeletal alignment and a relaxed but connected body structure. (Fig. 3) From here shite should be able reverse the movement, ascending into a fully upright posture.

tion created during body movement. Although the fasciae are involved in these tasks, current research indicates the fasciae have other integrated and active capabilities. Current understanding is that the fasciae form the largest, and perhaps the richest, sensory organ in the body, thanks to containing an abundant assortment of neurological receptors. Furthermore, the three-layer fasciae can stretch and contract similarly to muscles and thus store and release kinetic energy. The fasciae might also have proprioceptive and nociceptive properties in addition to interoceptive functions. Nairiki training (particularly the nairiki kunren) seeks to increase the tensile strength and plasticity of the fascia through the application of controlled-tension exercises. Diligent nairiki training leads to the manifestation of superior muscular dynamics supported by fascial development, which greatly increases the ability to physiologically sense, move and operate a unified and dynamic body structure.

手触り Tezawari (Touch/Feel)

Imagine deciding to purchase a fine silk scarf. To determine the highest-quality silk requires a light, delicate touch, so you might gently pass sections of various scarves lightly between your thumb and index and/or middle finger, being aware of feeling smooth, rough, sleek, slippery or velvety sensations. Now picture yourself trying to make these same distinctions by slapping scarves with the palm of your hand on a wooden table. The nerve receptors in your hands would become overwhelmed and unable to provide the information required to determine the desired outcome. This is the meaning of tezawari.

Human hands, particularly the palms and fingertips, have evolved throughout millennia into highly refined tactile receptors. This heightened tactile sensitivity of hands is an invaluable tool in the use of weaponry and the execution of grappling techniques in budō. Tezawari refers to the physiological fact that the nerve receptors in our palms and fingers operate most effectively within a particular range of pressure. These receptors become overloaded beyond a critical amount of pressure and lose their ability to detect increasing amounts of pressure. Eventually, increased pressure threatens to damage tissues, which causes the nervous system to convert pressure awareness into pain perception. Relaxing the body structure and keeping the touch of the hands and fingers as light as possible, allows a practitioner to utilize the entire range of tactile feedback. Conversely, direct strength and aggressive pressure can overwhelm manual nerve receptors in the hand, neurologically blinding the practitioner to valuable information needed during combat.

手の内 Te no Uchi (Gripping Hand)

A complementary skill to tezawari is te no uchi. The cultivation of precise grasping sensitivity is important in any weapons-based martial art. Muscular articulation of the fingers combined with pressure receptors in the palms allow a practitioner to develop a flexible, yet firm grip that is devoid of tension that can migrate up the arm and into the body structure. In classical weapons-based budō, one frequently hears the phrase "project ki through your weapon". This is a metaphorical expression related to developing such acute grip sensitivity that a practitioner can perceive the lightest touch or slightest change in the balance of a weapon in the hand. It is as if tactile sensitivity actually flows through the weapon. Grip sensitivity combined with internal body sensitivity can allow a weapon to be wielded with great force, precision, and speed without being dropped or knocked away. The weapon becomes a virtual extension of the practitioner's body.

竜捕り Tatsudori (Dragon Capturing)

Another complementary skill to tezawari is tatsudori. Similar to te no uchi but with an added dimension, tatsudori describes projecting force through the grip into the body structure of an adversary's body via direct connection, as opposed to simply grasping an inanimate object such as a sword or staff. The idea of tatsudori is to grab adversaries with a flexible, yet firm grip, projecting force into their bodies in a subtle spiral. Since the musculature can only contract in a linear fashion, a spiraling grip penetrates an adversary by circumventing linear resistance. When combined with a spiraling body structure, tatsudori becomes an effective tool in grappling attacks where a practitioner aims to take an adversary's center of gravity immediately upon physical contact.

呼吸 Kokyū (Breathing)

The breathing methods utilized in nairiki training are considered part of the TSYR okugi and are not discussed in depth outside the jōden level membership, but an outline of what they constitute can be examined. One of the foundational kokyū skills in TSYR is learning to isolate the body core musculature from the diaphragm so that these muscle groups can operate independent of one another. If the muscles of the body core cannot be isolated from the diaphragm, the act of breathing can create muscular tension that migrates through the body core. Such tension disrupts muscular pathways that are essential to the development and application of TSYR nairiki skills.

Other breathing methods like tatsu no iki (dragon breathing), where the breath is taken in through the nose and exhaled through the mouth, and tora no iki (tiger breathing), where the breath is taken in through the mouth and exhaled through the nose, are integrated with specific muscular dynamics that enhance the development of internal strength. A connected body core, increased internal sensitivity and mind/body integration can be greatly enhanced through specific breathing techniques.

Nairiki kunren demonstrated with force from uchite entering horizontally through the left arm, down the spine, across the pelvis and then dissipated down through shite's right leg and into his base.

Nairiki and Martial Application

Shindō Yōshin Ryū practitioners who manifest basic nairiki skills have expanded their corporeal sensitivity to a point where forces acting upon their structure are recognized and their source is consciously detected. They can also apply their own previously-cultivated sensitivity and proprioceptive awareness to channel, block or deflect power internally with minimal muscular investment.

At an intermediate level of internalization, Shindō Yōshin Ryū practitioners can project the sum of the power within their bodies into the body structure of an adversary in a pulse or wave that circumvents the adversary's defenses, while simultaneously engaging a sensitivity loop back into the adversary's power source, thus negating any attempt to counterattack. When an adversary grabs an advanced practitioner of Shindō Yōshin Ryū nairiki, the practitioner can instantly feel through the adversary's structure and identify the source of the forces acting on him. From there, the practitioner can intuitively select the most appropriate way to respond to the threat, compromising the adversary's center of gravity and rendering him unable to reverse the situation. Essentially, the act of an adversary touching the practitioner backfires because the forces the adversary attempts to project into the practitioner are immediately stripped of any structural support.

Ten Chi Jin Becomes Wa (Heaven, Earth, Man Becomes Martial Harmony)

At the highest levels of execution, training becomes a dynamic meditation. This level of study can last years, or even decades, depending on the inherent skill and dedication of the individual practitioner. As the practitioner progresses, he investigates the application of more sophisticated movement and power-channeling hidden within the Shindō Yōshin Ryū kata. This reinforces and projects the application of nairiki skills into a martial context. Finally the application of nairiki becomes completely formless, the spontaneous melding of external, internal, structural, and dynamic skills. This highest level of execution is a manifestation of marobashi, a concept that originated in the Shinkage Ryū schools of swordsmanship. Conscious thought is no longer involved as the body intuitively acts with instant flexibility, meeting and even preempting any internally-perceived threat. The mind and body are relaxed but physically, mentally and emotionally connected in a spontaneous and intuitive internalization of all Shindō Yōshin Ryū principles.

Kakugo 覚悟 (Resolve)

Not all budō practitioners can internalize or master nairiki skills. Nairiki training requires a significant investment in time and physical dedication. Some individuals simply do not possess the physical capability, the basic martial understanding, the intrinsic discipline, time, or inclination to pursue the acquisition of such esoteric skills. Considerable mental patience and resolve are needed. Repeated failure and thousands of hours of repetitive training must be endured to acquire these skills, with no guarantee of success.

"Superior jūjutsu is achieved when I can feel and control my opponent in every dimension, but he cannot feel or control me in any dimension."

- Takamura Yukiyoshi

Shindō Yōshin Ryū

Tekkyaku

Nairiki no Gyō

Tekkyaku, "Iron Legs", is the most fundamental exercise of all the Nairiki no Gyō. Proper execution of this form will improve the strength of the legs, back, chest and body core. It will also increase hip, shoulder and leg flexibility while supporting the development of internal structural sensitivity. Particular attention should be paid to forward/rearward balance during the execution of this exercise. The center of balance should remain at the front of the ankle throughout the raising and lowering motion. The exercise should be performed slowly and fluidly.

Fundamental to the efficient use of body mechanics is an intuitive awareness of how our skeleton supports our body structure. This kata utilizes movements that help the student identify flexibility limitations and muscular tension related to postural and skeletal misalignments.

1

The kata starts in shizenhontai with ankles shoulder-width apart and feet pointed outwards 30-45 degrees. The arms should hang naturally with palms resting on the thighs.

2

Bring the palms together in front of the pelvis, fingers pointed downwards. Next, extend the head of the humerus downward lowering the hands without straightening the elbows.

3

Extend the hands forward, raising the arms parallel to the floor with fingers extended outward. The head of the humerus should be extended forward in the shoulder socket without creating tension.

History And Technique

内力の形

鉄脚

4

While maintaining extension through the arms, now rotate the hands along the axis of the index finger so the palms are facing outward. It is important the deltoid muscle remain relaxed.

5

Extend the arms upward so the hands, palms out, are directly overhead. It is important to utilize the muscles of the back for this movement. Avoiding using the deltoid or trapezius, which creates undesirable tension.

6

Simultaneously start lowering the body and arms with the palms rotating along the coronal plane like they are following the shape of a ball. It is important the back remain straight during the lowering process.

7

Lower the body down the spinal plane with your weight dropping into the pelvis. Time the motion so the hands meet in front of the pelvis at the same time the drop is completed. The palms should be facing upward.

Shindō Yōshin Ryū

Tekkyaku

Nairiki no Gyō

8

With your body weight relaxed into the pelvis, extend the hands forward, raising the arms parallel to the ground, fingers extended outward. The head of the humerus should be extended forward.

9

While maintaining extension through the arms, rotate the hands through the axis of the index finger so the palms are facing outward. Take care to keep the spine as straight as possible during this motion.

10

Extend the arms upward so the hands, palms outward, are pointing 45 degrees up and forward. It is important to utilize the back muscles for this movement. Do not raise the hands higher than 45 degrees.

11

Simultaneously start raising the body and lowering the arms in an arc with the palms rotating like they are following the shape of a ball. It is important the spine remain as straight as possible during this motion.

History And Technique

内力の形　　　　　　　　　　　　　　　　　　　　　鉄脚

12

Raise the body all the way to shizenhontai, timing the lowering of the hands so they meet in front of the pelvis at the same time the rising is completed. The palms should be facing upward.

13

As before, extend the hands forward, raising the arms parallel to the ground with fingers extended outward. The head of the humerus should be extended forward in the shoulder socket devoid of tension.

14

While maintaining extension through the arms, rotate the hands through the axis of the index finger so the palms are facing outward. As previously, it is important that the deltoid be relaxed.

15

Extend the arms upward so the hands, palms outward, are pointing 45 degrees up and forward. It is important to utilize the muscles of the back for this movement. Do not raise the hands higher than 45 degrees.

Shindō Yōshin Ryū

Tekkyaku

Nairiki no Gyō

16
Simultaneously start lowering the body and arms with the palms rotating like they are following the shape of a ball. It is important the spine remains as vertically aligned as possible during the lowering process.

17
Lower the body all the way to a squatting position, timing the motion of the hands so they rest on the knees at the same time the drop is completed. The palms should be facing upward and the back straight.

18
Simultaneously start raising the body and arms in an arc, palms rotating like they are following a ball. The spine should remain straight during this rise. Imagine being pulled upwards from your crown.

19
Continue rising, extending the arms upward with the palms outward until they reach 45 degrees up and forward. Utilize the muscles in the back, while avoiding the use of the deltoid, which creates undesirable tension.

内力の形　　　　　　　　　　　　　　　　　　　　　鉄脚

20
While maintaining extension through the arms, lower the hands, inverted, with the palms facing outward until they are parallel with the floor. Maintain relaxed shoulders throughout this motion.

21
While continuing extension through the arms, rotate the hands on the axis of the index finger until the palms are touching one another.

22
Lower the arms, palms facing one another until they are resting in front of the pelvis.

23
Relax in proper structural alignment and allow the body to return to shizenhontai.

Shindō Yōshin Ryū

Banjaku

Nairiki no Gyō

Banjaku, "Immovable Stone", is an exercise whose proper execution improves lower body core strength, balance, control of one's center of gravity and proprioceptive awareness. It should be performed smoothly but crisply, with special attention given to keeping the spinal plane as straight as possible, particularly during the tilting motions.

A highly-developed sense of balance is required in all Shindō Yōshin Ryū techniques but the redirection of forces inside the body structure demands an extra level of sensitivity to both structure and balance. The regular performance of Banjaku helps develop and maintain this heightened level of body sensitivity.

1

The kata starts in shizenhontai with ankles shoulder-width apart and feet pointed outwards 30-45 degrees. The arms should hang naturally with palms resting on the thighs.

2

Bring the palms together in front of the pelvis, fingers pointed downwards. Next, extend the head of the humerus downward, lowering the hands without completely straightening the elbows.

3

Extend the hands forward, raising the arms parallel to the floor with fingers extended outward. The head of the humerus should be extended forward in the shoulder socket without creating tension.

内力の形　　　　　　　　　　　　　　　　盤石

History And Technique

4

Turn the palms parallel to the floor while maintaining extension through the fingertips.

5

Rotate the arms in the shoulder socket until they are extended straight to the sides. Try to keep the deltoids relaxed and the chest open.

6

Shift your weight to the left foot. Simultaneously lift the right foot until the thigh is parallel to the floor and bend the right arm until the fingertips align with your spine. Keep the right elbow extended during this motion.

7

Extend both hands outward rotating the palms forward. Tilt to the left keeping the back straight, while maintaining the shape of the upper body. Most of the rotation initiates in the hip socket with the right leg extended.

Shindō Yōshin Ryū

Banjaku

Nairiki no Gyō

8

Raise the right knee and start tilting back to vertical. Next, collapse the left leg allowing the body to fall. Catch the fall with the spine erect, hitting the floor abruptly, knees bent about 25 degrees.

9

Straighten the legs until almost straight while keeping the spine erect. Next, collapse both legs quickly until both knees are bent again to about 25 degrees. Repeat this dropping motion three times.

10

Shift your weight to the right foot. Simultaneously lift the left foot until the thigh is parallel to the floor and bend the left arm until the fingetips align with your spine. Keep the left elbow extended during this motion.

11

Extend the hands while rotating the left palm forward. Tilt slowly to the right with the back straight while maintaining the shape of the upper body. Most of the rotation initiates in the hip socket with the left leg extended.

History And Technique

内力の形

盤石

12
Raise the left knee and start tilting back to vertical. Next, collapse the right leg allowing the body to fall. Catch the fall with the spine erect, hitting the floor abruptly, knees bent about 25 degrees.

13
Straighten the legs until almost straight while keeping the spine erect. Next, collapse both legs quickly until both knees are bent again to about 25 degrees. Repeat this dropping motion three times.

14
Shift to the left until your weight is completely supported on the left foot and the right toes are just touching the ground.

15
Tilt quickly 45 degrees to the left keeping the back straight and extending the right leg out. Hold this position for five seconds and tilt abruptly back until the right toes touch the ground, shoulder-width apart.

Shindō Yōshin Ryū

Banjaku

Nairiki no Gyō

16
Now shift to the right until your weight is completely supported on the right foot and the left toes are just touching the ground.

17
Tilt quickly 45 degrees to the right keeping the back straight and extending the left leg out. Hold this position for five seconds and tilt abruptly back until the left toes touch the ground, feet shoulder-width apart.

18
Continue extending the hands outward while checking your structure and balance.

19
Rotate palms downward through the index finger.

内力の形　　　　　　　　　盤石

20

Rotate the arms forward in the shoulder socket with the index knuckles meeting on the center line, shoulder high.

21

Rotate the palms back to vertical through the index fingers on the center line (seichusen).

22

Lower the hands down the center line while extending through the fingertips until they are in front of the pelvis.

23

Relax in proper structural alignment and allow the body to return to shizenhontai.

Shindō Yōshin Ryū

Sarutahiko no Ōkami, ancestor of the earthly kami, and his wife Ame no Uzume no Mikoto, the kami of sensuality and revelry, are represented on this kakejiku, which hangs in the Takamura ha Shindō Yōshin Ryū Honbu Dōjō. These two kami, along with Amaterasu Ōmikami, the sun goddess enshrined at the Grand Shrine of Ise, and Takemikazuchi no Kami, the kami of thunder enshrined at Kashima Jingū, form the tutelary kami of Takamura ha Shindō Yōshin Ryū. Sarutahiko and Takemikazuchi are considered tutelary kami of all the martial arts.

History And Technique

On Shintō

Keidaichi (Shrine grounds) of Tsubaki Grand Shrine of America.

One characteristic of the ancient Japanese was their cultural tendency to see everything through the lens of spirituality. They viewed humanity as a spiritual conduit between the heavenly and earthly realms of existence. All Japanese budō is imbued in various and often subtle ways by Shintō and its spiritual underpinnings. In the case of Takamura ha Shindō Yōshin Ryū, Shintō was deemed by Takamura Yukiyoshi to be the vessel by which the inherent "Japaneseness" and ethos of the art could be passed to those practitioners beyond the shores of Japan. It was Takamura Sensei's belief koryū cannot be separated from its cultural foundation without betraying its deeper identity and without becoming a pursuit of corrupt self-indulgence.

What is Shintō?

Shintō or Kami no Michi (way of the spirits) is commonly thought of as the indigenous religion of Japan; however, most Japanese do not relate well to such a definition. Most Japanese view Shintō as a reflection of the Japanese people's intuitive connection to the universe via spirituality, nature, and ancestry. Shintō has no revealed religious dogma, no divinely-inspired scriptures, worships no supreme deity, and demonstrates little concern for moral idealism. In fact, Shintō is a somewhat generic term used to identify a diverse collection of local customs, beliefs, traditions, rituals, and cultural observances unique to Japan. Shintō is in many ways a form of animism, manifesting a ritualized celebration of life and living, and seeks to harmonize with the ceaseless flow of nature. Shintō is particularly sensitive to ritual, which recognizes the four seasons as part of divine nature. That does not mean Shintō ignores concepts like morality, death, or a person's spiritual qualities; it's just that Shintō approaches these concepts and ideals in a manner that is at once syncretic while also remaining uniquely Japanese.

Origins

The origins of Shintō are probably related to the arrival of the Yayoi culture to the Japanese islands around 300 BCE. The Yayoi were rice cultivators from the Asian mainland who left behind ceramic images of grain storehouses that bear a striking similarity to the architecture at the Grand Shrine of Ise. Associated with the Yayoi were ceremonial mirrors, jewels and swords; objects considered sacred in Shintō mythology. Today these items form the greater portion of Japan's imperial regalia. Shintō was unevenly influenced by Buddhism, Confucianism, and Taoism as these systems made their way to Japan from China during the sixth century. The name Shintō was coined during this period to identify itself as a belief system separate from these imported religious traditions.

Kami

To understand the Shintō concept of kami, a Westerner must be willing to step outside the restrictions of their own cultural indoctrination and view the world around them with a fresh perspective. Despite the western tendency to refer to kami as gods, such preconceptions are an impediment to understanding, because the Shintō concept of kami and the western concept of god/gods are not really comparable. Any Westerner seeking to understand Shintō must embrace a flexible view of spirituality, which allows them to transcend the limitations of intellect and feel with one's heart that which cannot be defined temporally. Only then can a non-Japanese begin to internalize the concept of kami and recognize its unique

History And Technique

Tōrō (lantern), torii (gate), and komainu (guardian dogs) at the entrance to the Tsubaki Grand Shrine of America in Granite Falls, Washington. This shrine is the only permanently-staffed Shintō shrine in the continental USA.

qualities. The Japanese tendency to view all things through a spiritual lens demonstrates that they do not draw boundaries between nature, humanity, objects, and actions. In Shintō, everything in existence is engaged in a complex dance that affects every aspect of existence, therefore Shintō is a ritualized expression of this dance.

Shintō beliefs and rituals revolve around the reverence of divine beings identified as kami, but the term more accurately refers to a diverse group of spirit beings, supernatural forces, and natural essences that create a sense of mystery, wonder, or awe. In Shintō, this sense of wonder harbors a transcendental aspect called, "kami nature" which can manifest itself in a person, place, or thing. Mootori Norinaga, a scholar of the late 18th century defined kami in this way:

> "Whatever seemed strikingly impressive, possessed of the quality of excellence and virtue, and inspired a feeling of awe was identified as kami."

Here Norinaga implies this sense of quality and otherworldly excellence wields enormous power, which goes far beyond the capabilities of mankind alone. As the children of kami, mankind can tap into this enormous power, but this power exists beyond mankind and is not of his creation.

All things that have a great effect on human existence, things like natural phenomena, objects of nature, and human beings can become kami. In the case of individual human beings, all are revered as ancestral kami among their families after their death. In very rare instances,

Shindō Yōshin Ryū

The haiden (hall of worship) and heiden (hall of offerings) of the Tsubaki Grand Shrine of America. This shrine, originally called the Kannagara Jinja, was constructed in 1992 by Rev. Kōichi Barrish. In 2001, 17 acres of adjacent land was donated to Tsubaki America by the Matsuri Foundation. At this time the decision was made to combine the Kannagara Jinja and Tsubaki America to create the Tsubaki Grand Shrine of America with Rev. Barrish as the head priest. Many members of the Takamura ha Shindō Yōshin Kai are official members of the Tsubaki Grand Shrine of America.
(Photo courtesy of Tsubaki Grand Shrine of America)

some individuals who have made a great contribution to a community or greater mankind can be enshrined as kami during a special ritual. In such cases, these kami are forever linked to a particular Shintō Shrine and hold a unique position among those kami revered in that shrine.

In 2009, Takamura Yukiyoshi's life and stewardship of the Takamura ha Shindō Yōshin Ryū was honored when his mitama (spirit) was enshrined as kami during a ritual performed at the Tsubaki Grand Shrine in Granite Falls, Washington. This was done in cooperation with the Tsubaki Ōkami Yashiro in Mie Prefecture, Japan. A mitamaya (altar) containing Takamura Sensei's mitamashiro (symbol of his spirit) now resides in the Takamura ha Shindō Yōshin Ryū Honbu Dōjō.

Harae and Misogi

Purity and cleanliness are vitally important in Shintō. It is the Japanese culture's connection to Shintō that has resulted in what appears to be an almost fanatical obsession with cleanliness. In accordance with Shintō ideals surrounding fastidious behavior, Japanese never wear their shoes in their homes, bathe daily, eat with hashi (chopsticks) and, until recently, did not allows pets like a dog into their homes. Before entering a Shintō Shrine, visitors will approach a temizuya (water basin) to ritually purify their hands and mouths with clean water.

In Shintō, the concept of cleanliness not only takes on a physical dimension but also manifests a spiritual one. Certain deeds are believed to create a form of impurity that can only be cleansed through a ritual of purification called harae. Harae can be used to purify spaces, objects, and people of spiritual corruption referred to as kegare. One specific type of individual harae is called misogi and involves the ritual use of water. Misogi is often led by a Shintō priest and takes place in waterfalls, rivers, or the ocean. The concept of Misogi comes from a story in Shintō mythology when Izanagi no Mikoto first performed ritual purification by entering the river Tachibana after returning from Yomi no Kuni (the land of the dead), where he sought to rescue his deceased wife, Izanami no Mikoto.

Another form of harae is embodied in the use of fire. Every year, numerous talismans or amulets in the form of ofuda, omamori, shimenawa etc., are purchased by followers of Shintō. These objects are used in the coming year and are believed to harbor specialized protective qualities which can include absorbing and identifying purified spaces. Every year amulets and talismans are returned to various Shintō Shrines and ritually burned in a ceremony of purification called Koshinsatsutakiageshiki.

Morality and Ethics

One of the most important ethical principles of Shintō involves the prioritization of group solidarity over individuality. This ethic demonstrates itself powerfully in Shintō's veneration of family and ancestral spirits. In Shintō, individual desire that conflicts with group solidarity threatens the concept of wa (natural harmony). The maintenance of wa is deemed indispensable, for without it many believe Japanese society and culture would disintegrate into chaos. Another important ethical principle of Shintō concerns a reverence for nature and the natural order of our universe. In Shintō, maintaining a harmonious balance between the natural world and human existence is paramount. This reverence of nature can be traced back to Shintō's origins amongst the Yayoi, who first began the systematic cultivation of rice in Japan. Early cultures like the Yayoi frequently developed animistic and shamanistic practices in response to observing the cycles of nature. In early Japan, the dependence of human existence on the cycles of the natural world led to formalized practices that still influence Japanese spirituality to this day through Shintō. In this way, the concepts of birth, purification, and renewal remain persistent themes in Shintō mythology, observance, and ritual.

Shintō in Takamura ha Shindō Yōshin Ryū

The connection to Shintō in Takamura ha Shindō Yōshin Ryū goes beyond simply being Japanese in origin and lies in bujutsu's origins as a codified method for combat. Inevitably, most warrior traditions around the world adopted a spiritual discipline as a portion of their greater

Misogi performed by deshi of the Takamura ha Shindō Yōshin Kai, led by Rev. Kōichi Barrish and Tobin Threadgill.
(Photo courtesy of John Lovato)

Ono no Takamura Shrine in Shiga Prefecture.
(Photo courtesy of John Lovato)

teachings. These spiritual disciplines frequently stress the transcendental nature of the human soul and the existence of a world beyond the temporal. In Takamura ha Shīndō Yōshin Ryū, our understanding of our transcendental nature is embodied in a branch of esoteric Minzoku Shintō (folk Shintō), whose origin is connected to the mystically-charged region surrounding Mount Kurama in Japan.

Takamura Yukiyoshi was born in Ono Village and spent much of his youth living with his grandparents near the shores of Lake Biwa and Ōtsu, Japan. This area, just northwest of Kyōto and due west of Mount Kurama, was rich in mythology and history, including stories of warfare, samurai exploits, and Shintō mysticism. As a boy, Yukiyoshi was taken on a Tango no Sekku (boys' day) pilgrimage to Mount Kurama by his grandfather, Obata Shigeta. They ventured from the base of Mount Kurama to the Yuki Jinja and Kurama-dera near its summit. During this pilgrimage Yukiyoshi was taught about spiritual transcendence and the magical tengu reportedly living in the forested slopes of the mountain. No one knows exactly what Yukiyoshi experienced or saw during that first pilgrimage to the summit of Mount Kurama, but the impression it left on him was pivotal. Throughout his life, Takamura Yukiyoshi returned to Mount Kurama on a schedule determined by way of kushiyo (numerology), ritually repeating the journey of his childhood until his death in 2000.

Shintō Ethos in Budō Culture

Many who undertake training in classical budō fail to appreciate that a spiritual discipline like Shintō is not mere window dressing. Some even see the inclusion of spiritual disciplines in budō training as an attempt to add an element of the exotic or to minimize the perception of a martial art's supposed violent nature. The truth is more complex. In Takamura ha Shindō Yōshin Ryū, Shintō is an integral part of the school's legacy because it functions as the foundation upon which the school's ethos resides. Without Shintō, it is believed the tradition's highest

History And Technique

level teachings are devoid of the spiritual context that defines the proper mindset and mental approach for training. Takamura Sensei's moral compass and view of life's destiny was difficult to understand without an appreciation of his Minzoku Shintō-dominated spirituality. Consequently, without Shintō as the vehicle to provide context for the art's unique ethos, Takamura ha Shindō Yōshin Ryū is difficult to comprehend, and the spiritual and emotional identity of the tradition could remain out of reach and therefore at risk of being lost or corrupted. In the expression of Shintō embraced by Takamura Yukiyoshi, the notions of pre-destiny and free will are not mutually exclusive. These seemingly at-odds concepts exist as companions in a complex dance of intellectual abstraction, which when viewed in the context of the Obata family's unique exposure to Shintō, are actually found to be both tangible and concrete.

The Dōjō

The Takamura ha Shindō Yōshin Ryū Honbu Dōjō is considered a sacred space, a place of learning and spiritual purification. Shintō ceremonies of purification are regularly performed there. Member dōjō are also considered sacred space if they house a kamidana. If possible, all member dōjō should contain a kamidana harboring the ujigami (protective kami) of the Takamura ha Shindō Yōshin Ryū, but it is recognized this is not always possible, or practical. The honbu dōjō is considered the spiritual center of the school and also operates as a minor Shintō shrine. As such, the kaichō is considered the school's official kannushi (Shintō priest) representing the members of the Takamura ha Shindō Yōshin Kai to the ujigami and school's ancestral spirits. Outside licensed Shintō priests, only specifically initiated jōden-licensed members of Takamura ha Shindō Yōshin Ryū are permitted to perform Shintō rituals and observances in the Takamura ha Shindō Yōshin Ryū Honbu Dōjō.

Takamura ha Shindō Yōshin Ryū members at the Tsubaki Grand Shrine participating in a Shintō ceremony conducted by Rev. Kōichi Barrish. The ceremony enshrined Takamura Yukiyoshi's mitama (spirit) as a Shintō kami.
(Photo courtesy of Miyamoto Kozue)

Takamura Yukiyoshi has joined his ancestors becoming an enshrined ujigami of the Takamura ha Shindō Yōshin Ryū. Going forward, Takamura Yukiyoshi no Mikoto, residing in a mitamaya containing his mitamashiro will be revered in the TSYR Honbu Dōjō. Into the foreseeable future, the Takamura ha Shindō Yōshin Kai will continue to maintain a formal relationship with

Shindō Yōshin Ryū

the Tsubaki Grand Shrine of America and its kannushi, Rev. Kōichi Barrish. Rev. Barrish visits the Takamura ha Shindō Yōshin Ryū Honbu Dōjō annually, and on special occasions related to Shintō celebratory rituals and observances.

The Tutelary Kami of the Takamura ha Shindō Yōshin Ryū

Takamura ha Shindō Yōshin Ryū venerates four Shintō kami, seeking their protection and transcendental counsel. Ofuda representing these four kami are enshrined inside the kamidana of the school's honbu dōjō.

Amaterasu Ōmikami

Amaterasu Ōmikami is the most important Shintō deity, endowed with the virtue of the sun. She also functions as the ancestral deity of Japan's imperial house. Amaterasu is identified as the kami who rules over Takamagahara, the heavenly plain. The Grand Shrine of Ise is dedicated to Amaterasu, and is the oldest and most important shrine in Japan. It houses the Yata no Kagami (the sacred mirror), which is part of Japan's Imperial Regalia.

Sarutahiko Ōkami

Sarutahiko Ōkami is a powerful guardian kami enshrined at Tsubaki Ōkami Yashiro in Mie Prefecture. He is the ancestor of all the Kinitsu Kami (earthly kami) and is the kami of guidance, strength, and ki (life force). He is the grandson of Amaterasu, who then descended from Takamagahara to rule over the earthly realm. He is depicted as a towering man with a large beard, jeweled spear, ruddy complexion, and long nose. At first, he was unwilling to yield his realm until persuaded by Ame no Uzume no Mikoto, the kami of dance and the arts, whom he later married. As a symbol of strength and guidance, Sarutahiko Ōkami is considered one of the patron kami of martial arts.

Ame no Uzume no Mikoto

Inari Shrine on the grounds of the Tsubaki Grand Shrine. Kitsune (foxes) take the place of Koma Inu (guardian dogs) in these popular shrines dedicated to Inari, the patron kami of fertility, rice, sake, tea, agriculture, and general prosperity.

Koma Inu and Kara Shishi are the guardians of most Shintō shrines in Japan. Their mouths, one open and the other closed, symbolize ah (beginning) and un (end).

History And Technique

Amaterasu Ōmikami, the kami of sunlight is emerging from a cave and returning light to the world after hearing the revelry caused by Ame no Uzume's erotic dancing. Standing to the right of Ame no Uzume is Sarutahiko Ōkami holding his hoko (spear). Sarutahiko will go on the marry Ame no Uzume. (Collection of the Takamura ha Shindō Yōshin Kai)

Sarutahiko Ōkami's wife, Ame no Uzume no Mikoto is the goddess of the dawn, sensuality, and revelry. In Shintō mythology, it was Ame no Uzume who enticed Amaterasu Ōmikami out of a cave with an erotic dance to return light to the world. Ame no Uzume is the patron kami of actors, performers, and negotiators.

Takemikazuchi no Kami

According to Shintō mythology, Takemikazuchi no Kami is a kami produced from the blood adhering to Izanagi no Mikoto's sword when he killed the fire kami Kagutsuchi. During the occasion of Emperor Jinmu's eastern campaign, Takemikazuchi sent his sword, Futsunomitama, to aid Jinmu's forces in their victory. The kami of thunder, Takemikazuchi, is revered at Kashima Jinja and due to his association with swordsmanship, Takemikazuchi no Kami is considered a patron kami of martial arts.

(Right) The kamidana on the upper shelf, and the mitamaya on the lower shelf, residing in the Takamura ha Shindō Yōshin Ryū Honbu Dōjō.

The kamidana houses ofuda representing the four tutelary Shintō kami associated with the school. Offerings of water, rice, sake, and salt are made to the kami before the beginning of every class.

The mitamaya houses the mitama-shiro of Takamura Yukiyoshi no Mikoto. The Takamura ha Shindō Yōshin Kai was greatly honored when Rev. Kōichi Barrish interceded on our behalf and engaged a shrine carpenter associated with The Grand Shrine of Ise to construct the mitamaya and mitamashiro for Takamura Yukiyoshi.

Shindō Yōshin Ryū

Jogensha - Rev. L. Kōichi Barrish

Rev. Kōichi Barrish is a licensed Negi (Senior Priest) of the Tsubaki Ōkami Yashiro of America, in Granite Falls, Washington. He was the first non-Japanese ever licensed as a Jinja Shintō Kannushi. Today, Rev. Barrishi is also a Jogensha, formal advisor on Jinja Shintō to the Takamura ha Shindō Yōshin Ryū.

Kaichō, Tobin Threadgill first met Rev. Barrish during an impromptu visit to the Tsubaki Grand Shrine in 2004. At this meeting Threadgill realized Rev. Barrish's knowledge and standing as a senior Shintō priest made him an ideal resource for consultation on the more esoteric aspects of Shintō included as part of the Takamura ha Shindō Yōshin Ryū mokuroku.

In 2009, Rev. Barrish honored Takamura Yukiyoshi by ceremonially enshrining his mitama (soul) as Shintō Kami. His name is now Takamura Yukiyoshi no Mikoto.

Eimeiroku, Kishōmon, Keppan

Instructor Karl Garrison's page in the school's eimeiroku.

A tradition that harkens back to Japan's feudal era, which is maintained in Shindō Yōshin Ryū is nyūmon, the process of becoming a formal disciple of the ryūha. Unlike modern budō, which anyone can join, a student of Shindō Yōshin Ryū must be invited into the school and take an oath sealed in his blood. The written oath is called a kishōmon. The act of placing one's blood seal upon the oath is called keppan. The kishōmon outlines the moral code members must adhere to as well ryūha-specific prescriptions and prohibitions. A historical record of every member's formal exploits, including his keppan are contained in a register book called an eimeiroku (catalog of distinguished persons). Names, dates, and hanko (seals) confirming the issuance of all formal documents related to each member's history in the ryūha are recorded in the eimeiroku.

In Takamura ha Shindō Yōshin Ryū, there are two levels of nyūmon. The first is undertaken when a member is initially accepted into the ryū and functions as general introduction into a koryū and its unique cultural identity. The second nyūmon is initiated prior to entering into gokui level instruction, and is much more comprehensive in its demands of service and duty to the ryū. Every member entering into gokui level training must demonstrate a durable and fierce sense of loyalty to the school, its traditions, its headmaster, as well as the founder's family. They must be willing to take upon their shoulders the burden of responsibility for the school and its survival into the future.

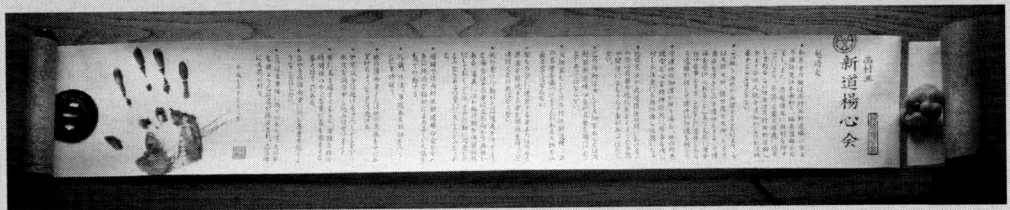

Kaichō, Tobin Threadgill's Jōden Kishōmon including a tegata (hand print) in his blood as its seal.

History And Technique

Koryū Densho

古流伝書

Koryū Densho - A Window Into The Past

To study koryū is to enter another world where old and new coexist. Koryū are not where history is preserved in musty old books on shelves gathering dust, or where it is fading from the memories of fewer and fewer elderly masters. Koryū are where history flourishes, living in the practice and passion of members around the world. The koryū community comprises vibrant international groups of historical preservation and research societies where members actively work to maintain a unique legacy for future generations.

Shindō Yōshin Ryū

The four most common formats for koryū densho. L to R, sasshihon, makimono, orihon and kirigami.
(Collection of the Takamura ha Shindō Yōshin Kai.)

The members involved in this pursuit are tasked with maintaining the wisdom and knowledge of the founders of their schools, as well as each subsequent generation of teachers. Because of this duty, members of koryū are required to see themselves as being involved in a reverent duality of past and present. Headmaster Takamura Yukiyoshi believed that to expand a sense of connection to the heritage of his particular art required access to relevant historical documents and other relics. He felt this would provide contemporary members of the tradition with more than simply historical context. He believed it would provide them with a tangible connection to the school and to those in the past who devoted much of their lives to the school. For this reason, he expended considerable effort into acquiring and preserving important historical documentation related to the history of Shindō Yōshin Ryū.

The Takamura ha Shindō Yōshin Kai is the custodian of a comprehensive collection of historical documents, including over 150 koryū densho (transmission scrolls) dating back to the early 17th century. Koryū densho represent the heritage and wisdom of a school of classical Japanese martial arts. They also serve as formal recognition of jikiden (direct transmission of knowledge from the headmaster of a school to students). Densho come in several forms, but the

Elaborate images of Marishiten and Mt. Kurama's tengu king Sōjōbō adorn this Akiyama Yōshin Ryū Kakugo no Maki. This densho of esoteric teachings was issued by 17th-generation shihan, Morimoto Tokiuemon in 1849.
(Collection of the Takamura ha Shindō Yōshin Kai.)

History And Technique

Beautiful technical illustrations of kata enhance this Akiyama Yōshin Ryū Inyō no Maki issued by 17th-generation shihan Morimoto Tokiuemon in 1845. Emakimono of this quality are quite rare. (Collection of the Takamura ha Shindō Yōshin Kai.)

most common is a makimono (hand-brushed scroll). Other formats include kirigami (a sheet of folded paper), orihon (accordion book) and sasshihon (bound codex). Densho are not encyclopedic as they were never intended for scrutiny by the general public. They were only available to, and passed between, members of a specific budō school. The most famous set of koryū densho is the Go Rin No Sho (Book of Five Rings), five scrolls inscribed by Miyamoto Musashi, the founder of Niten Ichi Ryū Kenjutsu.

Illustrated Musō Kenshin Ryū Torite no Maki, issued 1815.
(Collection of the Takamura ha Shindō Yōshin Kai.)

(Right) Kaichō Tobin Threadgill in the Takamura ha Shindō Yōshin Ryū Honbu Dōjō examining densho during an inventory of historic documents and records owned by the ryūha.

Muhen Mukyoku Ryū Sōjutsu no Maki, issued in 1831. This densho is illustrated in an elegant tonbo-e (dragonfly drawing) style, which captures the unique characteristics of utilizing a pole weapon.
(Collection of the Takamura ha Shindō Yōshin Kai.)

Shindō Yōshin Ryū

Akiyama Yōshin Ryū Jūjutsu Mokuroku issued by Santō Shinjurō Kiyotake in 1863. The manji in the middle of the scroll is a Buddhist symbol found on many martial arts densho. It represents the passage of time in the universe.
(Collection of the Takamura ha Shindō Yōshin Kai.)

Saburi Ryū Kagiso Kyō-Mokuroku issued by Takeuchi Kanesa in 1786. This refined densho is illustrated in a distinctive sumi-e (black ink) style.
(Collection of the Takamura ha Shindō Yōshin Kai.)

Akiyama Yōshin Ryū Yukiai no Maki. This densho is illustrated in a simple tonbo-e style including didactic aids.

Most densho serve as a simple catalog of techniques related to a particular level of teaching authority within a school. Some contain kishōmon (oaths) required for official membership in a school, while others represent the school's gokui or okuden (deepest secrets). The more secretive documents of a koryū are frequently cryptic, with some containing coded messages that can only be deciphered by an initiate into the highest level of instruction. Sometimes, these codes include proprietary characters called anjō moji and jindai moji. Others contain cryptic messages in the form of symbols like oshide or tegata (hand prints), manji (swastika-like crosses) or zuhyō (vital point illustrations). Some schools issued densho containing various didactic aids, which provide context or physical descriptions, particularly as most densho are written in kanbun, an older style of writing Japanese using Chinese grammar. Densho that include descriptions of techniques or technical clues occasionally have these clues inscribed in

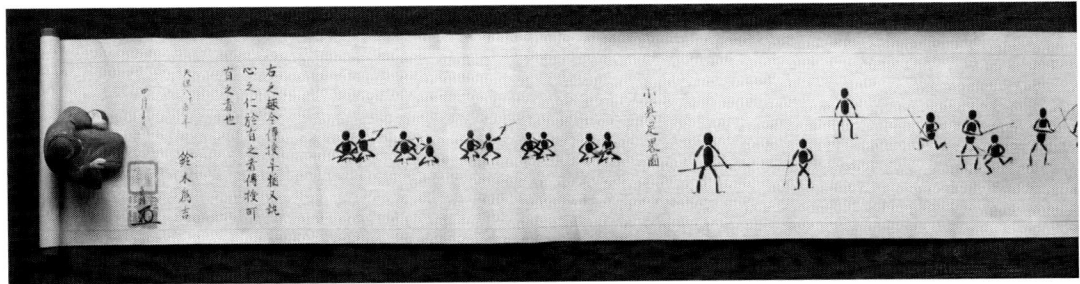

Muraku Ryū, Tachiai Hakari no Seki Mokuroku, issued 1837. This rare densho utilizes only tonbo-e

History And Technique

Shishin Nyukaku no Jo issued in 1705, signed Minamoto Oguri. This densho, issued over 310 years ago, is among the oldest and most refined densho in the Takamura ha Shindō Yōshin Kai collection, and due to the high quality of the paper this densho remains in very good condition. (Collection of the Takamura ha Shindō Yōshin Kai.)

Notice the elaborate kaō (personal monogram), hanko (personal stamp), and expensive gold leaf flower pattern in the paper. This is an exquisite example of a high-quality Hōei period densho.
(Collection of the Takamura ha Shindō Yōshin Kai.)

color alongside the kanji (Japanese/Chinese characters) written in the common black.

Not all densho were technical, tactical, or philosophical. Some were historical or biographical, chronicling a particular ryū's history or the life of its founder. The ryū that issued these documents are among those with the most complete and accurate surviving historical records. These documents go by names such as kogo den, hyōhō denki and taikeizu. Among the most noted of these is the Kashima Shinden Jikishikage Ryū Hyōhō Denki. (See: page 338)

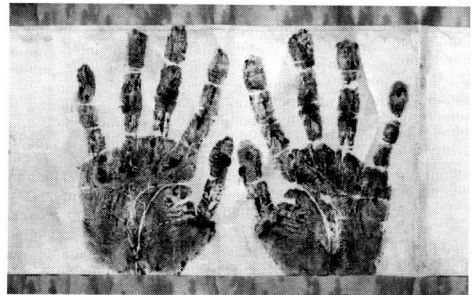

Symbolic oshide or tegata (hand prints) appearing on a Musō Kenshin Ryū Torite no Maki.
(Collection of the Takamura ha Shindō Yōshin Kai.)

The most distinctive and prized densho are emakimono (illustrated scrolls). The earliest versions of these enhanced teaching documents contained rudimentary stick drawings simply representing the positions of weaponry relative to one another. As time passed, the drawing styles on these documents became more detailed in an attempt to preserve the critical principles of combat particular to specific ryū. The most prevalent illustrations on densho are segmented line drawings, called tonbo-e (dragonfly drawings). They avoid detail and focus on basic body positioning. Properly executed, tonbo-e

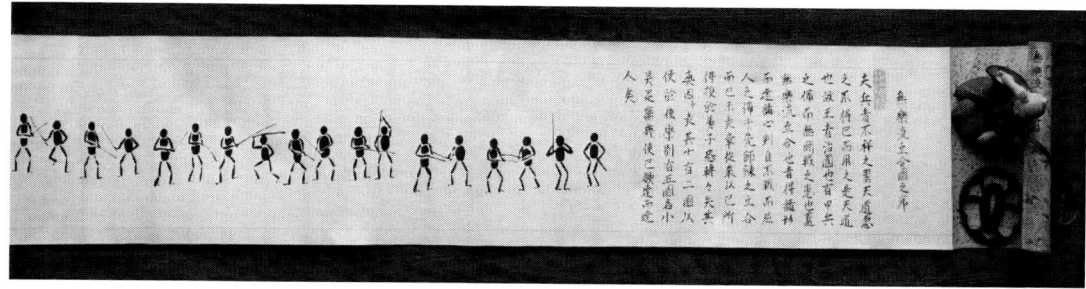

illustrations as a visual reference to the school's kata. (Collection of the Takamura ha Shindō Yōshin Kai.)

Shindō Yōshin Ryū

conveyed sufficient detail for an initiated practitioner to recall whatever is described without imparting too much information to an outsider who might gain access to the document. Conveying the defining characteristics of a kata or principle by way of artwork required not only familiarity with the subject matter, but also artistic sensibilities. For this reason, some ryū cultivated a student in the school who had artistic talent and made him responsible for producing densho.

Emakimono became far more elaborate during the Edo period, and evolved into a true representation of an art form, rather than persisting as a mere reference tool. Many of these more elaborate densho were full-color works, intricately drawn and illustrated with a painstaking

Hokushin Shinbu Ittō Ryū Hyōhō, kenjutsu densho
(Collection of the Takamura ha Shindō Yōshin Kai.)

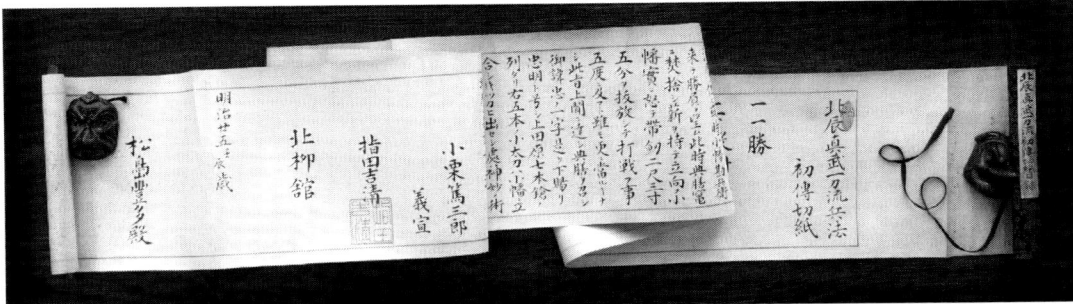

Hokushin Shinbu Ittō Ryū Kenjutsu, Shoden Kirigami, issued 1872.

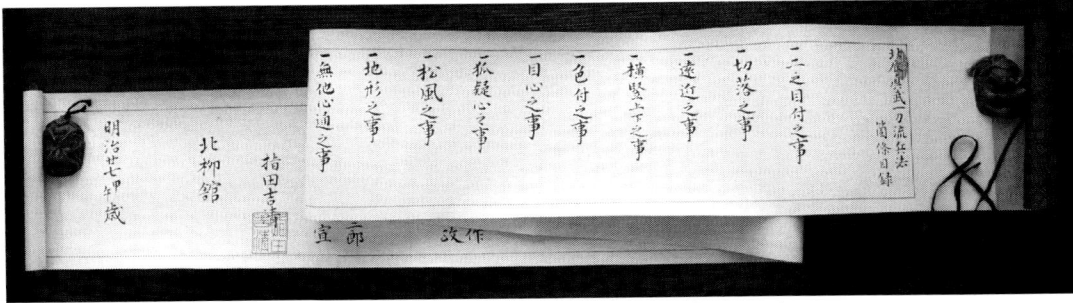

Hokushin Shinbu Ittō Ryū Kenjutsu, Kajō Mokuroku, issued 1874.

Shin Musō Yanagi Ryū, jūjutsu densho
(Collection of the Takamura ha Shindō Yōshin Kai.)

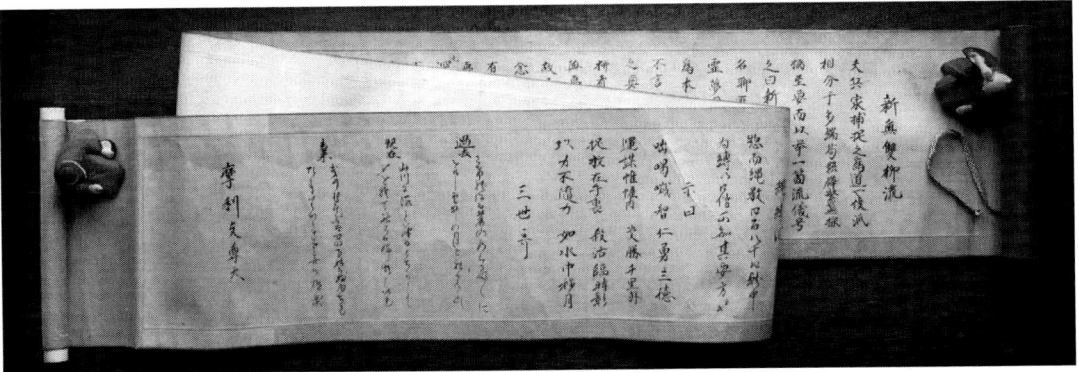

Shin Musō Yanagi Ryū Jūjutsu Mokuroku, issued 1815.

History And Technique

Kashima Shinden Jikishinkage Ryū, kenjutsu densho
(Collection of the Takamura ha Shindō Yōshin Kai.)

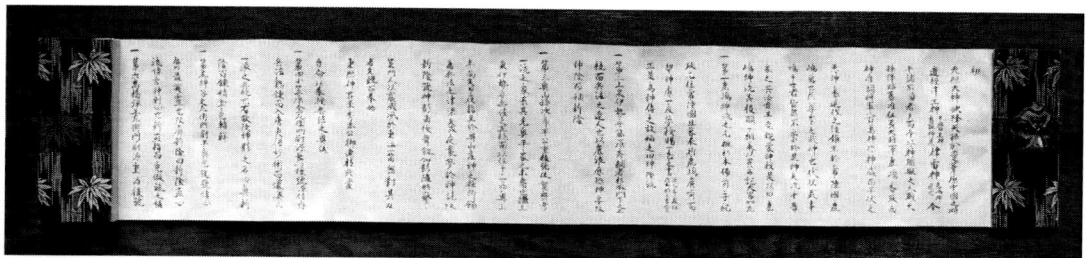
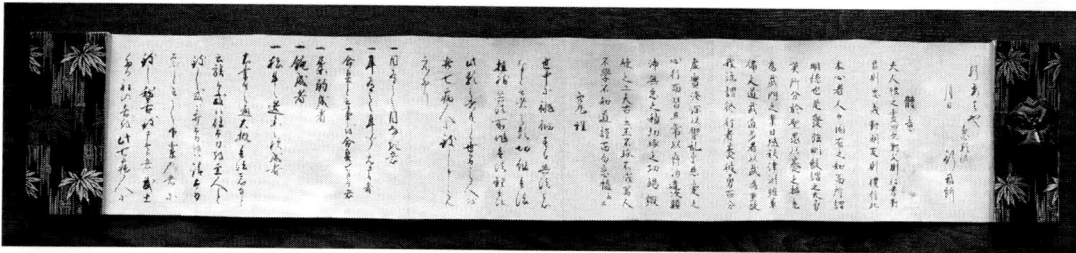
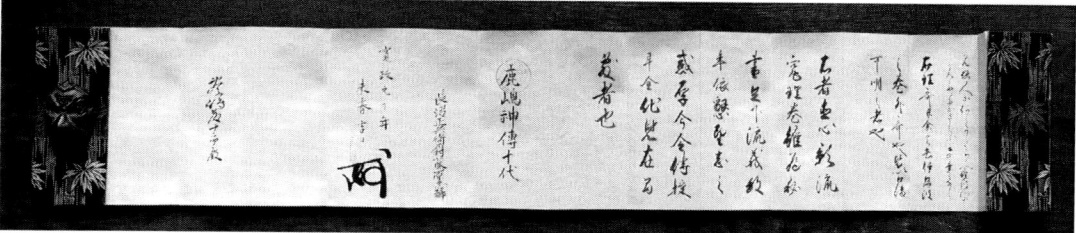

Kashima Shinden Jikishinkage Ryū Hyōhō Denki no Maki, issued 1797.

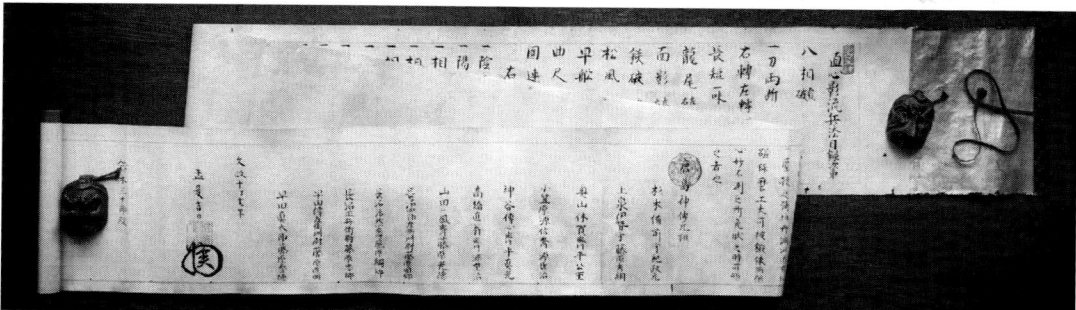
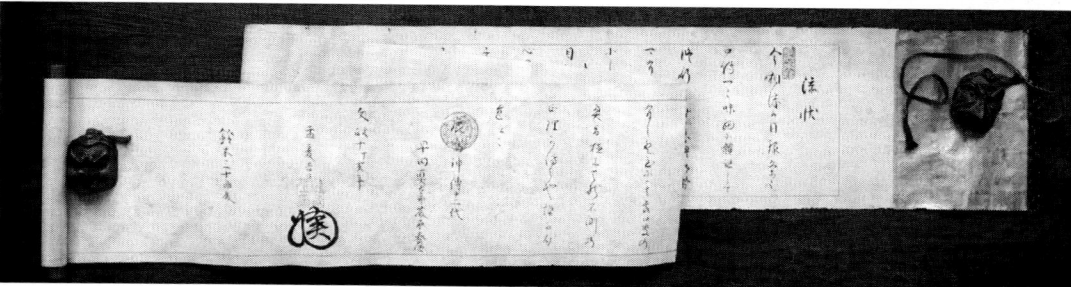

Kashima Shinden Jikishinkage Ryū Heihō Mokuroku Shidai and Ryūjō, issued 1828.

Shindō Yōshin Ryū

Shintō Ryū, kenjutsu densho
(Collection of the Takamura ha Shindō Yōshin Kai.)

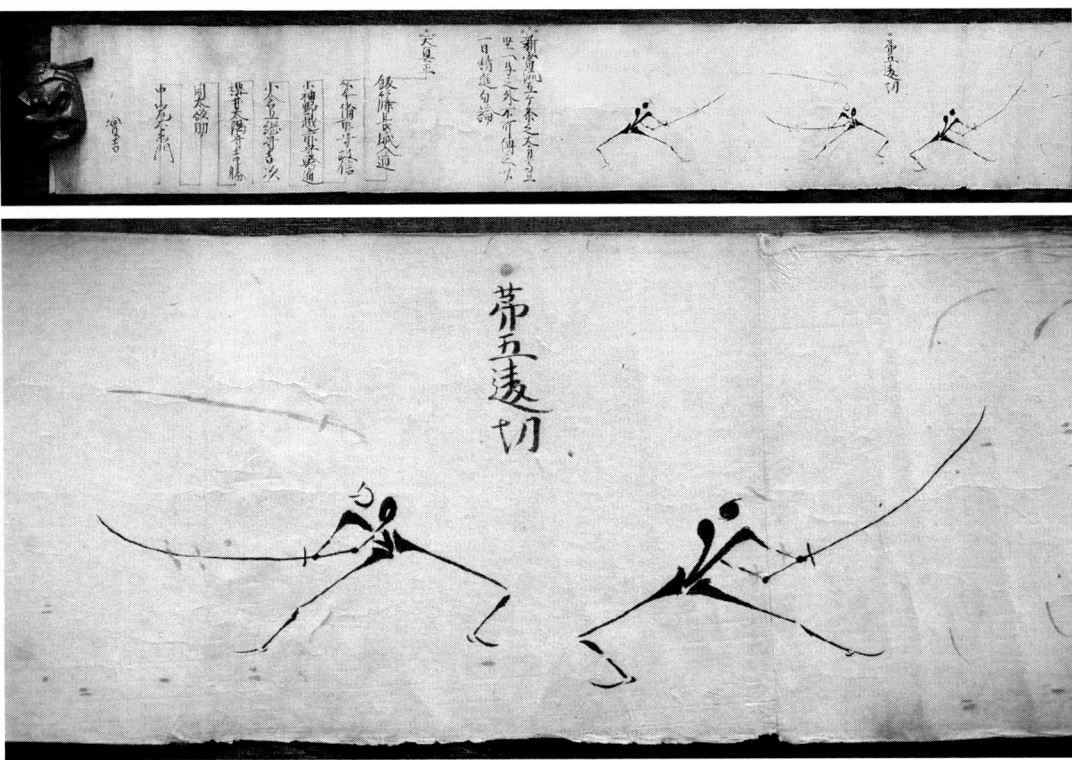

Elegant tonbo-e illustrations adorn this Shintō Ryū Kenjutsu mokuroku, issue date unknown.

Tōda Ryū, kenjutsu densho
(Collection of the Takamura ha Shindō Yōshin Kai.)

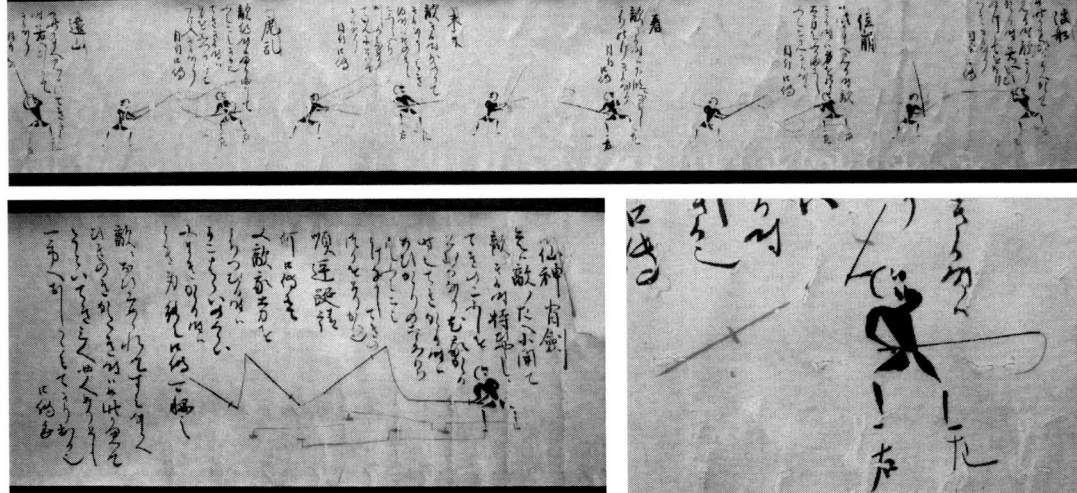

Tonbo-e Illustrations including didactic aids of Toda Ryū kenjutsu. The starting stances and weapon positions are rendered in black with movements and footwork rendered in red. This densho from the Keichō era is dated 1609, making it over 400 years old, among the oldest currently in the Takamura ha Shindō Yoshin Kai collection.

attention to detail. In the highest expression of Edo period densho, elaborated painted works were produced that included intricate facial details, and even richly-patterned clothing.

Imagery of a yamabushi tengu instructing kenjutsu included on a Hosatsu Ryū Torite no Maki, issued in 1849. Hosatsu Ryū Torite was an Edo period sōgō bujutsu derived in part from Akiyama Yōshin Ryū.
(Collection of the Takamura ha Shindō Yōshin Kai.)

Many traditional pursuits in Japan were neglected during the years immediately following the cultural upheaval that was the Meiji Restoration (1868). Koryū budō were one of these, and with that neglect came a substantial decline in the quality of koryū densho. The standard of makimono produced during the late 19th and early 20th centuries was much lower in terms of both materials and calligraphy. Because of this, many examples of densho from this period have deteriorated due to the use of inferior paper. For this reason their preservation has required intervention by remounting on an archival substrate.

The Takamura ha Shindō Yōshin Kai possesses an extensive collection of densho and kakejiku (hanging scrolls) related to the school's historical jūjutsu and kenjutsu roots. Included in this collection are over 50 Yōshin Ryū densho from the Akiyama and Miura lineages, plus another 25 from related traditions such as Shin no Shindō Ryū, Tenjin Shinyō Ryū, Shindō Goshin Ryū, Shin Musō Yanagi Ryū, Jikishinkage Ryū, Shinshinkage Ryū, and Hokushin Ittō Ryū. The school also holds over 35 kakejiku brushed by Bakumatsu period samurai and calligraphers including Yamaoka Tesshu, Katsu Kaishu, Takahashi Deishu and Nakahara Nantenbō.

In total, the Takamura ha Shindō Yōshin Kai collection comprises over 200 documents further including letters, dairies, books, poetry, other artwork including a signed banner brushed and presented to Obata Shigeta by Japanese Prince, Komatsu no Miya Akihito.

Shindō Yōshin Ryū

Yōshin Ryū, taijutsu, iaitachijutsu, naginatajutsu and jūjutsu densho
(Collection of the Takamura ha Shindō Yōshin Kai.)

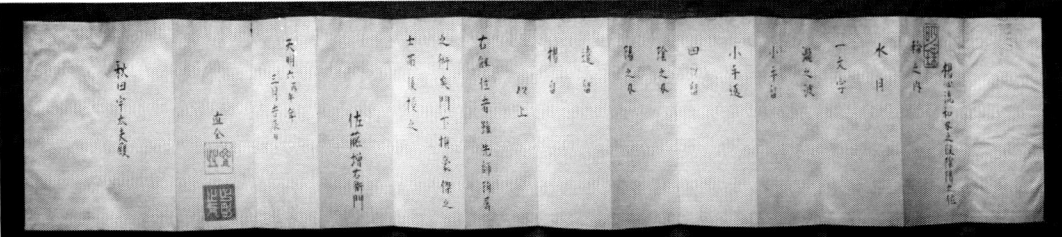

Akiyama Yōshin Ryū, Yawara Hanodan Inyō no Kurai, 1786.

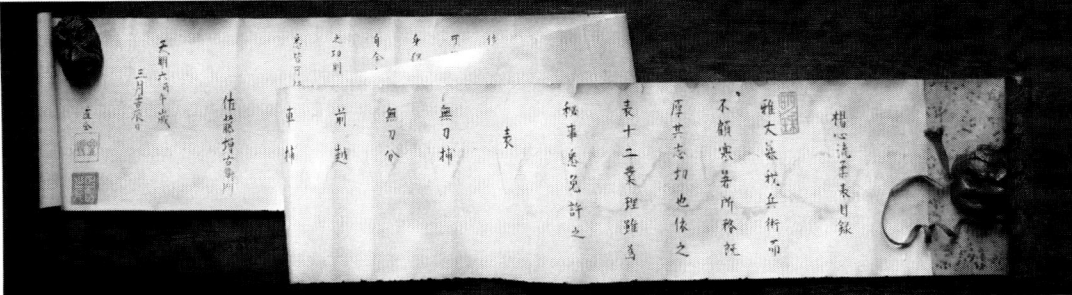

Akiyama Yōshin Ryū, Yawara Omote Mokuroku, issued 1786.

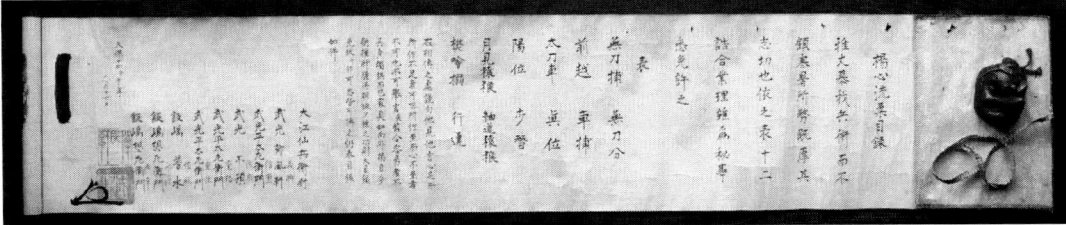

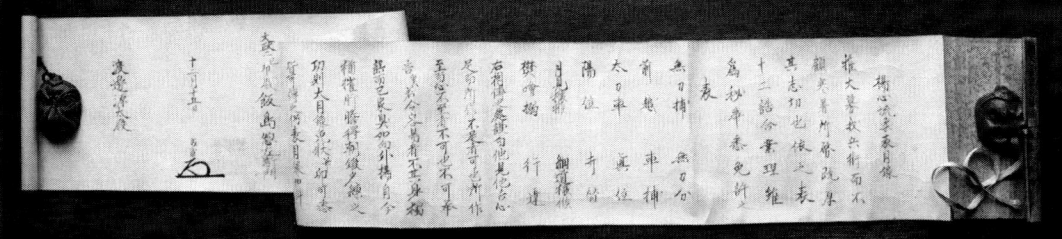

Akiyama Yōshin Ryū, Yawara and Yawara Omote Mokuroku, issued 1819 and 1843.

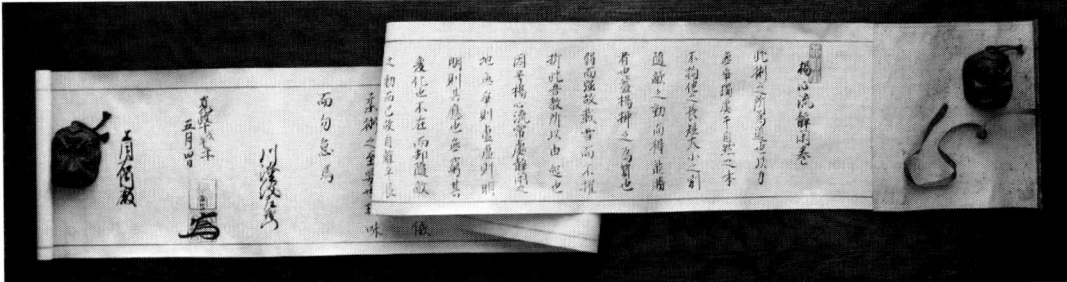

Akiyama Yōshin Ryū Seikan no Maki, issued 1798.

History And Technique

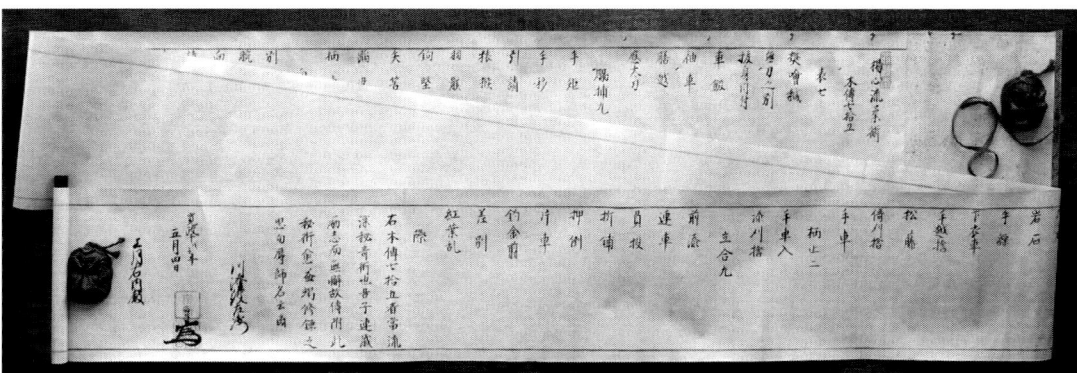

Akiyama Yōshin Ryū jūjutsu Honden Hichijūgo no Maki, issued 1798.

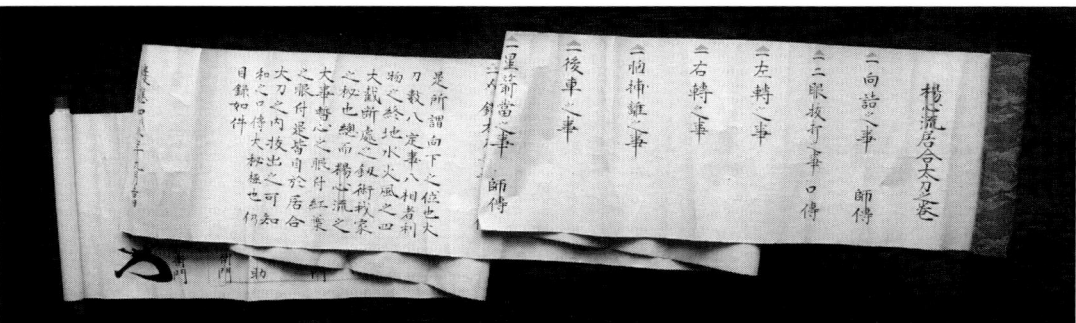

Akiyama Yōshin Ryū, Iaitachijutsu Mokuroku, issued 1866.

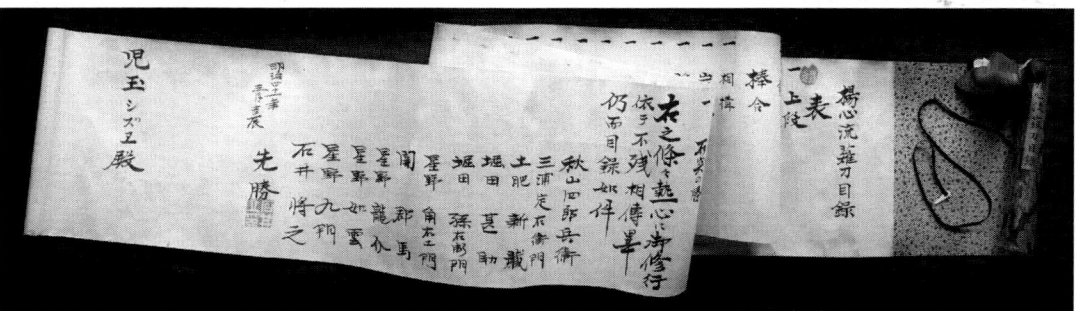

Akiyama Yōshin Ryū, Naginata Mokuroku, issued 1909.

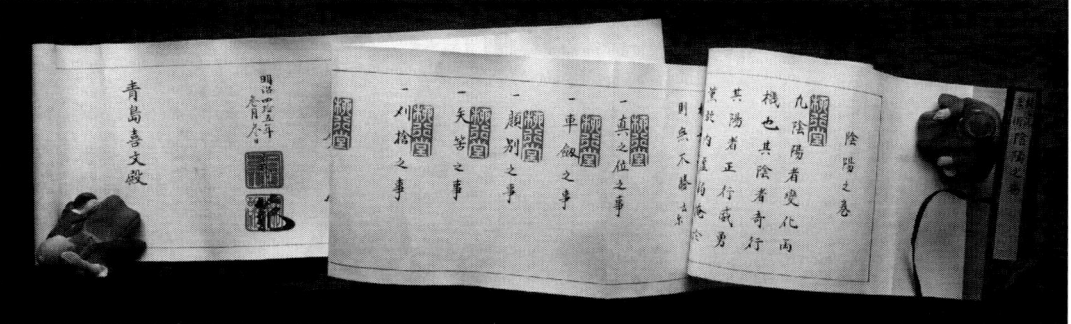

Akiyama Yōshin Ryū Jūjutsu, Inyō no Maki, issued 1871.

Shindō Yōshin Ryū

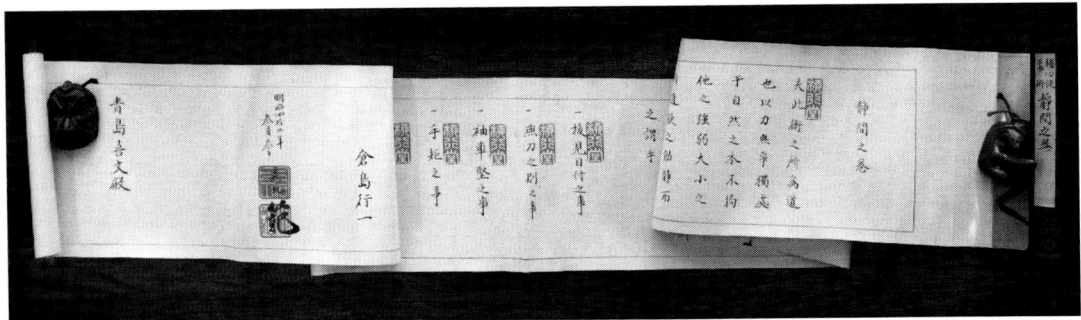

Akiyama Yōshin Ryū Jūjutsu, Seikan no Maki, issued 1871.

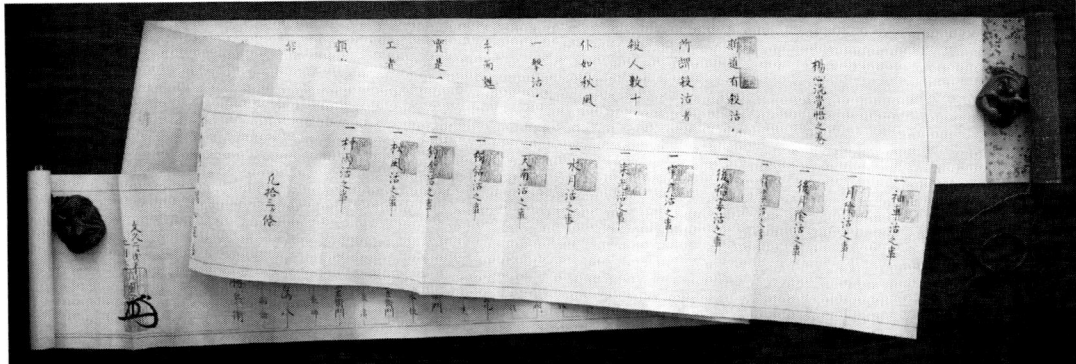

Akiyama Yōshin Ryū Jūjutsu, Kakugo no Maki, issued 1862.

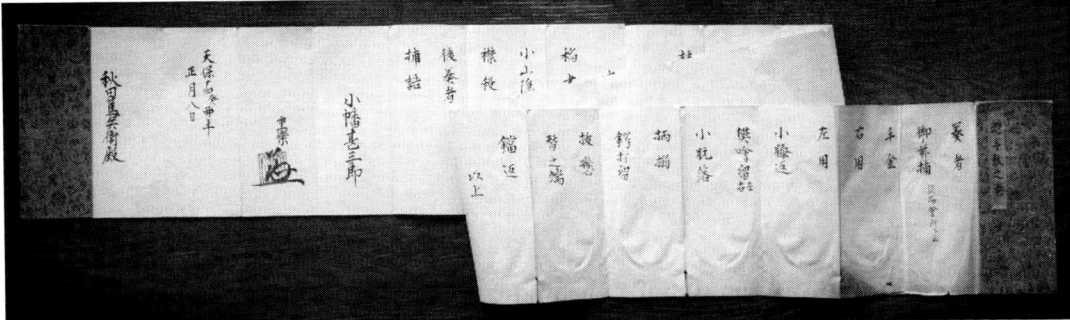

Akiyama Yōshin Ryū So Tekazu no Maki, issued 1843.

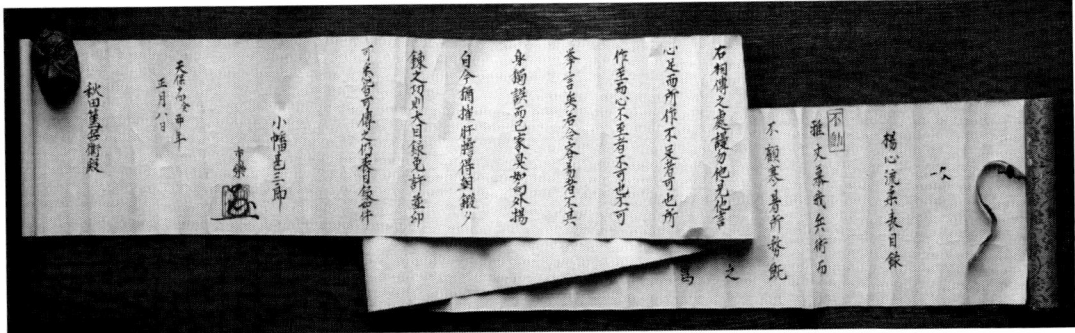

Akiyama Yōshin Ryū Yawara Omote Mokuroku, issued 1843.

Akiyama Yōshin Ryū densho, issued by Takahashi Heibei Hidetsugu in 1845. This densho is likely related to Dōjō Sōgon Gishiki, an intiation ceremony where secret teachings are passed from instructor to student.
(Collection of the Takamura ha Shindō Yōshin Kai.)

Shindō Yōshin Ryū

Recollections on Takamura Yukiyoshi

高村雪由

Following the interview that Stan Pranin published in Aikidō Journal in 1999, numerous individuals enquired about Takamura Sensei, curious about him and his unique perspectives on budō. Furthermore, a newer generation of TSYR students has asked me to put many of the stories and experiences I had training under him into writing. After much deliberation, I decided I was not capable of providing a sufficient picture of Takamura Sensei by myself. An earlier and dwindling generation of students had a more complete picture of him and his life. What follows is a short interview we arranged for this book. It eschews honorifics and reflects a casual discussion among old dōjō mates. The interviewees include David Maynard, Karl Garrison, Nanette Ōkura and me. The questions were compiled by Marco Ruiz, the gentleman who conducted the original interview that introduced Stan Pranin to Takamura Yukiyoshi.

- Tobin E. Threadgill

History And Technique

***Marco Ruiz:** Hello Everyone, I have only met Threadgill Sensei and Maynard Sensei personally, but it is an honor to participate in this forum with you esteemed people. I met Takamura Sensei around 1978 at a JACL [Japanese American Citizen's League] event in San Francisco where I was a representative for a local kendō dōjō. I was introduced to him by a local judōka whose name I have long forgotten.*

David Maynard: I think it was Mits Kimura [Kimura Mitsuho, ninth dan US Jūdō Federation].

***Marco Ruiz:** Yes, that's it. Let's start with how each of you met Takamura Sensei.*

David Maynard: I started training in jūdō under Mits Kimura at the San Francisco Jūdō Institute [SFJI] over in the Sunset District around 1966. I was just a kid. After a couple of years, I asked Kimura Sensei about self-defense. He told me jūdō was a sport, and that if I wanted to learn real self-defense I should go train in jūjutsu with a guy named Takamura across the bay in Hayward. An older guy in the dōjō named Fitz had seen Takamura and said he was fantastic. He gave me Takamura's dōjō address and I just showed up one Saturday morning to observe a class. Back then, Hayward was a small farming community out in the sticks. The dōjō was a hole in the wall, almost like a barn, with the words Obata Jūjutsu brushed beside the door. Once inside, it was actually pretty nice, with a sprung 24-tatami mat. Takamura Sensei was calling what he taught then Obata Jūdō/Jūjutsu. It was very different from the jūdō I was learning. I was immediately hooked when I saw him taking a huge marine to the floor without the least bit of difficulty. It looked faked, but the facial expression of the marine told me something else.

Karl Garrison: I originally tried my hand at boxing when I joined the Marines but I was too slow, so I was just a punching bag. Another marine introduced me to jūdō explaining that it was a new Olympic Sport. Once I tried it, I realized this was for me. I loved it. I started training in jūdō under Kimura Sensei at SFJI like David did. I also trained under Toshio Higashi when I could get out his way. There were not a lot of black men in jūdō back then, so I stood out and was not always welcomed. One day this scrawny teenager in class named David threw me with a wrist lock during randori and it hurt like hell. I asked him where he learned it and he told me about this guy Takamura. The next weekend, I went over to Hayward with David and was damned impressed by what I saw. The instructor, Yukio Takamura, was this ornery (sic) little guy, but he was totally color-blind. He invited me to put on my jūdō gi and get on the mat with him. I learned a hell of a lot about technique from Takamura in that one class. He had an unusual way of teaching things. He taught theory and technique together in a way the jūdō guys didn't. That type of teaching was something I could relate to. Also, the fact that I was black seemed to have zero effect on how he treated me, which impressed me a lot. I enrolled the next week. Unfortunately, I got orders six months later and shipped out. It was 1971 before I made my way back to Takamura's dōjō and jumped deep into TSYR.

David Maynard with Tobin Threadgill at the TSYR Japantown Dōjō in San Jose, CA. 1987.

Shindō Yōshin Ryū

Nanette Ōkura: I met sensei through my mother who worked with his wife Michiko at her antique store in San Francisco. My mother believed I should have a way to defend myself when I started dating boys. Sensei was very sweet to me and knew how to push me without intimidating me. I think my first class was around 1974.

Toby Threadgill: In 1985, I was a Wadō Ryū student under J. Gerry Chau and had been asked to write an article on Wadō Ryū history for a USKA [United States Karate Association] newsletter. In the process, I had been told Shindō Yōshin Ryū was no longer extant by a USKA/Wadō Ryū sensei named Cecil Patterson. By sheer chance, I was painting the interior of the Wadōkan Dōjō in Texas when someone knocked on the door. It was David Maynard. He was lost and looking for a hotel when he saw the Wadō Ryū sign and got curious. After a short introduction, he mentioned he trained in Shindō Yōshin Ryū jūjutsu. I was flabbergasted. He explained the main line of Shindō Yōshin Ryū was still active and led by Matsuoka Tatsuo in Tōkyō. He further explained that his teacher, Takamura Yukiyoshi in San Jose, California, led a separate line. I obtained Takamura Sensei's address from David and immediately sent him a letter. He responded providing an impressive amount of Wadō Ryū and Shindō Yōshin Ryū historical information. I made plans to visit Takamura Sensei's dōjō in San Jose several months later, and was very intrigued with the skills I observed. Many years previously, I had also trained in western fencing, so I had an appreciation of sword work. The mix of empty hand training and sword work really appealed to me. I suppose joining was inevitable.

Marco Ruiz: Garrison Sensei, you said something very interesting. You stated that Takamura Sensei treated you like anyone else. This was at a time when racial tensions were running high following the Civil Rights Movement. Takamura Sensei was harshly criticized by some budōka in Japan for teaching koryū to foreigners. Was he truly color-blind, and if so, how did he adopt this attitude, which would have been unusual for a man of his age and background?

Karl Garrison: Takamura was not your average Japanese guy. He had lived in the west for a long time. He came to realize people were just people regardless of where they lived, what color their skin was, or what shape their eyes were. I think we bonded in an American era when anyone who was Asian was viewed suspiciously because of the Vietnam War. Lots of white America wasn't interested in nationality, they just saw an Asian face as a potential threat. Because of this prejudice, we became soul brothers of a sort, but only off the mat. On the mat, he was sensei! There was no doubt who was the boss on the tatami. The man could be harsh, even to those students he liked. Ask Tobs! Takamura put the hammer to Toby so hard a couple of times we were surprised he stuck around.

Toby Threadgill: Yeah, he could really unload on you. I must admit that more than once I deserved getting hammered though. I was just dense back then and didn't understand the reigi. Takamura Sensei wasn't very touchy-feely, so if you violated dōjō protocol, you could really go for a nasty ride. I know I got knocked unconscious twice. But Karl, you were the senpai from hell. Imagine a 275 lb combat Marine as the dōjō enforcer. People were as intimidated by you as Takamura Sensei. We called you Professor Crush!

Nanette Ōkura: You guys are terrible. You make Sensei sound mean. He was never malicious. He did run the dōjō a bit like something from an old samurai novel, but to a young Japanese woman, I liked it. I always felt safe in the dōjō. Sensei would not tolerate any inappropriate behavior on the mat. That he enforced the rules strictly was understood. Because of the strict adherence to reigi, the dōjō was an oasis for me. I have never felt more comfortable or safe anywhere else in my life.

David Maynard: I think Takamura Sensei was a man ahead of his time as far as race relations were concerned. His first duty was to the school, and if that meant teaching the entirety of the ryū to non-Japanese students, so be it. Having left Japan at such a young age, he did not harbor many of the cultural prejudices most Japanese of his age did. His life overseas, particularly in progressive Sweden, encouraged him to become quite worldly in his perspective. Many Japanese sensei I've interacted with only lived in Japan. They had limited exposure to the outside world so they naturally developed provincial attitudes. Crikey, it's understandable. Takamura Sensei was unique in experience for a guy of his age and budō background, so he was a very different bloke from the Japanese budō guys living in Japan.

Marco Ruiz: This is fascinating stuff. It creates an interesting and complex picture of the man. However, there seems to be a slight disagreement concerning what Takamura Sensei was like on the mat. Can you guys clear this up a little? I don't want readers to get an incorrect impression of Takamura Sensei.

David Maynard: Let me start. There is no doubt Takamura Sensei was the picture of an old school budōka. He was tough as hell, but Nan is right, he was not malicious. There's a lot of romantic fiction spread around about "modern-day samurai" but it's all bunk. People who say such stuff are numptys who have no idea what they're talking about. I guess such romantic notions sell books and look good in movies, but the fact is guys like Takamura Sensei were just raised in an era where societal norms were very different. He adjusted the best he could to a very different culture, and in my opinion, did an admirable job. Great that he was, it doesn't mean today's koryū instructors should adopt societal norms from a man raised in another culture, in another era. In Takamura Sensei's case, the cultural adaptations he made could not as evenly transfer to a koryū dōjō, an environment where tradition is more deeply ingrained. Today's koryū budō teachers should not try to imitate how their Japanese teachers taught them, or related to their students. They must adjust in this respect or the koryū really will become a thing of the past. The challenge is managing and prioritizing those adjustments.

Karl Garrison: I agree. We've all seen guys pretending to act Japanese when they aren't. It's kind of embarrassing. Imagine me trying to act Japanese. I'd look a fool. Takamura was just the real deal, being himself. Yeah, he ran a very strict and formal dōjō. Being a marine, that environment really appealed to me. It felt familiar. You need to also remember that in the 1960s nobody knew what a koryū dōjō was. The environment and teaching method was totally foreign to Westerners. All the early students in the dōjō came from modern budō dōjō teaching jūdō, karate, and maybe kendō. The ones who liked the very strict environment in Takamura Sensei's dōjō stayed. The ones that didn't, and there were quite a few, left. Hell, I didn't really know what koryū was until I read Donn Draeger's books on classical budō and bujutsu, and I was doing it.

If I gave the impression Takamura was cruel or something, that was not my intention. Yeah, he could be harsh, but to a young marine, I was familiar with this level of intensity, just not outside the Corps. Compared to the environment in a commercial jūdō dōjō, it was far more strict and mentally demanding. Takamura would push us very hard sometimes, I mean to the edge, but I loved that. Maybe I was an adrenaline fiend but I loved being tested and driven to excel. I loved to find my personal limits and be pushed to surpass them. I don't think that was cruel at all. It was what I expected from a sensei.

David Maynard: How was Takamura Sensei on the mat? Demanding, uncompromising, and a stickler for detail. He hated mediocrity; could not stand it. When you walked through the dōjō genkan, you had better be ready to rock it because he was not there to watch you dawdle. You had better be prepared to train. Now, he did have an unusual tendency towards using wicked humor in his instruction during the last half of his teaching career, but in the early days he was just a hard-ass, and once class bowed in, it was bloody game on.

Toby Threadgill: You guys have a slightly different picture than I do because he was in his mid- to-late fifties when I met him. Takamura Sensei was certainly a package deal. You got what you got, warts and genius mixed together. I certainly saw the hard-ass side, but I also saw the brutally funny side. He had a knack for being funny and telling you how terrible your technique was in the same instant. I really admired that about him. He could let you know you needed to work on something, because you were doing it terribly wrong, without it feeling personal. He made you feel like we were all on a quest to preserve something bigger than both of us. You could feel it was a sacred trust to him, something he had devoted much of his life to. I heard him once describe koryū budō as a sacred trust passed to us by giants among men. I think that is exactly how he viewed it, and to be invited on that journey with him required some pretty serious dedication. I knew that going in and never regretted it.

The enforcement of reigi, that was different. I never took what he did to me personally, but there was a tinge of aggression that was probably out of place in this day and age. Like David said, he was a guy from a culture and time with different norms. He adapted as best as he could, but he was also a guy born into circumstances a modern Japanese cannot really imagine, much less a Westerner. Try to imagine being raised in Obata Shigeta's dōjō. That must have been wild. As Nanette implied, sure, he could be harsh, but if you knew the rules and obeyed them, all was good. Strictly enforcing the reigi made the environment predictable and safe to train in. No-one was going to pull any stupid nonsense in that dōjō, and if you did, it only happened once. I've seen lots of passive-aggressive nonsense tolerated in gendai dōjō, but if you saw that in Takamura's dōjō, you only saw it once.

David Maynard: Yeah, Takamura Sensei did not tolerate any passive-aggressive nonsense. It was pretty simple; you followed the bloody rules! If you didn't, there could be hell to pay. Between Takamura Sensei and Karl, you were walking in a minefield if you were a being a jerk, so jerks didn't last long. We took training intensity to a very high level, but the only reason we could do that safely was because funny business was not tolerated. Big ego? Trying to prove something? Wrong dōjō.

Toby Threadgill: No doubt about it, the training intensity could be incredible. It could sometimes catch me off guard. I had a lot of experience in hard contact martial arts such as karate and Muay Thai before I started Shindō Yōshin Ryū, but Takamura Sensei's dōjō was just as intense as anything I had ever experienced elsewhere, and he took me mentally to places I had never ventured. He'd line up across from you to do kumitachi and those crazy little grey eyes of his would look right through your soul. At that moment, you felt that if he cleaved your skull in half, he'd sleep like a baby. There was no emotion, just pure, precise and frightening technique. When he wanted to be intimidating, it was off the scale.

David Maynard: Absolutely! And his precision was bloody incredible. He had so much confidence in his technique and control that he could just mentally intimidate and overwhelm you. I met quite a few people from kendō who thought I was exaggerating until they met him and got a taste of what we called "Tak'd". He had this explosive attack that was on you before you knew it, and once it started, it was unrelenting. More than once, I witnessed people back peddling full speed into the dōjō wall trying to get away from him. It was raw but precisely applied aggression. And yeah, it was emotionless.

Nanette Ōkura: I suppose being a woman meant Sensei had different expectations of me. He did treat me different than he did you guys, but he let me know that his expectations for me were very high, even if they were different. I think the thing I most recall was his demand that I develop extreme precision and never flinch from doing what needed to be done. He told me that during kata I had to have ice in my veins. That I had to push my emotions and fears aside, and do what needed to be done, to prevail. He used to say: "Nan, you cannot match a man's power, but you can surpass his speed and precision. Let him come. When he presses you, yield and take a tendon so softly that he never knows what happened. You must strive to be deliberate, determined and dangerous. Sensei's skills in that arena were just remarkable. I was there when Sensei cut some hair off David's head with the Yamaura blade while executing a nito awase kata. I knew he did it intentionally. He was so precise that it was no accident.

David Maynard: Yeah, I remember that! It was his way of saying I needed a haircut. And by the way, where did he get that "deliberate, determined and dangerous" phrase? That could not have been him as he was not that creative with English. He got that phrase somewhere else.

Toby Threadgill: He got that from Michiko. I was there when she told Sensei that Nanette looked deliberate, determined and dangerous. Takamura Sensei loved it and recited it when Nanette put on her bōgu. Nanette, your kiai put us all to shame by the way. Takamura Sensei was absolutely smitten with it.

Nanette Ōkura: Well, he taught me that kiai. Sensei told me I needed to make a man's blood freeze in his veins if I was going to prevail over him. He made me practice screaming on every cut during private lessons in the dōjō. I would leave so hoarse I could barely talk.

Toby Threadgill: Although we all have slightly different impressions of Takamura Sensei on the mat, these differences highlight one of the least-understood aspects of koryū training, and that's the individualized teaching model. Unlike modern budō where people line up and train in unison, Takamura Sensei taught in a very individualized way. Every pair of students worked on something different and was taught slightly differently. I know he taught me a bit differently than he taught each of you. At first, that was confusing, because there seemed to be no orthodox standard. Later, I came to realize the orthodoxy was easier felt than seen. I was limiting myself because I am naturally so visual. I had to unlearn my dependency on visual reference.

Karl Garrison: Tobs, that's true but that came later. You and Nan benefitted from that teaching model more than Dave and I did. When Takamura first started teaching me, the class all trained on the same material.

David Maynard: That's true, but in the 1960s we were all beginners. Furthermore, we weren't really studying Shindō Yōshin Ryū yet. We were still really studying the abbreviated curriculum that Takamura Sensei called Obata Jūdō/Jūjutsu. Takamura Sensei was deciding how to teach and whether or not to teach us Obata ha Shindō Yōshin Ryū. Teaching non-Japanese, and in English, was really challenging for him. He was only 35 years old at that time. That's why he later put so much stock in cultivating teaching skills and principle-based instruction. Takamura Sensei, unlike many Japanese instructors I've met, really worked hard at developing a teaching process, and in my opinion he became a teaching savant. No-one else in Japanese budō I ever met was teaching like he was.

Marco Ruiz: I understand that Takamura Sensei made adjustments to the Shindō Yōshin Ryū curriculum in the 1960s. How does that work in koryū? I would assume the curriculum must remain unchanged for it to represent something that is really "old school".

David Maynard: This is a very complex question. First you need to understand what defines a koryū, and it is not the curriculum. It is the date the art was founded and the dependability of its transmission through time. Confusing this issue is the fact that Takamura Sensei's definition of koryū was different than is commonly accepted today. In his writings, koryū are defined as schools that were created during the Sengoku Jidai (1490 - 1603), classical schools were created during the Edo Jidai (1603 - 1868), while modern schools were created during the Mejij era (1868 - 1912) and beyond. A kendōka once asked Takamura Sensei if Shindō Yōshin Ryū was koryū, and he said no, that it was a classical school. Since the kendōka was not aware of Takamura Sensei's unique definition of koryū, he got the wrong impression. Shindō Yōshin Ryū was created in 1864 and the Obata/Takamura ha Shindō Yōshin Ryū has direct transmission via Menkyo Kaiden licenses back to the founder, Matsuoka Katsunosuke. So by the most commonly accepted definition, it is one of the last koryū traditions created.

As to the curriculum, yes, Takamura Sensei altered the curriculum in 1968, but nothing was eliminated. The entire koryū curriculum as passed to Takamura Sensei is intact and currently taught as part of the schools mokuroku. Areas of study were expanded as betsuden (auxiliary study). One of these is a goshinjutsu (modern self defense) curriculum taught as part of the shoden mokuroku. Other additions categorized as betsuden are teachings originating in Matsuzaki Shinkage Ryū. Most, but not all, of these additional teachings are taught as part of the jōden okugi chi no maki. As far as we can tell by examining the school's historical documentation, the only losses to the Obata/Takamura ha Shindō Yōshin Ryū curriculum are 15 naginata kata originating in Akiyama Yōshin Ryū, which were introduced by Obata Shigeta.

Toby Threadgill: As David says, this is a complicated subject. One has to remember that koryū schools were evolving technically all the time. It was only after the Meiji Restoration that the evolution of some koryū slowed and ceased their previous pace of change. Look at the Miura/Totsuka Yōshin Ryū for example. This school evolved drastically during the Edo period, so the specifics of evolution changed through time and from school to school. Altering the curriculum in a koryū today can be bad or good, depending on the school's traditions and who is doing the changing. Take Araki Ryū for instance. According to Ellis Amdur, Araki Ryū transmission permits significant changes to the mokuroku in each generation. Because of this, different lines of Araki Ryū can represent very different approaches to budō, but since they all share the same source and have direct transmission, each is considered a legitimate school of koryū. Alternatively, there is the Tenshinshō-den Katori Shintō Ryū, a school dominated by kenjutsu that follows a much more conservative approach to transmission and maintaining its curriculum. Nihon koryū can diverge significantly concerning curriculum and transmission.

Takamura sensei's admonition on this subject is very clearly outlined in the TSYR Kaiki. No kata can be intentionally eliminated from the Takamura ha Shindō Yōshin Ryū mokuroku. Kata can only be adjusted by the headmaster after intense review, and any alteration to the omote kata must be consistent with the underlying riai (principles) of the kata. This restriction does not apply to specific kata identified as betsuden that are currently included in the school's mokuroku, nor does it apply to a fuzoku bugei like Takagi Hachiho Ryū bōjutsu. Alterations or complete elimination of the betsuden and any fuzoku ryū are completely within the powers held by the headmaster. Despite these powers, it is my opinion as headmaster that any alteration of a kata should only be undertaken after intense long-term evaluation, a process that should span many years.

Marco Ruiz: What was Takamura Sensei like personally, off the mat? How did he relate to you as a fellow human being?

David Maynard: Well, like most Japanese men of his age, he was a hard drinker and smoker. My goodness, he could put away the Bushmills. It was his number-one choice for whiskey, and he only drank whiskey or beer. That said, I never saw him drink a drop before class. Only afterwards would he imbibe.

Although I was his longest training student and am senpai to everyone involved in this conversation, there was always a barrier between us. Perhaps being the dōjō senpai meant I was not allowed to get too close to him personally, but I don't know. We had a very at-arms-length relationship off the mat. It was different with Karl and Nan. I know he was personally close to them. That never bothered me though. Takamura Sensei was my budō teacher. We didn't need to be close personal friends.

Nanette Ōkura: It may not be fair to use me as a reference on this question because I had a personal relationship with Sensei and Michiko long before I became a dōjō member. I was close friends with them as a young girl. They were like my adopted grandparents. Michiko taught me to cook as a young lady and Sensei doted on me like a granddaughter. He taught me to garden and identify different birds. Rather incongruously, Sensei was an avid bird watcher. He loved to take me to feed the birds in a local park. He always had pet birds like canaries in the house. Out of the dōjō, he was a sweet but sometimes distracted man. He had a very focused intellect, and if he was studying something it was like he was in another world. I had to tap him on the shoulder to get his attention when he was doing research.

Karl Garrison: As I alluded to previously, I developed a close relationship with the man. I never intended to, but it just happened over time. We clicked. Maybe it was having stuff in common during the Vietnam War era. I enjoyed the hell out of just hanging with him and talking life. He was an interesting dude with some very thought provoking ideas to a young Marine like me. I was particularly interested in his ideas about life and death, and his Shintō-focused spirituality. Most Japanese are simultaneously Buddhist and Shintō. Takamura was exclusively Shintō. I can honestly say his opinions on life and living helped me get through the emotional challenges I confronted after returning home from combat duty. He believed we all experienced free will and predestination at the same time. This made sense to me given the pointless tragedies I witnessed during combat duty. His way of thinking led me to accept that my life story was written by me, and that my death was already set by me. This was a liberating way to live life. Fear left me after I accepted this, and I saw every day as an adventure, every day as a way to uncover who I really was. This was old samurai thinking. Some people think that considering yourself already dead is a downer, but that's just missing the point. Accepting your death as a set event releases you from the fear of it. You become fearless because you know there is nothing between you and living life to its fullest. Fearlessness is liberating. Death just comes when it's supposed to. This way of thinking changed my view of life.

I did not enter budō with any ideas about spiritual stuff. That stuff never crossed my mind until later. When students approached Takamura about that stuff early in their training, he would laugh and tell them to go to church or a Buddhist temple. He said joining a dōjō for spiritual enlightenment was the wrong way around the block. He believed you joined a dōjō to train hard, to experience shugyō. He also said the spiritual part would come or it wouldn't, but looking for it is just a distraction. Looking backwards at my experiences and how I approached mortality, well, it all ended up being pretty darned practical. As human beings, I think we draw up our own questions and then go about answering them. The dōjō was just one of my classrooms, while my combat experience was another one. The trick is, a dōjō has to really challenge you to be worth the time and trouble. That's what made Takamura's dōjō special. I guess the dōjō has always been my church.

Karl Garrison, demonstrating in Amsterdam, Netherlands, 1992.

Toby Threadgill: It's funny. When I first met Takamura Sensei I didn't like him because I could not figure him out. After receiving a very informative letter from him, our first meeting in person was bizarre. It was like he'd never corresponded with me. Maybe I made a bad first impression on him or he was just having a bad day, but he was very icy. During a later visit, he warmed up to me and we got along very well. Over time, we forged a very close friendship off the mat with me spending a lot of time with him and Michiko. I think the fact that I traveled so far on a regular basis to train with him did not go unnoticed, but one thing I never did was be presumptuous. Despite traveling from Dallas to San Jose every month, I never assumed he would have time to teach me outside regular class times. After showing up for several classes in a row, every month for about six months, he asked me why my schedule was so inconsistent. When I told him I was flying in from Dallas, his eyebrows almost popped off. Still, I always waited for him to ask me if I had time to train outside class, and never asked him to take time away from his day to accommodate me. Eventually, a private training pattern emerged during my monthly visits to San Jose, but I still never assumed it would happen. I always let him invite me to the dōjō to train. I always viewed the sessions as a special gift.

As far as his personality goes, I'd have to say I found him eccentric but fascinating. He definitely lacked a certain level of social sophistication, but he never seemed intimidated by people of wealth or position. He could be downright shy in some social situations, but other times it was Takamura Sensei being bored with superficial people. That's probably why he kept to himself later in life. He had no time for people playing games.

For a man who was not highly educated, he was very well informed on subjects that interested him. History, botany and ornithology, these were intellectual passions he studied deeply. He also followed politics closely. The nationalistic forces that took Japan into World War II were particularly disturbing to him, so he was a lifelong political observer and critic.

Similar to Karl's previous commentary, I found Takamura's ideas about spirituality, destiny and living fascinating. He really encouraged me to think deeply on this and throw away all my preconceived ideas on the subject. Starting from scratch spiritually and philosophically was something that appealed to me. That quest took me places I had never ventured, and it still influences me today.

Marco Ruiz: Did Takamura Sensei talk much about his early life? He must have had a very unique life and upbringing to end up where he did.

Dave Maynard: Some of this subject matter is not really appropriate for this forum. There are privacy issues to consider. Takamura Sensei has living descendants that are very sensitive to family honor and legacy. It's hard for many Westerners to understand this, but Japanese can be very protective of their family's history and legacies. Things that a Westerner would have no compunction to discuss openly, the average Japanese would find to be a gross invasion of privacy. I think all of us agree that we should honor such sensitivities.

Marco Ruiz: Understood, but surely there are things about Takamura Sensei's early training and life in Japan you can discuss without invading family privacy?

David Maynard: Of course, Yuki, as he was known as a young boy, was born to a very young mother named Hanako. His father left soon after marrying Hanako and joined the military, only occasionally returning home to visit. Because of this, Yuki's dominant male role model was his paternal grandfather, Obata Shigeta. Shigeta appears to have held spiritual ideas associated with esoteric Shintō and introduced these to his grandson. Shigeta took his grandson on many journeys around Japan visiting famous shrines and entertaining him with heroic stories of samurai and tengu. This aspect of his childhood had a big impact on his life. Shigeta encouraged his grandson to read classics like The Tales of the Heike and meditate on the themes hidden in these works. As an adult Takamura Sensei maintained a fascination with tengu mythology as well as a keen interest in folklore related to Minamoto Yoshitsune. He was a voracious reader who loved myths and was an avid fan of Joseph Campbell's writings.

Shindō Yōshin Ryū

Toby Threadgill: Takamura Sensei once told me the only places he felt connected to were Mt. Kurama and some of the shrines he visited with his grandfather as a boy. One was the small Ono no Takamura shrine near Lake Biwa, and another was the shrine on Mt. Tsukuba. One of the reasons Takamura Sensei took up photography as a hobby was to photograph all the shrines he visited as a child. I think he secretly wanted to snap a photo of a tengu (laughing). I know Takamura Sensei returned to Kurama-san frequently. He told me he felt spiritually re-charged after wandering the forests of Mt. Kurama or communing with the kami at the Ono no Takamura Shrine. This is important because these beliefs and interests drove him to train hard as a boy in his grandfather's dōjō. These tales gave him a powerful connection to the past and instilled in him the responsibilities of being the caretaker of the traditions passed to him by his grandfather. Shigeta was essentially grooming Takamura Sensei to be the caretaker of his martial legacy from a very early age.

Karl Garrison: I traveled to Mt. Takao with Takamura once to view the tengu statues and the shrine. During the visit, he told me tengu myths the whole time we were there. The tales that were introduced to him as a child were a really big deal to him. They stayed with him his whole life. I think they were the foundation of his character. They taught him right from wrong, responsibility, and influenced how he viewed his place in society. I gained a lot of respect for Shintō from the man because of the way he treated me. There is nothing more Japanese-centric than Shintō, but it was Shintō's underlying sense of respecting nature that made Takamura see all men as part of something miraculous, something spiritually pure and worthy of constant polishing. In western religions we are told we are all born tainted, but in Shintō we are all born pure. But Takamura was no Shintō zealot either. He was very critical of the way Shintō had been corrupted by the nationalist movement prior to World War II. He likened pre-war Shintō to a beautiful dōjō with a filthy floor. If anyone ever wondered why we cleaned the dōjō so much, there you have it. To Takamura, the dōjō was a place of purification, a place where the human spirit was separated from corrupting influences by challenge, cleaning and polishing. For this reason the dōjō had to be cleaned every day.

Toby Threadgill: I'd like to emphasize something Karl touched upon. When Takamura Sensei was discussing leadership in Shindō Yōshin Ryū with me, he was adamant any prejudices based on race, religion, sex or national origin, were unacceptable. All humanity in his mind was kami, miraculous and worthy of awe. He acknowledged that humans could become corrupted, but this had nothing to do with a person's race, religion, sex or nation of origin. It was his opinion that anyone demonstrating bigotry was spiritually corrupt and in violation of the blood oath they took to become a member of Shindō Yōshin Ryū. For this, they had to be severed from Shindō Yōshin Ryū and walk a different path to find redemption through spiritual purification.

Nanette Ōkura: This is misogi. Misogi and ethics go hand in hand. One thing I have always admired about many koryū and Shindō Yōshin Ryū in particular, is the overt demand that a code of ethics be maintained and reinforced by a blood oath. We are not living in 19th century Japan. As a woman in Nihon budō, I have been keenly aware of physical and sexual abuse in modern budō schools being ignored or covered up. Sexual abuse by the teachers of young women, and the physical hazing of young men by their seniors, is commonplace in many martial arts schools. Sensei had a zero tolerance policy for that sort of thing. I admired the way Sensei felt about this. I admired that he followed his own ethical path and did not allow others to influence his opinions, even if they were out of the norm. He was living a form of spiritual misogi and it was evident in the ethics he demanded in the dōjō. It's typically Japanese to believe there can be something spiritual about ethically cleaning your soul and physically cleaning your environment. Once everything is properly cleansed, you can feel the order of things. I find that sense of calm and tranquility related to cleanliness both spiritual and tangible.

Do you all remember the guy who brought a vacuum cleaner to the dōjō to clean the tatami? That poor guy, I thought Sensei would kill him when he heard it turn on and saw its wheels rolling on the tatami mats. I finally intervened and reminded Sensei the young man's intentions were admirable, and that he just didn't understand the difference between the western concept of cleaning and the Shintō concept of achieving cleanliness. They are not the same and it was our job to teach him that. Sensei calmed down and apologized, but the poor guy was tomadoi (totally bewildered).

David Maynard: Yes, I remember that Nan. Sensei was tapped! It was good you intervened. Sensei had unusual passions, and being very clean was one of them. He was a fanatic about it. If you didn't clean, you would not last long in the dōjō. Do you all remember Toby cleaning the dōjō bathroom? We were all gobsmacked. Cleaning the toilet with his bloody toothbrush! Takamura Sensei was ecstatic and made us all come peek through the door. He told us we must never let Toby escape. He announced that Toby was the kami of cleanliness. I've never let him live that one down. And the shoe rack! Oh my God, the shoes!

Toby Threadgill: No, you haven't Dave. And by the way, what kind of person lets expensive Italian loafers get that filthy? And how hard is it to line shoes up in straight rows? Barbarians!

David Maynard: (laughing) I don't know who was more obsessed with being clean and neat, you or Takamura? And thank you again for cleaning my expensive shoes. They looked great!

Marco Ruiz: I'm getting a good laugh here. You all were very fortunate to train under such an incredible budōka, and Takamura Sensei does sound like quite a character. I wish I had gotten to know him better. Why do you think he remained rather obscure before the Aikidō Journal interview? I knew of him because I lived in the area and was involved with the JACL, but I'm surprised Takamura Sensei was not more well known in the greater budō community.

David Maynard: Takamura Sensei certainly wasn't famous, but he was pretty well known. He just ran in strange circles. He was very selective about friends and not very social. I traveled around Japan several times with him when I lived in Matsudo in the 1970s. We attended a couple of enbu. At one enbu, I spied Donn Draeger and went over to introduce myself. I had recently read Donn's first couple of books, so he was a budō giant to me. Donn Draeger was standing with another jōdō student named Phil Relnick and a Japanese guy I later learned was Kaminoda Tsunemori! I turned around and Sensei was just watching from a distance. I introduced him to the group and he just bowed but didn't come over. He was weird like that. Someone he did fraternize with occasionally was Tobari Kazu of the Tenjin Shinyō Ryū down in Ōsaka, and some old-timers from up north in Morioka who were in Shoshō Ryū. Another group he fraternized with were some Okinawan Gōjū Ryū karate people in San Francisco. They were lunch chums. One old friend in Gōjū Ryū wrote a very touching obituary about Takamura Sensei after his death. In the obituary, he explained how he had decided to quit training in karate, but that a conversation with Takamura Sensei convinced him to continue.

Shindō Yōshin Ryū

Karl Garrison: I think Takamura was certainly better known in his early years of teaching, particularly among the Japanese jūdō instructors and some kendōka. You know, there just weren't many real jūjutsu people around in the 1960s and 70s, and koryū was unheard of. Outside jūdōka, who would have noticed him during the martial arts craze of the 1960s? By the 1980s, Takamura did keep more to himself. You know, you'd have thought the aikidō community would have discovered him earlier, but those people were hideabouts back then. Very few people from the aikidō community in America mixed with people in other arts.

Takamura also refused to do any promoting of the dōjō. The only sign on the front of the dōjō was in kanji and it just said Shindō Yōshin Ryū. It didn't even say jūjutsu. We had to lock the front doors because people would just walk in the dōjō out of curiosity or thinking the dōjō was a Chinese restaurant. If you wanted to find Takamura, you had to hunt him down and he liked it that way. Another thing that made us hard to find was that Takamura refused to teach youngsters or beginners. You had to have experience in another koryū or a yūdansha rank in a Japanese budō to get your foot in the dōjō door. Ranks in other arts like Gung Fu or Tae Kwon Do were not acceptable to him.

Nanette Ōkura: I have to agree with Karl. Sensei was better known in the early years, but as he got older he didn't socialize much. He liked dawdling around his garden and only teaching students who were seriously committed. As recently as the 1980s, koryū was still seen as exotic. The 1980s saw the last influx of serious students under Sensei's leadership.

Toby Threadgill: I wasn't around in the early years so I can't speak to that but I can say Takamura Sensei was better known in Europe than the US when I started teaching seminars abroad. The first time I taught a seminar in Germany, quite a few people approached me and told me about attending seminars or training under old students of his in the 1970s and 80s. These people were mostly in France or Belgium. I also corresponded with a gentleman in Sweden who trained under an early Shindō Yōshin Ryū student in Europe named Nils Thorsell. During a seminar in Florida I taught with JKF [Japan Karate Federation] Wadōkai's Takagi Hideo, a very adept karateka from New Zealand named Robbie Smith approached me about joining Shindō Yōshin Ryū. Later he told me had attended a seminar in London with Takamura Sensei, Karin Andersson and Karl Garrison. So, Takamura Sensei was not exactly a budō hermit. He just flew under the radar of the greater budō community, that is, until Stan Pranin of Aikidō Journal discovered him.

***Marco Ruiz:** I remember Stan Pranin calling me on the phone and suggesting the idea of expanding the original interview I had done with Takamura Sensei and then publishing it in Aikidō Journal. Who knew it would receive so much attention? How did things change for Takamura ha Shindō Yōshin Ryū after the interview appeared in Aikidō Journal?*

David Maynard: There were a lot of changes going on at that time, and the Aikidō Journal interview just added to it. Takamura Sensei was pretty ill with cancer so he was not up to teaching seminars or entertaining strangers who wanted to meet him. We must have received 100 emails. Furthermore, Takamura Sensei was not exactly computer literate, so the job of answering all the emails fell to Toby and me. A lot of the emails were just polite compliments, but others were from people who wanted to host a Shindō Yōshin Ryū seminar or just meet Takamura Sensei for coffee. Then there were the crazy people. The nutty things people can read into an interview amaze me. Takamura Sensei wrote something about being a pacifist in his interview and people twisted it into all sorts of crazy stuff. I thought his message was pretty straightforward, but some people interpreted his comments to imply things he did not intend.

Toby Threadgill: That is so true. It's still going on today. People have written to me or attended seminars and proceeded to tell me all about my teacher. When I finally ask them how long they knew Takamura Sensei, they respond that they never met him! It's bizarre. One guy actually started arguing with me about Takamura Sensei's budō philosophy. He admitted he never actually met Takamura Sensei, but told me that since he had read everything Sensei wrote, he was sure he understood him. I was astonished. This guy had turned Takamura Sensei into some sort of Ueshiba clone/holy man. Takamura Sensei was a lot of things, but he was no holy man. One sit-down over a whiskey would have dispelled that myth in a hurry.

There's another guy who promotes himself as an expert on samurai arts but does not have a single koryū teaching license. He talks about Takamura Sensei in a manner that implies they were very close friends. Some people who know this guy come away thinking he trained with Takamura Sensei. This guy never met Takamura Sensei. It's all talk. This guy corresponded with Takamura Sensei a couple of times and now he's using Takamura Sensei's reputation to bolster his own credibility. I suppose I shouldn't be surprised, but this sort of behavior is one reason Takamura Sensei didn't fraternize much as he got older. He stopped trusting people.

Karl Garrison: I was going to mention that earlier. Takamura did not have the personality to be in the public eye. He did not like big groups of students. He preferred small intimate groups. If we had more than 12 students on the mat you could tell Takamura didn't like it. Twenty drove him nuts. Tobs, I've seen the photos of the public seminars you teach with 100 plus Wadō Ryū people. I don't know how you do it. Takamura would have had a coronary. The seminar in London where I met Robbie Smith was maybe 35 people. Takamura Sensei just demonstrated a kata a few times and then wandered around shaking his head. Dave and I did the real teaching because Takamura Sensei just couldn't handle the numbers of people. He was overwhelmed.

David Maynard: Karl, that was one of the larger seminars Takamura Sensei ever taught, and yes, it drove him crazy. He just wasn't a seminar guy. He had no interest in a venue like that. He wanted to spend 30 minutes with every student, teaching them intricate technical details. That's just the kind of teacher he was. Very hands on and personal.

Marco Ruiz: Threadgill Sensei, you had a pretty close friendship with Stan Pranin didn't you?

Toby Threadgill: I suppose. I maintained regular contact with Stan until his recent death. If Takamura Sensei had lived longer I think he and Stan would have become close friends. I think they came to admire one another quite a bit during the process of doing the interview. Honoring Takamura's wishes, Stan was present when I received my Menkyo Kaiden.

I was indebted to Stan for his public support of Shindō Yōshin Ryū. He invited me to participate in all three Aiki Expo's. Stan also introduced me to a lot of wonderful people at those events, people like George Ledyard, Kayla Feder, Robert Mustard, Chuck Clark and Peter Goldsbury. Stan was a giant in the aikidō community who left an incredible legacy behind. Daitō Ryū owes him a great debt as well. Stan's promotion of Daitō Ryū as aikidō's progenitor was virtually unknown until Stan started writing well-researched articles about it.

Shindō Yōshin Ryū

Marco Ruiz: *Takamura Sensei was one of the pioneers of teaching koryū in the USA. Did he ever express his personal opinions on koryū and its growth outside Japan?*

David Maynard: Takamura Sensei openly expressed his opinion that koryū schools could not only survive outside Japan, but also thrive. The caveat is that a koryū school could only do so under very adept leadership. He did worry about a koryū school's ethos being lost, but this fear was not limited to outside Japan, it concerned dōjō inside Japan too. The problem is complicated. Japanese society drastically changed at the end of the Warring States era. Japanese society also changed significantly during the Meiji Restoration, and then again following World War II. Koryū schools were influenced in specific ways by each of these historical events. So exactly how did koryū maintain their ethos during these periods of upheaval? Is there a lesson to be learned from the past? Whatever the future holds, as koryū move into the 21st Century, they must be seen as worthy of being preserved? How do we achieve this? Since koryū is not flashy or really focused on modern self-defense, how do we convince potential students to take up such an antiquated and unusual pursuit? It's a difficult problem all koryū face.

Karl Garrison: In Japan, almost immediately after the fall of the Tokugawa Shogunate, jūdō exploded onto the scene. There are lessons to be learned there all right. With the cultural changes in Japan came inevitable changes to budō. Some jūdō people will argue Kanō was preserving jūjutsu through the Kōdōkan, but after being exposed to koryū, you can't seriously believe he was successful. Kanō's jūdō has become an Olympic sport. It developed its own identity, one very different from koryū jūjutsu. It is the same with kendō and koryū kenjutsu. One is not the other. Changing times have molded these modern budō schools into something only loosely connected to the schools they came from.

Nanette Ōkura: I think Shindō Yōshin Ryū is in a unique position. Like Daitō Ryū, Shindō Yōshin Ryū is in a good place to survive because of its historical link to a popular modern budō that has thousands of followers all over the world. Schools like Higo Ko-Ryū and Niten Ichi Ryū are at real risk of being lost because they do not have a similar link to a modern budō school. How tragic it would be to relegate Musashi's Niten Ichi Ryū to only being an entry in a history book. If koryū can thrive outside Japan, why not encourage this? These schools are historical treasures that we must attempt to preserve. Yes, it will be a difficult job, but I am convinced there are a lot of people who are capable of doing this task. Sensei once told me koryū are more likely to survive in Europe than the US. This was because after living in Europe and the US, he was convinced Europeans have a deeper appreciation of tradition.

Toby Threadgill: Nanette, Takamura Sensei told me the exact same thing. I almost asked him why he was choosing me for a Menkyo Kaiden.

Nanette Ōkura: Toby, you are not the norm. Sensei was generalizing, and I believe in general he was correct. You teach a lot overseas. What are your impressions?

Toby Threadgill: As far as specific people go, the answer is no. There are dedicated people everywhere. Generally however? Yes, Europeans demonstrate an edge, and sheer numbers support that conclusion. I have many exceptional students in the US, Canada, New Zealand and Australia, but there are a greater number of dedicated students in Europe. For instance, there are more students of Shindō Yōshin Ryū in Germany than anywhere in the world, and many of them are extremely dedicated. It is so humbling to teach a closed Shindō Yōshin Ryū seminar and see almost 60 familiar faces staring back at me from all over Europe. Yes, the popularity of Wadō Ryū in Europe has something to do with this, but it is more than just that. An impressive number of Europeans demonstrate a level of dedication to preserving Shindō Yōshin Ryū that is a cut above. Remember Shindō Yōshin Ryū is practically extinct in Japan, but it is thriving in Europe.

Every member in the Takamura ha Shindō Yōshin Kai is a valuable asset to me. The greater membership never ceases to amaze me in how hard they work, and how they demonstrate their passion for preserving koryū budō. I have several students who have built beautiful and costly private dōjō. Yes, koryū do face serious challenges both outside and inside Japan, but I believe there are individuals in the West who are not just dedicated to koryū, but are committed to acquiring the tools, the knowledge and the martial wisdom to properly pass these schools forward in a way that honors the members from the past generations. In reference to the question of koryū existing outside Japan, Takamura Sensei said, "What does the dirt under the dōjō floor have to do with proper koryū training?" He was right. There is so much more to it than just location. Koryū preservation is complex and nuanced, but it is not impossible outside Japan. I think the success of Shindō Yōshin Ryū and the growing popularity of koryū in general is proof of that.

Nanette Ōkura, practitioner of Takamura ha Shindō Yōshin Ryū, kendō and atarashi naginata, around 1984.
(Photo courtesy of Jen Yamada.)

Karl Garrison: Koryū schools will never be popular like modern budō, but I believe they will continue to be embraced by many people inside and outside Japan. I think some schools in Japan are already seeing foreign students become their top practitioners. Why this has raised eyebrows among some Japanese surprises me. It's only logical. I suspect Shindō Yōshin Ryū will someday be reintroduced to Japan, maybe by Toby, maybe by one of his successors. That would validate what Takamura believed and dedicated his life to.

Regardless, a belief that koryū are somehow the sole property of the Japanese is just as wrongheaded as the idea that the Japanese are the only ones who could excel at jūdō or sumo. Yeah, it's true the Japanese-ness of koryū must remain and be cultivated as part of the art's overall character, but preserving the essence of these schools is not beyond someone properly taught and keenly aware of the arts martial and cultural underpinnings. As long as enough people are dedicated to an art, and it is properly taught and conveyed, these schools can survive outside Japan. I am convinced of it.

Marco Ruiz: *It's good to hear Shindō Yōshin Ryū is healthy, but what are the criteria for quantifying health? What did Takamura Sensei think would indicate his success when he decided to transplant the Obata/Takamura ha Shindō Yōshin Ryū Honbu Dōjō outside Japan?*

David Maynard: The benchmark Takamura Sensei had for determining success changed over time. Initially, he imagined he would sow seeds of the art in Japan and eventually move back there to cultivate its growth. This was particularly true after Iso Sensei, who was living in Ōsaka, and Takamura Sensei were reunited by Namishiro Matsuhiro in the early 1960s. Eventually he realized moving back to Japan was not an option. His wife Michiko was not keen on the idea, and honestly, neither was Takamura Sensei. The more he traveled to Japan, the more he realized his impressions of Japan were idealized due to his childhood. As an adult, he really preferred living in the west. Iso Sensei, for all his technical skills, did not have the required teaching skills or personality to cultivate a strong dōjō. By the mid-1970s, Takamura Sensei started contemplating how to transplant the art outside Japan because the most dedicated and talented students were in the US and Europe. When I lived in Matsudo in the 1970s, Takamura Sensei specifically rejected the idea of transferring the honbu dōjō back to Japan, even if I continued living there. That is one reason I returned to the US when a business opportunity came up in California. Takamura Sensei's opinion on this became irreversible as western students continued to demonstrate a very high level of dedication and technical ability.

Karl Garrison: When Iso Sensei brought a group of his Japanese students over in the 1990s, he was shocked by the skills of the western students. I don't know what he expected, but after he got hands-on with each of us here, you could tell he had to reconsider his opinions. I also remember his shock at hearing David reciting norito at the beginning of class. He could not believe it; and Takamura's skills at that point were in the stratosphere. In the realm of jūjutsu, Takamura was so beyond Iso Sensei's skills that Iso would just laugh after being thrown. He had no idea what happened. He just shook his head and said mahō [magic]. In Iso's defense, he was always a weapons guy first, particularly a bōjutsu guy, but he knew great jūjutsu when he felt it, and he was feeling it outside Japan. If you want a measure of Takamura's success or failure at teaching outside Japan, this is it. The western students clearly had the goods.

Toby Threadgill: Something else that needs to be remembered is that technical competence is not the only metric of health in a koryū. You also have to have students. Each koryū has its own opinion of what constitutes an ideal number of students, but there must be a balance of several, sometimes conflicting factors. Everyone who joins a koryū is not going to be a top-tier athlete. This fact means the organization must recruit enough students so it has access to a competent talent pool. If the ryū is too small, it will struggle to have enough physically talented members to represent the mokuroku at the highest technical level. However, if the school is too large, the honbu dōjō will not be able to provide enough instructional control over the mokuroku to maintain a consistent technical standard.

Takamura Sensei was also very clear in his demand that the ryū never develop a complex organizational structure, something that inevitably seeds an organization with political stresses. When any organization reaches a certain size it must adopt a hierarchy to manage itself or it will become cumbersome. As outlined in the TSYR Kaiki, the Takamura ha Shindō Yōshin Kai cannot adopt an authoritative chain of command beyond the honbu dōjō. Every student is expected to maintain a direct relationship with the honbu dōjō and the honbu dōjō is expected to maintain a direct relationship with every student. As the present kaichō, I must be able to recognize every deshi of our organization by name, and on sight. Currently, the Takamura ha Shindō Yōshin Kai has around 20 dōjō and active study groups comprising 200 members. I do not see the organization growing significantly beyond its current size or it would become both technically and administratively unmanageable.

(Left to Right) Kuroda Yasumasa, Kuroda Tetsuzan, Tobin Threadgill at the 10th Nuit Des Arts Martiaux Traditionnels demonstration in, Paris, France, 2016. (Photo courtesy of Kuroda Tetsuzan.)

Nanette Ōkura: When I was in Japan, I was saddened to realize how many koryū were barely surviving. Some schools have only a handful of members preserving them.

Marco Ruiz: Ōkura Sensei, I understand you are no longer involved in Takamura ha Shindō Yōshin Ryū, while Maynard Sensei and Garrison Sensei function as official advisors.

Nanette Ōkura: Around 1995, my career took off and now I travel almost five days a week. I just don't have time to train any longer. Besides, after Michiko's passing and Sensei closed the San Jose dōjō, I had nowhere to train. I did try some local aikidō dōjō, but they were not to my liking. I came to realize Sensei was a meijin, a budō genius. When you've trained with such a person, it sets the bar at a level hard to match. If the Takamura ha Shindō Yōshin Ryū Honbu Dōjō was around the corner, and I didn't travel so much, I'd definitely be training with Toby, but that's life. I have accepted that my budō days are over. Naginata and jūjutsu enriched my life and made me a more confident woman. Besides, Shindō Yōshin Ryū is in capable hands, so I would not bring much to the table. I hear the new generation of students is very talented. I'm sure Sensei is very happy with how Shindō Yōshin Ryū has grown under the new generation of instructors. Two hundred members is something Sensei could not have imagined.

David Maynard: Nan is right. Shindō Yōshin Ryū is in good hands. The new generation of teachers and students appear very talented. The quality of the teaching within the individual dōjō has managed to attract shihan level instructors from Wadō Ryū and Aikidō into Shindō Yōshin Ryū. People are also hosting cooperative seminars with us and Japanese instructors like Shimura Koichi, the JKF Wadōkai General Secretary. Twenty years ago, this sort of cooperation would have been unthinkable. Cooperation between the leadership of these organizations is a good sign for the future of both Wadō Ryū and Shindō Yōshin Ryū.

Karl Garrison: The relationships Toby has cultivated between Shindō Yōshin Ryū and other budō schools is also impressive. Given my health these days, I'll never be able to get on the mat again, but I read a review of a seminar taught by Toby Threadgill and Yōshinkan eighth Dan, Robert Mustard recently that made me wish I could. Imagine the information made available at a gathering like that? In my days of budō, a cooperative event by two such people just did not happen. Minds were too closed and egos too frail. The NAMT (Nuit Des Arts Martiaux Traditionnels) event in Paris, France, in 2016, which included Toby Threadgill and Kuroda Tetsuzan, made me wish I were a younger man. It is heartening Toby and Tetsuzan Kuroda maintain the kind of friendship they do. Their friendship represents the future of koryū.

Marco Ruiz: Garrison Sensei and Maynard Sensei, what do you gentlemen do as advisors to the Takamura ha Shindō Yōshin Ryū Honbu Dōjō?

David Maynard: Sometimes Karl tells me I'm a bloody nuisance, but the idea is that we answer questions and act as a sounding board when some administrative issue comes up that the honbu dōjō feels it needs feedback on. There are a lot of years of experience between the two of us, so we do have some depth of perspective. I must add that it's very respectful for Toby to keep a couple of old-timers like us in the administrative loop. A lot of people in his position would never allow it; they would not be as gracious or accommodating.

Karl Garrison: Yes, it's nice to be reminded that our combined 100 years of experience in Nihon budō can still be of benefit to the honbu dōjō. If needed, Toby, as kaichō, can call upon us to contribute advice and counsel. However, we must stay on the sidelines as much as possible. When a previous generation of students maintain too high a profile it can inadvertently cause political difficulties best avoided. We are only advisors and must remain only advisors. Advisors must recognize their boundaries and respect what Takamura Sensei envisioned for the future of Shindō Yōshin Ryū. As long-time members of a koryū both Dave and I understand that the honbu dōjō must speak with only one voice. Furthermore, as an old school Marine, I understand how a vertical chain of command operates, and that disparate voices can result in confusion and even fratricide. David and I will not allow that to happen while we are advisors. We both took a blood oath to the school and we intend to honor that oath as long as we live.

Marco Ruiz: How did the transition of leadership in Shindō Yōshin Ryū work following Takamura Sensei's passing? Was everyone in agreement with how the transition took place?

Karl Garrison: Takamura Sensei compiled a list of rules and regulations called the TSYR Kaiki. It clearly outlined how transitions of authority would be managed in the kai. Every koryū school should do this but most of them do not, which commonly creates a political crisis and even schisms. It is inevitable that if a leader as charismatic as Takamura

Tobin E. Threadgill and Yōshinkan Aikidō eighth dan, Robert Mustard teaching a cooperative seminar in London, 2013.

passes away, there will be those who resist the mandated change in leadership. This is why Takamura so clearly outlined how all transitions of authority would take place in Takamura ha Shindō Yōshin Ryū. If someone didn't approve of the process or the person selected, they would be asked to resign.

David Maynard: Initially, the three Menkyo Kaiden holders were supposed to administratively oversee three geographical areas. I was selected as the kaiden shihan (chief instructor), and Toby as kanjichō (honbu administrator). Unfortunately, events such as my car accident and Iso Sensei's illness made that option untenable. Toby was then selected by Iso Sensei and myself to become the kaichō, combining the positions of kaiden shihan and kanjichō.

Karl Garrison: Shindō Yōshin Ryū was really in a precarious position at that point in time. Membership was never large and there had been an exodus of people from the organization following Takamura Sensei's death. When Toby was asked to take the reins of Shindō Yōshin Ryū, he gave up a lucrative photography career and decided to run the kai full time. What has followed is a pretty impressive turn-around. Toby runs a doggone tight ship. People know what is expected of them because he makes it plain as day. Every administrative decision that affects the public face of the organization must go through the honbu dōjō. Nothing anyone does can be allowed to embarrass the Matsuoka or Obata descendants. If you flagrantly violate your kishomon, you are out!

Nanette Ōkura: That is the only way to successfully run a koryū. The authority is top down, succession is clearly defined, the ethical code must be observed, and the honor of the school must be preserved and protected. I know that sounds autocratic, but that is what koryū are, old Japanese autocratic institutions. They are not democratic.

Toby Threadgill: Nanette is correct. Takamura Sensei once told me that a koryū must function as a benevolent dictatorship. The trick is always the benevolent part. A power-hungry or egotistical member must never be chosen to lead Takamura ha Shindō Yōshin Ryū. Such a person would marginalize the school for selfish gain.

Shindō Yōshin Ryū is certainly healthier than it was in 2003 when I ascended to the position of kaichō, but there is still a lot of work to do. Takamura Sensei told me I should have six or seven jōden licensed instructors before I step down. He added that the reason for so many was attrition, that I would lose two or three of them. I thought he was being a bit theatrical and then tragedy struck twice. Two of our most senior instructors died a year apart: Robbie Smith and Kim Henderson. Robbie Smith was a budō prodigy and Wadō Ryū seventh Dan from New Zealand who learned Shindō Yōshin Ryū faster than anyone I've ever seen. Kim Henderson was a very close friend I had known for almost 30 years. She was a top instructor at the honbu dōjō here in Colorado and the administrative face for the organization. I never imagined I would lose two of my top instructors, and worse, in such a short span of time. Shindō Yōshin Ryū was almost lost during World War II, and it is still on shaky ground today. I now take Takamura's admonition very seriously. I am pushing hard to get a group of our students initiated into the upper level teachings. Currently, we only have two, Brent Carey and Marco Pinto.

Karl Garrison: Toby, I never had the pleasure of meeting Kim Henderson, but I had the honor of meeting Robbie Smith. I met him in 1994 at Takamura's last seminar in London. As I sat in the training hall waiting for Takamura, a wiry and chiseled-looking guy came in and started warming up by going through karate forms. I'm certainly no karate expert, but what I observed was a damned impressive demonstration of body control. His movements were something to see, and in no time a group of us were watching him, curious who he was. During the seminar, he asked David and I about some paired kata done in Wadō Ryū, and at that point I asked him his name. He chatted with Takamura for a few minutes after the seminar and said he was interested in Shindō Yōshin Ryū. We encouraged him to stay in touch. I was not surprised when I heard he had hunted you down. I was really sad to hear of his passing. You never know what tomorrow brings. I saw completely incompetent soldiers survive intense combat. I also saw fantastic soldiers die in the most pointless and random ways imaginable. That is the reality of violence and warfare. It is a reality every real budōka should confront because it should keep us humble. Training gives us an edge but brings no guarantees. We can all fall in a myriad of ways.

Marco Ruiz: *When corresponding with Takamura Sensei during the original interview he discussed how risky it was for a koryū to hold it's knowledge back; limiting its high-level teachings to too few students. It's good to hear your organization is trying to address this issue.*

David Maynard: This is a huge problem directly related to hoarding knowledge. The resistance of some teachers in Japan to promoting foreign students into positions of authority has only made the risks associated with koryū survival and knowledge transmission worse. There is one koryū in Japan whose Japanese headmaster passed away, leaving the school's designated leader a European. Instead of honoring the demands of the deceased headmaster and recognizing this foreign student as the ryūha's leader, a cabal of instructors from one of the koryū preservation organizations conspired to hijack the school and attempted to insert an unqualified Japanese instructor into position as a faux-headmaster. This was a gross violation of responsibility and duty. The organization in question had no business trying to interfere with the leadership transition of a member school. The arrogance is bloody appalling. This is how a koryū is destroyed or lost, not preserved. Fortunately, this fraud has been publicly exposed. The European shihan now leads what is broadly recognized as the legitimate line of this ryūha.

When Takamura Sensei confronted the issue of teaching foreign students, he recognized that honoring his oath to the school meant being color-blind. He also recognized that hoarding knowledge was frequently an issue of ego, not an issue of a student's dedication. He believed the ideal age for a student to receive full transmission of a koryū was in their mid-40s. This coincides with a student's physical prime. I was 44 when Takamura Sensei issued my Menkyo Kaiden and Toby was 42. It is all too common these days for headmasters to hold on to advanced knowledge too long, rationalizing this behavior by saying the student isn't ready for it yet. If a student has 20 years of consistent training behind him, he should be ready. If he isn't ready, something is either wrong with him, or something is wrong with the teaching. In Takamura Sensei's opinion, holding knowledge back from advanced students was a violation of his kishomon (oath of loyalty). Takamura Sensei discussed this issue clearly in an article he wrote on Shu Ha Ri.

Toby Threadgill: I would like to clarify something related to the subject of advanced training and knowledge transmission. Takamura Sensei did not think every long-term student of Shindō Yōshin Ryū was worthy of receiving full transmission. But a problem becomes critically obvious when you have multiple long-term students and none of them are on a path of receiving full transmission. This is a sign that someone's ego is in the way and they are using knowledge as leverage to maintain authority. There are numerous legitimate reasons a long-term student may not be worthy of the authority that comes with receiving full transmission. A lack of properly-cultivated teaching skills, disloyalty or compromised respect from the school's greater membership are but a few reasons a long-term student might be denied access to the most advanced teachings in a koryū. Full transmission should be reserved for only those individuals who demonstrate all the requisite qualities and requirements of holding such authority. There is also the issue of dilution. Too many individuals at the top of an organization will make the school top-heavy increasing the potential for political struggles. Takamura Sensei told me very distinctly that anyone receiving a jōden mokuroku had to demonstrate a flexible spirit and emotional balance. They had to demonstrate the quality of self-sacrifice. They had to be able to compromise for the good of the group. Anyone demonstrating the qualities of a lone wolf, or someone convinced their opinions eclipsed those of their peers was unsuitable for jōden level instruction. The jōden level instructors must represent a unified group of like-minded and emotionally-balanced budōka, whose most important focus is the kai, not themselves.

Marco Ruiz: To finish up is there anything else you would like to add about Takamura Sensei or your experience in koryū budō that the readers might find interesting?

Karl Garrison: Mixed martial arts are all the rage today, but I'm not impressed. I was doing pretty intense shiai in jūdō/jūjutsu into my early 60s. I still love to watch competition, but I see it for what it is, and it's not real. It's great play fighting but it's still a game. Koryū is different. Koryū, properly approached, can challenge you physically, emotionally and intellectually. These are the challenges most valuable in real life. When I returned from combat duty in the early 70s, my eyes were opened and life took on a different meaning to me. Around this time, I got to know Takamura Sensei and we became close friends. Through his teaching and friendship, my view of life and human beings changed. We fought, argued and trained, but through it all I knew he was on my side, he had my back. To a Marine, that is everything. It was not easy, but Shindō Yōshin Ryū forced me to challenge my ego and my perception of what real goodness is. I'm not some enlightened being or nothing, but I do have a handle on things that has made me appreciate my journey in a way I couldn't have without the influence of budō. Like I said earlier, the dōjō became my church and gave me the tools I needed to navigate my way through life. I'll never be a perfect man. I still have a temper and allow the passions of my past to control me in ways I shouldn't, but I am a better man now than I would have been without budō. I guess budō became the anchor of my rowdy spirit and that has been a good thing.

Toby Threadgill: If you are looking for a real budō sensei, look for someone who cares about his students. Look for someone who is not hung up on being the best, but helping you hone your personal expectations. A real sensei must challenge you and motivate you to find those things that make you a complete human being. A real sensei will at times scare you, threaten you and make you want to run away. That is his job, to force you to confront your fears and accept them. This is part of shugyō. Shugyō is what gives you confidence and makes you strong. Shugyō is what allows you to confront any challenge life can throw at you and still be compassionate. I think there is too much mollycoddling in most budō today. Too many students take up budō to feel good about themselves, and when they are challenged, pressured, or feel threatened, they quit. Because of this, many teachers are more concerned about paying rent than being good teachers. They water down what they teach and make budō into a commodity. The student becomes a consumer who must be catered to. Real budō is not a business arrangement. It is not something you can buy with money. Real budō rests on the model of

Shindō Yōshin Ryū

Tobin Threadgill and Nanette Ōkura in Nihonmachi, San Jose, California, 1994
(Photo courtesy of Karl W. Garrison)

an old-fashioned apprenticeship. The teacher offers to teach you, but you must promise to train hard and learn. David said something earlier I really liked. He said that once you bowed in, it was game on. That is the way it should be. That doesn't mean you should be ready to go full bore and fight to the death. It means you should be mentally present and ready to train. You must be prepared to follow your teacher's directions with 100% commitment. It is not your teacher's job to force you to train diligently. You must commit yourself to the pursuit of learning and accept that as a student you do not get to decide what, when, or how you will be taught. You are there to follow your teacher's directions. As a student you are an investment in your teacher's life. Reward your teacher and those teachers that came before him by dedicating yourself, heart and soul, to the tradition you are learning. If you do that, budō really can benefit you in powerful ways that go far beyond the dōjō door. You will also be part of a gift to future generations, something that should not be allowed to slip away. There are too few pursuits left in the world like koryū budō. Once lost, living traditions like this cannot be reconstituted.

Nanette Ōkura: I would encourage people interested in budō to seriously consider studying koryū. It is definitely a bigger commitment than modern budō, but I believe there are bigger payoffs for the investment. Koryū are also in danger of being lost. This breaks my heart. These traditions harbor incredible wisdom and knowledge that cannot be found anywhere else. To lose them due to neglect would be tragic. When I studied kendō and atarashi naginata as a youngster, I enjoyed it immensely. When I was introduced to Higo Ko-Ryū naginata in Japan, I realized atarashi naginata was just a game. Do not misunderstand. Atarashi naginata is a wonderful game and I still harbor lovely memories of my time in the art, but being exposed to koryū exposed me to a richness of tradition and thought I had never experienced before. When I returned to California, my mother told me she wanted me to study karate to learn to defend myself. I said I would only study koryū jūjutsu from Mr. Takamura. By this way, I became the youngest student to ever start training in Takamura Sensei's dōjō. It was one of the best decisions of my life, and as a Nisei, it became the connection that allowed me to understand my mother and what it is to be Japanese. Koryū has provided me with so many positive experiences I cannot possibly list them all, but I can list these gifts that koryū has instilled in me: confidence and poise. These things have followed me my whole life and made me the woman I am today. The seeds of their growth started under the watchful gaze of an intense and striking example of a man. Through his teachings, he convinced me I was the match of anyone if I applied myself passionately and refused to accept mediocrity in myself. Some will say you can achieve the same goals in other pursuits, and that is probably true, but there is an intangible quality to koryū that can only be felt. It is that intangible mark on my soul that will be with me for the rest of my life. You can have it too if you are willing to follow a very old and noble path.

David Maynard: When you join a koryū budō like Shindō Yōshin Ryū, you are becoming part of a historical legacy. The Yōshin Ryū legacies started in the 1600s. Our branch of the legacy started with a samurai named Matsuoka Katsunosuke. From there it passed to Obata Shigeta and then to his grandson, Takamura Yuikiyoshi. There are few pursuits like koryū left anywhere in the world. The very act of joining a koryū means you must put your ego away and accept the fact that a group endeavor supersedes your individual desires. This is difficult for people to accept who stubbornly embrace individualism. Japanese society thrives on the concept of group benefit over individuality. After living in Japan for several years, I came to appreciate how well such a system can work. It's actually symbiotic. The benefit works both directions. It is the same with koryū. Their very existence in this day and age means the benefit works pretty well both directions. Takamura Sensei personally sacrificed a great deal for Shindō Yōshin Ryū, as did every teacher that came before him. Without the individual sacrifice of each previous teacher, the rich knowledge and wisdom existing within Shindō Yōshin Ryū would have been lost. Each of us involved in this arcane pursuit has made a conscious decision to dedicate a portion of our lives to preserving this knowledge for people we will never know because we realize the school is bigger than any one of us. When I'm long gone, I do not imagine anyone will remember me beyond my name appearing in some book like this one, but I hope Takamura ha Shindō Yōshin Ryū is still around having a positive impact on people's lives while preserving the wisdom hidden in its mokuroku. In that way each of us will enjoy just a little immortality.

> *"It is an all-too-common cliché to describe any accomplished Japanese budō man as a samurai, but in the case of Mr. Takamura such a description is not far off. He was a man of a different era and way of thinking, a man who did not see the world as most of us do. I never met another man like him. Polite and worldly, he possessed the most intense nature I've ever known. During a disagreement over tea one afternoon, he cast a cold disapproving gaze at me and it sent a shiver running through my body. I had never experienced such an intimidating force of spirit in my life. It was if I was staring into the eyes of a dragon. At that moment I thought it a very good thing that we were not enemies. You would never want to be on the other end of that man's sword."*
>
> *- Ōba Hideo, Lifelong friend and associate of Takamura Yukiyoshi.*

In Memoriam

Robbie Smith (1964-2014)

Watch me.
I will go to my own sun.
And if I am burned by its fire,
I will fly on scorched wings.

- Segovia Amil

Kim Henderson (1964-2015)

Bibliography

Shindō Yōshin Ryū

Chapter 1- Studying Koryū Budō Outside Japan

Clark, Chuck E. (1999) *Jyushinkai: Guide for New Members,* Jiyushin Press

Friday, Karl F. and Seki, Humitake (1997) *Legacies of the Sword,* University of Hawai'i Press

Lowry, Dave (1998) *The Classical Japanese Martial Arts in the West: Problems with Transmission,* Furyū: The Budō Magazine #9

Lowry, Dave (2006) *In the Dōjō: A Guide to the Rituals and Etiquette of the Japanese Martial Arts,* Weatherhill

Muramoto, Wayne (1998) *Real or Fake? Is Your Martial Arts School Legitimate?* Furyū: The Budō Magazine #9

Reynosa, Larry and Joseph Billingiere (1988) *A Beginners Guide to Aikidō,* R & B Publishing

Skoss, Diane, editor (1997) *Koryū Bujutsu: Classical Warrior Traditions of Japan Vol.1.* Koryū Books

Skoss, Diane, editor (1999) *Sword and Spirit: Classical Warrior Traditions of Japan Vol.2.* Koryū Books

Skoss, Diane, editor (2002) *Keiko Shōkon: Classical Warrior Traditions of Japan Vol.3.* Koryū Books

Takamura, Yukiyoshi (1990) *TSYR Dōjō Reigi,* TSYR Newsletter #21

Takamura, Yukiyoshi (2011) *Takamura ha Shindō Yōshin Ryū Kaiki,* New Willow Press

Threadgill, Tobin E. (2009) *Takamura ha Shindō Yōshin Kai Student Handbook,* New Willow Press

Chapter 2 -The Origins of Jūjutsu

Akima, Toshio (1993) The Myth of the Goddess of the Undersea World and the Tale of Empress Jingū's Subjugation, JJRS

Aston, W.G. (2011) *Nihongi: Chronicles of Japan from the Earliest of Times to A.D. 697,* Charles E. Tuttle

Clements, Jonathon (2010) *The Samurai: A New History of the Warrior Elite,* Running Press

Cunningham, Don (2000) *Secret Weapons of Jūjutsu.* Budō Kai, Ltd.

Davis F. Hadland (1992) *Myths and Legends of Japan,* Dover Publications

Draeger, Donn F. (1973) *Classical Bujutsu: The Martial and Ways of Japan, Vol 1,* Weatherhill

Draeger, Donn F. (1974) *Modern Budō and Bujutsu: The Martial and Ways of Japan, Vol 3,* Weatherhill

Hall, David A. (2012) *Encyclopedia of Japanese Martial Arts,* Kōdansha

Hillsborough, Romulus (2005) *Samurai Tales: Courage, Fidelity, and Revenge in the final years of the Shōgun,* Charles E. Tuttle

Imamura, Yoshio (1982) *Nihon Budō Taikei, Vol.6, Vol. 8,* Dōhosha

Kimbrough, R. Keller (2006) *The Tale of the Fuji Cave,* Published Online http://nirc.nanzan-u.ac.jp/welcome.htm.

Kimbrough, R. Keller (2008) *Preachers, Poets, Women, and the Way,* University of Michigan

Kimbrough, R. Keller (2012) *Battling Tengu, Battling Conceit: The Tale of the Handcart Priest,* Japanese Journal of Religious Studies

Kimbrough, R. Keller and Haruo Shirane (2018) *Monsters, Animals, and Other Worlds,* Columbia University Press, New York

McCullough, Helen Craig (1966) *Yoshitsune: a 15th Century Chronicle,* Stanford University Press

McCullough, Helen Craig (1990) *The Tale of the Heike,* Stanford University Press

Mol, Serge (2001) *Classical Fighting Arts of Japan: A Complete Guide to Koryū Jūjutsu.* Kōdansha International

Mol, Serge (2010) *Classical Swordsmanship of Japan: A Comprehensive Guide to Kenjutsu and Iaijutsu.* Eibusha

Murasaki, Shikibu, translated by Dennis Washburn (2016) *The Tale of Genji,* W.W. Norton & Company

Musashi, Miyamoto, translated by William Scott Wilson (2002) *The Book of Five Rings,* Kodansha

Nawa, Yumio (1977) *Zukai Kakushibuki Hyakka,* Shin Jinbutsu Ōraish

Nihon no Budō (1983) *Budō of Japan, Jūjutsu - Vol. 5,* Kodansha

Nihon Kobudō Kyōkai (1989 & 2005) *Nihon Kobudō Sōran,* Shimazu Shobō

Phillippi, Donald L. (2015) *Kojiki,* Princeton University Press

Skoss, Diane, editor (1997) *Koryū Bujutsu: Classical Warrior Traditions of Japan Vol.1.* Koryū Books

Takenouchi-Ryū Hensan Linkai (1978) *Nihon no Jūjutsu,* Nichibō Shuppan-sha

Yokose, Tomoyuki (2000) *Nihon No Kobudō,* Nihon Budōkan

Chapter 3 - The Origins of Shindō Yōshin Ryū

Amdur, Ellis (2013) *Old School: Essays on Martial Arts Traditions,* Freelance Academy Press

Amdur, Ellis (2009) *Hidden in Plain Sight: Tracing the Roots of Ueshiba Morihei's Power,* Edgework Publishing

Deal, William E. (2005) *Handbook to Life in Medeival and Early Modern Japan.* Oxford University Press

Draeger, Donn F. (1973) *Classical Bujutsu: The Martial and Ways of Japan, Vol 1,* Weatherhill

Draeger, Donn F. (1974) *Modern Budō and Bujutsu: The Martial and Ways of Japan, Vol 3,* Weatherhill

Draeger, Donn F. and Robert W. Smith (1969) *Asian Fighting Arts,* Kōdansha

Fujiwara, Ryōzō (1983) *Shindō Yōshin Ryū Reikishi to Gihō,* Sōzō

Hall, David A. (2012) *Encyclopedia of Japanese Martial Arts,* Kōdansha

Higo Budōshi (1974) *Budō History in Higo (Kumamoto),* Kyōshinsha

Higo Hosokawa (Hosokawa Samurai), (http://www.shinshindōh.com/samurai/01-a.htm)

Iguchi, Matsunosuke and Hisatomi, Tetsutarō (1898) *Hayanawa Kappō Kenpō Kyōhan Zukai, Zen,* Kinseidō

Kanō, Jigorō and Kanō Yukimitsu (2005) *Mind Over Muscle: Writings from the Founder of Jūdō,* Kōdansha

Kazuhiko, Kuboyama (2014) *Historical research; Derived from the Mokuroku of Yōshin Ryū Jūjutsu,*

Matsuda, Ryuchi (1978) *Hiden Nihon Jūjutsu,* Shin Jinbutsu Ōraisha

Murata Naoki (2001) *Kanō Jigorō Shihan ni Manabu,* Budōkan

Mol, Serge (2001) *Classical Fighting Arts of Japan: A Complete Guide to Koryū Jūjutsu.* Kōdansha International

Nanbara Misao (1993) *Chin Genpin/Genpin Ryū,* vol. XI, pp.112, Rekishi Dokuhon

Osano, Jun (1991) *Yōshin Ryū Jūjutsu Denshoshū,* Nihon Sōgō Budō Kenkyūjo

Pranin, Stan (1999) *Interview with Takamura Yukiyoshi, Part #1,* Aiki News #121

Pranin, Stan (1999) *Interview with Takamura Yukiyoshi, Part #2,* Aiki News #122

Skoss, Diane, editor (1999) *Sword and Spirit: Classical Warrior Traditions of Japan Vol.2.* Koryū Books

Skoss, Diane, editor (2002) *Keiko Shokon: Classical Warrior Traditions of Japan Vol.3.* Koryū Books

Takamura ha Shindō Yōshin Kai Collection: Over 50 Akiyama Yōshin Ryū, Miura/Totsuka Yōshin Ryū Shikage Ryū related densho.

Takamura Yukiyoshi (1984) *Transcribed Diary Entries of Obata Shigeta,* TSYR Newsletter #14

Takamura Yukiyoshi (1976) *The life of Obata Shigeta,* TSYR Newsletter #2

Watatani, Kiyoshi and Yamada Tadashi (1978) *Bugei Ryūha Daijiten,* Tōkyō Kopī Shuppanbu

Shindō Yōshin Ryū

Chapter 4 - The History of Shindō Yōshin Ryū

Amdur, Ellis (2013) *Old School: Essays on Martial Arts Traditions,* Freelance Academy Press

Amdur, Ellis (2009) *Hidden in Plain Sight: Tracing the Roots of Ueshiba Morihei's Power,* Edgework Publishing

Baelz, Erwin (1931) *Awakening Japan: The Diary of a German Doctor,* Viking Press

Draeger, Donn F. (1973) *Classical Bujutsu: The Martial and Ways of Japan, Vol 1,* Weatherhill

Draeger, Donn F. (1973) *Classical Budō: The Martial and Ways of Japan, Vol 2,* Weatherhill

Draeger, Donn F. (1974) *Modern Budō and Bujutsu: The Martial and Ways of Japan, Vol 3,* Weatherhill

Egami, Shigeru (1972) *Karate-Dō, Beyond Technique,* Kodansha

Fujiwara, Ryōzō (1983) *Shindō Yōshin Ryū Reikishi to Giho,* Sōzō

Fujiwara, Ryōzō (1994) *50 Year Anniversary Program, History of Wadōkai,* JKF Wadōkai

Fujiwara, Ryōzō (1990) *Kakutōgi no Reishiki,* Baseball Magazine

Funakoshi, Gichin (1935) *Karate-Dō Kyōhan,* Kōdansha

Gekkan Karatedō (1980-Jan) Interview with Ōtsuka Hironori & (1998 Feb.) Interview with Ōtsuka Jiro.

Gima, Shinken and Fujiwara Ryōzō (1986) *Kindai Karate-dō no Rikishi wo Kataru,* Baseball Magazine

Hall, David A. (1979) *Bujutsu and Esoteric Tradition, 1 & 2,* Hoplos 1- 5,6

Hall, David A. (2012) *Encyclopedia of Japanese Martial Arts,* Kōdansha

Hane, Mikiso (1972) *Japan; A Historical Survey,* Scriber & Sons

Higo Budōshi (1974) *Budō History in Higo (Kumamoto),* Kyōshinsha

Hillsborough, Romulus (1999) *Ryōma: Life of a Renaissance Samurai,* Ridgeback Press

Hillsborough, Romulus (2005) *Shinsengumi: The Shōguns Last Samurai Corps,* Charles E. Tuttle

Hiragami, Nobuyuki (1992) *Hiden Koryū Jūjutsu Gihō,* Airyūdō

Hiragami, Nobuyuki (1999) *Koryū Jūjutsu Sento Riron,* Airyūdō

Hiragami, Nobuyuki (1993) *Hiden Jūjutsu,* Airyūdō

Inose Katsui, *School Records and Iou Newsletters #15-37 (1905-1910),* Shimotsuma Middle School, Ibaraki

Iwasa, Masaru (2005) *Kashima Shinden Jikishinkage Ryū: The Origin of Samuraihood from Kashima Shrine,* Shuppan-sha

JKF Wadōkai (1984) *Wadō Ryū 50 Year Special Program,* JKF Wadōkai

JKF Wadōkai (1989) *Shūnenshi/50 Year Anniversary Program,* JKF Wadōkai

JKF Wadōkai (1999) *Shūnenshi/60 Year Anniversary Program,* JKF Wadōkai

JKF Wadōkai (2004) *Shūnenshi/65 Year Anniversary Program,* JKF Wadōkai

Kazuhiko, Kuboyama (2014) *Historical research; Derived from the Mokuroku of Yōshin Ryū Jūjutsu,*

Keio Daigaku Karatebu (1974) *50 Year Anniversary Book, Keio University Karate Club,* Keio University Press

LaFleur, William R. (1983) *The Karma of Words: Buddhism and the Literary Arts of Medieval Japan,* University of California Press

Kenpō Kaiho, (1965) *Ōtsuka Hironori, Tōkyō University,* Issue #6 (1976) *Ōtsuka Hironori.* Issue #15

Matsuda, Ryuchi (1978) *Hiden Nihon Jūjutsu,* Shin Jinbutsu Ōraisha

Matsuoka (1987) *Shiawase to Heiwazukuri, Matsuoka Tatsuo-shi no Ayumi,*

Mol, Serge (2001) *Classical Fighting Arts of Japan: A Complete Guide to Koryū Jūjutsu.* Kōdansha International

Mol, Serge (2010) *Classical Swordsmanship of Japan: A Comprehensive Guide to Kenjutsu and Iaijutsu.* Eibusha

Monthy Kendō Japan (1997) *Edo Sanjyo Dōjō,* Tsuki Journal

Monthy Kendō Japan (2002) *Kendō History Nogi 45th Ōsaka,* Tsuki Journal

Nakasone, Genwa (1938) *Karatedō Taikan,* Tōkyō Tosho

Nakazawa Sohaku (1924) *Goshinjutsu Gokui,* Shindō Yōseikai (Hoshino Sentarō, Shindō Yōshin Ryū kyōshi, advisor)

Nanbara Misao (1993) *Chin Genpin/Genpin Ryū,* vol. XI, pp.112, Rekishi Dokuhon

Noguchi, Kiyoshi (1913) *Jūjutsu Kyōjusho Shindō Rikugō Ryū,* Teikoku Shōbukai

Noguchi, Kiyoshi (2001) *Footsteps of Ōtsuka Hironori,* Karatedō Kenkyukai, Japanese Budō Academy

Nihon Kobudō Kyōkai (1989) *Nihon Kobudō Sōran,* Shimazu Shobū

Nihon Kobudō Kyōkai (2005) *Nihon Kobudō Sōran,* Shimazu Shobū

Osano, Jun (1988) *Nippon Jūjutsu Atemi Kenpō,* Airyūdō

Osano, Jun (1991) *Yōshin Ryū Jūjutsu Denshoshū,* Nihon Sōgō Budō Kenkyūjo

Osano, Jun (1994) *Zusetsu Nippon Bunka Gairon,* Airyūdō

Osano, Jun (1996) *Koryū Jūjutsu Gairon,* Airyūdō

Ōtsuka, Hironori (1969-1979) *Private letters to Ohgami Shingo*

Otsuka, Hironori (1979) *Wadō Ryū,* Gekkan Karatedō, November Issue

Otsuka, Hironori (1970) *Karate-Dō, Vol #1,*

Ōtsuka, Hironori (1986) *Karate-Dō, Vol #2,*

Pranin, Stan (1999) *Interview with Takamura Yukiyoshi, Part #1,* Aiki News #121

Pranin, Stan (1999) *Interview with Takamura Yukiyoshi, Part #2,* Aiki News #122

Sasamori, Junzō (1986) *Ittō Ryū Gokui,* Reigakudō

Skoss, Diane, editor (1997) *Koryū Bujutsu: Classical Warrior Traditions of Japan Vol.1.* Koryū Books

Skoss, Diane, editor (1999) *Sword and Spirit: Classical Warrior Traditions of Japan Vol.2.* Koryū Books

Skoss, Diane, editor (2002) *Keiko Shokon: Classical Warrior Traditions of Japan Vol.3.* Koryū Books

Terao, Masamichi (1998) *Koryū Jūjutsu,* Airyūdō

Takamura Yukiyoshi (1984) *Transcribed Diary Entries of Obata Shigeta,* TSYR Newsletter #14

Takamura Yukiyoshi (1976) *The life of Obata Shigeta,* TSYR Newsletter #2

Takamura Yukiyoshi (1982) *Den Sanna Historien bakom Shindō Yōshin Ryū och dess kopplingar till Wadō Ryū,* TSYR Newsletter #10

Tokinotsuke, Hisamatsu (1901) *Jyūjutsu Gokuhi Shinden,* Bunoyōdō Shoten

Tobe, Shinjuro (1991), *Nihon Kengō Tan/ Matsuzaki Namishirō, 1-4,* Monthly Magazine "Budō".

Tōykō University Karate Club (1962-2016) *Kenpō Kaihō, Karate Club Magazine,* Tōkyō University

Tōykō University Karate Club (1988) *Tōkyō Daigaku Karate Gijutsu Kenkyu Vol.3.* Tōkyō University

Ueno Sonshi (1954) *History of Ueno Village,* Local

Wadō Ryū Renmei (1984) *Anniversary Program, Wadō Ryū Championships,* Wadō Ryū Renmei

Wadō Ryū Renmei (2016) *Wadō Ryū 80 nenshi (Wadō Ryū 80 Years History),* Wadō Ryū Renmei

Watatani, Kiyoshi and Yamada Tadashi (1978) *Bugei Ryūha Daijiten,* Tōkyō Kopī Shuppanbu

Yoshida Chiharu and Iso Mataemon (1894) *Tenjin Shinyō Ryū: Jūjutsu Gokui Kyōju Zukai,* Shūeidō

Yokose, Tomoyuki (2000) *Nihon No Kobudō,* Nihon Budōkan

Shindō Yōshin Ryū

Chapter 5 - The Technical Legacy of Shindō Yōshin Ryū

Draeger, Donn F. (1974) *Modern Budō and Bujutsu: The Martial and Ways of Japan, Vol 3,* Weatherhill

Fujiwara, Ryōzō (1983) *Shindō Yōshin Ryū Reikishi no Giho,* Sōzō

Hall, David A. *(2012) Encyclopedia of Japanese Martial Arts,* Kōdansha

Iwasa, Masaru *(2005) Kashima Shinden Jikishinkage Ryū: The Origin of Samuraihood from Kashima Shrine,* Shuppan-sha

Nihon Kobudō Kyōkai (1989) *Nihon Kobudō Sōran,* Shimazu Shobō

Sasamori, Junzō *(1986) Ittō Ryū Gokui,* Reigakudō

Shinjurō, Tobe *(1991), Nihon Kengō Tan/Matsuzaki Namishirō,* 1-4

Takamura ha Shindō Yōshin Kai Collection: *Over 50 Akiyama Yōshin Ryū, Miura/Totsuka Yōshin Ryū and Shikage Ryū related densho.*

Takamura Yukiyoshi (1984) *Transcribed Diary Entries of Obata Shigeta,* TSYR Newsletter #14

Takamura Yukiyoshi (1976) *The Life of Obata Shigeta,* TSYR Newsletter #2

Takamura Yukiyoshi (1982) *Den Sanna Historien bakom Shindō Yōshin Ryū och dess kopplingar till Wadō Ryū,* TSYR Newsletter #10

Threadgill, Tobin: *Personal Densho Collection: Shoden, Chūden, Jōden Gokui & Okugi, Menkyo Kaiden*

Watatani, Kiyoshi and Yamada Tadashi (1978) *Bugei Ryūha Daijiten,* Tōkyō Kopī Shuppanbu

Chapter 6 - Nairiki: Internal Power

Amdur, Ellis (2009) *Hidden in Plain Sight: Tracing the Roots of Ueshiba Morihei's Power,* Edgework Publishing

Gumiberteau, Jean Claude and Colin Armstrong (2015) *Architecture of the Human Living Fascia,* Handspring Publishing

Myers, Thomas, (2001) *Anatomy Trains,* Churchill Livingston

David Lesondak (2017) *Fascia: What It is and Why It Matters,* Handspring Publishing

Takamura ha Shindō Yōshin Kai Collection: *Over 50 Akiyama Yōshin Ryū, Miura/Totsuka Yōshin Ryū Shikage Ryū related densho.*

Threadgill, Tobin: *Personal densho collection: Shoden, Chūden, Jōden Gokui & Okugi, Menkyo Kaiden*

Chapter 7 - On Shintō

Cali, Joseph and John Dougill (2013) *Shintō Shrines,* University of Hawai'i Press.

Hall, David A. (2012) *Encyclopedia of Japanese Martial Arts,* Kōdansha

Hitoshi, Miyaki and Gaynor Sekimori (2005) The Mandala of the Mountian, Keiō University

Little, Frederick Alan (2012) *Lost in Translation:The Anglo-Japanese Productions of Minakata Kumagusu,* UMI Publishing

Littleton, C. Scott (2002) *Shintō Rituals, Festivals, Spirits, Sacred Places,* Oxford University Press.

Kitagawa, Joseph M. (1987) *On Understanding Japanese Religion*, Princeton University Press.

Mason J.W.T. (2006) *The Meaning of Shintō*, Tenchi Press.

Nelson, John K. (1996) *A Year in the Life of a Shintō Shrine,* University of Washington Press.

Takamura, Yukiyoshi (1980) *Folk Shintō and its Rituals in Shindō Yōshin Ryū,* TSYR Newsletter #8

Yamakage, Motohisa (2007) *The Essence of Shintō: Japan's Spiritual Heart,* Kōdansha.

Yamamoto, Rev. Yukitaka (1998) *Kami no Michi, The Way of the Kami,* Tsubaki America Publications.

Ueda, Kenshi (1989) *Shintō,* Kokugakuin University.

Chapter 8 - Koryū Budō Densho

Hall, David A. (1979) *Bujutsu and Esoteric Tradition, 1 & 2*, Hoplos 1- 5,6

Hall, David A. (2012) *Encyclopedia of Japanese Martial Arts*, Kōdansha

Irie, Kōhei (1987) *Kinsei Budō Bunken Mokuroku*, Daiichi Shobō

Mol, Serge (2013) *Bujutsu Densho: Exploring the Written Tradition of Japan's Martial Culture*, Eibusha

Nihon Kobudō Kyōkai (2005) *Nihon Kobudō Sōran*, Shimazu Shobō

Osano, Jun (1991) *Yōshin Ryū Jūjutsu Denshoshū*, Nihon Sōgō Budō Kenkyujo

Watatani, Kiyoshi (1962) *Nihon Bugei Shōden*, Jinbutsu Ōraisha

Informants, Conversations and Correspondence

Amdur, Ellis (2000-2019) Shihan, Toda ha Bukō Ryū. Shihan, Araki Ryū torite-kogusoku. Conversations & correspondence.

Arakawa Tōru (2008-2012) JKF Karate 9th dan, Hanshi. Conversations in Montreal, Canada. Conversations and exchange of documentation in Longmont, CO.

Delaney, Steve (2006-2019) Conversations & correspondence on Tenjin Shinyō Ryū and Sosuishi Ryu.

Foster, Norma (2003-2017) JKF Wadōkai Karate 7th dan. Training, conversations & correspondence.

Fujiwara, Ryōzō (1995-2008) Menkyo Kaiden, Shindō Yōshin Ryū. Kōdōkan Jūdō 7th dan, JKF Wadōkai 8th dan Conversations & correspondence.

Garrison, Karl (1986-2017) Chūden Menkyo, Takamura ha Shindō Yōshin Ryū, Kōdōkan Jūdō 4th dan.

Hakoishi, Katsumi (2008) JKF Wadōkai Karate 8th dan. Conversations & correspondence.

Inose, Katsuei (2008) Principal, Shimotsuma Daiichi High School. Conversations and correspondence.

Kobayashi, Toshishirō (2013) Densho and kakejiku expert and collector. Correspondence.

Kuroda Tetsuzan (2002-2017) Sōke of the Shinbukan Ryūgi including Komagawa Kaishin Ryū, Tamiya Ryū, Shinshin Takuma Ryū, and Tsubaki Kotengu Ryū. Conversations & correspondence.

Maynard, David (1985-2017) Menkyo Kaiden, Takamura ha Shindō Yōshin Ryū. Training, conversation and correspondence.

Nakayama, Tsuyuko (2005) Granddaughter of Nakayama Tatsusaburō. Conversations and correspondence.

Nash, Bob (2002-2017) JKF Wadōkai Karate 7th dan. Training, conversations & correspondence.

Ōta, Frederick (1990-2018) Personal friend of Takamura Yukiyoshi, conversations. correspondence and interview in Aug, 2018.

Pranin, Stanley (1998-2017) Budō historian and archivist, publisher of Aikidō Journal. Conversations & correspondence.

Relnick, Phil (2001-2017) Shidōsha Menkyo, Tenshin Shōden Katori Shintō Ryū. Menkyo Kaiden, Shintō Musō Ryū. Kōdōkan Jūdō 4th dan. Founder, Japan Martial Arts Society. Conversations & correspondence.

Saitō, Takao (2005-2008) Teacher, Shimotsuma Daiichi High School. Conversations and correspondence.

Skoss, Diane (1994-2017) Shihan, Toda ha Bukō Ryū. Menkyo Kaiden, Shintō Musō Ryū. Conversations & correspondence.

Skoss, Meik (1994-2017) Shihan, Toda ha Bukō Ryū. Licensed in Tendō Ryū, Shintō Musō Ryū and Yagyū Shinkage Ryū. Conversations & correspondence.

Smith, Robert (2005-2014) JKF Wadōkai Karate 7th dan. Takamura ha Shindō Yōshin Ryū Shoden Mokuroku. Training, conversations & correspondence.

Takagi, Isoga (1990 & 1994) Menkyo Kaiden, Takamura ha Shindō Yōshin Ryū. Founder, Takagi Hachiho Ryū. Conversations, 1990 and 1994 in San Francisco, CA.

Takamura, Yukiyoshi (1985-2000) Kaichō, Takamura ha Shindō Yōshin Kai including Takamura ha Shindō Yōshin Ryū and Takagi Hachihō Ryū. Direct instruction, conversations & correspondence.

Glossary

History And Technique

A

age	上	Upward or rising.
agura	胡座	Cross-legged sitting position.
aihanmi	合半身	A position where adversaries facing one another have the same foot forward. *See: gyaku hanmi.*
aiki	合気	Harmonizing energy. As a martial concept, aiki represents the harmonizing of physical movement, breathing, intent or spirit.
aikuchi	合口	A dagger usually around 28cm without a tsuba. In this style of mounting, the tsuka aligns smoothly with the mouth of the saya.
ainuke	相抜	Concept of mutual escape. It originated in the Okuyama line of Shinkage Ryū, particularly with Harigaya Sekiun of Sekiun Ryū.
aki	秋	Autumn. In Takamura ha Shindō Yōshin Ryū, one of four kata sets named after the seasons and usually performed with bokken.
aku	悪	Concept of evil or malice.
akusho	悪所	In Takamura ha Shindō Yōshin Ryū, a vital point that if attacked or stimulated, always results in harm.
antehō	安定方	Direction of stability. In Shindō Yōshin Ryū it is the strong line of the base passing through the feet.
ashi sabaki	足捌	Footwork. Movement of the feet.
atemijutsu	当身術	Body striking. A comprehensive system and study of attacking vital points of the body with hands, feet and weaponry.
atoyaku	後やく	The year following the unlucky ages associated with Yakuyoke Taisai. Atoyaku is the 26th 43rd and 62nd year for men, and the 20th 34th, 38th and 62nd year for women.
awasema	合間	In Takamura ha Shindō Yōshin Ryū, a distance of engagement. In kenjutsu sword blades are crossed about 4-6 inches. In taijutsu the hands are crossed at the wrists.
ayumi ashi	歩足	Walking. An alternating stride.

B

Bakumatsu period	幕末	The period from 1853-1867. It generally references Japan's forced opening to the West following Admiral Perry's negotiations, and the collapse of the Tokugawa Shōgun.
battōjutsu	抜刀術	One of several terms referencing combative quick-draw swordsmanship. In Shindō Yōshin Ryū, battōjutsu is performed standing. A variation of the same kata performed kneeling is identified as iaijutsu.
Battōtai	抜刀隊	A samurai Japanese police unit established in the 1870s.
betsuden	別伝	Auxiliary teachings. Teachings added to and separate from the regular curriculum.
Bishamonten	毘沙門天	A Buddhist deity functioning as tutelary protector of the Japanese warrior class.

Shindō Yōshin Ryū

bōgu	防具	Protective training armor.
bokken	木剣	A wooden training sword.
bu 1.	武	Martial, military or pertaining to warfare.
bu 2.	分	A Japanese unit of measurement equal to .12 inches or 3mm.
budō	武道	Bu=Martial, Dō=Way. Martial arts originating in Japan. In modern times budō is defined as a way of life influenced by the study of bujutsu. Classically, budō is the study of conflict including technique, tactics, strategy and psychology, which includes the political ramifications of conflict.
budōka	武道家	An individual dedicated to the study of Japanese martial arts.
budōkan	武道館	A building where Japanese martial arts are taught.
bugei	武芸	Martial art. An older term synonymous with classical budō. The term implies the study of conflict beyond technique and tactics including strategy, psychology and politics.
bujutsu	武術	The study of the techniques and tactics of war. A subset of classical budō, bujutsu is the art of the battle-hardened samurai devoid of the distractions of politics and the cultural intricacies of conflict. The study of bujutsu is characterized by the single-minded determination to perfect the techniques of combat.
buki	武器	Weapons or weaponry.
Buki no Maki	武器の巻	Weapons scroll. In Takamura ha Shindō Yōshin Ryū the shoden and chūden weapons curriculum is included on a separate scroll from the taijutsu curriculum.
bushi	武士	Japanese medieval term for warrior.
bushidō	武士道	"The way of the warrior." A warrior code of ethics, attitudes and cultural behaviors that evolved during the Edo period.

C

chakuchi ashi	着地足	An instantaneous reversal of the feet that does not move the seichūsen.
chiburi	血振	A technique for removing blood from a sword. As part of the Takamura ha Shindō Yōshin Ryū battō/iaijutsu kata, chiburi identifies the initiation of zanshin. In a practical sense, chiburi is followed by washiseisō, a wiping of the blade with paper to remove blood before returning the sword to the saya.
chikama	近間	Distance of combat engagement where a cut or strike can reach the target but requires a partial step.
chinkon	鎮魂	Deepening the soul. An esoteric Shintō spiritual exercise intended to heal and direct the soul by making a guided connection to outside spirits. Chinkon is included as part of the Takamura ha Shindō Yōshin Ryū gokui.
Chi no Maki	地の巻	Earth Scroll. In Takamura ha Shindō Yōshin Ryū, one of two okugi level teaching documents.
chōjiabura	丁子油	Clove-scented oil used to prevent the rusting of Japanese blades.

chūdan 中段		Middle or intermediate level.
chūdan gamae 中段構え		In Takamura ha Shindō Yōshin Ryū, a kenjutsu stance with the sword tsuka parallel to the floor on the seichūsen, at the level of the tanden.
Chūden Buki no Maki 中伝武器の巻		In Takamura ha Shindō Yōshin Ryū, the intermediate weapon techniques scroll.
Chūden Taijutsu no Maki 中伝体術の巻		In Takamura ha Shindō Yōshin Ryū, the intermediate body techniques scroll.
chūshin wo tadasu 中心を正す		Properly aligned body posture.

D

dai	大	Large or great.
Dai Nippon Butokukai 大日本武徳会		Classical martial arts promotion and preservation organization founded in 1895, in Kyōto. The original organization was disbanded in 1946 by the Allied GHQ and no longer exists.
daishō	大小	Large and small. The term references a matched set of swords, a long sword (daitō or katana), and a short sword (shōtō, kodachi or wakizashi). Only warriors of samurai status were allowed to wear multiple swords.
daitō	大刀	Long sword. Generally a sword longer than 60cm. A daitō can be mounted as a tachi or a katana. Sometimes a daitō is distinguished from a katana by having a handle longer than 25cm.
dan'i	段位	Level or grade.
den	伝	Teachings.
densho	伝書	Transmission document, usually in the form of a scroll. They come in a variety of designations: kirigami (cut paper), mokuroku (catalog), menjō (certificate), menkyo (license), menkyo kaiden (license of full transmission) and inka (seal of confidence).
deshi	弟子	Disciple. A student who is formally accepted as a member of a school.
dō	胴	Torso of the body. Also, armor protecting the body core.
dō	道	Way or path. Used as a suffix, it recognizes following a pursuit.
dōjō	道場	A sacred place where learning a path of life is pursued.
dōjōchō	道場長	Chief instructor in a dōjō.
dōka	道歌	Didactic poem. *Also koka.*
dōshin	道心	Edo period police constable.

E

Edo Jidai	江戸時代	Period from 1603 until 1868. Named after national seat of the Tokugawa shogunate. Edo is the old name for Tōkyō.
emaki	絵巻	An illustrated densho.

Shindō Yōshin Ryū

eimeiroku	英名録	Register book of a school's official disciples.
ekisho	益所	In Takamura ha Shindō Yōshin Ryū, a vital point that if stimulated, always results in benefit.
enbu	演武	Martial arts demonstration. If done as a demonstration for tutelary kami or at a shrine, it is referred to as a hōnō enbu.
eri	襟	Collar.

F

fuantehō	不安定方	Direction of instability. In Shindō Yōshin Ryū, it is a direction 90 degrees in opposition to a line passing through the feet.
fudōshin	不動心	Immovable mind. A state of mind so focused and disciplined that it transcends any and all outside influences.
fukuro shinai	袋竹刀	A bamboo practice sword covered in a leather sheath. In Takamura ha Shindō Yōshin Ryū the weapon is covered in white doeskin.
fundoshi	ふんどし	A traditional Japanese loin cloth.
fusahimo	房紐	The tasseled cord used to tie a sword bag closed.
fuyu	冬	Winter. In Takamura ha Shindō Yōshin Ryū, one of four kata sets named after the seasons and usually performed with bokken.

G

gaiden	外伝	Outside teachings. Gaiden teachings are allowed to be demonstrated to a public audience as a means of promoting the school.
gaikikaku	外気覚	External sensitivity. A highly-developed perception of touch and tactile sensitivity.
gaeshi	返し	To turn back or reverse. *Also: kaeshi*
gedan	下段	Lower level. Usually in reference to a physical position.
gedan gamae	下段構	Lower stance. In Takamura ha Shindō Yōshin Ryū, a seldom-utilized stance with the sword in front on the center line with the kissaki approximately 6 inches above the ground.
gehanen	下半円	Kenjutsu reigi performed before specific TSYR kumitachi. It is an homage to Kashima Shinden Jikishinkage Ryū.
gekiken	撃剣	Aggressive sword. A form of freestyle training with protective bōgu and bamboo weapons. It was greatly influenced by the schools of Shinkage Ryū and Ittō Ryū.
gekikenkai	撃剣会	An organization created by Sakakibara Kenkichi in 1873. Its aim was to increase the popularity of classical martial arts through public competitions called Gekiken Kōgyō. These events were very popular with the masses and attracted thousands of observers.
gendai	現代	Modern day.
gendaitō	現代刀	New sword. Japanese swords produced after 1876.

History And Technique

genkan	玄関	Building entrance. in būdō, a room dedicated to removing shoes before entering the main training area of a dōjō.
genri	原理	Principle.
giri	義理	Obligation or personal debt.
gishiki	儀式	Ceremony or ceremonial behavior.
go	五	Five.
gofu	護符	A wooden Shintō talisman hung in dōjō to impart protective qualities.
gohei	御幣	Zigzag strips of paper attached to a shimenawa (braided rope) or harai gushi (purification wand). Symbolic of lightening, gohei are associated with purified areas and purification ceremonies.
gōhō	業報	Shintō concept of kamic destiny.
gokui	極意	Significant knowledge. Important teachings or mysteries. In Takamura ha Shindō Yōshin Ryū there are two jōden gokui level scrolls, the Ten no Maki (Scroll of Heaven) and Jin no Maki (Scroll of Man).
go no sen	後の先	Reactive initiative. One of the three basic forms combat initiative.
goshin jutsu	護身術	Self-defense techniques.
gyaku	逆	Reverse.
gyaku hanmi	逆半身	A stance where adversaries facing one another have the opposite foot forward. *See: aihanmi*
gyakute	逆手	Reverse hand. Also, a taijutsu technique where the hand is placed into a reversed direction.
gyaku kyōtō kamae 逆脅刀構		Reversed threatening sword. An aggressive stance with the sword held on the left side of the body with the tsuba at face level, tilted to the side 30-45 degrees outward and 45 degrees backward.

H

ha 1.	派	Suffix, meaning branch, division or group.
ha 2.	刃	The cutting edge of a Japanese blade.
habikitō	刃引刀	Pulled-edge sword. A steel training sword with a dulled edge.
hachimaki	鉢巻	A white cotton headband associated with shugyō. Hachimaki should only be worn during training that requires great physical or mental exertion.
hakama	袴	Short for hanbakama, hakama are skirt-like divided pants originally worn by the warrior class of Japan.
hakkai shiki	発会界式	Ceremonial beginning of a martial arts class.
hakuda	白打	Older name for a jūjutsu-like pugilistic art imported from China in the early 1600s.
hamon	破門	Formal expulsion or excommunication from a Nihon koryū school.

Shindō Yōshin Ryū

han	藩		A warlords domain during the Tokugawa shogunate.
hanashi	放		Escaping. Techniques of escape or employed in countering.
hankō	判子		A stamp or personal seal traditionally made of soapstone. In Japan they function as a legal signature.
hanmi	半身		A half body stance. A stance with the hips turned 45 degrees.
hanshi	範士		In Takamura ha Shindō Yōshin Ryū, hanshi is an honorific that references a retired headmaster who is no longer actively teaching.
hantai	反対		Opposite. Turning the opposite direction without moving the feet. Pivot.
happō	八方		Eight directions. In Takagi Hachihō/Happō Ryū, the term is symbolic of awareness in all directions. It is related to cardinal and ordinal points on a compass.
hara	腹		Lower abdomen and center of gravity. *Also: tanden* 丹田.
harae 1.	払		Suffix usually meaning to sweep or brush away.
harae 2.	祓		To purify or exorcise corrupting influences. To cleanse.
haramaki	腹巻		Abdomen wrap. A long white cotton cloth wrapped tightly around the abdomen, sometimes concealing chain mail. In Takamura ha Shindō Yōshin Ryū haramaki are worn during misogi and other Shinto-associated purification ceremonies.
haraigushi	祓串		A wooden wand with gohei attached at one end. Haraigushi are used by Shintō priests during various purification ceremonies where they are waved over the items to be purified.
haragei	腹芸		Gut intuition and personal fortitude.
haru	春		Spring. In Takamura ha Shindō Yōshin Ryū, one of four kata sets named after the seasons and usually performed with bokken.
hassō kamae	八租構		Facing eight directions stance. Symbolic of being able to strike in any direction. *Also: happō*
hassōkudai			An eight-legged table used in various Shintō ceremonies.
hasuji	刃筋		Blade alignment. A sword's angle of trajectory through a target.
heihō	兵法		Methods of war. Principles of military strategy. Heihō is synonymous with bugei, military arts *Also: hyōhō.*
heiza gamae	兵座構		In Takamura ha Shindō Yōshin Ryū, a seated position with the knees on the ground, legs approximately 45 degrees apart, and the toes overlapping to form a crescent under the hips. Similar to seiza but with the knees spread in a manner that creates a larger base and greater stability.
henka	変化		A variation or individually-evolved version of a kata.
hi	火		Fire. In Takamura ha Shindō Yōshin Ryū, one of four kata sets named after the elements and usually performed with bokken.
hidari	左		Left.
hiden	秘伝		Secret teachings or a category of advanced kata.
hijutsu	秘術		Secret techniques. In Takamura ha Shindō Yōshin Ryū these teachings

are used along with norito (prayers) and koka (poems) to identify a student's initiation into a specific level of training.

hibuki	秘武器	Secreted weapons. In Takamura ha Shindō Yōshin Ryū, a series of 15 kata in three sets included on the Chūden Buki no Maki. They are kōgai, tetsubō, and torinawa.
hinoki	檜	The sacred wood of Shintō, known for its aromatic qualities. A false cypress, it is known as Port Orford Cedar in the USA, the only other place in the world where it is considered native.
hira kamae	開構	Kneeling position with both feet up on the balls of the feet and under the hips. Legs are 90 degrees apart with the right leg forward, knee up. The left knee is on the ground and perpendicular to the right. If the right leg is outstretched with the heel touching the ground, and the knee slightly bent, the position becomes hira ichimonji kamae.
hishigi	拉技	Crushing or overwhelming spirit.
hissatsu	必殺	Death blow. The focus point of a decisive technique.
hiza	膝	Knee.
hō	法	Suffix meaning way or method.
hobaku	捕縛	Older name for a jūjutsu-like capturing art from the Muromachi period.
hoko	矛	An old style Japanese spear with a socketed blade that fit over the shaft.
hoko kamae	矛構	A middle guard stance similar to seigan with the sword blade angled diagonally left to right.
hokote	矛手	Spear hand. Strike using the tips of the fingers against a soft target.
honbu	本部	Headquarters dōjō.
hongi	本義	A foundational principle or concept.
honne	本音	True intent or genuine motive.
hyōshi	拍子	Rhythm, cadence or timing.

I

iaijutsu	居合術	One of several terms referencing combative quick-draw swordsmanship. In Takamura ha Shindō Yōshin Ryū, iaijutsu kata are considered the ura variation of an omote kata performed standing. The standing versions are identified as battōjutsu.
iaitō	居合刀	A training sword with an unsharpened alloy blade. *Also: mogito.*
ichi-tai-gi	位置体技	Position, body, technique. Yōshin Ryū derived principle of tactical engagement related to flexibility.
ichimonji kamae	一文字	A standing kamae with the feet widely spaced and hands placed in front of the tanden forming a triangle symbolizing ten chi jin.
idori	居捕	Kneeling techniques. Takamura ha Shindō Yōshin Ryū idori kata begin in either heiza no kamae or hira no kamae.
igen	威厳	The sense one feels when entering a proper dōjō. Similar to shibusa, but associated with a feeling rather than an object or place.

Shindō Yōshin Ryū

ihira kamae	威開構		Kneeling half-open stance. The same stance as hira kamae with a bladed weapon in the obi. *See: hira kamae*
iki no gyō	息の形		Breathing forms. In Takamura ha Shindō Yōshin Ryū there are seven specific breathing methods utilized. Four of these methods are included in okugi level study.
inasu	往なす		Deflecting an attack while using a body drop to enter or slip into a tactically superior position.
inkajō	印可状		Authority of the seal. In Takamura ha Shindō Yōshin Ryū, inkajō is passed automatically with a Menkyo Kaiden, authorizing the holder to pass the ryūha in its entirety to another generation. Only the holder of a Menkyo Kaiden receives inkajō in the Takamura ha Shindō Yōshin Kai.
in'yō	陰陽		The Japanese version of duality or the dual forces of nature (yin/yang).
irimi	入身		Entering body. A tactic that includes stepping into an attack a fraction of a second before it is launched.
ishizuki	石突		Metal end-cap on a pole arm such as a spear or naginata. Sometimes ishizuki were pointed and virtually as dangerous as the kissaki.
itten	一点		One point. The center of gravity.

J

jikideshi	直弟子		A student of the honbu dōjō or a student who studies directly under a school's headmaster.
jinja/jingū	神社/神宮		A Shintō shrine.
jōdan	上段		High or upper level.
jōdan kamae	上段構		A stance with a sword held on the center line above the head, and tilted back at 45 degrees.
jōge	上下		Up and down.
jōhanen	上半円		Kenjutsu reigi performed before specific TSYR kumitachi. It is an homage to Kashima Shinden Jikishinkage Ryū.
jōseki	上席		The mat area to the right side of the dōjō when facing the kamiza.
jū 1.	十		Ten.
jū 2.	柔		Martial principle of flexibility or pliability.
jūji	十字		Crossed.
jūjutsu	柔術		Form of budō incorrectly associated with unarmed grappling. Authentic Nihon jūjutsu is a sōgō bujutsu incorporating weapons as well as unarmed combat methods. Flexibility is its foundational principle.
jū no ri	柔の理		Martial principle of flexibility, both mentally and physically.

K

kaeshi	返し		To turn back or reverse. *Also: gaeshi*

kaeshizuno	返し角	A hook on a sword saya that catches on the obi preventing it from moving when the sword is drawn. They are commonly used on shorter weapons that are drawn by one hand. *Also: soritsuno and origane.*
kagami biraki	鏡開き	Mirror opening. Shintō ritual symbolizing the end of the Japanese New Year's celebrations. Usually celebrated on the second weekend of January.
kage 1.	陰	Darkness, secret or something obscured.
kage 2.	影	Shadow or silhouette.
kaichō	会長	Leader of a group or organization.
kaiden	皆伝	Complete transmission.
kaisetsu	解説	Explanation or investigation. The process of evaluating the underlying teachings and principles of a kata.
kaiten	回転	To rotate or pivot.
kaji	鍛治	A shortened term for katana kaji, a sword smith.
kake	掛	Hook. A rack used to hold weapons in a dōjō.
kakegoe	賭け声	Shout (kiai). The four basic kiai used in Shindō Yōshin Ryū kata.
kakei	家系	Lineage or genealogy list included on a densho.
kaku obi	角帯	Stiff Belt. A cloth belt around 10cm wide and 400cm long, it is used to hold a keikogi or kimono closed and hold a swordsman's weapons. They are usually made of stiff cotton or heavy silk.
kamae	構	Stance.
kami	神	A Shintō spirit or supernatural phenomena. Kami include landscape, natural forces and beings of unique qualities. Kami are considered to be manifestations of nature, and as such frequently represent the duality of positive and negative traits.
kamidana	神棚	A miniature Shintō altar located in a home or dōjō. The kamidana and associated offerings should reside on a shelf higher than any other object on the wall. Talisman called ofuda representing specific kami are housed inside the kamidana and replaced annually.
kamiza/jōza	神座/上座	The upper seat of a dōjō. The kamidana always resides on kamiza, which faces east or south in the northern hemisphere, or east or north in the southern hemisphere. This location is determined as light from the rising sun should fall of the kamiza. *Also: shinza.*
kansetsu	関節	Joint locking. Rotating or bending a joint to its maximum flexion.
kappō	活法	Resuscitation methods usually included in Nihon jūjutsu schools.
karajishi	唐獅子	Chinese lion residing on the left side of a Shintō shrine or dōjō entrance. Karajishi has an closed mouth and is represented saying "um".
Kashima Jingū	鹿島神宮	Shrine founded in the 7th century located northeast of Tōkyō in Ibaraki prefecture. The tutelary deity at the shrine is Takemikazuchi no Mikoto making it one the three primary warrior shrines in Japan.
kasumi	霞	Fog. A kyūsho point on the skull just outside the eye socket.

kasumi kamae	霞構	In Takamura ha Shindō Yōshin Ryū, a stance with the sword inverted, parallel to the ground and head high, kissaki towards an adversary.
kata	形	A pre-arranged combative form that functions as pedagogical device to convey principles, theories, and tactics.
katana	刀	A single-edged long sword intended to be worn thrust through an obi with the cutting edge facing upwards. Katana were designed for foot-soldiers and are less curved than their predecessor, the tachi, a weapon created during an era where mounted calvary dominated the battle-field.
katate	片手	A single hand wrist grab.
katchū	甲冑	Armor. Techniques either practiced or assumed to include armor.
katsujinken	活人剣	The life-giving sword. A nuanced moral principle embraced in the Shinkage Ryū schools of swordsmanship related to sparing an enemy's life in the service of overcoming evil. *See: setsunintō.*
kawari	変	Changing or altering an enemy's perception of reality.
kaze	風	Wind. In Takamura ha Shindō Yōshin Ryū, one of four kata sets named after the elements and usually performed with bokken.
kazoedoshi	数え年	The Japanese tradition of being born age one and then one year added every New Year's day.
keiko	稽古	Study. Martial arts training.
keiko shōkon	稽古照今	Studying the past to understand the present. This is a common subject of Akiyama Yōshin Ryū esoteric teachings.
ken 1.	剣	Sword. A term originally referencing a tsurugi or double-edge straight sword. In time it developed into a general term for all types of swords.
ken 2.	拳	Fist.
kendō	剣道	Kendō is a modern sport descended from Nihon koryū kenjutsu. Kendō descended from gekiken and shinaigeiko, Edo period evolutionary training methods that sought to replicate combative engagement utiliz-ing bamboo staves and protective armor.
kenjutsu	剣術	Combative sword arts. Kenjutsu was the primary weapons system em-braced by the warrior class of feudal Japan. Because the sword was symbolic of the warrior's role in society, swordsmanship was the well-spring from which all the other arts descended.
keppan	血判	Blood seal. The act of taking a oath and sealing it with your own blood. Keppan was required in many Nihon koryū schools and is still required in Takamura ha Shindō Yōshin Ryū.
keri	蹴	Kick or kicking techniques.
ki	気	Life force of vital energy.
kiai	気合	Vital energy projection. In Takamura ha Shindō Yōshin Ryū, methods to dominate an adversary through vocalizations, controlled breathing and exhalation.
kigaku	気学	Japanese numerology or divination. *Also: reikigaku*
kihon	基本	Basic movement, pattern training, and technique.

kime	極め	Mental and physical focus.
kiri ippatsu	切一発	To cut instantly from the subconscious.
kirigami	切り紙	Cut paper license. The first license issued to a student.
kirioroshi	切下し	Powerful downward cut performed from jōdan.
kishōmon	起請文	Oath or vow. The document outlining the requirements adhered to when undergoing keppan.
kiza gamae	跪座構	A kneeling position similar to heiza gamae but with the feet turned under and vertical, with the weight resting on the balls of the feet.
ko 1.	古	Old, or ancient.
ko 2.	小	A prefix meaning small or lesser.
koden	古伝	Old teachings.
koken fukuro no gyō 古剣袋の形		A series of Takamura ha Shindō Yōshin Ryū kata listed on the Okugi Chi no Maki, which are performed with fukuro shinai. The kata are strongly influenced by Kashima Shinden Jikishinkage Ryū.
koken nitō awase no gyō 古剣二刀合の形		A series of 16 Takamura ha Shindō Yōshin Ryū kata listed on the Okugi Chi no Maki which are performed with fukuro shinai. The kata are strongly influenced by Matsuzaki Shinkage Ryū.
kōbō itchi	攻防一致	Combat tactic meaning attack and defense are one.
kobudō	古武道	Old or ancient martial arts. Generic term for classical martial arts.
kodachi	小太刀	Short sword.
kōgai	笄	A small metal skewer sometimes carried in a special pocket carved into a sword saya. There are five kōgai kata in Takamura ha Shindō Yōshin Ryū.
kogatana 1.	小刀	A smaller and lighter than normal katana (45-55cm) with a short tsuka. Usually wielded with one hand. They were frequently carried as an auxiliary weapon by foot-soldiers whose primary weapon was a pole arm. Sometimes called a chisagatana.
kogatana 2.	小刀	A small utility knife carried in a small slot of a sword saya. The knife blade is mounted in a decorative handle called a kozuka.
kogusoku	小具足	In Takamura ha Shindō Yōshin Ryū, a taijutsu kata set assumed to be practiced in light armor.
kohai	後輩	Junior. The junior member in a dōjō student relationship.
koiguchi	鯉口	The opening of a sword saya.
kokoro	心	Heart. Term referencing mind, intent emotions or spirit. In the context of budō, kokoro is what binds the mind and body together.
kokyū	呼吸	Breath. Kokyū in the context of budō is a nuanced term. It can mean breathing, timing, emotional control or source of power.
koma inu	狛犬	Korean dog. Korean dog-like creature residing on the right side of a Shinto shrine or dōjō entrance. Koma Inu has an open mouth and is represented saying "ah".
koryū	古流	Old School. The term generally refers to classical Nihon bujutsu schools founded prior to the Meiji Restoration in 1868.

Shindō Yōshin Ryū

koshirae	拵	The mounting furniture of a Japanese sword when being used as opposed to being stored. When being stored, the furniture is called tosogu.
kōshōma	交渉間	Negotiating distance. Distance of engagement in idori kata equal to the width of a tatami.
kote	小手	Small hand. Kote refers to the wrist or forearm closest to the hand.
kozuka	小柄	The decorative metal handle mounting for a kogatana.
kuden	口伝	Oral teachings. Teachings of special significance taught verbally from teacher to student.
kujiki	挫	To bend or strain.
kumitachi	組太刀	A pre-arranged combative form performed between two swordsmen.
kumiuchi	組打	Armored grappling.
kuzushi	崩し	Off-balancing or disrupting.
kushiyō	駆使曜	Astrological and numerological methods utilized in some Yōshin Ryū traditions for divination and knowledge transmission.
kyōtō kamae	脅刀構	Threatening sword. In Takamura ha Shindō Yōshin Ryū there are three variants of this combative stance. *See: gyaku kyōtō and tate kyōtō.*
kyūsho	急所	Vital point. A point on the body that can potentially damage or heal depending on how it is stimulated.

M

maai	間合	Distance of combat engagement.
mae	前	Forward.
makimono	巻物	Scroll.
manji gamae	万字構	A stance where the thigh and shin are bent at 90 degrees. One leg's shin is vertical while the other is parallel to the ground. The legs replicate the shape of a manji. 卍
Marishiten	摩利支天	A Buddhist bodisatva and one of many protective deities of the Japanese warrior class.
marobashi	転	A state of formlessness. To transcend form and internalize the deepest secrets of a ryūha without conscious thought.
mawashi	回し	Circular.
meijin	名人	Master or expert level instructor.
menkyo	免許	A license reflecting a particular level of proficiency.
menkyo kaiden	免許皆伝	A license of complete transmission. In Takamura ha Shindō Yōshin Ryū a Menkyo Kaiden symbolizes not only the highest level of technical authority but also represents a level of administrative authority determined by the honbu dōjō.
metsuke	目付	Focus of, or on the eyes.

migi	右		Right.
mikkyō	密教		Esoteric knowledge. Mikkyō is usually associated with teachings in the Shingon and Tendai sects of Buddhism.
minari	身なり		Appearance.
misekake	見掛け		Feint.
misogi	禊		Purification.
mitama 1.	御霊		Human spirit.
mitama 2.	御魂		Spirit of a deceased ancestor recognized as kami.
mitamaya	御霊屋		Spirit house. A Shintō alter similar to a kamidana used to house deceased ancestors. When displayed with a kamidana it rests on a smaller shelf directly below the kamidana.
mitamashiro	霊代		A talisman residing in a mitamaya believed to be inhabited by a deceased ancestor. Often the ancestor inhabiting a mitamashiro is recognized as kami.
mitsudogu	三道具		Three tools of arresting. Three pole arms used by Edo period arresting police. They are sodegarami (sleeve entangler), sasumata (spiked fork), and tsukubō (spiked T-bar).
mizu	水		Water. In Takamura ha Shindō Yōshin Ryū, one of four kata sets named after the elements and usually performed with bokken.
mokuroku 1.	目録		Catalog or index.
mokuroku 2.	目録		Transmission document including a list of the school's techniques.
mon	紋		Family crest similar to western heraldry.
montsuki	紋付き		A formal kimono that includes a kamon (mon).
mune 1.	胸		Chest or breast.
mune 2.	棟		Back edge of a sword.
mune uchi	棟打		A strike with the back edge of a sword blade. In Takamura ha Shindō Yōshin Ryū kenjutsu using the mune of a blade to abruptly deflect an adversaries sword is a frequently employed tactic.
mushin	無心		No mind. A detached state of mind devoid of conscious thought, fear, or victory. Behavior based on intuitive influences instead of active reasoning.
musubi	結び		To link or connect two things.
myōden	妙伝		Mysterious teachings. A category of advanced teachings included in the Takamura ha Shindō Yōshin Ryū Gokui Ten no Maki.

N

nagashi	流し		Blend. To evasively flow and avoid an attack, often while simultaneously launching a counter attack. Foundational principle of Yōshin Ryū.
nage	投げ		Throw.
naginata	薙刀		Japanese long-shafted weapon similar to a western glaive.

Shindō Yōshin Ryū

naname	斜め		Diagonal.
naiden	内伝		Inside teachings. Naiden teachings are restricted and rarely demonstrated to a audience outside the ryūha membership.
naikikaku	内気覚		Internal sensitivity. The development of body sensitivity beneath the skin and inside the structure of the body.
nairiki	内力		Internal power.
natsu	夏		Summer. In Takamura ha Shindō Yōshin Ryū, one of four kata sets named after the seasons and usually performed with bokken.
newaza	寝技		Grappling techniques.
ni	二		Two.
Nihon	日本		Japan. (Older pronunciation, Nippon).
nobashi	伸ばし		To stretch out or extend.
nodowa	咽喉輪		A throat protector used as part of Japanese armor.
nogare	逃れ		To avoid or escape.
noru	乗る		Softly maintaining contact with an adversary as he moves to control or dominate him.
nōtō	納刀		Re-sheathing a sword.
nuki	抜き		Drawing a sword.
nukiashi	抜き足		A pulling step. Movement initiated by pulling with the forward leg.
nyūnanshin	柔軟心		Flexible mind. A mental state devoid of predisposition. Nyunanshin is required for proper learning.

O

obi	帯		Belt or sash.
o fuda	御札		Shintō amulet issued by a shrine. The name of a specific tutelary kami is written on it and it is placed inside a kamidana.
okuden	奥伝		Secret or inner teachings.
okugi	奥義		Similar to okuden. Okugi are a category of advanced and proprietary teachings. In Takamura ha Shindō Yōshin Ryū there are two jōden okugi level scrolls, the Chi no Maki (Scroll of Earth) and Tengu Tobi no Maki (Flying Goblin Scroll).
okuriashi	送り足		A type of sliding step. In Takamura ha Shindō Yoshin Ryū, a sliding step in which movement is initiated by dropping the body and driving the front foot forward and then drawing up the rear foot. In appearance okuriashi looks like tsugiashi but is dynamically reversed.
o mamori	御守		A protective amulet issued by a Shintō shrine.
omote	表		The obvious or easily observed. In Takamura ha Shindō Yōshin Ryū, the teaching version of a form is identified as the omote kata as opposed to the ura kata, which is usually related to practical application.
oroshi	下し		Downward, drop or lower.

osae	押え	To press or push.
otoshi	落し	To drop or allow to fall.
owari	終り	Completed. Bring to an end.
ōyoroi	大鎧	Great armor. Full suit of armor worn by a high-ranking bushi.

R

rei	礼	Bow. Etiquette.
reigi/reishiki	礼義/礼式	Etiquette. Ritual formalities performed before or after martial arts training or demonstration.
riai	理合	Fundamental principles that underlie kata or techniques.
ryōte	両手	Two-hand grab.
ryū	流	Literally, flow. In the context of martial arts, ryū references a tradition that flows from generation to generation through time.
ryūha	流派	School branch. An independent branch or separate line of an already existing martial arts school. Frequently a ryūha is a school still closely identified with its progenitor art but reflects additions or subtractions to the main line's original curriculum. Sometimes ryūha are the result of succession issues or internal political turmoil.

S

sabaki	捌き	Movement.
sagamae kamae	下前構	Hanging forward. A sword kamae where the kissaki rests forward on the center line at approximately knee level.
sageo	下緒	A cord that secures the sword to the obi.
sagetō shisei	提刀姿勢	Hanging sword. A posture where the sword is held in the left hand, arm relaxed and hanging downward with the hand at mid-thigh.
sakura		Ritual of seating the sword in the saya following nōtō. In TSYR the hand symbolically replicates a falling cherry blossom.
samegawa	鮫皮	Hide of a stingray or shark. Extremely tough and strong, samegawa was used in sword handles and occasionally sword scabbards.
san	三	Three.
sansenjin	三戦神	The three Buddhist war gods: Fudō Myōō, Aizen Myōō and Marishiten.
saya	鞘	Scabbard.
sayabiki	鞘引	Pulling the saya backwards. A movement used during the drawing and re-sheathing of a sword.
sayaoshi	鞘押	Pushing the saya forward. A movement that initiates the draw.
seigan gamae	正眼構	A combative posture where the sword tip is pointed towards the eyes of his adversary.
seikotsushi	整骨師	A bonesetter. An Edo period equivalent of a modern physiotherapist.

seiryoku	精力		The efficient use of energy, a foundational principle of jūjutsu.
seiza	正座		A sitting posture where both legs are folded under the torso, knees together, and the hips resting on the soles of the feet. It was a posture not commonly used by samurai. In Takamura ha Shindō Yōshin Ryū a similar but more stable and mobile posture called heiza, with knees spread wide making a triangle shaped base.
senpai	先輩		Senior.
sen	先		Initiative.
sen no sen	先の先		Simultaneous action that prevents an adversary from taking the initiative.
sensei	先生		Honorific title used when addressing one's teacher or teachers of other traditions. As an honorific it is never used in reference to one's self.
sen sen no sen	先先の先		Preemptive action or initiative to overwhelm an adversary before he can contemplate an attack.
setsunintō	殺人刀		The life-taking sword. A nuanced moral principle associated with taking a life in pursuit of eliminating evil. *See: katsujinken*
shaku	尺		A Japanese unit of measurement equivalent to 30.3cm.
shiai	試合		A contest or competition. To test each other.
shibori	絞り		Wringing action of the hands used during a sword cut.
shibuchō	支部長		A branch director. A title that reflects administrative authority over a group of dōjō.
shibumi	渋味		Restrained elegance. An aesthetic cultivated in a traditional Japanese dōjō. *Also: shibui.*
shihan	師範		Master level instructor. In TSYR this honorific is only used in official written correspondence.
shime	絞め		Strangle or choke.
shimenawa	注連縄		A straw rope with white zigzag paper strips attached. Its presence identifies sacred places or areas purified by a Shintō ritual.
shimoseki	下席		The lower seat of a dōjō. The wall to the right of the kamiza.
shimoza	下座		The wall directly opposite the jōza or kamiza.
shin 1.	心		Heart, spirit or soul.
shin 2.	新		New or modern.
shinkiritsu kamae	芯起立構		A preparatory upright stance, half open, with the feet shoulder-width apart. In taijutsu, the hands are placed on both sides of the tanden (lower abdomen). When wielding a bladed weapon, the left hand secures the saya and the right hand rests on the right side of the tanden.
shinryoku tanren 心力鍛錬			Spiritual forging. The shinryoku tanren is a physical and mental test a deshi must pass before being allowed entry into advanced level study.
shintai 1.	芯体		Body core.
shintai 2.	真体		Correct body posture or structure.

shingi ittai	心技一体		Body and mind are one. Term coined by Yamaoka Tesshū and embraced by Jikishinkage Ryū. Technical and spiritual mastery.
shirasaya	白鞘		White wooden unfinished scabbard for the storage and transportation of a sword blade.
shiroi	白い		White. Symbolically related to purity.
shisei	姿勢		Posture.
shishi	獅子		Lion dogs motif as commonly used in Japanese art.
shitachi	仕太刀		Active sword. The person responding to an attack in paired weapon forms. (In jūjutsu the term is shite, meaning active hand - 仕手).
shizen hontai	自然本体		Natural stance.
sho 1.	初		First.
shō 2.	小		Small or minor.
Shoden Buki no Maki 初伝武器の巻			In Takamura ha Shindō Yōshin Ryū, the basic weapon techniques scroll.
Shoden Taijutsu no Maki 初伝体術の巻			In Takamura ha Shindō Yōshin Ryū, the basic body techniques scroll.
shoji	障子		Sliding paper screens commonly used in Japanese homes and dōjō.
shōkaijō	紹介状		Introduction letter.
shoshin	初心		Beginner's mind.
shōtō	小刀		Short sword.
shugyō	修行		To cultivate one's spirit through austere training.
shu ha ri	守破離		To embrace, to break from, and to transcend. A traditional Japanese learning process through which a classical martial arts student develops expertise.
shuriken	手裏剣		Metal spike thrown as a projectile or employed in the hand to momentarily distract or mentally disarm an adversary.
sode	袖		Sleeve.
sōden	相伝		Direct transmission of knowledge or authority.
sōgō bugei/bujutsu 綜合武芸/武術			A classical comprehensive martial arts tradition.
sōhei	僧兵		Warrior monks.
sōji	掃除		Cleaning the dōjō before or after class. Seen as a form of misogi or spiritual purification.
sōjutsu	槍術		Spear arts.
soto	外		Outside.
suigetsu	水月		Water moon. Kyūsho point just below the sternum.
suihei	水平		Horizontal.

suki	隙		Gap. An opening or flaw in an executed technique.
sun	寸		A Japanese unit of measurement equal to about 3.03cm.
suriashi	摺足		An alternating sliding step.
sutemi	捨身		In budō, sacrificing or throwing away.

T

tabi	足袋		Split-toed socks.
tachi 1.	太刀		A Japanese long sword with a single cutting edge. A tachi was usually mounted to be drawn with the edge facing down. Generally, the tachi was longer, with a deeper curve than a katana.
tachi 2.	立ち		Standing or stance.
tachikaze	太刀風		Sword wind. The whistling sound of a sword as it passes through the air with proper hasuji (blade alignment).
tai	体		Body.
taijutsu	体術		Body techniques. Unarmed martial art based on seizing, grappling and throwing.
tai otoshi	体落とし		Principle of dropping the body to generate power.
taisabaki	体捌き		Body management. The tactic of moving the body to avoid an attack.
taiyaku	体厄		Time of great risk or misfortune. In Shintō, great misfortune is associated with the ages 42 for men, and 33 for women.
tameshigiri	試し切		Test-cutting. Evaluating cutting technique by cutting bamboo or rolled straw mats.
tanren	鍛錬		Forging.
tantō	短刀		Short dagger usually between 30-40 cm in length.
taoshi	倒し		To tip over or topple to the ground.
tasuki-gake	襷掛		To tie one's kimono sleeves up with a cord to facilitate combat.
tate	縦		Vertical.
tatehanen	縦半円		Shoden level kenjutsu reigi performed before kumitachi. It is an homage to Matsuzaki Shinkage Ryū.
tateken	縦拳		Vertical fist.
tate kyōtō kamae 立胥刀構			A stance with the sword in a position similar to kyōtō but with the sword positioned vertical relative to the target.
tatsujin	達人		Master level swordsman or strategist.
tatsumaki	竜巻		Dragon coil. Tornado.
te	手		Hand.
tegatana	手刀		Hand sword. A strike with the edge of the hand.

tehanare	手離		Placing the right hand on the tsuka before drawing a sword. Perceived as an overt threat.
te hodoki	手解		Hand untying. In Takamura ha Shindō Yōshin Ryū te hodoki is a category of study in how to escape from grips and restraints.
teitō shisei	堤刀姿勢		Hand carrying sword. A posture where the sword is held in the left hand with the sword at the left hip.
teko	挺		Moving the sword by exerting leverage between the hands on the tsuka.
tekubi	手首		Wrist.
temizuya	手水舎		Ablution basin at a Shintō shrine for purification by water of the hands and mouth.
tenchi	天地		Heaven to earth. Symbolic name for any technique or sword cut that travels from an upper position to a lower position.
ten chi jin	天地人		Heaven, earth, man. An esoteric concept identifying man as the primordial link between heaven and earth.
tengu	天狗		Mountain and forest goblins associated with magical powers and swordsmanship. Sōjōbō, the tengu king of Mount Kurama plays an important role in Yōshin Ryū and Shinkage Ryū mystical traditions.
tenkai	転回		Rotation or pivot.
tenouchi	手の内		Hand grip. The technique of properly gripping a sword handle.
tenugui	手拭		A small cotton towel wrapped on the head and worn under a men.
tessen	鉄扇		An iron fan.
tetsubō	鉄棒		A short metal bar, sometimes with a hook. Used in a manner similar to a jutte, they were usually around 30cm long.
tettsui uchi	鉄槌打		Iron hammer, or hammer-fist strike.
tobi	飛び		Flying or jumping.
togimonoshi	研物師		Sword polisher.
Tokugawa bakafu 徳川幕府			Government of the Tokugawa Shōgun's who ruled Japan from 1603-1867.
tōma	透間		In Takamura ha Shindō Yōshin Ryū, a distance of combat engagement that is the length of two full tatami. It assumed the attacker must aggressively engage his adversary by covering the distance between them.
torima	取間		Grabbing distance. Combative distance of engagement where a grab can be achieved with a single step or less.
torinawa	捕縄		Ensnaring or capturing cord.
tsubazeriai	鍔迫り合い		Crossed or locked tsubas. Close quarter combat where the sword's hand guards are pressed towards one another. Also tsubajiku.
tsuchi	土		Earth. In Takamura ha Shindō Yōshin Ryū, one of four kata sets named after the elements and usually performed with bokken.

Shindō Yōshin Ryū

tsugiashi	継足	A type of sliding step. In Takamura ha Shindō Yōshin Ryū, a sliding step in which movement is initiated when the rear foot is drawn forward before the front foot is extended forward. In appearance tsugiashi looks like okuriashi but is dynamically reversed.
tsuka	柄	Sword handle.
tsuki	突き	A thrust with a sword.
tsukisasu	突き刺す	The act of stabbing.
tsukuri	作り	In budō, creating a position of advantage by fitting to an adversary.

U

uchi 1.	内	Inside.
uchi 2.	打ち	Strike.
uchideshi	内弟子	Inside student. A live in apprentice.
uchiko	打粉	Powdered limestone inside a pompom used to clean and lightly polish a sword blade.
uchima	打間	Striking distance. Combative distance of engagement where a strike or cut can be achieved.
uchimata	打股	Striking inside the thigh. A common target in swordsmanship as it is the location of the femoral arteries.
uchitachi	打太刀	Attacking sword. The person initiating an attack in paired combative forms. (In jūjutsu the term is uchite, meaning attacking hand - 打手).
ude	腕	Arm.
ukemi	受身	Receiving body. The techniques of proper rolling and falling skills.
uke	受	To block.
ura	裏	Hidden or obscured.
ushiro	後	Back or to the rear.

W

wa	和	Harmony, soft, Japanese. Also yawara.
wajutsu	和術	Older name for a jūjutsu-like grappling art.
waki gamae	脇構	A posture of engagement with the sword to the right side of the body, edge down and the kissaki pointing to the rear, knee high.
wakizashi	脇差し	Another name for shōtō or short sword.
washiseiso	和紙清掃	The act of wiping blood from a sword with a piece of soft paper called nuguigami, which was carried in the kimono or keikogi.
waraji	草鞋	Straw sandals worn with tabi. Waraji's very long laces were frequently wrapped over the hakama and secured just beneath the knee to prevent becoming entangled in the excess fabric.

waza	技		Technique.

Y

ya	矢		Arrow.
yakuyoke taisai 厄除け大祭			Time of risk or misfortune. In Shintō, misfortune is associated with the ages of 25, 42 and 61 for men, and 19, 33, 37 and 61 for women.
yamatoma 山刀間			Distance of combat engagement with the swords in seigan gamae making the shape of a mountain.
yanagi	柳		A weeping willow tree. A flexible willow tree whose branches hang downward as opposed to rise upwards. A frequently used metaphorical name in several Japanese budō schools that implies physical and mental combat flexibility.
yari	槍		Spear.
yawara	柔		Older alternative pronunciation of jūjutsu.
Yayoi	彌生		Iron age Asians who immigrated to Japan and introduced rice cultivation around 300 BCE. The Yayoi absorbed and overwhelmed the native Ainu population, which were predominantly a hunter-gatherer culture.
yō 1.	揚		To raise or lift up. A frequently-used metaphorical name in several Japanese budō schools that implies positive or upward evolution.
yō 2.	楊		Purple Willow. A flexible willow tree whose branches rise upwards as opposed to the variety of willow tree that has branches hanging downward (yanagi). A frequently-used metaphorical name in several Japanese budō schools that implies physical and mental combat flexibility.
yō 3.	陽		Positive. A frequently-used metaphorical name in several Japanese budō schools that implies positive qualities or evolution.
yō 4.	養		Cultivate. A frequently-used metaphorical name in several Japanese budō schools that implies positive cultivation or evolution.
yoko	横		Side or horizontal.
yoko jōdan kamae 横上段構			Upper level stance with the sword tsuka over the forehead tilted to the right 30-45 degrees.
yoriki	与力		A mid-level Edo period police officer of lower samurai status.
yūgen	幽玄		Mysterious skills. In Takamura ha Shindō Yōshin Ryū, yūgen is related to developing intuition and freedom of movement during combat that transcends the purely evaluative.
yumiya	弓矢		Bow and arrow.

Z

zanshin	残心		Combative awareness. Having a focused and intense level of situational awareness.
zarei	座礼		To bow from a seated posture.
zenpō	前方		Forward.
zuhyō	図表		Diagram, often identifying vital points on the body to strike or cut.

Index

A

Abe Kanryū 30, 52
Akiyama Yōshin Ryū **33, 34–38**
   See also jūjutsu early schools 24
   and Chinese medicine 29, 30, 31, 34–36, 140
   .... See also kyūsho & nairiki
   and go-no-sen 140
   and nairiki 34, 35, **299**
   .... See also kyūsho & nairiki
   and Miura Yōshin Ryū 30, 33, 54
   and naginata 35–38
   and Obata Shigeta 104, 106, 130, 140
   and the Takeda 49
   curricula 47, 48
   densho 31–34, 334, 335, 341–344
   famous early students 32
   influence on TSYR 104, 140, 291, 300, 301
   lineages 39–46
Akiyama Yoshitoki 31, 49, 139, 300
   and Wadō Ryū 94
Amaterasu Ōmikami 12, 321, 329,
.... See also Kami
amatsukitsune 16,
.... See also tengu
Amdur, Ellis 7, 351
Ame no Uzume no Mikoto 321, 329, 330,
.... See also Kami
Andersson, Karin 112, 114, 357,
.... See also TSYR first generation
Angier, Don 106, 121, 123
Araki Ryū 26, 351
Arakawa Tōru 125
.... See also Wadō Ryū
Asano clan 33, 49, 52, 104
atemi kyūsho zuhyō 23, 35,
.... See also kyūsho
Azukizaka, Battle of 15

B

Baelz, Erwin Dr. 24, 53, 60–62
   and Sakakibara Kenkichi 60
Bakufu Kōbusho 50, 53, 64, 76, 136
Batton, Louis 114,
.... See also TSYR first generation

Bishamonten 16, 17, 378
Boshin Wars 73, 105, 118, 136
Bugei Jūhappan 20

C

Carey, Brent 364
Ch'en Yuang Ping .... See Chin Genpin
Chau, J. Gerry 120, 121, 123, 347
Chelstowski, Piotr 201
Chiba Shūsaku 64, 76, 137,
.... See also Hokushin Ittō Ryū
Chin Genpin 29, 30
...... See also Miura Yōshin Ryū and Chinese medicine
Clark, Aaron 201
Clark, Chuck 358

D

Dainichi Buddha 18
Dai Nippon Butokukai Conclave 51
Daitō Ryū 25, 33, 106, 107, 358, 359
daitengu .... See tengu types
Dan-no-ura, Battle of 17
Douglass, Kathryn 140
Draeger, Donn 7, 348, 356

E

Egami Taketsune 52,55,
.... See also Miura Yōshin Ryū
Enomoto Takeaki 77
Eriguchi Eiichi 94
Ermita, Ronaldo 114,
.... See also TSYR first generation

F

Feder, Kayla 358
Fujiwara Ryōzō, Dr. .... xi, xiii, 26, 73, 85, 91, 136
Fukuda Hichinosuke 64,
.... See also Tenjin Shinyō Ryū
Funakoshi Gichin 91–94,
.... See also Ōtsuka Hironori

Shindō Yōshin Ryū

Funakoshi Yoshitaka 93,
.... *See also* Ōtsuka Hironori
Fusen Ryū .... *See* Motsugai Ryū

G

Ganjin 14
Gantei 14
Garrison, Karl W. **175**, 331, 353,
.... *See also* TSYR first generation
   as sōdansa 363
   on Takamura Sensei's dōjō etiquette 348
   on meeting Takamura Yukiyoshi 346
   recollections on Takamura Sensei 345–68
Gembelliot, Henri 114, 115, 116
Gempei Wars 15
Genji .... *See* Minamoto clan
Genkō Wars 15
Gohō Maōson 16
Goldsbury, Peter 358

H

Hakomori Yosaburō 86, 88,
   See also Nakamura Tatsusaburō & Shinkage Ryūha
Hakuten 31,
See also Akiyama Yōshin Ryū and Chinese medicine
Hamaguri Rebellion 104
Harigaya Sekiun 138,
.... *See also* Shinkage Ryūha
Heiji Rebellion 17
Heike .... *See* Taira clan
Henderson, Kim 364
   in memoriam 369
Hiei, Mt. 15
Hieizan Enryaku-ji 14
Hiratsuka Katsuta 51, 106, 107,
.... *See also* Obata Shigeta travels
Hitotsu Oribei 63,
.... *See also* Tenjin Shinyō Ryū
Hokushin Ittō Ryū **137**
   and Shindō Yōshin Ryū 64, 72, 76
   densho 137, 337
   influence on TSYR 137

Hokushin Musō Ryū 137,
.... *See also* Hokushin Ittō Ryū
Honma Masatō 63,
.... *See also* Tenjin Shinyō Ryū
Hōzōin Ryū 20

I

Ichi-no-Tani, Battle of 17
Ikkō .... *See* koryū and Buddhism
Inazu Masamizu 51, 106, 107,
.... *See also* Obata Shigeta travels
Inose Motokichi 73, **79–81**, 101, 102, 126, 129
   and jūdō 114
   and Nakayama Tatsusaburō 88
   and Obata Shigeta 78, 101, 105
   Shindō Yōshin Ryū curriculum 129–130
Ishii, Fred 123
Ishijima Yoshi 76,
.... *See also* Matsuoka Katsunosuke
Ishikawa Gotō 107, 119, 138, 139,
.... *See also* Shinkage Ryūha
Ishikawa Jōzan 29
Iso Masatomo 64, 75, 137
.... *See also* Matsuoka Katsunosuke
Iso Mataemon Minamoto no Masatari 64,
.... *See also* Tenjin Shinyō Ryū
Iwasa Matabei 18, 19

J

Jikishinkage Ryū **136**,
.... *See also* Shinkage Ryūha
   and Matsuoka Katsunosuke 72, 75, 76, 129,
.... *See also* Shinkage Ryūha
   and Nakayama Tasusaburō 86, 88, 94
.... *See also* Shinkage Ryūha
   and Obata Shigeta 78, 104, 130, 136–137,
.... *See also* Shinkage Ryūha
   and Ōtsuka Hironori 90, 94
   and Sakakibara Kenkichi 76, 85, 104, 136, 249
   and Shindō Yōshin Ryū 133
.... *See also* Shinkage Ryūha

Jikishinkage Ryū (continued)
    and Takamura Yukiyoshi ....
    .... See also Shinkage Ryūha
    and Yamaoka Tesshū 103. 119
Jinmu 13, 330
Jirōbō 21
    .... See also tengu
JKF Wadōkai .... See Wadō Ryū
Jōdo .... See koryū and Buddhism
jūjutsu 23–26
    active classical schools 25, 26
    and Chinese medicine 31–32, 34–36
    and the police 24, 55, 63
    early schools 24
    nagashi 23
    vs. jūdō .. 24, 51, 53, 55, **59–62**, 65, 82, 114, 359

K

Kamakura Shogunate 15
Kami 12, 13, 17, 321, **323–325**,
    .... See also tengu
    influence on Takamura Yukiyoshi 109, 111,
    in TSYR 329–331
Kami no Michi .... See Shintō
Kamiizumi Ise no Kami 31, 136, 138, 139, 249,
    .... See also Shinkage Ryūha
Kaminoda Tsunemori 356
Kamiya Denshinsai Naomitsu 138,
    .... See also Shinkage Ryūha
Kanaya Motoo 53, 54,
    .... See also Totsuka ha Yōshin Ryū
    and Ōtsuka Hironori 91, 92
Kanaya Motoyoshi 53,
    .... See also Totsuka ha Yōshin Ryū
Kanō Jigorō 59–62, 129
    and Obata Shigeta 107
    and Tenjin Shinyō Ryū 59, 64–66
    Dai Nippon Butokukai Conclave 51
    influence on Shindō Yōshin Ryū 129
    kuzushi 164
karasu .... See tengu types
Karuraten .... See Goho Maōson
Kashima Jingū 13, 25, 26, 321
Kashima Shin Ryū 20

Kashima Shinden Jikishinkage Ryū **136–138**
    .... See also Shinkage Ryūha
    and Shindō Yōshin Ryū 80
    densho 338
    influence on Obata Shigeta 104
Katayama Takayoshi 51, 56, 107,
    .... See also Obata Shigeta travels
Katōda Heihachiro 118, 138,
Katōda Shinkage Ryū 118, 138,
    .... See also Shinkage Ryūha
    densho 339
Katsu Kaishū 119, 340
    and Obata Shigeta 1, 103
    and Matsuoka Katsunosuke 77
Kawabata, Al 115
Kawakami Daisaburō 93,
    .... See also Ōtsuka Hironori
keppan 4, 83, 122, **331**, 335
Kinitsu Kami .... See Sarutahiko Ōkami
Kinuhikihime .... See Sōjōbō
kishomon-dai 122
Kojiki, The 12–13
Kokusai Budōin 95
    .... See also Ōtsuka Hironori
Kokushōji 29
Komazawa Yoshitsugu 75,
    .... See also Hōzōin Ryū and Shindō Yōshin Ryū
Kominami Yasutomo 119,
    .... See also Yamaoka Tesshū
Konishi Yasuhiro 91,
    .... See also Kanaya Motoo
Konjaku Monogatari, The 16
konoha .... See tengu types
koryū **3–4**, 351
    and Buddhism 14–16
    and loyalty 6–7
    densho 332–344
    finding a school 7–11, 368
    mythological roots 12–13
    oldest surviving traditions 3
    organizational structure 4, 101, 363, 364
    outside Japan 2, 112, 113, 127, 348, 359, 360
    study 2, 3,5, 163, 227, 366, 367
    tengu influences 33, 70, 354, 355
    training & commitment 4–6, 113, 122
    vs. gendai budō 5–8, 114, 348–350, 359, 360

Kurama, Mt. 14, 33, 327
    and Takamura Yukiyoshi 109, 111, 328, 355
    and tengu 16, 17–19, 31, 333
Kuriyama Mataemon 64,
.... See also Tenjin Shinyō Ryū
Kuroda clan 50
    and Matsuoka Katsunosuke 50, 73, 75, 76
Kuroda Tetsuzan 163, 362, 363
kyūsho **22**, 23, 301
    in Akiyama Yōshin Ryū 22, 34–36, 301
    in Shindō Yōshin Ryū 129–131, 135, 150, 202
kyūsho kiri zuhyō 23, 36

L

Ledyard, George 358

M

Marume Tessai 139,
.... See also Shinkage Ryūha
Matsumoto Bizen no Kami 136,
.... See also Shinkage Ryūha
Matsuoka Chau 77, 78,
.... See also Matsuoka Katsunosuke
Matsuoka Chiyo 77, 78,
.... See also Matsuoka Katsunosuke
Matsuoka Dōrin 75,
.... See also Matsuoka Katsunosuke and Chinese medicine
Matsuoka Katsunosuke 73, **75–79**, 80, 126, 128
    and Chiba Shūsaku 64, 76, 137
    and Chinese medicine 75, 77
    and Hokushin Ittō Ryū 64, 72, 76
    and Hōzōin Ryū 72, 75, 76
    and Jikishinkage Ryū 72, 75, 76, 136,
.... See also Shinkage Ryūha
    and Katsu Kaishū 77
    and Obata Shigeta 23, 37, 77, 78, 101, 105
    and Sakakibara Kenkichi 76, 136, 137
    and Tenjin Shinyō Ryū 64, 72, 74–76, 129, 137
    and the Bakufu Kōbusho 75–77, 136
    and the Kuroda clan 50, 73, 75, 76

Matsuoka Katsunosuke (continued)
    and the Tokugawa Shōgun 73, 75–77, 136
    and Totsuka ha Yōshin Ryū 72, 74, 76, 77
    founding Shindō Yōshin Ryū .. 72, 74, 76, 128, 129
Matsuoka Matsu 77, 78,
.... See also Matsuoka Katsunosuke
Matsuoka Nobuatsu 83, 84
    and Ōtsuka Hironori 83, 90, 91
    and Takamura Yukiyoshi 114, 126
Matsuoka Takeshi 83, 84, 125,126
.... See also Threadgill and Ohgami in Japan
Matsuoka Tatsuo 81–83
    and Obata Shigeta 114
    and Takamura Yukiyoshi 114
    and mainline Shindō Yōshin Ryū 85
Matsuoka Teisaburō 77–79, 82,
.... See also Matsuoka Katsunosuke
Matsuzaki Namishirō **118–119**, 139,
.... See also Shinkage Ryūha
    and Obata Shigeta 105, 118
    and the Boshin Wars 118
Matsuzaki Shinkage Ryū **118–119**, 139
.... See also Shinkage Ryūha
    influence on TSYR 110, 112, 130, 249, 351
Maynard, David 114, 123, 175
    as kaiden shihan 124
    as sōdansa 175, 363
    meeting Donn Draeger 356
    meeting Tobin Threadgill 115, 121, 347
    menkyo kaiden 115, 175, 365
    on meeting Takamura Yukiyoshi 346
    on Takamura Sensei's dōjō etiquette 348, 349
    on Wadō Ryū 362
    recollections on Takamura Sensei 345–68
    steps down 123–124, 175, 364
Mifune Kyūzō 95,
.... See also Ōtsuka Hironori and the Kokusai Budōin
Minamoto clan 14, 15, 17, 18
    and the Takeda 33
Minamoto no Yoshitomo 17, 18
Minamoto no Yoshitsune............... 17–19, 109, 354
Miura Sadauemon 30, 32, 41, 42,
.... See also Miura Yōshin & Nakamura Yoshikuni
Miura Yojiuemon 29
Miura Yōshin 30, 52
......See also Miura Sadauemon
......See also Nakamura Yoshikuni

Miura Yōshin Ryū **52–56**
    and Akiyama Yōshin Ryū 30, 33, 54–55
    curriculum 58
    lineage 57
Montagne, David 114,
    .... *See also* TSYR first generation
Mootori Norinaga 324,
    .... *See also* Kami & Shintō
Morinaga Shinnō 15
Motobu Chōki 91, 93,
    .... *See also* Ōtsuka Hironori
Motsugai Ryū 104
Motsugai Zenji 104
Mukan 31
    .... *See also* Akiyama Yōshin Ryū
Mustard, Robert 358, 362, 363

N

nairiki 299, **300–308**
    and martial application 307–308
    chūshin wo tadasu (skeletal posture) 302
    dokikaku (dynamic/kinesthetic) 303
    gaikikaku (external/tactile sense) 302
    in Akiyama Yōshin Ryū 34, 35, **299**
    kakugo (resolve) 308
    kokyū (breathing) 307
    naikikaku (proprioception) 302–303
    tai no musubi (connected body) 305–306
    tatsudori (projecting force) 307
    te no uchi (gripping hand) 306
    ten chi jin wa (dynamic meditation) 308
    ten chi jin (redirecting force) 304
    tezawari (touch/feel) 306
nairiki kunren 299, 300–308,
    .... *See also* nairiki & nairiki no gyō
nairiki no gyō 299, 309–20
    banjaku (immovable stone) 315–320
    tekkyaku (iron legs) 309–314
Nakamoto, Daniel 115
Nakamura Yoshikuni 30, 33, 52
.... *See also* Miura Sadauemon & Miura Yōshin
Nakanishi ha Ittō Ryū 137,
    .... *See also* Hokushin Ittō Ryū
Nakayama Hakudō 95

, ... *See also* Ōtsuka Hironori and the Kokusai Budōin
Nakayama Tatsusaburō 73, 80, **86–89**
    and Inose Motokichi 88
    and Obata Shigeta 106
    and Ohgami Shingo 125
    and Ōtsuka Hironori 73, 88, 90, 91, 98, **101**
Namishiro Matsuhiro 107, 113, 361
    and Takamura Yukiyoshi 110, 111, 123
Nash, Bob 124, 125
Nihon Shoki, The 13
Ninigi no Mikoto 13
Nippon Budō Kyōgikai 25
Nippon Budōkan 25, 35, 98
Nippon Kobudō Kyōkai 25, 26, 85, 95
Nippon Kobudō Shinkōkai 25, 95, 98
Nishida, Makio 123
Nishimura Tokinosuke 64,
    .... *See also* Tenjin Shinyō Ryū
Nomi no Sukune .... *See* sumō

O

Obata Hideyoshi 107–110
Obata Shibuharu 104, 140,
    .... *See also* Obata Shigeta
Obata Shigeta 73, **104–108**
    and Akiyama Yōshin Ryū 104, 130, 351
    and Inose Motokichi 78, 101, 106
    and Jikishinkage Ryū 130, 136–137
    .... *See also* Shinkage Ryūha
    and Kanō Jigorō 107
    and Katsu Kaishū 1, 103
    and Matsuoka Katsunosuke 23, 37, 77, 78, 105
    and Matsuzaki Namishiro 105, 118
    and Miura Yōshin Ryū 104
    and Sakakibara Kenkichi 105, 137
    and Takamura Yukiyoshi 109–110, 127
    and the Takeda/Takeda Ryū 104
    and the Shinkage Ryūha 105, 130
    and Totsuka ha Yōshin Ryū 54, 62, 104, 105
    on Ōtsuka Hironori 91
    travels 107–108
    Shindō Yōshin Ryū curriculum 129, 130–132
    Shindō Yōshin Ryū menkyo kaiden 101

Shindō Yōshin Ryū

Oda Nobunaga 15, 52
Odani Nobutomo 75, 136
.... See also Matsuoka Katsunosuke & Shinkage Ryūha
Ōe / Ōi Senbei 30, 32, 38–46, 63
Ogasawara Genshin Nagaharu........................ 138,
.... See also Shinkage Ryūha
Ogawa Yozaemon 75,
.... See also Matsuoka Katsunosuke and Chinese medicine
Ohgami Shingo..................................**v, xii–xiii**
   and Dr. Fujiwara Ryōzō 88
   and Nakayama Tatsusaburō 89, 125
   and Ōtsuka Hironori .... xii, xiii, 91, 92, 94, 97
   and T. Threadgill in Japan .... xi, 83, 84, 87–89, 126
   and Yukiyoshi Takamura 116
   letter from Ōtsuka Hironori 98
   and Wadō Ryū .... xii, xiii, 94, 97, 99, 101, 124
   publications v
Ōkura, Nanette 114, 115, 360
   and Takamura Michiko 347, 352, 362
   on meeting Takamura Yukiyoshi 347
   on Takamura Sensei's dōjō etiquette 347–348
   recollections on Takamura Sensei 345–68
Okuyama Masatari 63, 64
.... See also Tenjin Shinyō Ryū
oldest surviving bujutsu ryūha 20
Ono no Takamura 111, 327, 355,
.... See also Takamura Yukiyoshi changing his name
Ono-ha Ittō Ryū 86,
.... See also Nakamura Tatsaburō
Ōtomo Sōrin 75,
.... See also Matsuoka Katsunosuke
Ōtsuka Hironori **90–98**
   and jūdō 83, 91
   and jūjutsu 53, 94
   and Kanaya Motoo 91, 92
   and Matsuoka Nobuatsu 83, 91
   and Nakayama Tatsusaburō 88, 90, 91, 98, 101
   and Obata Shigeta 91
   and Ohgami Shingo .... xii, xiii, 91, 92, 94, 97
   and Shindō Yōshin Ryū 93–96, 101–102, 121
   and Tenjin Shinyō Ryū 91
   and the Kokusai Budōin 95
   letter to Ohgami Shingo 98
   made Meijin... 95
   resigns as head of JKF Wadōkai 95

Ōtsuka Kazutaka 95,
.... See also Wadō Ryū

P

Pranin, Stanley .... x, xi
   Aiki Expo 124, 358
   and Daitō Ryū 358
   and Tobin Threadgill .... x, 123, 358
   Takamura interview 116, 124, 345, 357
   and Daitō Ryū 358
Pinto, Marco 364

R

Recio-Coll, Oscar 124,
.... See also TSYR Europe & beyond
Relnick, Phil .... vii, x, 8, 201, 356
Rikkokushi, The 13
Robbins, Bryan 121, 122
Ryūkansai 64,
.... See Tenjin Shinyō Ryū

S

Sakakibara Kenkichi 136–137
   and Dr. Erwin Baelz 60
   and Jikishinkage Ryū 76, 85, 104, 136, 249
   and Matsuoka Katsunosuke 76, 136, 137
   and Odani Nobutomo 136
   and Obata Shigeta 104, 105, 136
   and the Shōgun 136
sakoku 29
Sarutahiko Ōkami 17, 321, **329**, 330
Sekigahara, Battle of 15
sen wo toru 137
Sente Kanzeon Bosatsu 16
Shimura Koichi 362
.... See also Wadō Ryū
Shin no Shindō Ryū 63, 64, 68
.... See also jūjutsu and the police

Shin no Shindō Ryū *(continued)*
    and Tenjin Shinyō Ryū 24
    and Shintō Rikugo Ryū 56
    densho 340
Shin Shinkage Ryū 138,
    densho 339,
    .... *See also* Katōda Shinkage Ryū
Shindō Yōshin Ryū **72–88**
    and Hokushin Ittō Ryū 64, 72, 76
    and Hōzōin Ryū 72, 75, 76
    and Tenjin Shinyō Ryū 64, 72, 74–76, 129, 137
    and the Shinkage Ryūha 105, 130, 138, 139
    and Totsuka ha Yōshin Ryū 72, 74, 76, 129
    Inose line curriculum 129–130
    kanji spelling 74
    lineage 71
    mainline curriculum 133–134
    Obata line curriculum 130–132
    Takamura ha curriculum 135
Shindō Yōshin Ryū Dōmonkai 26, 85
    in decline 114
Shinkage Ryūha 136–139
    and Matsuoka Katsunosuke 75, 76
    and Obata Shigeta 104, 105, 130
    and TSYR 129, 130, 138, 139
    densho in TSYR collection 338–339
    influence on TSYR 105, 130, 138, 139
    influences on Shindō Yōshin Ryū 136
    Shinryoku Tanren 122
    Shinsen Bujutsu Ryūsoroku, The 31
Shintō **322–331**
    and the dōjō 328–329
    ethos on budō culture 327–328
    harae and misogi 325–326
    influence on Takamura Yukiyoshi 109, 111 322, 328–329, 352–355
    influence on TSYR 123, 329
    kami 323–325, 329
    morality and ethics 326
    origins of 323
Shintō Rikugo Ryū **56**
    and Miura Yōshin Ryū 54, 55
shisei no shin (body mechanics) **283–298**
    antehō (strong line) 286
    chūshin wo tadasu (correct center) 285
    fuantehō (weak line) 286
    hiki ashi (pulling foot) 295

shisei no shin *(continued)*
    jiku (rotational axis) 291
    jūji (body symmetry) 288
    kaimon (opening the gate) 293
    koshi otoshi (hip drop) 290
    mae-kado (front balance limit) 287
    mon (gates) 292
    oshi te (pushing hand) 296
    rasen no tai (spiraling body) 298
    seichūsen (centerline) 284
    tai no kaiten (body rotation) 294
    tai-otoshi (body drop) 289
    tanden dori (center capturing) 297
    ushiro-kado (back balance limit) 287
Smith, Robbie 125, 127, 357, 364
    and Takamura Yukiyoshi 364–365
    in memoriam 369
sōhei .... *See* koryū and Buddhism
Sōjōbō **17–19**, 31, 109
    illustration 333
Sōjōgatani 111
sumai no sechie .... *See* sumō
sumō 13
Suzuki Tatsuo 94, 96,
    .... *See also* Wadō Ryū

T

Taima no Kehaya .... *See* sumō
Taira clan 14–15, 17–18
Taira no Kiyomori 17
Taisha Ryū 139
Takagi Hideo 125, 357
    .... *See also* Wadō Ryū
Takagi Iso 5, 113, 115
    meeting Takamura Yukiyoshi 113
    menkyo kaiden 115, 123
    steps down 123, 364
Takamagahara 329,
    .... *See also* Kami
Takamura Michiko 113, 115, 361
    and Nanette Ōkura 347, 352, 362
    and Tobin Threadgill 353
Takamura Yukiyoshi **109–117**

Takamura Yukiyoshi *(continued)*
    Aikidō Journal interview 116, 124, 345, 357
    and Jikishinkage Ryū 110
    and Matsuoka Nobuatsu 114, 126
    and Matsuoka Tatsuo 114
    and Mt. Kurama 109, 111, 328, 355
    and Namishiro Matsuhiro 110, 111, 123
    and Obata Shigeta 109–110, 127
    and Shintō 109, 111, 322, 328, 329, 352–355
    and Takagi Iso 113, 115, 123
    and tengu 109, 327, 354, 355
    changing his name 111
    early students 113, 114
    final years 117
    in the US 113–116
    leaving Japan 113
    made a Kami 328–329
    menkyo kaiden 110
    Obata ha becomes Takamura ha 114
Takeda clan 33
    and Akiyama Yōshin Ryū 49
    and Miura Yōshin Ryū 30, 52
    and Obata Shigeta 104
    and the Minamoto clan 33
Takeda Ryū 104, 107
Takeda Sōkaku 33, 106, 107,
    .... *See also* Obata Shigeta travels
Takemikazuchi no Kami 12, 13, 321, 330
    .... *See also* Kami
Takeminakata no Kami 12, 13
    .... *See also* Kami
Takenouchi Ryū 21, 22, 51
    .... *See also* jūjutsu early schools
Tarōbō 19,
    .... *See also* tengu
Tatsuno Yorihisa 85
Tendai .... *See* koryū and Buddhism
tengu **16–20**
    depictions 16, 17, 18, 19, 20, 31, 333, 340
    influence on Takamura 109, 327, 354, 355
    influence on koryū 33, 70, 354, 355
    influence on TSYR 20, 130, 132, 135
    types 16–17
Tengu no Dairi, The 17–19
Tenjin Shinyō Ryū **64–70**
    .... *See also* jūjutsu early schools

Tenjin Shinyō Ryū *(continued)*
    and Kanō Jigorō 59, 64–66
    and Ōtsuka Hironori 91
    and Shin no Shindō Ryū 24
    and Shindō Yōshin Ryū 64, 72, 74–76, 129, 137
    curriculum 68–69, **73**
    densho 340
    influence on TSYR 129
    lineage 67
Tenjin Shinyō Ryū Gokui Kyōju Zukai, The 31
Tenjin Shinyō Ryū Tai-i Roku, The 31, 63
Tenmangū Shrine 32
Threadgill, Tobin .... **v, x–xii, 120–27**
    and Chau, J. Gerry 120, 121, 123, 347
    and Matsuhiro Namishiro 123
    and Ohgami S. in Japan ..... xi, 83, 84, 87–89, 126
    and TSYR 121–27
    and Western fencing 120
    becoming kaichō .... x, 124
    becoming shibuchō 116
    meeting David Maynard 115, 121, 347
    menkyo kaiden 116, 123, 365
    on meeting Takamura Yukiyoshi 121, 347
    on Takamura's dōjō etiquette 347, 349
    on Wadō Ryū 96, 121
    recollections on Takamura Sensei 345–68
    training in other disciplines 121, 349
tō no mae (sword forward) 139
Toba-Fushimi, Battle of 73, 129
Tobari Kazu 64, 65, 356
Tobari Takisaburō 64,
    .... *See also* Tenjin Shiyō Ryū
Todaiji Temple 14
Tokugawa Iemitsu 29
Tokugawa Iemochi 136
Tokugawa Ieyasu 15, 29, 52
Tokugawa Yoshinobu 76
torimono-dōshin .... *See* jūjutsu and the police
Totsuka ha Yōshin Ryū **52–56**
    and the police 24, 55
    and Obata Shigeta 54, 62, 104, 105
    and Shindō Yōshin Ryū 72, 74, 76, 129
    curriculum .... *See* Miura Yōshin Ryū curriculum
    influence on TSYR 72, 74, 76, 104, 105, 129
    lineage 75, 79
    vs. jūdō 53, 60, 62
Totsuka Hidesumi 52–53, 55, 57
    .... *See also* Totsuka ha Yōshin Ryū

Totsuka Hidetoshi 24, 52, 53, 60
.... *See also* Totsuka ha Yōshin Ryū
    and Matsuoka Katsunosuke 76
Totsuka Hideyoshi 51–53, 62, 104, 140,
.... *See also* Totsuka ha Yōshin Ryū
Toyotomi Hideyoshi 15, 52
Tsubaki Ōkami Yashiro 325, 329, 331,
.... *See also* Shintō & Kami & Sarutahiko Ōmikami
TSYR
    and Akiyama Yōshin Ryū 104, 140, 291, 300–01
    and go-no-sen 140
    and Hokushin Ittō Ryū 137
    and Hōzōin Ryū 104, 129
    and nairiki .... *See* nairiki & nairiki no gyō
    and Shintō 123, 329
    and tengu 20, 130, 132, 135
    and Tenjin Shinyō Ryū 129
    and the Shinkage Ryūha 105, 130, 138, 139
    and tō no mae 139
    and Totsuka ha Yōshin Ryū 72, 74, 76, 104,
    .... 105, 129
    and Wadō Ryū 125, 126, 362
    .... *See also* Wadō Ryū and Shindō Yōshin Ryū
    curriculum 135
    Europe & beyond 73, 124–126, 359–360
    first generation 113, 114
    honbu dōjō 8, 73, 114, 115, 116, 123,
    .... 124, 325, 328, 329, 334, 361
    kami 331
    preference for longer tsuka 138
TSYR mokuroku (curriculum) 141–282
    (Battō torikaeshi) 274–282
        hiji kujiki 277
        hiji otoshi 279
        saya oshi 275
        tekubi giri 281
    (Battōjutsu / Iaijutsu) **264–272**
        men 269
        seishi 265
    (Idori te hodoki) **142–152**
        kami / tamusa 151
        morote 147
        ryōmune 149
        ryōte 143
        uchite 145
    (Idori) **176–200**
        ashi dori 181
        eri guruma / kinsha dori 177

(Idori) (continued)
    gozen dori 179
    gyakute dori 189
    hiki dori 187
    kanegi dori / shumoku dori 193
    kasumi dori 185
    nukimi no metsuke 199
    ryote dori 191
    tobi chigai dori 197
    ushiro dori 195
    zu soe 183
(Ken toriage) **240–248**
    iri sumigaeshi 241
    kosoto gari 245
    tachi otoshi 247
    te gaeshi 243
(Kenjutsu / kumitachi) **250–262**
    ate 259
    gyaku aku / nigiri 253
    isoku no tsume 251
    kurabatsu 255
    nebari (shōtō) 257
    saegiri 261
(Tachiai kuzushi / Te dori) **164–174**
    atama osae 169
    hiji otoshi 173
    kubi osae / oshi 167
    mae kata osae 171
    ude osae 165
(Tachiai taijutsu) 202–226
    gyakute gaeshi 213
    harai goshi 223
    hidari mune dori 215
    hiki tate 203
    kinomuguri 211
    kinukatsugi 209
    kinukuguri 207
    koshi nage 221
    ranshō 219
    soto ude garami 217
    soto ude otoshi 205
    yoko otoshi 225
(Tachiai te hodoki) **153–162**
    age nuki 153
    sode nuki 155
    te gaeshi 157
    ude kujiki 159
    ushiro kubishimi 161

Shindō Yōshin Ryū

(Tantō toriage) **228–238**
    age nagashi 237
    hiji kujiki 233
    soto ude garami 231
    te gaeshi 229
    uchi ude garami 235

U

uchiwa kagami 17
Udo Dai Gongen 138,
.... See also Shinkage Ryūha
Ueno, Battle of 73, 74, 77, 129
Ueshiba Kisshōmaru 95,
...... See also Ōtsuka Hironori and the Kokusai Budōin
Ushiwakamaru 17, 18,
.... See also Minamoto no Yoshitsune

V

Vlacht, Johan 114,
.... See also TSYR first generation

W

Wadō Ryū **94–99**
    and Akiyama Yōshin Ryū 94
    and Shindō Yōshin Ryū 73, 96, 124
    and TSYR 125, 126, 362
    curriculum 99
    official acceptance 95
    naming 94–94
    schism 95
Wicks, John 96

Y

yamabushi 17
yamabushi tengu 17, 31, 340
.... See also tengu depictions

Yamada Kiyoko 110,
.... See also Takamura Yukiyoshi
Yamamoto Hidehaya 24, 63,
.... See also Tenjin Shinyō Ryū & jūjutsu and the police
Yamaoka Tesshū 77, 118, 393
calligraphy 103, 340
Yashima, Battle of 17
yoriki .... See jūjutsu and the police
Yoshida Kōtarō 106, 107,
.... See also Obata Shigeta travels
Yōshin Koryū .... See Totsuka ha Yōshin Ryū
Yōshin Ryū 30–33, **49**, 72
.... See also Ōe / Ōi Senbei
    and tengu 18
    kanji spelling 29
    willow parable 32
Yumoto, Annaue 114,
.... See also TSYR first generation

History And Technique